They Dare to Speak Out

PEOPLE AND INSTITUTIONS CONFRONT ISRAEL'S LOBBY

by Paul Findley

Lawrence Hill Books

Published in the United States of America
by Lawrence Hill Books, an imprint of Chicago Review Press, Incorporated
814 North Franklin Street, Chicago, Illinois 60610

6 7 8 9

Printed in the United States of America

Library of Congress Cataloging in Publication Data

Findley, Paul, 1921—
    They dare to speak out.

    Includes bibliographical references.
    1. United States—Foreign relations—Israel.
    2. Israel—Foreign relations—Unites States.
    3. Zionists—United States—Political activity.
    4. Findley, Paul, 1921—
    5. Legislators—United States—Biography. I. Title
E183.8.I7F56 1984   327.7305694   84-28977
    ISBN 1-55652-073-5

*To our grandchildren
Andrew, Cameron, Henry, and Elizabeth
may they always be able
to speak without fear*

Contents

Preface to the 1989 Edition

One day in early December 1982, I was called to the Republican cloak-room, an area just off the floor of the House of Representatives where Congressmen may receive telephone calls, have a light lunch, or watch television. The House was engaged in the post-election "lame duck" session, finishing up legislative business which had been put off by campaign pressures. Waiting on the phone was a prominent citizen I had known and admired for years. He expressed his regret at my defeat at the polls the previous month, then made the surprising suggestion that I write a book about Israel's lobby. He even suggested the title.

That telephone call started me down a fascinating trail that absorbed most of my time and energies for the next two years and culminated in this volume. The journey elicited great support from many people and entailed, from others, many frustrations. The magnitude and diversity of cooperation I received were surprising. The frustrations were not. Although there were many dark moments when I harbored evil thoughts about my friend for luring me into writing this book, there were rewards aplenty, and now I wish I could thank him by name in this space for making the suggestion. I cannot, for I promised him anonymity.

I can name only one of the five people who contributed the most in the preparation of my manuscript — Robert W. Wichser, a good friend and for fourteen years director of my Washington staff, who perished in flood waters in December 1985. While the other four are enthusiastic about the text and convinced the book meets a long-standing need, they unanimously asked that their names not be mentioned in these acknowledgments. Recognizing the Israeli lobby's potential for malice, they agreed that such mention might jeopardize their careers. One said bluntly, "In helping you, I'm taking a big chance. If this gets out, I will be fired from my job." Others who helped expressed similar concern. Much of the information provided here is volunteered by career government officials who want the public to be aware of how the lobby functions but insist that their own names be withheld. These requirements tell a lot about the sensitivity of the subject matter.

Happily, I can acknowledge by name several people who provided yeoman support. I am especially indebted to Washington journalist Donald Neff, former Middle East correspondent for *Time* magazine and author of *Warriors at Suez* and *Warriors for Jerusalem*, and George W. Weller, former foreign correspondent for the *Chicago Daily News* who now lives in Rome, for their extensive and valuable suggestions on organization and style. If you detect a professional touch here and there, credit these gentlemen. My gratitude also extends to a number of my former colleagues in Congress and many citizens around the United States and elsewhere who provided both encouragement and cooperation, especially former Senator James Abourezk.

I must also thank the word processor to which I was glued for eighteen months. The attachment was so constant that my wife, Lucille, occasionally described herself—without really complaining—as a Wang widow. In fact, when she first learned that I was thinking of writing this book, she offered to live on beans and water if need be to see the project to completion.

The Spartan diet was unnecessary, thanks to a grant provided by Sangamon State University, Springfield, Illinois, and funded by the American Middle East Peace Research Institute, a nonprofit organization based in Boston, Massachusetts. The grant covered most of the expenses I encountered in the preparation of the text. During this period I also received helpful income by speaking at chapter meetings of the American-Arab Anti-Discrimination Committee.

My quest for a publisher began in March 1983 and was predictably long and frustrating. Declining to represent me, New York literary agent Alexander Wylie forecast with prophetic vision that no major U.S. publisher would accept my book. He wrote, "It's a sad state of affairs." Bruce Lee of William Morrow and Company called my manuscript "outstanding," but his company concluded that publishing it "would cause trouble in the house and outside" and decided against "taking the heat." Robert Loomis of Random House called it an "important book" but reported that the firm's leadership decided the theme was "too sensitive." Twenty other publishers also said no.

In July 1984, veteran publisher Lawrence Hill agreed to take the gamble. When he died in March 1988, I lost a friend, and the cause of human rights lost an able advocate. He would rejoice, I am sure, that this book now appears in a new updated edition.

The response since publication of the first edition in June 1985 has been substantial. Despite informal but effective attempts to curtail its sale in the early months, *They Dare to Speak Out* became a best seller—nine weeks, for example, among the *Washington Post* top ten. Thanks in great measure to the enthusiasm of readers themselves, over 70,000 copies have been sold. Scores of readers made bulk purchases for distribution to their friends, business associates, and public libraries. It elicited reviews in fifty-two periodicals, invitations to appear on over eighty television and radio programs, including NBC's "Today Show" and PBS's "Late Night America," and lectures on twenty-five campuses.

In another heartening response, more than eight hundred readers have taken the trouble to locate me by telephone or mail. Most of them, concerned over the damage being done by Israel's lobby, ask, "Where do we go from here?"

Many, I hope, will support the Council for the National Interest, Post Office Box 53048, Washington DC 20009, the newly-formed citizens' lobby mentioned in the last chapter of this new edition. Other worthy groups include the American-Arab Anti-Discrimination Committee, Suite 500, 4201 Connecticut Avenue NW, Washington DC 20008; the Arab American Institute, Suite 501, 918 16th Street NW, Washington DC 20006; the National Association of Arab Americans, 2033 M Street NW, Washington DC 20036; The American Educational Trust, 1900 18th St. NW, Washington DC 20009, toll-free 1-800-368-5788; and the National Council on U.S.-Arab Relations, Suite 515, 1735 Eye Street NW, Washington DC 20006.

To keep up to date on Middle East developments, I suggest the monthly *Washington Report on Middle East Affairs*, Box 53062, Washington DC 20009; the monthly *Israeli Foreign Affairs*, Box 19580, Sacramento CA 95819; the fortnightly *Middle East International*, Suite 306, 1700 17th Street NW, Washington DC 20009; the quarterly *Arab American Affairs*, Suite 411, 1730 M Street NW, Washington DC 20036; the quarterly *Journal of Palestine Studies*, Georgetown Station, Post Office Box 25301, Washington DC 20007.

Paul Findley
1040 West College
Jacksonville, IL 62650

June 1, 1989

Introduction

A Middle West Congressman Meets the Middle East

"How did a Congressman from the corn-hog heartland of America get entangled in Middle East politics?" people ask. Like most rural Congressmen, I had no ethnic constituencies who lobbied me on their foreign interests. As expected, I joined the Agriculture Committee and worked mainly on issues like farming, budget and welfare reform.

Newly appointed in 1972 to the subcommittee on Europe and the Middle East, I had represented the Springfield, Illinois, area for 12 years without attracting much attention at home or abroad.

Eight short years later, my involvement in Middle East politics would bring me infamy among many U.S. Jews, notoriety in Israel and applause throughout the Arab world. By 1980, in urban centers of pro-Israel activism—far from the local Jews in central Illinois who knew and trusted me, I found myself in the most expensive Congressional campaign in state history. Thanks to a flow of hostile dollars from both coasts and nearby Chicago, I became "the number one enemy of Israel" and my re-election campaign the principal target of Israel's lobby.

Prodded by a professor at Illinois College, I had already begun to doubt the wisdom of United States policy in the Middle East when I first joined the subcommittee. For the most part, I kept these doubts private, but not because I feared the political consequences. In fact, I naively assumed I could question our policy anywhere without getting into trouble. I did not realize how deeply the roots of Israeli interests had penetrated U.S. institutions.

Congressmen generally heard only the Israeli case. Arab American lobbies, fledgling forces even today, were nonexistent. Arab embassies, which even today hire public relations experts only with reluctance, then showed little interest in lobbying. Even if a Congress-

1

man had wanted to hear the Arab viewpoint, he would have had difficulty finding an Arab spokesman to explain it.

My personal involvement with Middle East politics started with a constituent problem that had no direct connection with the Arab-Israeli conflict. It began in the spring of 1973 when a letter arrived from Mrs. Evans Franklin, a constituent who wrote neighborhood news for a rural weekly newspaper I once edited. In this letter, she pleaded for my help in securing the release of her son, Ed, from a faraway prison. He had been convicted of espionage and sentenced to five years' solitary imprisonment in Aden, the capital of the Marxist People's Democratic Republic of (South) Yemen. After reading her plea, I had to consult a map. I knew only that Aden once had been a major British base.

Had it not been for a series of cancelled airline flights, his mother told me, Franklin would never have set foot in Aden. Returning from Ethiopia to his teaching post in Kuwait, he was rerouted through Aden and then delayed again by the cancellation of his departing flight. His luck worsened. A camera buff and unaware of local restrictions, he photographed a prohibited area. The Adenese were still nervous about blonde-haired visitors, remembering the commando raid the British had conducted shortly after they left Aden six years earlier. When Franklin snapped the pictures, he was immediately arrested, kept in an interrogation center for months, and finally brought to trial, convicted and sentenced. My efforts to secure his release proceeded for the most part without aid from the State Department. Our government had had no relations, diplomatic or otherwise, with Aden since a 1969 coup moved the regime dramatically to the left. This meant the State Department could do nothing directly. I asked a friend in the Egyptian embassy in Washington to help. Franklin's parents, people of modest means living in a rural crossroads village, sent a request to Salim Rubyai Ali, South Yemen's president, seeking executive clemency. I sent a similar request. Our government asked the British to intervene through their embassy in Aden. There was no response to any of these initiatives.

In December 1973 I visited Abdallah Ashtal, Aden's ambassador to the United Nations in New York, to ask if I could go personally to Aden and make a plea for Franklin's release. Ashtal, a short, handsome, youthful diplomat who was taking evening graduate courses at New York University, promised a prompt answer. A message came back two weeks later that I would be welcome.

If I decided to go, I would have to travel alone. I would be the first Congressman—House or Senate—to visit Aden since the Republic was established in 1967 and the first United States official to visit there since diplomatic relations were severed in the wake of the coup two years later. Although this was an exciting prospect, it also caused me some foreboding. Moreover, I had no authority as an envoy. South Yemen, sometimes called the Cuba of the Arab world, was regarded by our State Department as the most radical of the Arab states. A State Department friend did nothing to relieve my concern when he told me that Aden's foreign minister got his job "because he killed more opponents than any other candidate."

Troubling questions came to mind. How would I be received? I discussed the trip with Alfred L. Atherton, Jr., assistant secretary of state for Near East and South Asia affairs. I asked him, "If they lock me up, what will you do first?" He smiled and said, "Look for another Congressman to come get you out!"

Still, I was probably the only person able to help. Franklin's mother told me, "I doubt if Ed can survive five years in a Yemen jail." My wife, Lucille, expressed deep concern over the prospects of the trip but agreed that I had little choice but to go.

I also thought the trip might be an opportunity to open the door to better relations with a vital but little-known part of the world. With the imminent reopening of the Suez Canal, better relations with Aden could be important to United States interests in the Indian Ocean. After all, Aden, along with French-held Djibouti, was a guardian of a world-famous and vitally important strait, the gateway to the Suez Canal. If the Soviets, already present with aid missions and military advisers, succeeded in dominating the Aden government, they could effectively control the canal from the south. It was obvious that, beyond the release of Franklin, the United States needed good relations.

I decided that I must go. The trip was set for late March 1974.

From Middle East scholars, I learned that Secretary of State Henry Kissinger, who was soon to begin shuttle negotiations between Israel and Egypt, was held in high esteem in Aden. I asked him for a letter that I could take with me which would be as explicit as possible about United States-Aden relations. A personal letter arrived three days before I left. In it, Kissinger said he welcomed my "humanitarian mission" to Aden and added: "Should the occasion arise, you may wish to inform those officials whom you meet of our continuing commitment to work for an equitable and lasting Middle East peace and of our desire to strengthen our ties with the Arab world."

The letter was addressed to me, not to the Aden government. It was a diplomatic "feeler." I hoped it would convince any officials I met that the United States wanted to establish normal relations.

A good traveler always brings gifts. At the suggestion of an Egyptian friend, I secured scholarships from three colleges in Illinois to present to South Yemeni students. I also located and had specially bound two Arabic language translations of Carl Sandburg's biography of Lincoln, *The Prairie Years.* In addition, I also carried two small busts of Lincoln—my most celebrated constituent—hoping he would be known even in Aden.

I left Washington early enough to visit Syria before heading south to Aden. Syria had not had normal diplomatic relations with the United States since the 1967 war with Israel, and despite its growing importance, no member of the House of Representatives had visited there for five years. To my surprise, President Hafez Assad of Syria agreed to receive me without advance appointment. Perhaps he was intrigued with the presence of a United States Congressman who said he had an open mind about Middle East issues.

Assad received me in the spacious second-floor reception room of his offices. A tall, thickset man with a prominent forehead and a warm, quiet manner, Assad made his points forcefully but without a hint of hostility. While sipping small cups of rich Syrian coffee, he voiced his pain over United States support of Israel's actions: "We are bitter about the guns and ammunition you provide to Israel, and why not? But bitterness is not hostility. In fact, we have very warm feelings about the American people. Despite the war, the Syrian people like Americans and have for years."

While sympathizing, I took the initiative, urging him to restore full diplomatic relations and to take a page from the public relations book of the Israelis. I suggested that he come to the United States and take his case directly to the American people over television.

Assad responded, "Perhaps we have made some mistakes. We should have better public relations. I agree with what you say and recommend, but I don't know when I can come to the United States."

As I rose to leave, Assad said, "You have my mandate to invite members of your Congress to visit Syria as soon as possible. They will be most welcome. We want those who are critical as well as those who are friends to come."

While I later extended Assad's invitation personally to many of my colleagues and, in a detailed official report, to all of them, few accepted. The first Congressional group did not arrive until 1978, four years later.

After my interview with Assad, I was driven late at night from Damascus to Beirut for the flight to Aden. As our car approached the Syria-Lebanon border, I could hear the sound of Israel's shelling of Lebanon's Mt. Hermon, a sobering reminder that seven years after the 1967 war the fighting still continued.

In 1974, Beirut was still the "Paris of the Middle East," a western-like city with a lively night life and bustling commerce. A new Holiday Inn had just opened near the harbor. Every street seemed to boast two international banks, at least three bookstores and a dozen restaurants. A year later the Holiday Inn became a battleground between Phalangist militia, backed by Israel, and the Lebanese left coalition, including Palestinians, helped by various Arab governments and by Moscow. Its walls were ripped open by shells, its rooftop pavilion littered with the bodies of fallen snipers. The vicious civil war, which began in 1975, had turned Beirut into a city of rubble.

But even in 1974, the Palestinians in the refugee camps did not share the prosperity of the city. I passed the hovels of Sabra and Shatila, where, nine years later, the massacre of hundreds of Palestinian civilians would shock the world. My embassy escort said, "These miserable camps haven't improved in 20 years."

I also passed the Tel Zaatar refugee camp, whose wretched inhabitants would soon suffer a fate even more cruel. A year later that camp was besieged for 45 days by rightist "Christian" militias, armed and advised by Israel's Labor government. Fifteen thousand Palestinians died, many of them after the camp surrendered. Virtually every adult male survivor was executed. That slaughter was little noted by the world press. Hardly anyone, save the Palestinians, remembers it.

At that time, the spring of 1974, I had no premonition of the tragedies to follow. I boarded the Aden-bound plane at Beirut with just one person's tragedy on my mind—that of Ed Franklin.

Mission in Aden

In Aden, to my surprise and pleasure, I was met by a delegation of five youthful officials, three of them cabinet ministers. Mine was the only gray hair in sight that night. The group had stayed up until 2 A.M. to meet the plane. "Welcome. We have your quarters ready," said the government's chief of protocol. Good news! This meant, I felt, that I would not be stuck off in a hotel room. My quarters turned out to be a rambling old building which years ago, in imperial days, was the residence of the British air commander. A tree-shaded terrace—a rarity in Aden—looked over the great harbor, a strategic prize ever since white men first rounded the Cape of Good Hope in the sixteenth century. Blackbirds chattered overhead.

I received permission to visit Franklin at 7:15 that first night. I found him under guard in an apartment on the second floor of a small modern building. When I entered, he was standing by a couch in the livingroom. We had never seen each other before.

"I presume you are Congressman Findley."

Despite the emotion of the occasion, I smiled, sensing how Dr. Livingston must have felt years before in Africa.

After 16 months of confinement, Franklin was thin, almost gaunt. His trousers were several sizes too big, his blonde hair was neatly combed, his face cleanly shaved and he was surprisingly well tanned. He looked much older than his 34 years.

We were able to talk alone. I said, "You're thin, but you look well." He answered, "I'm very glad you came, and I feel pretty well. Much better now that you're here. A few days ago when I used a mirror for the first time in months, I was shocked at how I look." He said he had got the tan from daily exercise in the prison yard, adding that he had been transferred to the flat two days before, obviously because authorities did not want me to see the prison.

"Here is a box of food items your family asked me to deliver." When I said that, his face, which until then had displayed no emotion, fell. "I guess this means I am not going home with you."

I said, "I don't know."

Franklin changed the subject. "I had to leave my Bible at the prison. I hated to, because I like to read it every day."

I said, "Many people have been praying for you."

He responded, "Yes, I knew at once, even before I got word in letters from home. I could feel it."

Franklin told me he had not been physically abused but said the food was terrible and some of the rules bothered him. "I am not allowed to have a pen and paper. I like to write. I once wrote poetry on a sack, but then my pencil was discovered and taken from me. I don't know why." Still, he seemed to hold no grudge against his captors. "I like the Arab world. Maybe someday when the American embassy is reopened, I could even get a job here."

I assured him: "I'll do my very best to secure your release, or at least shorten your term. That's why I'm here, and I'll try to see you again before I leave. I'll also try to get approval for you to have pencil and paper."

On the way back to my quarters, I passed on Franklin's request for writing materials to my escort officer, who answered simply, "I will report your request." I spent Friday, a Moslem day of worship, touring the nearby desolate countryside. The main tourist attraction is an ancient, massive stone well built to store the area's scarce rainfall. That evening the British consul, a compassionate man who had occasionally delivered reading material to Franklin, joined me for dinner. The British long ago understood the importance of maintaining diplomatic relations even with hostile regimes and, shortly after their stormy departure from Aden, they had established an embassy there.

Saturday morning Foreign Minister M. J. Motie came to my quarters for a long discussion of United States–Yemen relations. The plight of the Palestinians under Israeli occupation was at the top of his agenda, Franklin at the top of mine. He charged, "The United States is helping Saudi Arabia foment subversion along Yemen's borders." I told him I was troubled by this charge, was unaware of such activity and I hoped to help improve relations. Motie responded, "While the past is not good, the present looks better, but we need a substantial sign of friendship. For example, we need aid in buying wheat."

After the discussion, I spent a long and fruitless afternoon trying to fill a shopping list my family had sent with me. The bazaar had little but cheap Japanese radios and a few trinkets. It had even fewer shoppers. I returned to the guest house, finding, to my astonishment, an assortment of gifts, each neatly wrapped—among them a jambia, the traditional curved Yemeni dagger, and a large ceremonial pipe. The gifts were accompanied by a card: "With the compliments of the president."

Were these gifts merely sweeteners to take the place of Franklin on my homeward journey? Or were they a harbinger of success? I dared not believe the latter. I had received no hint that the government would even shorten Franklin's sentence, but, at least, it acceded to his request for paper and pencil.

My second visit with Franklin was more relaxed than the first. He accepted the pencils and paper I brought him with the comment, "I hope I won't need them except for tonight." I responded that I had no reason to hope he would be able to leave with me, but, strictly on my own hunch, felt that he would be released soon.

I met with President Ali the night before my scheduled departure inside the heavily guarded compound where the president both lived and had his offices. I was ushered into a long reception hall adorned with blue flowered carpeting and gold drapes down three sides. The fourth side opened into a large courtyard. Two rows of ceiling fans whirred overhead. In the center of this large hall was a lonely group of gold-upholstered sofas and chairs.

By the time I reached the circle of furniture, President Ali, the foreign minister of Aden and an interpreter were walking through the same door I had entered. I needed no introduction. I had seen Ali's picture many places around Aden, but frankly it did him little justice. He was a tall, well-built man of 40. His black hair had a touch of gray. His skin was dark, his bearing dignified. He was soft-spoken, and two gold teeth glistened when he smiled.

After exchanging greetings, I thanked him for his hospitality and for the gifts. Then I launched into my own presentation of gifts: first, the Lincoln book and bust, then the scholarships.

What he was waiting for, of course, was the letter from Kissinger which would indicate the weight the United States gave my mission. When I handed it to him, I tried to broaden its importance.

"Perhaps your excellency will permit me to explain," I said. This letter presents formally the desire of the U.S. to re-establish diplomatic relations. This is important. Our government needs these relations in order to understand Aden's policies and problems. The president of the United States and the secretary of state are limited in foreign policy. They can do only whatever the Congress will support, so it is also important for Congressmen to gain a better understanding of Aden's situation and of the Arab world in general."

Ali responded: "Aden is the shining example of the Republic. Other areas of our country are quite different. The people are much poorer." I gulped. I had seen only Aden, Ali's "shining example" which struck me as very poor, so I could only guess at conditions elsewhere.

While I took notes, Ali told me that the anti-poverty efforts of his government were handicapped by "subversion" from neighboring states. He said, bluntly, "The belief is held by the people of our country that all suffering, all damage caused by subversives, is really the work of the United States government. All military equipment we capture is United States equipment." Some of it, he said, was outside this building for me to examine.

I interjected that this information was not known in the United States, underscoring the need for diplomatic relations, so this sort of injury would stop. He nodded. "I favor relations with the United States, but they must relate to grievances now seen by my people." He added, "Aden does not wish to be isolated from the United States."

Ali thanked me for the gifts, indicating the interview was over. I sensed this was my long-awaited opportunity, my chance to launch into an appeal for Franklin.

It was not needed. Ali interrupted by saying simply, "Regarding the prisoner, as soon as I heard of your interest in him, I saw to it that he received preferential treatment. I have carefully considered your request and your desire that he be released. I have decided to grant your request. When you want him, you may have him."

I could scarcely believe what I had heard. "When you want him, you may have him." I was so overcome with joy I half-stumbled leaving the room. Franklin was free. In fact, he was waiting at my quarters when I returned. We were on the plane at 6 o'clock the next morning, headed for Beirut, New York and then St. Louis—where a joyous family welcomed Franklin home.

I am convinced the main reason for Franklin's release was the decision by the government to probe ever so cautiously for better relations with the United States. Caution was necessary, because there were those in both nations who did not wish to see relations improved. Ali was the least Marxist of a three-man ruling junta. In the State Department, even some "Arabists," still resentful over the Yemeni expulsion of the United States presence years before, rejected Aden as nothing but a "training ground for PLO terrorists." Others, such as Kissinger, felt differently. Ed Franklin had provided the opportunity to begin the probing.

But the United States government fiddled, hedged and delayed three years. Jimmy Carter replaced Gerald R. Ford in the White House, and Cyrus Vance became secretary of state. Our government turned down Aden's request to buy wheat on credit, then refused to consider a bid to buy three used airliners. The United States kept putting off even preliminary talks. At a second meeting with me in September 1977—this time in New York where he addressed the United Nations—Ali restated his desire for renewed relations with the United States and suggested that I report our discussion to Secretary of State Cyrus Vance. I did so, and after my report, Vance and Foreign Minister Motie of South Yemen agreed to exploratory talks. To me, this appeared like a momentous breakthrough. The talks were to begin in Aden in just a few weeks, shortly after New Year's Day. Sadly, procrastination took over.

No precise date for the meetings had been set when I returned to the Middle East with a number of other Congressmen in January 1978. I altered my own itinerary long enough for a side trip to Aden. Before I left the group, we met with Secretary of State Vance, whose travels happened to cross ours, and with Saudi Arabia's Crown Prince Fahd— a large, impressive man who spoke eloquent English and was to become the Saudi monarch. Fahd spoke approvingly of my efforts in Aden and asked me to tell officials in Aden that Saudi Arabia was ready to resume sending them economic aid.

"It's a Good Omen"

When I arrived, the scene in Aden had improved. South Yemen had already exchanged ambassadors with its former arch-enemy, Saudi Arabia—even though the two nations still had disputes over territory. Aden had also just agreed to diplomatic relations with Jordan. The local radio station no longer harangued American and Saudi "imperialists." This time my wife, Lucille, accompanied me. We were assigned to the same guest house I had used before, where the principal change was the presence of a well-stocked refrigerator.

President Ali received us in the same spacious hall, along with an honor guard. Although he avoided comment on Saudi Arabia's offer of aid, Ali spoke of Crown Prince Fahd with great warmth.

Then he added, "We are looking forward to the expected arrival of the diplomatic delegation from the United States before the end of the month." I am sure my face fell. I knew the delegation was not coming that month. In fact, the mission had been delayed indefinitely. A few days before, Vance had told me the bad news but had not explained why. When I expressed the hope that Ali had been notified of the delay, Vance had replied, "We will take care of it." But, unfortunately, no one did.

Ali was left waiting, day by day, for a group that did not arrive. I did not feel free to tell him of the change, so I listened and tried to look hopeful. I knew the delay would strengthen his critics who opposed reconciliation with the United States.

I changed the subject: "Some of our strategists say you have let the Soviets establish a naval base here. Do you have a comment?"

He strongly protested: "That is not true. We do not allow the Soviets, or any foreign nation, to have a military base in our territory. But we do cooperate with the Soviets because they help us." Ali concluded our discussion by giving me a message to take to Washington:

Please extend my warm greetings to President Carter. Kindly inform him that we are eager to maintain smooth and friendly relations between Democratic Yemen and the United States. We recognize that President Carter is concerned about maintaining friendly relations with all countries. We feel that is a positive policy. We believe our relations should be further strengthened.

As we parted, I gave Ali a pottery vase our daughter, Diane, had made for him. He said, "That's very nice. Please thank your daughter. I admire it." Then he stepped to the door to admire something else, rain, which is a rarity in Aden.

"It's a good omen," he said.

I left Aden more convinced than ever that diplomatic relations would help the United States and our friends in the region. The United States and Saudi Arabia had a common interest in minimizing the Soviet presence in South Yemen. We needed a diplomatic mission there. Back in Washington, I missed no opportunity to press this recommendation on Secretary Vance and on the White House staff.

At the White House a month later I was able to make a personal appeal to President Jimmy Carter. Carter said he was "surprised and pleased" by Ali's message.

"His words are surprisingly warm," he observed. "We've been hoping to improve our situation there." I urgently argued that there should be no further delays: "Another cancellation would be baffling to President Ali, to say the least."

Carter thanked me, and, as Vance had earlier, told me he would "take care of the matter."

Carter was true to his word. Five months after my last meeting with Ali, a team of State Department officials arranged to visit Aden on June 26, 1978, for "exploratory talks" to discuss in a "non-committal way" the resumption of diplomatic negotiations. Ali was to meet them on the day of their arrival.

It was too late. Aden's Marxist hardliners decided to act. Concerned by Ali's probing for improved relations with the United States and Saudi Arabia, radicals seized fighter planes, strafed the presidential quarters, took control of the government, and on the day the U.S. delegation was scheduled to arrive, arrested Ali. He was executed by a firing squad. Ambassador Ashtal called from New York to tell me the delegation would still be welcome, but the mission was scrubbed. The group, after traveling as far as Sa'ana, capital of North Yemen, returned to Washington. Distressed over the execution of Ali, I asked Ashtal for an explanation. He told me, "It's an internal matter of no concern to the outside world."

Still, Ali's fate concerned me deeply. And still does. I have often wondered whether my goodwill and his merciful act toward Ed Franklin contributed to his downfall.

My journeys to Aden had broader personal importance than my ultimately unsuccessful efforts to re-establish diplomatic relations. After years on Capitol Hill, I had heard for the first time the Arab perspective, particularly on the plight of the Palestinians. I began to read about the Middle East, to talk with experts and to begin to understand the region. Gradually, Arabs emerged as human beings.

The word of my experiences got around, and soon my office became a stopping place for people going to and from the Middle East—scholars, business people, clerics, government officials. It was unusual for anyone in Congress to visit Arab countries and take an interest in their problems. I began to speak out in Congress. I argued from what I considered to be a U.S. viewpoint—neither pro-Israel nor pro-Arab. I said that our unwillingness to talk directly to the political leadership of the Palestinians, like our reluctance to talk to President Ali in Yemen, handicapped our search for peace. Diplomatic communication with other parties, however alien, however small, is a convenience to our government. It does not need to be viewed as an endorsement. Thus, I asked, why not talk directly to PLO Chairman Yasser Arafat, the acknowledged political voice of the Palestinians? One reason, I discovered, was that Henry Kissinger, who had provided help on my long road to Aden, had, yielding to an Israeli request, agreed not to communicate formally with the PLO until they recognized the right of Israel to exist—a tough demand, especially in light of Israel's flat refusal to accept a new Palestinian state as its neighbor!

I decided to communicate with Arafat to help break the ice. I had first met the PLO leader in January 1978 during that Congressional mission to the Middle East when I saw Ali for the last time. Joining me were several colleagues, Democrats Leo Ryan of California, who was later to die in the violence at Jonestown, Guyana, and Helen Meyner of New Jersey. A Republican Congressman also attended, but, fearful that the news would cause him problems with Israeli activists in his district, asked me not to mention his presence. Before the meeting, I had many of the same misgivings that I felt before going to Aden four years earlier. I was wary, because meeting Arafat crossed the chalkline which Kissinger, at Israel's demand, had drawn.

"I Stand Behind the Words"

When I crossed the line, to my surprise I discovered that Arafat, who received us in a heavily guarded second-floor apartment, was not a wild-eyed, gun-waving fanatic. He spoke softly and listened attentively. He met us bare-headed—he was nearly bald. This took us by surprise, because in public he was always attired in the Palestinian headdress or military cap. To questions about PLO terrorism, he repeated his usual litany, but coming from the depth of his experience it seemed somewhat more forceful: "I am a freedom fighter. We are fighting for justice for our people, the four million Palestinians dispossessed and scattered by three decades of war."

Later that year, I had a second and more productive meeting with Arafat. This time I was alone. We met in the same apartment as before. With him were Abu Hassan, his security leader who was soon to die in a car-bombing in Beirut, and Mahmoud Labadi, his public affairs officer, who later deserted Arafat and joined Syrian-supported hardliners. Such was the ferment in that tortured group. I wanted Arafat to clarify the terms under which the PLO would live at peace with Israel. Was he ready to recognize Israel? In a four-hour discussion late into the night, he provided the answer. Working carefully word by word, and phrase by phrase, he fashioned a statement and authorized me to report it publicly.

I wrote the words and read them back several times so he could ponder their full meaning. When it was done I asked Arafat if he would sign his name on the paper bearing the words. He answered, "No, I prefer not to sign my name, but I stand behind the words. You may quote me."

The declaration Arafat gave me follows:

The PLO will accept an independent Palestinian state consisting of the West Bank and Gaza, with a connecting corridor, and in that circumstance will renounce any and all violent means to enlarge the territory of that state. I would reserve the right of course to use non-violent, that is to say diplomatic and democratic means, to bring about the eventual unification of all of Palestine. We will give de facto recognition to the State of Israel. We would live at peace with all our neighbors.—Damascus, November 30, 1978.

I was elated—perhaps too much so. Arafat's pledge contrasted sharply with the harsh rhetoric of earlier Palestinian public statements which called, in effect, for the elimination of the state of Israel. It was not, of course, everything Israel or the United States would want, but it was an encouraging start. If true, it belied the image of the fanatic who believed only in violence. During the long interview we covered many points, and, determined to protect my credibility, I asked Arafat to identify statements he did not wish to make public. The carefully-drafted pledge was not one of these. He wanted the world to know, and, clearly, he expected a positive response from President Carter. To use one of the PLO leader's favorite expressions, he had "played a card" in authorizing me to transmit this statement. It was a step beyond anything his organization had officially proclaimed.

Tragically, it brought no reaction from the U.S. government. I later learned that Secretary of State Vance privately recommended that the administration "take note" of it, though no public announcement was made. In subsequent public interviews, Arafat—always a nimble actor—sidestepped questions about the pledge.

Nevertheless, Carter's newly-appointed special ambassador to the Middle East, Robert Strauss, a prominent Democrat who had previously been chairman of the Democratic National Committee, was intrigued with my communication with Arafat and became a frequent visitor to my office. I often thought that bringing Arafat and Strauss together would be important to the peace process.

The fact that Strauss is Jewish would have helped thousands of Jews in Israel to put aside their government's hard line. But Strauss, despite his unique intimate relationship with Carter and his demonstrated ability to negotiate complicated problems on both the international and domestic scene, never received full presidential backing on the Middle East. Late in his diplomatic mission, just before he was shifted to the chairmanship of Carter's ill-fated campaign for re-election, Strauss told me, "If I had had my way, I would have been talking directly to Arafat months ago."

I found myself being drawn deeper and deeper into Middle East politics. Early one Sunday morning in August 1979, Assistant Secretary of State Harold Saunders called me in Illinois to ask for my help. At Arafat's behest, Kuwait was demanding consideration of a United Nations resolution sympathetic to the Palestinians. The United States, because of Israel's objections, would not support this resolution but did not want to go on record against it. The vote was scheduled for the following Tuesday. Given more time, Saunders hoped to find a formula which would satisfy both the Arab states and the United States. Mindful of President Carter's rule against even informal talks with the PLO, he carefully avoided directly asking that I call Arafat. Nevertheless, I knew Saunders well enough to grasp the purpose of his call. He hoped I could persuade Arafat to cancel the scheduled vote.

My call to Arafat's office in Beirut went through instantly, unusual for the chaotic Beirut exchange. I urged Arafat to delay the U.N. confrontation, arguing that this would cost him nothing while winning him the gratitude of the United States. Two hours later Arafat sent word to Kuwait causing the vote to be postponed. This spared the U.S. an embarrassing public spat with Arab friends. That same weekend, Carter's ambassador to the United Nations, Andrew Young, acted less cautiously than Saunders and met on the same issue with Zuhdi Terzi, the PLO observer at the United Nations. So firm was Carter's edict against talking with the PLO that this incident led to Young's resignation.

I was soon on the phone again with the State Department. This time my help, through Arafat, was needed in getting the U.S. hostages out of our embassy in Tehran. In our 1978 meeting, the PLO leader had told me of his close relationship with the revolutionaries in Iran, and I saw this crisis as an opportunity for Arafat to help in a humanitarian cause and perhaps open the door for peaceful negotiations on a broader scale. This time Arafat was away from headquarters, but I had a long talk with his deputy, Mahmoud Labadi, whom I had met during my second interview with Arafat.

He reminded me that Arafat had taken my advice on the United Nations confrontation but, in Labadi's words, "got nothing in return." He was right. No compromise resolution was ever accepted, and Arafat got little thanks. Labadi told me he disagreed with me regarding the situation in Iran but would report my arguments and recommendation carefully to his leader. Once more Arafat cooperated. He sent an envoy to Khomeini, and, according to Saunders, that envoy successfully arranged the release of the first eleven hostages.

For this, the Carter Administration thanked Arafat privately— very privately. Publicly, Carter spokesmen did nothing to discourage the unfounded speculation that the PLO had actually conspired with

Iran to seize the hostages. CBS's Marvin Kalb reported darkly that "someone" had been heard speaking Arabic (Iranians speak Farsi, a different language altogether) inside the embassy compound. This somehow seemed to mean that the PLO was responsible. Yet the reverse was true. Just before he left office, Secretary of State Vance told me that he was in "almost daily" communication with Arafat and his staff enlisting PLO help during the protracted Iranian hostage ordeal, but he never said so in public.

On several occasions during off-the-record meetings at the White House, I pleaded with the president to acknowledge publicly the moderate cooperative course chosen by Arafat and warned that failure to do so would strengthen more radical forces. Carter listened but never followed my advice. I learned later that Vice President Walter Mondale, more than any other personality in the Administration, had argued persuasively against any public statements which acknowledged PLO cooperation.

Mahmoud Labadi never forgave Arafat for this cooperation. Three years later he deserted the PLO leader and joined the rebels laying siege to Arafat in Tripoli. In explaining his defection, Labadi denounced Arafat by denouncing the aid Carter had ignored, "He [Arafat] gave far too many concessions to the U.S. and to the Israelis and he got nothing back. We think that we should step up armed resistance against the Israeli occupation." Labadi and his defecting comrades turned their weapons against Arafat, predicting—wrongly—that military measures could deliver for the Palestinian people what the PLO chief's diplomacy apparently could not.

Throughout 1979 and 1980, while deploring Palestinian violence, I also did my utmost to get the Carter Administration to pressure Israel to halt its repeated military attacks on Lebanon. Israel had begun periodic heavy bombing of villages and even areas in Beirut. The bombings were killing innocent civilians. Also, the planes and bombs were supplied by the United States. Finally Secretary of State Vance took an unusual step. He issued a formal written report to Congress stating that Israel "may have violated" the United States law which declared that United States-supplied weapons could be used only in self-defense. While the Administration did not take the next logical step of suspending military aid to Israel because the law was violated, the "may have violated" announcement made a point. It was one of those rare occasions when a United States administration has publicly rebuked Israel.

Behind the scenes, Carter was tougher—but not for very long. He sent a diplomat to Israeli Prime Minister Menachem Begin's office during the summer of 1980 with a warning that U.S. aid to Israel would be imperiled if Israel's air attacks against Lebanon continued. The ultimatum got results. Begin backed down, immediately phoned his Air Force chief and ordered the attacks stopped.

Later that summer Carter's resolve faded as the November elections approached. Israel resumed its use of U.S.-supplied weapons against Lebanon, but Carter fell silent. My protests were lonely on Capitol Hill and largely ignored by the makers of policy in the Administration.

My efforts did not, however, go unnoticed elsewhere. I became something of a curiosity, if not a celebrity, appearing on national television, interviewed on the radio and quoted in newspapers and magazines internationally. At times it was heady stuff. Ed Franklin's mother must have marveled at how her letter had changed my life.

Turmoil in the Middle West

While I was organizing my one-man peace initiative, my critics were organizing to put me out of office. Partisan critics back home, who had watched my re-election margins reach landslide proportions—I received 70 percent of the votes cast in 1978—correctly surmised that my unusual activities in foreign policy would provide them with the money to attack me in the upcoming elections. Beginning in the spring of 1979, an aggressive former state legislator, David Robinson, strongly encouraged by pro-Israel activists, began campaigning fulltime for the Democratic nomination for the Congressional seat I had held for nineteen years. Then, three months before the March 1980 primary, David Nuessen, the popular Republican mayor of Quincy, Illinois, entered the primary election, challenging my renomination in a professionally managed campaign that was supported substantially by pro-Israel political action committees and individuals. The contributions financed a relentless pummeling that bruised me more than I realized. I squeaked through the Republican primary with only 55 percent of the vote.

It was a year of surprises, the greatest being the reaction to my candidacy of Dr. Arthur Burns, former chairman of the Federal Reserve Board and now ambassador to the Federal Republic of Germany. Just after the primary election, I explained my campaign plight during a telephone conversation on legislative matters, and Burns responded generously, "We simply cannot afford to lose you. Your re-election is very important to the entire nation." Gratified, I made a modest request: "If you would put those sentiments in a letter that I could use in the campaign, that would be a great help."

His endorsement was not a high priority objective. In fact, I did not even think to ask for it until he praised my record. But I expected Burns to agree without hesitation. Why not? The courtesy was routine for a Republican as senior as I, and Burns had been not only a lifelong and outspoken Republican, but a close friend throughout my career in Congress. Several years earlier, at my request, he had spoken at the commencement program of my alma mater, Illinois College. Our views on economic and fiscal issues were the same.

His answer was the deepest wound of a traumatic year: "Oh, I couldn't do that. It's your views on the PLO. I'm sorry."

I was stupefied. I am used to surprises—and disappointments— but this refusal left me speechless.

A lesson? No event, before or since, disclosed to me so forcefully the hidden leverage of the Israeli lobby on the U.S. political scene. This great, kind, generous Jewish elder statesman, a personal friend for twenty years, could not ignore the lobby and say a public good word for my candidacy. I report this episode because, when a great man like Arthur Burns feels he must keep his views private, lesser men and women who would speak out face an enormous challenge.

Meanwhile, Democrat Robinson solicited campaign contributions through advertising in Jewish newspapers from coast to coast, stirring up interest by calling me a "practicing anti-Semite, who is one of the worst enemies that Jews and Israel have ever faced in the history of the U.S. Congress." He drew funds from each of the fifty states. In all, the campaign cost $1.2 million—the most expensive in Illinois history. We each spent about $600,000. University students from New York and California, as well as other states, came to central Illinois to staff Robinson's phone banks and handle other campaign chores.

"Dirty tricks" dogged me even when I wasn't campaigning and away from my district. The Chicago Council on Foreign Relations asked me to speak on foreign policy, and midway through my lecture on foreign policy one evening in Chicago, a man shouted from a door-way: "We've received a call. There's a bomb in the room." The crowd of 500 made a fast exit. The police later found a pipe loaded with bubble gum placed in the grand piano on the stage. Later, Robinson activists drove all the way to Detroit, Michigan, where I was a delegate to the Republican convention, to picket and to amuse onlookers with the chant, "Paul, Paul, he must go. He supports the PLO."

Trapped on a Bus with Percy

At first, my plight escaped the attention of the Reagan presidential campaign. In fact, when his scheduling office learned that I was having a fund-raising luncheon in Springfield, his manager asked if Reagan could stop by since he would be nearby that day. That unsolicited warmth quickly chilled. When he was scheduled to visit Illinois, New York City organizers warned Reagan's managers: "Appear friendly with Findley and you lose New York." This led them to take unusual measures to keep their candidate a safe distance from me.

Springfield, located in the heart of my district, posed a problem, because it is the home of the first Republican president, Abraham Lincoln, and therefore a Mecca for Republicans. During a day in Illinois, a Republican presidential candidate simply could not pass by Springfield. The Reagan camp was concerned about how to make the expected pilgrimage and still keep me at arm's length.

Greg Newell, chief of scheduling, first planned to finesse the problem by having Reagan deliver a major address from Lincoln's home at the very moment he knew I would be attending my major fundraiser of the year halfway across town. Just for insurance, Newell made it a deep finesse by moving Reagan's Springfield appearance all the way across town to the Lincoln Tomb instead of the home. He also scrubbed Reagan's speech, a decision to minimize press interest in the Springfield stop.

I realized, however, that many of my supporters would also want to see Reagan when he came to town. To accommodate them (and ensure good attendance at my own function), I rescheduled my fundraiser early enough so those attending—myself included—could attend the Reagan appearance at the tomb.

Reagan's manager passed an order quietly, or so they thought: "Under no circumstance is Findley to get near Reagan," even though elsewhere in Illinois, Congressional candidates were to appear on speaking platforms with him. Learning of the order, my manager, Don Norton, vented his outrage to Reagan headquarters. The Reagan team shifted gears again. This time they declared that all Congressmen were to be treated alike during the day in Illinois. None was to share the speaking platform with Reagan. Congressman Ed Madigan, irritated when told he must either speak before Reagan's arrival in Bloomington that day or wait until Reagan had left the platform, made no speech at all.

At Springfield, Reagan campaign staffer Paul Russo had only one assignment, but it was an important one. He was to keep me out of camera range when Reagan was nearby. I was literally coralled behind a rope 50 feet away while Reagan was photographed in the ceremonial "rubbing Lincoln's nose" on a statue at the tomb entrance.

At the next stop, a coal mine near Springfield, Russo's team tried to keep me on a bus and in the process trapped my friend, Senator Charles H. Percy, too. The purpose was to keep only me away from

Reagan during his remarks to the crowd. But Percy had the misfortune to be on the bus with me, so he too was detained. Together we managed to force the door open but only after Reagan had concluded his remarks and left the area.

Bob Hope Backs Out

The "panic" even spread to Hollywood. Bob Hope, who never wavered under enemy fire on war fronts in World War II and Korea and withstood heavy criticism for his support of President Nixon's Vietnam policies, encountered a new and more devastating line of fire when he agreed to appear at a fund-raising event for me in Springfield.

Two years earlier I had organized a 75th birthday party for Hope in the House of Representatives. It was the most fun-filled moment in the House I can remember. Hope and his wife sat in the gallery as one Congressman after another voiced their praise of the great entertainer. The tributes filled 14 pages of the *Congressional Record*.

Gratefully recalling the unique party, Hope agreed to help in my 1980 campaign. His manager, Ward Grant, knowing from the start that I was being opposed by pro-Israel activists because of my work on Middle East policy, declared, "We need men in Congress who speak their mind."

Coast-to-coast pressure quickly brought a change. Don Norton recalls an urgent telephone message he received from Hope's manager:

Grant told me that Hope was getting tremendous pressure from Jews and non-Jews all over the country. He said it's gone to the point where Hope's lawyer of 35 years, who is Jewish, has threatened to quit. The pressure was beyond belief, like nothing they had ever experienced before, and Hope just couldn't come.

Stunned, Norton pleaded that the event was widely publicized, all arrangements made, tickets sold and enthusiasm high. His plea was to no avail. When Norton told me of the crisis, I tried repeatedly to get a phone call through to Hope himself, hoping to persuade him to reconsider.

Failing to get a call through, I wrote a confidential letter, giving Hope details of my unpublicized endeavors the year before to promote understanding between PLO leader Yasser Arafat and Robert Strauss, President Carter's special emissary to the Middle East. I sent him copies of messages I had transmitted at the request of the two leaders. I asked Hope to keep the information confidential, because then—as now—our government was maintaining a public posture of refusing to communicate with the PLO. This letter brought no response, nor were my phone calls answered.

A happy surprise. Strauss, himself Jewish and a prominent Democrat, agreed to help. Encountering Strauss one afternoon on the steps of the House of Representatives, I explained my problem and asked him if he would be willing to talk to Hope and explain to him that I got in hot water with certain Jews simply by trying to work for my country and for peace in the Middle East.

By then Strauss had left his diplomatic post and was serving as chairman of Carter's ill-fated campaign for re-election. In a remarkable gesture of magnanimity to a Republican in the midst of a hotly contested election, Strauss agreed, adding: "Maybe I can help him understand the 'crazy' pressure he's getting." He gave me phone numbers where Hope could reach him.

In a wire to Hope I said: "[Strauss] will be glad to talk with you or anyone about the value of my work and what he described as the 'crazy pressure' you have been receiving."

By then, however, the "crazy" pressure had taken its toll, and Hope never made the call. I still have a souvenir of my chat with Strauss. It bears the phone number he gave me and my record of his parting words: "I wish you the best. I hope we both make it November 4, because we need to work together on the problems that remain."

A few days later, I finally got a call through to Hope. He was not his usual bubbly self. I assured him it had never occurred to me that he would have such an avalanche of protest calls, but now that the event had been scheduled it would hurt if he failed to come.

Hope interjected, "I read those letters you sent me. You should go public on this. Defend yourself with the facts." I said, "I just can't do that. It is highly secret information, and releasing it might hurt the peace process Carter is trying to advance." He paused, then said, "I just don't need this problem. I've been getting all these calls. It's too much pressure. I don't want to get involved."

Hope did not come, but, happily, only one ticket holder asked for a refund. The sell-out crowd heard a stirring address by Congressman Guy Vander Jagt, who filled in at the last minute.

Lobby pressures also intruded when former President Gerald R. Ford agreed to appear in my behalf, this time in Alton, Illinois.

The first sign of trouble was a call from Palm Springs in which Ford's secretary reported that the former president had to cancel his date because his staff had mistakenly booked him to speak at a meeting of the Michigan Bar Association the same day. There was no other time that Ford could help me, the caller said, before election day. To determine if some accommodation was possible, my assistant, Bob Wichser, called the Michigan Bar Association, only to learn that there was no conflict—no event was scheduled.

I was puzzled. I had worked closely with Ford during the 16 years he was Republican leader of the House, noting with admiration that he had never let disagreement on a policy issue keep him from campaigning for Republican Congressmen seeking re-election. When I finally reached Ford by phone, he said: "Paul, I've got to be up front with you. I've got to be candid. My problem is your relationship, your activities with the PLO and Arafat."

The day before, Reagan had lambasted Carter for refusing to brand the PLO a terrorist organization. "This puts me in a difficult position," said Ford. "I'm trying to help Reagan. If I come out and support you, at every press conference, I will be badgered and dogged with the question of how I could campaign for Reagan and then go and support Findley with his views on the PLO."

Despite these setbacks and the nationwide campaign against me, I won in 1980 with 56 percent of the vote. I felt that the worst was over—what more could the pro-Israeli activists do? Thus, I continued my peace endeavors. I did not anticipate the severe new challenges related to the Arab-Israeli dispute that were yet to come. In late 1981 a federal court, responding to shifts in population, ordered boundary changes in my district that eliminated Jacksonville, my old hometown, and added Decatur, the city with the nation's highest unemployment. Marginally Democratic before, my district was now substantially so. Then, too, recession fever was high and farmers were restless.

When election time came around again two years later, I was unopposed in the primary, but a strong Democratic opponent, Richard Durbin, emerged in the general election. More experienced and popular, he quickly picked up the resources Robinson had amassed, including Robinson's list of nationwide contributors. The Associated Press reported that: "Israel's American supporters again are pouring money into an emotional drive to unseat Central Illinois Representative Paul Findley." On the plus side, Reagan lieutenants were helping this time. My former House colleague, Vice-President George Bush, brushed aside pro-Israeli complaints from Texas and appeared at an event in my behalf in Springfield.

This time re-election was not to be. I lost by 1,407 votes, less than one percent of the total cast. In a vote that close, almost any negative development could account for the difference. The attack by pro-Israel activists was only one of several factors. Nevertheless, the American Israel Public Affairs Committee (AIPAC), Washington's principal pro-Israel lobby, claimed credit for my defeat. In a report to a Jewish gathering in Austin, Texas, a few days after election day, Thomas A. Dine, the organization's executive director, said his forces brought 150 students from the University of Illinois to "pound the pavements and knock on doors" and concluded, "This is a case where the Jewish lobby made a difference. We beat the odds and defeated Findley." He later estimated that $685,000 of the $750,000 raised by Durbin came from Jews. With my supporters raising almost exactly the same sum, the contest once again set a new state record for total spending.

No Ready Answers

The campaign to remove me from Congress had started early in 1979 and covered most of the next four years. It attracted the attention and resources of people in every state in the Union. Reports from friends suggested its national scope. Senator Bob Dole of Kansas, for six years my colleague on the House Agriculture Committee, said he heard pro-Israel leaders in Kansas speak with great emotional intensity about my candidacy both before and after election day. Clarence Palmby, former undersecretary of agriculture, learned that my defeat was the principal 1982 political objective of the partners in a large New York City law firm.

After my twenty-two years in Congress, losing was, of course, a disappointment. But my main reaction was wonderment. I was puzzled by the behavior of the pro-Israel activists. Why did they go to such trouble to eliminate me from Congress? Why did people from all over the country who did not know me personally and very likely knew little of my record dig so deeply in their own pockets—many of them contributing $1,000 to my opponents? What sustained this commitment for a four-year period?

Israeli activists could find few flaws in my voting record. Over the years I had voted consistently for aid to Israel. Sometimes I was highly critical of Egypt and other Arab states. Even when I was trying to get President Carter to suspend aid, as a temporary device to force Israel to halt its attacks on Lebanon, I had voted for all measures in Congress which authorized future Israeli military and economic assistance. Interestingly, many Israelis shared my views. According to polls, so did many U.S. Jews. Beyond Middle East policy, I had supported causes most Jews applauded: civil rights, community action programs, equal rights for women, a freeze on nuclear weapons and normalization of relations with China.

Moreover, I was but one of 435 Members of the House of Representatives. While senior among the Republicans, I was just one of nine on the Foreign Affairs subcommittee dealing with the Middle East. More often than not I stood completely alone when I criticized Israel, whether I spoke in committee or on the floor of the House of Representatives. Surely they realized that I posed no serious threat. Could Israel's supporters not tolerate even one lonely voice of dissent?

Or was the lobby's purpose to make an example of me in the Elizabethan manner? (According to legend, Queen Elizabeth occasionally hanged an admiral, just as an example to the others). Was I chosen for a trip to the political gallows to discourage other Congressmen from speaking out?

I could not reconcile the harsh tactics I had experienced with traditional Jewish advocacy of civil liberties, a record I had admired all my life. In Congress, I had worked closely in support of human rights causes with Jewish Congressmen like Allard Lowenstein, Stephen Solarz and Ben Gilman. In my wonderment, I pressed Doug Bloomfield, a friend on the AIPAC staff, for an explanation. He shrugged, "You were the most visible critic of Israeli policy. That's the best answer I can give." It was hardly adequate.

The unanswered question led to others.

Do other Congressmen have similar experiences? To be sure, those who speak out are few in number, but it seemed implausible that the lobby would target me alone. I wanted the facts.

Beyond Congress were the president and the vast array of "movers and shakers" in the executive branch. What pressures, if any, do they experience? A lobby formidable enough to frighten off a presidential campaign team and a former president of the United States—as Reagan and Ford had been in my 1980 election—must have great leverage at the highest levels of government.

What of other occupations? The lobby had intimidated Bob Hope. Did it have similar power over people in different professions? On campus, for example, does the tradition of academic freedom give immunity to teachers and administrators from the kind of pressure I had received from the pro-Israeli activists? Do clergymen escape? How about people in business, large and small? And, vitally important in our free society, is there intimidation of reporters, columnists, editorial writers, publishers, the commentators on television and radio?

Deep questions. To me, crucial questions.

There were no ready answers, so I decided to seek them. I began my quest by calling at the Capitol Hill offices of the American Israel Public Affairs Committee.

Chapter 1

King of the Hill

Washington is a city of acronyms, and today one of the best-known in Congress is AIPAC. The mere mention of it brings a sober, if not furtive look, to the face of anyone on Capitol Hill who deals with Middle East policy. AIPAC—the American Israel Public Affairs Committee—is now the preeminent power in Washington lobbying.

In 1967, as a fourth-term Congressman just named to the House Foreign Affairs Committee, I had never heard of it. One day, in private conversation in the committee room, I voiced a brief criticism of Israel's military attack on Syria. A senior Republican, William S. Broomfield of Michigan, responded with a smile, "Wait till 'Si' Kenen over at AIPAC hears what you've said." He was referring to I. L. Kenen, the executive director of AIPAC, whose name was just as unfamiliar to me as the organization he headed. I learned later that Broomfield was not joking. AIPAC sometimes finds out what Congressmen say about Middle East policy even in private conversations, and those who criticize Israel do so at their political peril.

AIPAC is only a part of the Israeli lobby, but in terms of direct effect on public policy it is clearly the most important. The organization has deepened and extended its influence in recent years. It is no overstatement to say that AIPAC has effectively gained control of virtually all of Capitol Hill's action on Middle East policy. Almost without exception, House and Senate members do its bidding, because most of them consider AIPAC to be the direct Capitol Hill representative of a political force that can make or break their chances at election time.

Whether based on fact or fancy, the perception is what counts: AIPAC means power—raw, intimidating power. Its promotional literature regularly cites a tribute published in *The New York Times:* "The most powerful, best-run and effective foreign policy interest group in

25

Washington." A former Congressman, Paul N. "Pete" McCloskey puts it more directly: Congress is "terrorized" by AIPAC. Other Congressmen have not been so candid on the public record, but many House and Senate members privately agree.

AIPAC's preeminence is relatively new. Only a few years ago the Conference of Presidents of Major Jewish Organizations was regarded as the strongest pro-Israel voice in Washington, speaking as it did for the leadership of the 38 main Jewish groups. The Anti-Defamation League, American Jewish Committee and AIPAC were generally in its shadow. The latter two organizations have about 50,000 members each. The Anti-Defamation League is technically subordinate to B'nai B'rith with its worldwide membership of 500,000, but it raises its own funds and has attained substantial independence. Although prominent in their younger years, Washington representatives Hyman Bookbinder of the American Jewish Committee and Dave Brody of the Anti-Defamation League are now substantially eclipsed by AIPAC.

The Washington presence is only the most visible tip of the lobby. Its effectiveness rests heavily on the foundation built nationally by U.S. Jews, who function through more than 200 national groups. A professional on the AIPAC staff says:

I would say that at most two million Jews are interested politically or in a charity sense. The other four million are not. Of the two million, most will not be involved beyond giving some money.

Actually, those who provide the political activism for all organizations in U.S. Jewry probably do not exceed 250,000. The lobby's most popular newsletter, AIPAC's *Near East Report,* goes to about 60,000 people, a distribution that the organization believes is read by most U.S. citizens who take a responsibility in pro-Israeli political action, whether their primary interest is AIPAC, B'nai B'rith, the American Jewish Committee, the Anti-Defamation League, the Jewish National Fund, the United Jewish Appeal or any of the other main national groups. The newsletter also goes without charge to news media, Congressmen, key government officials, and other people prominent in foreign policy. AIPAC members get the newsletter as a part of their $35 annual dues.

In practice, the lobby groups function as an informal extension of the Israeli government. This was illustrated when AIPAC helped draft the official statement defending Israel's 1981 bombing of the Iraqi nuclear reactor, then issued it the same hour as Israel's embassy.

No major Jewish organization ever publicly takes issue with positions and policies adopted by Israel. Thomas A. Dine, executive director of AIPAC, spoke warmly of President Reagan's peace plan when it was announced in September 1982, but as soon as Israel rejected the plan, Dine fell silent.

This close coordination sometimes inspires intragovernment humor. "At the State Department we used to predict that if Israel's prime minister should announce that the world is flat, within 24 hours Congress would pass a resolution congratulating him on the discovery," recalls Don Bergus, former ambassador to Sudan and a retired career diplomat.

To Jewish organizations, however, lobbying Washington is serious business, and they look increasingly to AIPAC for leadership. Stephen S. Rosenfeld, deputy editor of *The Washington Post* editorial page, rates AIPAC as "clearly the leading Jewish political force in America today."

AIPAC's charter defines its mission as legislative action, but it now also represents the interests of Israel whenever there is a perceived challenge to that country's interests in the news media, the religious community, on U.S. college campuses—anywhere. Because AIPAC's staff members are paid from contributions by American citizens, they need not register under the Foreign Agents Registration Act. In effect, however, they serve the same function as foreign agents.

Over the years the pro-Israel lobby has thoroughly penetrated this nation's governmental system, and the organization that has made the deepest impact is AIPAC, to whom even the president of the United States turns when he has a vexing political problem related to the Arab-Israeli dispute.

The Ascendancy of Thomas A. Dine

Faced with rising public opposition to the presence of U.S. Marines in Lebanon, President Ronald Reagan in October 1983 sought help from the American Israel Public Affairs Committee. The terrorist bombing which killed more than 200 Marines asleep in their barracks at the Beirut airport was yet to come. Still, four Marines had already died, three by sniper fire, and Congressional concern was rising. Democratic Congressman Sam Stratton of New York, a veteran known for his "hawkish" views, called the Marines "sitting ducks" and predicted heavy casualties. He wanted them out.

Others cited the War Powers Resolution and questioned whether the president had authority to keep forces in a hostile environment such as Beirut for more than 90 days without the express approval of

Congress. Some Congressmen began drawing parallels between the Marine presence in Lebanon and the beginnings of the disastrous U.S. experience in Vietnam.

President Reagan objected, as did his predecessors, to the restrictions imposed by the War Powers legislation. If he accepted its terms, he would have to withdraw the forces within 90 days or get Congress to approve an extension. If he insisted that the law did not apply because the situation was not hostile, events might quickly prove him wrong and, regardless, he would have a rebellious Congress on his hands.

He decided to finesse the problem. He asked Congress for legislation letting him keep the existing force of Marines in Lebanon for 18 months. This would please the "strict constructionists" who felt the chief executive must live with the War Powers Resolution. It would suit his own needs, because he was confident that the orderly removal of the Marines would occur within the 18-month period.

Thanks to extraordinary help from an unlikely quarter, Reagan's plan had relatively clear sailing in the House of Representatives. Speaker Thomas P. "Tip" O'Neill, the most prominent elected Democrat in the nation, gave the legislation his strong support. To O'Neill, it was a question of patriotism, and enough Democrats answered his call to assure passage in the Democrat-controlled body.

But the Senate, although controlled by his fellow Republicans, posed a more difficult problem for the president. A "nose count" showed a close vote and probably even defeat. The president decided he needed help and enlisted the cooperation of Thomas A. Dine, the slender, aggressive, dark-haired young Capitol Hill staff veteran who has headed AIPAC since 1981.

Reagan's appeal to Dine for support on the Marine issue was without precedent. The pending bill contained no money for Israel, and AIPAC and other Israeli lobby groups had kept hands off the Lebanon controversy. Pro-Israeli forces did not want other Americans to blame Israel if the Marines should encounter more trouble. Certainly Israel already bore responsibility enough for U.S. problems in Lebanon. It had discreetly but effectively helped to engineer the original Marine presence in Beirut by agreeing to withdraw its forces from Beirut in favor of a multinational force provided the United States were included. (The multinational force would have been unnecessary had Israel not invaded Lebanon in the first place.) Though AIPAC privately wanted the Marines to stay in Lebanon, under the circumstances its leadership preferred to stay in the background.

The White House call to Dine was exceptional for another reason: Reagan needed help with Senators who were normally his most stalwart supporters. The president was unsure of the votes of twelve Republicans, among them John Warner of Virginia, Dan Quayle of Indiana, William Cohen of Maine and James A. McClure of Idaho. All were generally regarded as "hawkish" on military questions and, except for McClure, strong supporters of Israel. Learning of the presidential plea, one AIPAC staffer said: "If the White House is worried about those votes, the bill is going down."

Despite its reluctance to get involved publicly in the sensitive issue, AIPAC made the calls. Nine of the twelve Senators, including the four mentioned above, voted with the president and helped him win a narrow 54 to 46 victory.

AIPAC's role in the outcome was not noted in most media reports on the dramatic event, but an elated President Reagan called Dine personally to express his thanks. Michael Gale, then handling White House relations with the Jewish community, provided a transcript of the conversation with the suggestion that AIPAC publicize it. AIPAC declined, preferring to maintain its low profile on the issue, so Gale gave the text to Wolf Blitzer of *The Jerusalem Post,* who formerly wrote for AIPAC's *Near East Report.* The *Post* quoted Reagan as saying to Dine, "I just wanted to thank you and all your staff for the great assistance you gave us on the War Powers Act resolution. . . . I know how you mobilized the grassroot organizations to generate support."

"Well, we try to use the telephone," responded Dine. "That's part of our job. And we wanted to do it and will continue to do it. . . . We want to work together, obviously."

Work together they have. The Reagan executive branch established a relationship with AIPAC of unprecedented intimacy. It was not the first time the White House or the State Department had turned to the lobbying group for help. Although these high level approaches are little known even on Capitol Hill, they actually occur every time foreign aid legislation is up for a vote. Whoever controls the White House finds that securing Congressional approval of foreign aid is a challenge and, as the legislation includes economic and military aid to Israel, naturally looks to AIPAC for help. Except for a few humanitarian and church-related organizations, AIPAC serves foreign aid's only domestic constituency.

Without AIPAC, foreign aid legislation would not be approved at the $7 billion-plus level of 1983 and might have difficulty surviving at all. A candid tribute to the lobby came from John K. Wilhelm, the executive director of the presidential commission that made recommendations in late 1983 on the future direction of foreign aid. Briefing a world hunger board at the State Department in January 1984, Wilhelm, a career veteran in the Agency for International Development, said the active support of the pro-Israeli lobby was "vital" to Congressional approval of foreign aid. In the early 1960s when aid to Israel was modest—less than $100 million a year—a foreign-aid bill squeaked through the House of Representatives by a scant five votes. AIPAC was then in its infancy.

AIPAC also crafted the strategy which produced a $510 million increase in 1983 aid for Israel—an increase which was astonishing because it came just after the indiscriminate bombing of Beirut and the failure of Israeli forces to halt the massacre of Palestinian refugees in the Sabra and Shatila refugee camps, events that aroused unprecedented public criticism of Israeli policy.

The administration opposed the increase but was outmaneuvered. By the time Judge William Clark, at the time National Security Adviser to President Reagan, sent an urgent appeal to Republican Senator Mark Hatfield to block the increase, the issue was settled. AIPAC had already locked in support by persuading a majority on the Appropriations Committee that the add-on was a simple question of being for or against Israel. No one wanted to champion the negative side.

AIPAC had already confounded the administration on the House side, where the White House had argued against the increase for budgetary reasons, contending it would be at the expense of other needy countries. This argument was demolished when AIPAC lobbyists presented elaborate data showing how the extra aid to Israel could be accomplished without cutting support for other countries. An AIPAC lobbyist summed up: "The administration lobbyists really didn't do their homework. They didn't have their act together." By 1984 the aid level had risen to over $2 billion a year—all of it in grants with no repayment—and the approval margin was 112.

In February 1983, Secretary of State George Shultz named a "blue ribbon" panel of prominent citizens to recommend changes in the foreign aid program. Of the 42 on the commission, 27 were Senators or House members with primary responsibility for handling foreign aid legislation. The others had prominence in administering foreign aid in years past.

Only one full-time lobbyist was named to the panel: AIPAC's executive director, Thomas A. Dine. It was the first time to my knowledge that a lobbyist had been selected for such a prestigious government assignment, and Dine's selection was particularly surprising because it put him in a close working relationship with the handful of people who formulate and carry out policy on the very matter AIPAC was set up to influence—aid to Israel.

A more enviable position for a lobbyist could hardly be imagined. Former Senator James Abourezk, head of the American-Arab Anti-Discrimination Committee, commented:

It would make as much sense to let the president of Lockheed Corporation serve on a Defense Department board which decides what planes our air force will buy.

In November, Dine took an even bigger step up the ladder of Washington prestige and influence. He was invited to the White House for a private meeting with National Security Adviser Robert C. McFarlane, President Reagan's closest advisor on day-to-day policy in the Middle East. On the agenda were two foreign policy topics of great sensitivity: the Lebanese situation and the proposal to help Jordan establish a rapid deployment force. Both of these issues, of course, were of vital interest to Israel. Dine's invitation came just a week after he received the President's jubilant phone call.

In January 1984 *Washingtonian* magazine listed Dine among the most influential people in the nation's capital.

Dine's reputation has even stirred Arab capitals. In mid-March 1984 King Hussein of Jordan publicly blamed AIPAC, in part, for the decline in U.S. influence and leadership for peace in the Middle East. He also criticized the inordinate influence of the Israeli lobby on U.S. presidential candidates. He said the candidates had to "appeal for the favors of AIPAC, Zionism and Israel."

One development which especially provoked the king was that, for ten days beginning in mid-March 1984, Dine personally took part in direct foreign policy negotiations with Undersecretary of State Lawrence S. Eagleburger and National Security Adviser McFarlane. During one session, Eagleburger offered to withdraw a widely publicized proposal to sell antiaircraft missiles to Jordan if AIPAC would drop its support of legislation requiring the removal of the U.S. embassy in Israel from Tel Aviv to Jerusalem.

By then, King Hussein's sharp criticism of the United States—and AIPAC—had appeared in U.S. newspapers, and Dine knew it had strengthened Congressional opposition to the sale. At the time Eagleburger made his proposition, AIPAC already had 48 Senators committed in opposition and received pledges from six more the next day. Thus AIPAC was able to kill the sale without cutting a deal on other issues.

After he rejected Eagleburger's offer, Dine promised that AIPAC would cease active opposition to a proposal to help Jordan establish a rapid deployment force and would lobby to work out a compromise on the bill to transfer the U.S. embassy from Tel Aviv to Jerusalem if the administration would take two important steps: first, refuse to sell Stinger antiaircraft missiles to Saudi Arabia, and, second, issue a public letter announcing that it would engage in no further indirect communications with the Palestine Liberation Organization. Although the public letter did not appear, the administration backed away from the Stinger sales to both Saudi Arabia and Jordan.

Dine emerged from these negotiations with his prestige greatly enhanced. Richard Murphy, assistant secretary of state for Near East and South Asia affairs, the official charged with the development and administration of United States policies relating to the Middle East, was not invited to the Eagleburger-McFarlane-Dine negotiations, nor was he notified of the administration decision to cancel the proposed sale of Stinger missiles until twelve hours after AIPAC received the information.

The Washington Post concluded that the episode "raised questions about the propriety of the administration's making deals on foreign policy issues with a private, special-interest organization." Dine had a ready response: "We think it's better to be strong and criticized, than weak, ignored and not respected."

In part, the unprecedented presidential consideration was a tribute to Dine's combination of ingratiating manner, tough, relentless spirit and sheer dynamism. Under Dine, AIPAC's membership has risen from 11,000 to over 50,000, and its annual budget from $750,000 to more than $3,000,000.

Dine's influence is felt in power centers beyond the Oval Office. He receives calls from presidential candidates as well as presidents and reports that former Vice-President Walter Mondale "bounces ideas off us" before he issues statements on Middle East policy.

Most Congressional actions affecting Middle East policy are either approved or initiated by AIPAC.

Broadening the Network

To accomplish these feats for Israel—sometimes cooperating with the president of the United States, sometimes not—AIPAC director Dine utilizes a team of hard-driving, able professionals and keeps them working together smoothly.

He keeps policy lines clear and the troops well-disciplined. AIPAC's role is to support Israel's policies, not to help formulate them, so AIPAC maintains daily telephone communication with the Israeli embassy, and Dine meets personally with embassy officials at least once a week.

Though AIPAC has a staff of only 60—small in comparison to other major U.S. Jewish organizations—it taps the resources of a broad nationwide network of unpaid activists. Annual membership meetings in Washington are a major way to rally the troops. Those attending hear prominent U.S. and Israeli speakers, participate in workshops and seminars, and contribute financially to the cause. The conferences attract top political talent: the Israeli ambassador, senior White House and State Department officials, prominent Senators and House members. Recent conferences featured Senators Paul Laxalt of Nevada, Joseph Biden of Delaware, Robert Kasten of Wisconsin, Christopher Dodd of Connecticut, Robert Packwood of Oregon, Robert Dole of Kansas, and Daniel Inouye of Hawaii.

The White House is also well represented at such conferences. Vice-President George Bush recently assured AIPAC delegates that the Reagan administration will keep fighting against anti-Semitism at the United Nations and criticized the three Democratic presidential candidates—Walter Mondale, Gary Hart and Jesse Jackson—for being "soft on anti-Semitism."

More than 1,200 representatives from 41 states attended AIPAC's 1983 national gathering. They heard Congressman Jack Kemp of New York, chairman of the Republican caucus in the House of Representatives, describe himself as "a de facto member of AIPAC." Forty-three House members and sixteen Senators attended the conference banquet.

Art Chotin, deputy executive director of AIPAC, reported to the group that during the previous year ten different statewide workshops on political involvement had given the "pro-Israeli community" the "skills they need to have an impact." Ten more were planned for 1984. Chotin illustrated the national impact of these local events by pointing out that a 1982 workshop in New Mexico had helped elect Democrat Jeffrey Bingaman to the Senate. Bingaman, described by Chotin as "a strong pro-Israeli voice in Washington," was among the 100 "pro-Israeli citizens" attending the 1983 affair.

Tightly scheduled workshops, similar to the national conferences, are conducted annually in each of five regions. The "capitals" are Atlanta, Fort Worth, Hollywood, Des Moines and Chicago, and from each a chairperson coordinates all AIPAC regional activities. To help these outreach programs, AIPAC now has full-time staff located in New York, New Jersey and California.

Chotin told the conference that during the 1982 Congressional elections, 300 candidates "came to visit AIPAC" to explain their positions on "foreign aid, arms sales to Arab nations, and the general nature of U.S.-Arab relations."

Ties with other interest groups are carefully cultivated. Christian outreach was announced as AIPAC's newest national program, and Merrie White, a "born-again Christian," was introduced as the director of relations with the Christian community. According to Chotin, the goal was nothing less than to "bring that community into AIPAC." He noted the presence of 50 Christians representing 35 states as evidence of progress already made toward this end. White helped organize the annual Religious Roundtable Prayer Breakfast for Israel the following February (see chapter nine). Chris Gersten, AIPAC's political director, came to the position after seven years as special assistant to the president of the International Union of Operating Engineers.

AIPAC's coast-to-coast outreach is enhanced by its speaking program. Its officers, staff members and representatives filled over 900 dates in 1982 alone. Receptions are held in scores of smaller cities. "Parlor briefings" in the homes of Jewish leaders nationally help raise money to supplement revenue from membership dues. Social events on Capitol Hill help spread the word to the thousands of high school and college students who work as interns in the offices of Senators and Congressmen or in committee offices.

Tours of Israel which other Jewish groups arrange help to establish a grassroots base for AIPAC's program. For example, in April 1982, the Young Leadership Mission, an activity of United Jewish Appeal, conducted 1,500 U.S. Jews on one week tours. "The visitors were given a view of the magnificence you will find in any country," observes an AIPAC staff member. He said the tour had profound impact: "It built spirit for the cause, and it raised money. The pitch for funds was the final event. It came right after the folks walked out of the memorial to the Holocaust." The effect was awesome: "The tour directors have it down to a science," he reports. "They know how to hit all the buttons." The United Jewish Appeal and Israel share the proceeds. Larry Kraftowitz, a Washington journalist who attended a similar tour, calls the experience "profound." He adds, "I consider myself more sympathetic to the New Jewish Agenda goals [than current Israeli government policy], but I must say I was impressed."

Tours are not just for Jews. Governors, members of state legislatures, and community leaders, including news media personnel, are also given the opportunity for expense-paid tours of Israel. Trips are also arranged for leaders nationally, especially those on Capitol Hill. While AIPAC does not itself conduct the tours, it facilitates the process. Over half the membership of Congress has traveled to Israel, about half going on what is deemed official business at the expense of the U.S. government. With few exceptions, Jewish organizations or individuals paid the expenses of the rest.

Another group of potentially influential—but often overlooked—Washington functionaries that AIPAC tries to influence is made up of Congressional staffers. AIPAC works with Israeli universities who arrange expense-paid tours for staff members who occupy key positions. These annual trips are called the Hal Rosenthal program, named for a staff aide to former Republican Senator Jacob Javits who was gunned down by a Palestinian terrorist on the first such trip. By 1984 over 50 Congressional staffers had participated.

AIPAC is as successful at keeping lawmakers from visiting Arab countries as it is in presenting only Israel's views. When the National Association of Arab Americans, working through the World Affairs Council of Amman, invited all Congressmen and their spouses to an expense-paid tour of Jordan with a side trip to the West Bank in 1983, a notice in AIPAC's *Near East Report* quickly chilled prospects for participation. It questioned how Amman, without Israeli cooperation, could get the tourists across the Jordan river for events scheduled in the West Bank. It also quoted Don Sundquist, a Republican Congressman from Tennessee, as expressing "fear" that if any of his colleagues accepted the trip they would be "used" by anti-Israeli propagandists. Only three Congressmen made the trip. A 1984 tour was cancelled for lack of acceptances.

AIPAC's outreach program is buttressed by a steady stream of publications. In addition to "Action Alerts" and the weekly *Near East Report,* it issues position papers and monographs designed to answer, or often discredit, critics, and advance Israel's objectives.

The most controversial publication of all is an "enemies list" issued as a "first edition" in the spring of 1983. A handsomely printed 154-page paperback entitled *The Campaign to Discredit Israel,* it provides a "directory of the actors": 21 organizations and 39 individuals AIPAC identified as inimical to Israeli interests.

Included are such distinguished public servants as former Undersecretary of State George W. Ball, retired ambassadors Talcott Seelye, Andrew Killgore, John C. West and James Akins, and former Senator James Abourezk. There are also five Jewish dissenters and several scholars on the list.

Seemingly unaware of the AIPAC project, the Anti-Defamation League of B'nai B'rith almost simultaneously issued its own "enemies list": *Pro-Arab Propaganda in America: Vehicles and Voices.* It too is identified as a "first edition," and lists 31 organizations and 34 individuals. These books are nothing more than blacklists, reminiscent of the worst tactics of the McCarthy era.

A similar "enemies list" is employed in AIPAC's extensive program at colleges and universities (see chapter seven).

"They Get the Word Out Fast"

Through "Action Alert" mailings AIPAC keeps more than one thousand Jewish leaders throughout the United States informed on current issues. An "alert" usually demands action to meet a legislative challenge on Capitol Hill, requesting a telephone call, telegram or, if need be, a personal visit to a reluctant Congressman.

The network can have almost instantaneous effect. One day I

whispered to a colleague in the Foreign Affairs Committee I might offer an amendment to a pending bill cutting aid to Israel. Within 30 minutes two other Congressmen came to me with worried looks, reporting they had just had calls from citizens in their home districts who were concerned about my amendment.

Paul Weyrich, who worked as a Senate aide before becoming a political analyst, details the effectiveness of AIPAC:

It's a remarkable system they have. If you vote with them, or make a public statement they like, they get the word out fast through their own publications and through editors around the country who are sympathetic to their cause.

Of course it works in reverse as well. If you say something they don't like, you can be denounced or censured through the same network. That kind of pressure is bound to affect Senators' thinking, especially if they are wavering or need support.

This activism is carried out by an elaborate system of officers, committees and councils which give AIPAC a ready, intimate system for political activity from coast to coast. Its nineteen officers meet once a month to confer with Dine on organization and management. Each of its five vice-presidents can expect eventually to serve a term as president. A large executive committee totaling 132 members is invited to Washington every three months for briefings. A national council lists over 200 names. These subgroups include the leadership of most major U.S. Jewish organizations.

The AIPAC staff is not only highly professional and highly motivated but also thoroughly experienced. Director Dine worked in several Capitol Hill jobs, first on the staff of Democratic Senator Edward Kennedy, later on the Foreign Relations Committee under Democratic Senator Frank Church of Idaho, and finally as staff director on foreign policy for the Senate budget committee.

AIPAC's four lobbyists are Douglas Bloomfield, Ralph Nurnberger, Esther Kurz and Leslie L. Levy. All but Levy worked in foreign policy for a Senator or Congressman before joining AIPAC. Levy came to AIPAC as a student intern and advanced within the organization.

Bloomfield, once an intern under Democratic Senator Hubert Humphrey of Minnesota, worked for 10 years for Democratic Congressman Ben Rosenthal of New York. Nurnberger worked for several years on the Senate Foreign Relations Committee and for Republican Senator James Pearson of Kansas. Kurz worked, in succession, for Democratic Congressman Charles Wilson of Texas, and Republican Senators Jacob Javits of New York and Arlen Specter of Pennsylvania.

The four divide up the membership of the House and Senate. Actually, only a handful of legislators are keys to success, so each of the four lobbyists needs to watch carefully only about thirty lawmakers. They concentrate on legislators from the twelve states which have a Jewish population of at least three percent: New York, New Jersey, California, Massachusetts, Ohio, Illinois, Michigan, Pennsylvania, Maryland, Delaware, Florida and Connecticut.

The movement from Congressional staff job to AIPAC also occasionally works the other way. A few veterans of AIPAC have moved to government assignments, among them Jonathan Slade, now with Democratic Congressman Larry Smith of Florida, and Marvin Feuerwerger, who was with Democratic Congressman Stephen Solarz of New York before he joined the Policy Planning Staff at the State Department. Both Smith and Solarz are members of the Foreign Affairs Committee, and both are passionate supporters of Israel.

Lobbyists for AIPAC have almost instant access to House and Senate members and feel free to call them at their homes in the evening. Republican Congressman Douglas Bereuter of Nebraska, an exception, will receive no lobbyists, AIPAC or otherwise, but the doors are wide open to AIPAC lobbyists at the offices of almost all other Congressmen. A Congressional aide explained why:

Professionalism is one reason. They know what they are doing, get to the point and leave. They are often a useful source of information. They are reliable and friendly. But most important of all, they are seen by Congressmen as having direct and powerful ties to important constituents.

The result is a remarkable cooperation and rapport between lobbyist and legislator. Encountered in a Capitol corridor one day, an AIPAC lobbyist said, "Tomorrow I will try to see five members of the House. I called this morning and confirmed every appointment, and I have no doubt I will get in promptly." Two days later, even he seemed somewhat awed by AIPAC's clout. He reported, "I made all five. I went right in to see each of them. There was no waiting. Our access is amazing."

This experience contrasts sharply with the experience of most other lobbyists on Capitol Hill. One veteran lobbyist reflected with envy on the access AIPAC enjoys: "If I can actually see two Congressmen or Senators in one long day, it's been a good one."

Despite its denials, AIPAC keeps close records on each House and Senator member. Unlike other lobbies, which keep track only of a few "key" issues voted on the House or Senate floor, AIPAC takes note of other activities, too—votes in committees, co-sponsorship of bills, signing of letters and even whether speeches are made. "That's depth!" exclaims an admiring Capitol Hill staff member.

An illustration of lobby power occurred October 3, 1984, when the

House of Representatives approved a bill to remove all trade restrictions between the United States and Israel; 98.5 percent (416) voted affirmative, despite the strong opposition of the AFL-CIO and the American Farm Bureau Federation. The vote was 416 to 6 on legislation that normally would elicit heavy reaction because of its effect on markets for commodities produced in the United States.

As they voted, few were aware of a Commerce Department study which found that the duty-free imports proposed in the bill would cause "significant adverse effects" on U.S. producers of vegetables. Because the White House wanted the bill passed, notwithstanding its effects on jobs and markets, the study was classified "confidential" and kept under wraps. One Congressman finally pried a copy loose by complaining bitterly—and correctly—to the White House that AIPAC had secured a copy for its own use.

"I Cleared It with AIPAC"

Until his defeat in an upset on November 6, 1984, Congressman Clarence D. "Doc" Long, a 74-year-old Democrat of Maryland, exemplified the strong ties between AIPAC and Capitol Hill. He delivered for Israel as chairman of the House Appropriations Subcommittee which handles aid to Israel.

The tall, gray-haired, former economics professor at Johns Hopkins University trumpeted his support: "AIPAC made my district their number one interest." AIPAC supported Long for a good reason: He held the gavel when questions about funding Israeli aid come up. The lobby wanted him to keep it. Chairmanships normally are decided by seniority, and next in line after Long is David Obey of Wisconsin, who earned lobby disfavor in 1976 by offering an amendment to cut aid to Israel by $200 million. "Doc" Long never had any misgivings about aid to Israel and helped his colleagues defeat Obey's amendment, 342 to 32.

Sitting at a table in the House of Representatives restaurant during a late House session in 1982, Long explained,

Long ago I decided that I'd vote for anything AIPAC wants. I didn't want them on my back. My district is too difficult. I don't need the trouble [pro-Israeli lobbyists] can cause. I made up my mind I would get and keep their support.

The conversation turned to one of Obey's questions about the high levels of Israeli aid. Long said, "I can't imagine why Dave would say things like that." A colleague chided: "Maybe he's thinking about our own national interest."

In September 1983, Long led a battle to get U.S. Marines out of

Lebanon. He proposed an amendment which would have cut funding for the operation in 60 days. John Hall, a reporter who knew Long's close ties with the lobby, asked Long, "Are you sure this amendment won't get you in trouble?" Without hesitation, the Congressman replied: "I cleared it with AIPAC." He was not joking. Though this was not the first Congressional proposal to be cleared in advance with the Israeli lobby, it was the first time the clearance had been specifically acknowledged in the public record. The proposal to cut aid to Lebanon provoked a lively debate but, opposed by such leaders as Speaker "Tip" O'Neill and Lee Hamilton of Indiana, chairman of the Subcommittee on Europe and the Middle East, the measure failed, 274-153.

Although heavily supported by pro-Israeli interests—18 pro-Israel political action committees chipped in $31,250 for Long's 1982 re-election campaign—Long denies a personal linkage:

Nobody has to give me money to make me vote for aid to Israel. I've been doing that for 20 years, most of the time without contributions.

The money and votes Israel's supporters provided to Long's candidacy were insufficient in 1984. Although pro-Israel PACs gave him $155,000—four times the amount that went to any other House candidate—Long lost by 5,727 votes, less than three percent of those cast. A factor in his defeat was advertising sponsored by people prominent in the National Association of Arab Americans which attacked Long for his uncritical support of Israel's demands. Obey, Long's likely successor as chairman, was the only Democrat on the panel who did not accept money from pro-Israel political action committees.

Outreach on an International Scale

AIPAC not only champions Israel's causes in the U.S., but its international ambitions as well. The lobby recently began an international outreach program, serving Israel's interests by facilitating U.S. aid to other countries. In 1983 it tried to help Zaire, Israel's new African friend. Israel wanted Zaire to get $20 million in military assistance requested by President Reagan, but AIPAC decided against assigning the lobbying task to its regular staff. Instead, it secured the temporary services of a consultant who button-holed members of the House Committee on Foreign Affairs. The amendment failed, but the effort helped to pay Israel's obligation incurred when Zaire extended full diplomatic recognition to Israel the previous year.

Columnists Rowland Evans and Robert Novak viewed the initiative as the first step in an Israeli program "to broker aid favors for other pariahs on the congressional hit list to enhance its influence." They described this new effort by Israel as "an exercise of domestic political power by a foreign nation that raises troubling questions."

While branching out internationally, AIPAC maintains strong influence in domestic partisan campaigns. It took a major role in the intense 1984 contest for the Senate in North Carolina, which involved an expensive showdown between Jesse Helms, the Republican incumbent, who is proud to be viewed as the apostle of conservatism, and Democratic Governor Jim Hunt, who sees himself as a leader in the progressive politics in the "New South." These adversaries were of one mind, however, in soliciting the pro-Israel vote, and the endeavor led Helms into surprising activity. The contest took on special national importance because Helms, as second-ranking Republican on the Senate Foreign Relations Committee, could have chosen to head the committee after the defeat of Senator Charles Percy (see chapter three).

In his program to win pro-Israel support, Helms had to overcome major obstacles. In a 1979 speech, Helms had warned that Israeli West Bank policies were "the block to a comprehensive settlement" of the Arab-Israeli dispute. During Israel's invasion of Lebanon in 1982, Helms made a speech in which he suggested that the United States might ultimately need to "shut down" relations with Israel.

High on Helms's hate list is foreign aid, which he considers to be the "the greatest racket of all time." He proclaims proudly, "I have not voted to send one dime overseas for these programs."

Because aid to Israel is included in the foreign aid he opposed, Hunt charged that Helms had voted against Israel no fewer than 25 times. He also criticized Helms sharply for voting in favor of controversial military sales to Saudi Arabia.

Hunt's campaign team sought to exploit these "mistakes" with a letter to pro-Israel financial prospects mailed in an envelope conspicuously labeled: "Caution: the enclosed information is extremely damaging to the state of Israel." The damage was identified as the prospect that Helms might become an anti-Israel chairman of the Foreign Relations Committee. This form of fundraising brought good results: a Helms staff member said, "We calculate that 60 percent of Hunt's money is from the Jewish community." By mid-August Hunt had received $130,350 from pro-Israel political action committees, Helms zero.

Helms launched a counterattack designed to mend his relations with backers of Israel. In May he personally introduced a visiting Likud member of the Israeli parliament on the Senate floor and had the text of his guest's foreign policy statement inserted in the *Congressional Record*. He seemed to contradict an earlier statement criticizing Israeli policies in occupied areas when he told the Senate that the

United States "should never pursue any plan that envisions a separation of the West Bank from Israel."

Helms's skill in playing both sides was demonstrated in his stand on a proposed bill to move the U.S. embassy from Tel Aviv to Jerusalem. Although he declined to co-sponsor the bill because of "grave legal questions" and its "uncertain" constitutionality, Helms urged President Reagan to order the removal of the embassy without special legislation.

In a remarkable countermove, Helms's campaign sent a fund appeal to Jewish citizens which expressed anguish that any Jew would consider opposing Helms in light of his "friendship" for Israel.

In the contest, the most expensive non-presidential campaign in history, Helms spent over $13 million and Hunt over $8 million. When the polls closed, Helms had eked out a narrow victory.

Beyond AIPAC to the PACs

AIPAC differs from most lobbies, in that it avoids endorsing candidates publicly and does not raise or spend money directly in partisan campaigns. Campaign involvement is left officially to pro-Israel political action committees (PACs). Over 3,000 PACs are registered under federal law, and almost all are directly affiliated with special-interest lobbies. There are 75 PACs which focus on support for Israel, though none lists an affiliation with AIPAC or any other Jewish organization.

Prior to 1979, pro-Israeli financial support to candidates and party organizations came entirely from individuals. Some of these individuals focused heavily on an Ohio Congressional race in 1976, the candidacy of Mary Rose Oakar, who was to become the first person of Syrian ancestry elected to Congress. A popular member of the Cleveland city council, she confronted a field of twelve male Democrats and an avalanche of Jewish money in the primary election race. Pro-Israeli interests selected State Senator Tony Celebreze, regarded as a "comer" in Ohio politics, as the candidate with the best chance to nudge her from the nomination.

During the campaign Dennis Heffernan, a fundraiser for Celepreze, was asked by a surprised and uneasy colleague to explain why more than thirty "Jewish-appearing" names were each recorded as donating $1,000.

"What's going on here?" he asked, wondering aloud if his friend Celebreze had "caved in" to a special interest. He asked bluntly: "Is Tony selling himself out, or is this money given in a worthy cause?" Heffernan responded, "Well, is Israel a worthy cause?"

Oakar found the focus by pro-Israel forces "upsetting." She explained, "I hadn't said a word about the Middle East, so it had to be because of my ethnic background. My father served in World War II and my brother in the Army later, but you would think we were less American."

The money helped Celebreze defeat the other eleven men, but Oakar won the nomination. Noting the district was overwhelmingly Democratic, the pro-Israel group sensed a hopeless situation and made no fight against Oakar in the fall or in subsequent elections.

The prominence of "Jewish-appearing" names in the Ohio race may have been a factor in encouraging Jews nationally to organize the first pro-Israel political action committees in 1979. By 1982 they had mushroomed to a total of thirty-one. Pro-Israel PACs contributed more than $1.8 million dollars to 268 different election campaigns during the 1981-82 Federal Election Commission reporting cycle, putting them in the highest political spending range. By mid-August 1984, the list had increased to 75 PACs, and they had accumulated $4.25 million for the 1984 federal elections.

None of them carried a name or other information which disclosed its pro-Israeli interest, nor did any list an affiliation with AIPAC or other pro-Israeli or Jewish organization. Each chose to obscure its pro-Israel character by using a bland title, like the "Committee for 18," "Arizona Politically Interested Citizens," "Joint Action Committee for Political Affairs," or the "Government Action Committee." Yet all are totally committed to one thing: Israel.

"No one is trying to hide anything," protests Mark Siegel, director of the pro-Israeli National Bipartisan Political Action Committee and a former White House liaison with the Jewish community. He insists that the bland names were chosen because "There are those in the political process who would use the percentage of Jewish money [in a given race] as a negative." The PAC Siegel heads was formed originally to help in the late Senator Henry Jackson's 1978 presidential bid.

Norman Silverman, who helped to found the Denver-based Committee for 18, is more explicit, saying the name selection became "an emotional issue." Some of the organizers, mainly younger people, wanted Jewish identity plainly set forth in the name. "Others," Silverman noted, "said they didn't want to be a member if we did that."

Whatever their names, pro-Israel PACs enlarge the opportunities for individual supporters of Israel to back candidates. An individual may contribute up to $5,000 to a political action committee but only $1,000 to a candidate in each election. PACs, in turn, may contribute $5,000 to a candidate in each election. Individuals often contribute the $1,000 limit directly to a candidate and also the $5,000 limit to a PAC supporting the same candidate. *The Wall Street Journal,* reviewing the growth of pro-Israel PACs in August 1983 reported that Lawrence and Barbara Weinberg of Beverly Hills, California, gave $20,000 to the Citizens Organized Political Action Committee, based in Los Angeles, over a period that encompassed both the primary and general elections in 1982 and gave $2,000 to Democrat Richard J. Durbin, the man who defeated me in 1982. The PAC also contributed $5,000 to Durbin. That kind of generosity is not ignored by your average politician.

The largest pro-Israel PAC is the National Political Action Committee (NatPAC), headquartered in New York with Marvin Josephson, head of a theatrical and literary talent agency, as chairman. Its Washington-based executive director is Richard Altman, who previously worked as political director of AIPAC. It draws money heavily from the entertainment industry and got off to a fast start in 1982 when Woody Allen signed its first nationwide fund-raising appeal. *The National Journal* rates it as the nation's largest non-labor, non-business political action committee.

In 1982, NatPAC raised $1.04 million and spent $547,500 on 109 candidates for Congress. It gave the $5,000 legal limit to each of 31 Senate candidates. Twenty-eight of these were elected. On the House side, 57 of the 73 candidates it supported won. In the wake of those successes, NatPAC ran a full-page advertisement in *The New York Times* inviting further support and declaring that it was "helping to elect officials in all fifty states who realize that Israel's survival is vital to our own."

A recent fund-raising letter carried an appeal by Republican Senator Robert Packwood of Oregon and Democratic Senator Patrick Moynihan of New York, both ardent supporters of Israel: "If you believe, as we do, that Israel is a great strategic asset to the United States and its most reliable ally in that part of the world, please read this letter." The letter asked for support so NatPAC can "take on the Petrodollar interests."

Five colleagues help Josephson decide which candidates receive funds. They are Barry Dillar, chairman of Paramount Pictures Corporation, George Klein, a New York City developer, James Wolfensohn, a New York investment banker, Martin Peretz, editor of *The New Republic,* and Rita Hauser, a New York lawyer who is prominent in the work of the American Jewish Committee.

Executive director Richard Altman calls NatPAC a "grassroots movement." By late 1983 he had signed up over 20,000 members, with his goal for 1984 goal set at 100,000. NatPAC strives for "ecumenical fund-raising," he says, noting the presence of Methodist Bob Hope among the one hundred prominent Americans listed as charter members.

He is candid: "Money makes the political engine run. To elect a friend, you have to pay for it—and we're not the only ones who know that."

Altman declares that participating in PACs "is quintessentially both American and Jewish, as an expression of our involvement in political life."

Small PACs sometimes focus on candidates far from their locales. Robert B. Golder, a Philadelphia businessman, organized the Delaware Valley Political Action Committee (Del-Val PAC) in 1981, recruited 160 members, and dispensed $58,000 to 32 widely scattered candidates. Twenty-eight of them won. Golder explains that his goal is to elect pro-Israel Congressmen "in faraway places who don't have Jewish constituencies." For example, his PAC sent $1,500 to Jeffrey Bingaman, the Democrat elected to the Senate in 1982 from New Mexico. In late 1983 it sent $5,000 to Tom Corcoran, the unsuccessful challenger of Republican Senator Charles Percy of Illinois. A 12-person executive committee decides where the money is spent.

A San Francisco-based PAC concentrates on contests outside California. Melvin Swig, who is chairman of the Bay Area Citizens Political Action Committee, says: "There are enough people locally who do enough for their constituency. We look for areas that have less Jewish visibility than others, places where there are fewer Jews."

Golder explains the aims of such groups:

We feel we are getting more Jewish people involved. . . . Look how much we can get from the United States government by being politically active. This is the key thing about PACs. We're trying to get those candidates [elected] who will vote 'Yes' on foreign aid.

Golder, Swig and other PAC leaders receive guidance from AIPAC, which keeps them up to date on votes cast and statements made by Senate and House members as well as positions taken on the Middle East by candidates seeking office for the first time.

AIPAC sometimes drops all pretense at staying apart from fund raising. For instance, a pro-Israel political action committee was organized in Virginia in 1983 during a workshop sponsored by AIPAC.

Financial help does not stop at United States borders. Jewish Americans living in Israel are solicited for political action in the United States. Newton Frolich, a former Washington lawyer who moved to Israel eight years ago, is heading a Jerusalem-based political action committee. In June 1984, his committee mailed a solicitation letter to some 11,000 U.S. families living in Israel and expects to approach, in all, the estimated 50,000 U.S. citizens living there, many of whom also claim Israeli citizenship. His organization is called Americans in Israel

Political Action Committee. Through the committee, he explains, Americans in Israel can "keep making their contribution" to the U.S. political process. The contribution comes back, of course, in the form of enormous U.S. grants to Israel—greater than to any other country.

A lobby veteran who is now engaged fulltime in fund-raising worries about appearances. AIPAC's former executive director, Morris J. Amitay, feels that smaller local PACs are best and fears that large well-publicized national PACs may create the impression that Jews exercise too much political power. He operates the relatively small Washington Political Action Committee, which dispensed $89,075 in 158 races during the 1982 campaigns.

Too much or not, Jewish influence in fund raising is widely recognized. In August 1983 the *Wall Street Journal* reported,

Several ranking Congressmen—most of whom wouldn't comment on the record for this story—say they believe the political effect of Jewish PAC money is greater than that of other major lobbies because it is skillfully focused on one foreign policy issue.

Focused it is. The pro-Israel PACs concentrate exclusively on federal elections and focus heavily on Senate races and on House members who occupy key foreign policy assignments.

PAC leader Mark Siegel says the PACs concentrate on the Senate, because it is the "real battleground" on questions of foreign policy. In 1982, they invested $966,695 in Senate races, with $355,550 going to key House contests.

Guided by AIPAC, PACs choose their targets with care. When Lynn Adelman, a Jewish state senator in Wisconsin, in 1982 mounted the first primary election challenge that Democrat Clement J. Zablocki had experienced in thirty years, AIPAC recommended against an all-out effort. AIPAC was unhappy with Zablocki's record, but did not consider him a problem; furthermore, it concluded that Adelman could not win. Adelman received only $9,350 from thirteen pro-Israel political action committees. The contest made national news, because Zablocki was chairman of the House Foreign Affairs Committee, through which all Israeli aid measures must go (see chapter two). Despite AIPAC's low-key recommendation, a letter soliciting funds for Adelman cited two "gains" if Zablocki lost: "Adelman's election not only means a friend of Israel in Congress, but also that the House Foreign Affairs Committee will have a friend of Israel as its new chairman," referring to Dante Fascell of Florida, the Democrat who was next in line to succeed Zablocki. Zablocki was re-elected by a two-to-one margin.

Meanwhile, Fascell, the "other friend" cited in the fund-raising

appeal, was receiving strong support from pro-Israel PACs in his successful campaign for re-election in a Florida district that includes part
of Miami. Twenty-two of these PACs provided Fascell with a total of
$43,250, the second highest amount to a House candidate that year.
These funds helped him survive a challenge by a former television
newsman.

My successor, Richard Durbin, topped all House candidates, receiving $103,325 from pro-Israel political action committees. Other
House Members receiving in excess of $10,000 were Sam Gejdenson of
Connecticut, $30,175; Clarence Long of Maryland, $29,250; Ike Skel-
ton of Missouri, $20,000; Martin Frost of Texas, $18,300; Thomas Lantos of California, $15,500. Most of the big money went to Senate races.
Eighteen Senators who were elected in 1982 received over $10,000
from pro-Israel PACs. Five received more than Congressman Fascell.
The top 10 were: George Mitchell, Democrat of Maine, $77,400; James
Sasser, Democrat of Tennessee, $58,250; David Durenberger, Repub-
lican of Minnesota, $56,000; Robert Byrd, Democrat of West Virginia,
$55,500; Paul Sarbanes, Democrat of Maryland, $48,500; Chic Hecht,
Republican of Nevada, $46,500; Quentin Burdick, Democrat of North
Dakota, $44,775; Lowell Weicker, Republican of Connecticut, $42,075;
Jeffrey Bingaman, Democrat of New Mexico, $36,575; Howard Met-
zenbaum, Democrat of Ohio, $35,175; Dennis DeConcini, Democrat of
Arizona, $32,000; and Donald Riegle, Democrat of Michigan, $29,000.
Eight others received in excess of $10,000 each.

In the 1984 elections, by July 1 pro-Israel PACs had distributed
$1.49 million to Senate candidates and $684,465 to House candidates.

That year, Paul Simon, Democratic challenger to Republican
Senator Charles Percy, topped the Senate list with $147,870. Next in
line were Carl Levin, Michigan, $140,063; James B. Hunt, North
Carolina, $130,350; Rudolph E. Boschwitz, Minnesota, $95,100;
George J. Mitchell, Maine, $77,400; James Sasser, Tennessee, $58,250;
Albert Gore, Tennessee, $57,450; Thomas Harkin, Iowa, $57,250;
David Durenberger, Minnesota, $56,750 and Robert C. Byrd, West
Virginia, $55,500. Mitchell, Sasser, Durenberger and Byrd will not be
up for re-election until 1988. All but Boschwitz and Durenberger are
Democrats. Sixteen other Senators received over $30,000.

Of 17 House Members who received $10,000 or more, 11 were on
panels which handle foreign aid. One of them, Lee Hamilton of Indiana, chairman of the Middle East Subcommittee, received all but
$500 of the $14,500 in pro-Israel PAC money that went to Indiana
House contests. The top House recipients: Clarence Long, Maryland,
$97,500; Charles Wilson, Texas, $21,750; Ben Erdreich, Alabama,
$21,250; Ronald L. Wyden, Oregon, $18,000; Mark Siljander, Michigan, $16,800; Dante Fascell, Florida, $16,750; Robert G. Torricelli,

New Jersey, $16,500; Harry M. Reid, Nevada, $15,500; Cardiss Collins, Illinois, $14,250; Lee Hamilton, Indiana, $14,000. All but Siljander are Democrats.

Despite the dramatic growth of these PACs—a development that has occurred entirely since 1979—most of the contributions to candidates still come directly from individual pro-Israel activists.

Democratic candidates are especially dependent on contributions from Jewish sources. A non-Jewish strategist told Stephen D. Isaacs, author of *Jews and American Politics:* "You can't hope to go anywhere in national politics, if you're a Democrat, without Jewish money." In 1968, 15 of the 21 persons who loaned $100,000 or more to presidential candidate Hubert Humphrey were Jewish. According to Isaacs, the Democratic National Committee, whose principal charge is the advancement of Democratic Party prospects for the White House, for years received about 50 percent of its funds from Jewish sources.

After the 1982 election—a year before he was elected chairman of the Foreign Affairs Committee after the sudden death of Zablocki—Fascell remarked:

The whole trouble with campaign finances is the hue and cry that you've been bought. If you need the money, are you going to get it from your enemy? No, you're going to get it from your friend.

"Our Own Foreign Policy Agenda"

Much of the American Israel Public Affairs Committee's work in 1982 centered on expanding grassroots support, enlarging outreach programs to the college and Christian communities, and helping pro-Israel political action committees sharpen their skills. These efforts were largely aimed at increasing the lobby's influence in the Senate. AIPAC wanted no repetition of its failure to block the 1981 AWACS sale to Saudi Arabia.

One way in which AIPAC increases the number of its Senate friends is illustrated by its interventions in a critical race in Missouri. AIPAC stood by a friend and won. Republican Senator John C. Danforth, an ordained Episcopal minister, was opposed for re-election by a Jewish Democrat, Harriett Woods. In the closely fought contest, the non-Jewish Danforth found that an unblemished record of cooperation brought him AIPAC support even against a Jewish challenger. The help was crucial, as Danforth won by less than one percent of the vote.

AIPAC also weighed in heavily in Maine, helping to pull off the upset victory of Democratic Senator George Mitchell over Republican Congressman David Emery. The *Almanac of American Politics* rated Mitchell "the Democratic Senator universally regarded as having the least chance for re-election." He had never won an election. Defeated for governor by an independent candidate in 1974, he was appointed to fill the Senate vacancy caused when Senator Edmund Muskie resigned in 1980 to become President Carter's Secretary of State.

Encouraged by AIPAC, 27 pro-Israeli political action committees, all based outside Maine, contributed $77,400 to Mitchell's campaign. With this help Mitchell, who has Lebanese ancestry, fooled the professionals and won handily. In a post-election phone call to AIPAC director Thomas A. Dine, Mitchell promised: "I will remember you."

In another example, Republican Senator David Durenberger of Minnesota received for his 1982 re-election bid $57,000 from 20 pro-Israeli political action committees, with $10,000 of this total coming from the Citizens Organized PAC in California. This PAC contributed $5,000 during a breakfast meeting four months after he voted against the sale of AWACS planes to Saudi Arabia, and added $5,000 more by election day. Directors of the PAC include Alan Rothenberg, the law partner of Democratic National Chairman Charles Manatt.

In close races, lobby interests sometimes play it safe by supporting both sides. In the 1980 Senate race in Idaho, for example, pro-Israeli activists contributed to their stalwart friend, Democrat Frank Church, chairman of the Senate Foreign Relations Committee, but also gave to his challenger, Republican Congressman Steven D. Symms.

One reason for the dual support was the expected vote in the Senate the next year on the AWACS sale to Saudi Arabia—during the campaign both Symms and Church were listed as opposing it. With the race expected to be close, the lobby believed it had a friend in each candidate and helped both.

Symms defeated Church by a razor-thin margin; but the investment in Symms by pro-Israel interests did not pay off. By the time the new Senator faced the AWACS vote he had changed his mind. His vote approving the AWACS sale helped to give AIPAC one of its rare legislative setbacks.

In a post-election review in its newsletter, *Near East Report,* AIPAC concluded that the new Senate in the 98th Congress would be "marginally more pro-Israel." As evidence, it noted that two of the five new Senators were Jewish: Frank Lautenberg, Democrat of New Jersey, and Chic Hecht, Republican of Nevada, each "with long records of support for Israel." It could also count as a gain the election of Democrat Jeffrey Bingaman of New Mexico, who defeated Republican Senator Harrison Schmitt. Voting for the AWACS sale to Saudi Arabia and opposing foreign aid had given Schmitt bad marks, and AIPAC gave its support to his challenger, Bingaman, in the campaign.

Because favored candidates need more money than PAC sources

provide, AIPAC also helps by providing lists for direct mail fundraising. The appeal can be hard-hitting. An example is the literature mailed in early 1984 on behalf of Republican Senator Rudy Boschwitz of Minnesota. Fellow Republican Lowell Weicker wrote the introductory letter, citing him as a "friend of Israel in danger." He noted Boschwitz's key position as chairman of the subcommittee "that determines the level of aid our country gives to Israel," and praised his efforts to block military sales to Saudi Arabia. The appeal included tributes by Senator Bob Packwood and Wolf Blitzer, Washington correspondent for *The Jerusalem Post*.

AIPAC has convinced Congress that it represents practically all Jews who vote. Columnist Nat Hentoff reported this assessment in the New York *Village Voice* in June 1983 after a delegation of eighteen dissenting rabbis had scoured Capitol Hill trying to convince Congressmen that some Jews oppose Israeli policies. The rabbis reported that several Congressmen said they shared their views but were afraid to act. Hentoff concluded: "The only Jewish constituency that's real to them [Congressmen] is the one that AIPAC and other spokesmen for the Jewish establishment tell them about."

An Ohio Congressman speaks of AIPAC with both awe and concern:

AIPAC is the most influential lobby on Capitol Hill. They are relentless. They know what they're doing. They have the people for financial resources. They've got a lot going for them. Their basic underlying cause is one that most Americans sympathize with.

But what distresses me is the inability of American policy-makers, because of the influence of AIPAC, to distinguish between our national interest and Israel's national interest. When these converge—wonderful! But they don't always converge.

After the 1982 elections, Thomas A. Dine summed up the significance of AIPAC's achievements: "Because of that, American Jews are thus able to form our own foreign policy agenda."

Later, when he reviewed the 1984 election results, Dine credited Jewish money, not votes: "Early money, middle money, late money." He claimed credit for defeating Republican Senators Charles Percy of Illinois and Roger Jepson of Iowa and Democratic Senator Walter Huddleston of Kentucky, all of whom incurred AIPAC wrath by voting for the sale of AWACS planes to Saudi Arabia.

Dine said these successes "defined Jewish political power for the rest of this century."

Chapter 2

Stilling the Still, Small Voices

The youthful Congressman from California listened as his House colleagues expressed their views. His earnest manner and distinctive
shock of hair roused memories of an earlier Congressman, John F.
Kennedy. For more than an hour, between comments of his own, Representative Paul N. "Pete" McCloskey yielded the floor to other Congressmen, 23 in all. While they cooperated by requesting from Speaker
"Tip" O'Neill allocations of time for the debate, most of them did so in
order to avoid a sticky issue. They were ducking legislative combat, not
engaging in it.

Real debate was almost unknown on the subject McCloskey had
chosen—aid to Israel. Most Congressmen, fearing lobby pressure,
carefully avoid statements or votes that might be viewed as critical of
Israel. Not McCloskey. Admired for his courage and independence, he
began opposing the Vietnam war long before most Americans, withstood the lobbying of Greek Americans to cut off military aid to Turkey, consistently supported controversial civil rights measures, and
now challenged conventional wisdom on Middle East policy. He and I
were members of a tiny band of Congressmen willing to criticize Israel
publicly, and both of us would soon leave Capitol Hill involuntarily.

On that June afternoon in 1980, most of McCloskey's colleagues
provided him with debate time—and joined him in the discussion—
because they saw this as the only way to keep him from forcing them to
vote on an amendment cutting aid to Israel. Some of them privately
agreed with McCloskey's position but did not want his amendment to
come to a vote. If that happened, they would find themselves in the
distressing circumstance of reacting to the pressure of Israel's lobby by
voting against McCloskey's amendment—and their own conscience.

In offering his amendment, McCloskey called for an end to the
building of Israeli settlements in the territory in the West Bank of the

50

Jordan river which Israel held by force of arms. To put pressure on Israel to stop, he wanted the U.S. to cut aid by $150 million—the amount he estimated Israel was annually spending on these projects. In the end, tough realities led him to drop his plan to bring the amendment to a vote:

Friend and foe alike asked me not to press the amendment. Some of my friends argued that if I did get a roll call, the amendment would have been badly defeated. If that happened, they argued, Israel would take heart—saying "Sure, somebody spoke out, but look how we smashed him." Every Jewish Congressman on the floor of the House told me privately that I was right.

Representative James Johnson, a Republican from Colorado and one of the few to support McCloskey, was aware of the pressure other Congressmen were putting on him. Johnson declared that many of his colleagues privately opposed Israel's expansion of settlements but said Congress was "incapable" of taking action contrary to Israeli policy: "I would just like to point out the real reason that this Congress will not deal with the gentleman's amendment is because [it] concerns the nation of Israel."

It was not the first time peer pressure had stopped amendments viewed as anti-Israeli, and McCloskey was not the first to back down to accommodate colleagues. Such pressure develops automatically when amendments restricting aid to Israel are discussed. Many Congressmen are embarrassed at the high level of aid—Israel receives one-fourth of all U.S. foreign aid—and feel uncomfortable being recorded as favoring it. But, intimidated by Israel's friends, they are even less comfortable being recorded in opposition. How much of the lobby's power is real, and how much illusion, is beside the point. Because they perceive it as real, few Congressmen wish to take a chance. Worrying endlessly about political survival, they say: "Taking on the Israeli lobby is something I can do without. Who needs that?" On several occasions, sensing I was about to force a troublesome vote on aid to Israel, a colleague would whisper to me, "Your position on this is well known. Why put the rest of us on the spot?"

Most committee action, like the work of the full House, is open to the public, and none occurs on Israeli aid without the presence of at least one representative of AIPAC. His presence ensures that any criticism of Israel will be quickly reported to key constituents. The offending Congressman may have a rash of angry telephone messages to answer by the time he returns to his office from the hearing room.

Lobbyists for AIPAC are experts on the personalities and procedures of the House. If Israel is mentioned, even behind closed doors, they quickly get a full report of what transpired. These lobbyists know that aid to Israel, on a roll call vote, will receive overwhelming support. Administration lobbyists count on this support to carry the day for foreign aid worldwide. Working together, the two groups of lobbyists pursue a common interest by keeping the waters smooth and frustrating "boat rockers" like McCloskey.

Assaulting the Citadels

For McCloskey, compromise was an unusual experience. Throughout his public career he usually resisted pressures, even when his critics struck harshly.

This was true when he became nationally prominent as a critic of the Vietnam war—an effort that led him in 1972 to a brief but dramatic campaign for the presidency. His goal was a broad and unfettered discussion of public issues, particularly the war. The wrong decisions, he believed, generally "came about because the view of the minority was not heard or the view of thinking people was quiet." He contended that the Nixon administration was withholding vital information on a variety of issues. He charged it with "preying on people's fear, hate and anger."

When McCloskey announced for president, his supporters sighed, "Political suicide." His opponents, particularly those in the party's right wing, chortled the very same words. Although the Californian recognized that his challenge might jeopardize his seat in Congress, he nevertheless denounced the continuation of the war: "Like other Americans, I trusted President Nixon when he said he had a plan to end the war." McCloskey agonized over the fact that thousands of U.S. soldiers continued to die, and United States airpower, using horrifying cluster bombs, rained violence on civilians in Vietnam, Laos and Cambodia.

McCloskey knew war's effects firsthand. As a Marine in Korea he was wounded leading his platoon in several successful bayonet assaults on entrenched enemy positions. He emerged from the Korean war with a Navy Cross, Silver Star and two Purple Hearts. He later explained that this wartime experience gave him "a strong sense of being lucky to be alive." It also toughened him for subsequent assaults on entrenched enemies of a different sort—endeavors which brought no medals for bravery.

For protesting the war, McCloskey was branded "an enemy of the political process," and even accused of communist leanings. "At least fifty right-wing members of the House believe McCloskey to be the new Red menace," wrote one journalist. The allegation was ridiculous, of course, but party stalwarts in California clearly were restive. So much so, according to the *California Journal,* that he "needed the personal intervention of then Vice-President Gerald R. Ford to save him in the 1974 primary."

His maverick ways exacted a price. He was twice denied a place on the Ways and Means Committee. Conservatives on the California delegation rebuffed the liberal Republican's bid for membership, even though he was entitled to the post on the basis of seniority.

By the time of his ill-fated 1980 amendment on aid to Israel, McCloskey had put himself in the midst of the Middle East controversy. After a trip to the Middle East in 1979, he concluded that new Israeli policies were not in America's best interests. He was alarmed over Washington's failure to halt Israel's construction of West Bank settlements—which the Administration itself had labeled illegal—and to stop Israel's illegal use of U.S.-supplied weapons. The Congressman asked, "Why?"

The answer was not hard to find. The issue, like most relating to the Middle East, was too hot for either Congress or the White House to handle. A call for debate provoked harsh press attacks and angry constituent mail. To McCloskey, the attacks were ironic. He viewed himself as supportive of both Jewish and Israeli interests. As a college student at Stanford University in 1948, he had helped lead a successful campaign to open Phi Delta Theta fraternity for the first time to Jewish students. He reminded a critic, Earl Raab of the *San Francisco Jewish Bulletin,* that he had "voted for all the military and economic assistance we have given to Israel in the past." McCloskey also vigorously defended Israel's right to lobby: "Lobbying is and should be an honorable and important part of the American political process." He described the American Israel Public Affairs Committee as "the most powerful [lobby] in Washington," insisting there was "nothing sinister or devious" about it.

Still, McCloskey had raised a provocative question: "Does America's 'Israeli lobby' wield too much influence?" In an article for the *Los Angeles Times* he provided his answer: "Yes, it is an obstacle to real Mideast peace." McCloskey cited the risk of nuclear confrontation in the Middle East and the fundamental differences between the interests of Israel and the United States. He observed that members of the Jewish community demand that Congress support Israel in spite of these differences. This demand, he argued, "coupled with the weakness of Congress in the face of any such force, can prevent the president, in his hour of both crisis and opportunity, from having the flexibility necessary to achieve a lasting Israeli-Palestinian peace."

He pleaded for full discussion:

If the United States is to work effectively toward peace in the Mideast, the power of this lobby must be recognized and countered in open and fair debate. I had hoped that the American Jewish community had matured to the point where its lobbying efforts could be described and debated without raising the red flag of anti-Semitism. . . . To recognize the power of a lobby is not to criticize the lobby itself.

The article appeared shortly before McCloskey's bid for his party's nomination for the 1982 Senatorial race in California. It was an unorthodox opening salvo, to say the least, and most of the reaction was critical. One of the exceptions was an analysis by the *Redlands Daily Facts* (California) which called his campaign a "brave but risky business." The newspaper described him as "the candidate for those who want a man with whom they will disagree on some issues, but who has the courage of his intelligent convictions."

On the other hand, Paul Greenberg, in a syndicated article in the *San Francisco Examiner,* wrote that McCloskey had accused the Israeli lobby of "busily subverting the national interest" and linked him with notorious anti-Semite Gerald L. K. Smith. This time, McCloskey did not need to fight back. A few days later, the same newspaper published an opposing view. Columnist Guy Wright noted that Greenberg had accused McCloskey of McCarthy era tactics without quoting "a single line from the offensive speech." Wright observed that this was itself a common tactic of McCarthyism. He cited with approval several of McCloskey's recommendations on foreign policy and concluded: "Now I ask you. Are those the ravings of an anti-Semite? Or fair comment on issues too long kept taboo?"

Such supportive voices were few. An article in the *B'nai B'rith Messenger* charged that McCloskey had proposed that all rabbis be required to register as foreign agents, declaring that he had made the proposal in a meeting with the editors of the *Los Angeles Times.* The author assured his readers that the tidbit came from a "very reliable source," and the charge was published nationally. The charge was a complete fabrication, and *Times* editor Tony Day was quick to back up McCloskey's denial.

The *Messenger* published a retraction a month later, but the accusation lingered on. Even the Washington office of the Israeli lobby did not get the retraction message. In an interview about McCloskey two years later, Douglas Bloomfield, legislative director for AIPAC, apparently unaware of the retraction, repeated the accusation as fact. Such false information may have colored his view of McCloskey, whom he described as "bitter" with "an intense sense of hostility" toward Jews:

I hestitate to use the term that he was anti-Semitic. Being anti-Israeli is a political decision. Being anti-Semitic is something totally different. I think he did not just creep over the boundary.

Despite the *Messenger*'s retraction, there was no letup in criticism of McCloskey. The *Messenger* charged McCloskey with denigrating "the Constitutional exercise of petitioning Congress," with "obstreperous performances," and with marching on a "platform of controversy unmindful of the fact that the framework of his platform is dangerously undermined with distortion, inaccuracy and maybe even malicious mischief." Another Jewish publication published his picture with the caption, "Heir to Goebbels." An article in the *Heritage Southwest Jewish Press* used such descriptive phrases as "No. 1 sonovabitch," "obscene position against the Jews of America," "crummy" and "sleazy" in denouncing him.

Although used to rough and tumble partisanship, McCloskey was shocked at the harshness of the attacks. No rabbis or Jewish publications defended him. One of a small number of individual Jews who spoke up in his behalf was Merwyn Morris, a prominent businessman from Atherton, California. Morris argued that "McCloskey is no more anti-Semitic than I am"—but he still switched his support to McCloskey's opponent in the Senatorial election.

Josh Teitelbaum, who had served for a short time on McCloskey's staff and was the son of a Palo Alto rabbi, resigned from McCloskey's staff partly because he disagreed with the Congressman's attitude toward Israel. But he also defended his former employer: "McCloskey is not anti-Semitic, but his words may give encouragement to those who are."

McCloskey's views on Israel complicated—to put it mildly—campaign fund raising. Potential sources of Jewish financial support dried up. One former supporter, Jewish multimillionaire Louis E. Wolfson, wrote: "I now find that I must join with many other Americans to do everything possible to defeat your bid for the U.S. Senate and make certain that you will not hold any future office."

Early in the race, when McCloskey was competing mainly with Senator S. I. Hayakawa for the nomination, he felt he had a chance. Both were from the northern part of the state, where McCloskey had his greatest strength. After Hayakawa dropped out and Pete Wilson, the popular mayor of San Diego, entered the contest, McCloskey's prospects declined.

When the primary election votes were counted, McCloskey had won the north but lost the populous south. He finished 10 percentage points behind Wilson. Still, his showing surprised the experts. Polls and forecasters had listed him third or fourth among the four contenders right up to the last days. Congressman Barry Goldwater Jr., the early favorite, emerged a poor third, and Robert Dornan, another Congressional colleague, finished fourth.

The final tally on election day was close enough to cause a number of people to conclude that without the Jewish controversy McCloskey might have won. All three of McCloskey's opponents received Jewish financial support. Stephen S. Rosenfeld, deputy editorial page editor of the *Washington Post,* drew a definite conclusion: "Jewish political participation" defeated McCloskey.

The lobby attack did not end when the polls closed, nor did McCloskey shun controversy. On September 22, 1982, a few days after the massacre of hundreds of Palestinians in the refugeee camps at Beirut, McCloskey denounced a proposed new $50 million grant for Israel in a speech on the House floor. He warned that the action "might be taken as a signal of our support for what Israel did last Thursday in entering West Beirut and creating the circumstances which led directly to the massacre." Despite his protest, the aid was approved.

In the closing hours of the 97th Congress, after 15 years as a member of "this treasured institution," McCloskey invoked George Washington's Farewell Address in his own farewell, citing the first president's warning that "a passionate attachment of one nation for another produces a variety of evils."

McCloskey found this advice "eminently sound" and said that Congress, in action completed the day before, had demonstrated a "passionate attachment" to Israel by voting more aid per capita to that country "than we allow to many of the poor and unemployed in our own country," despite evidence that "Israel is no longer behaving like a friend of the United States."

McCloskey's Academic Freedom

With his political career interrupted, if not ended, McCloskey planned to return to a partnership in the Palo Alto law firm he helped John Wilson, a fellow graduate of Yale Law School, establish years before. "Many of my old clients are still clients," he said, "and I wanted to go back to them. I never thought of going anywhere else."

But others had different thoughts about McCloskey's future. Ken Oshman, president of the Rolm Corporation, the firm's biggest client, warned that his company "might take their law business elsewhere" if

McCloskey were to rejoin the firm. The senior partners invited McCloskey to lunch and told him the episode would not cause them to withdraw their invitation, but they wanted McCloskey to be "aware of the problem." McCloskey's response, "I don't want to come back and put you under that burden." In a letter to Oshman, McCloskey expressed his dismay. In reply, the industrialist said his company really wouldn't have taken its business elsewhere but reiterated his disagreement with McCloskey's views on Israel.

McCloskey accepted a partnership with the San Francisco law firm of Brobeck, Phleger and Harrison, but the pressures followed him there. The firm received a telephone call from a man in Berkeley, California, who identified himself only as a major shareholder in the Wells Fargo Bank, one of the law firm's major clients. He said that he intended to go to the next meeting of the shareholders and demand that the bank transfer its law business to another firm. The reason: the San Francisco firm was adding to its partnership a "known anti-Semite" who supported the Palestine Liberation Organization and its chairman, Yasser Arafat. McCloskey's partners ignored the threat, and the bank did not withdraw its business.

A tracking system initiated by the Anti-Defamation League of B'nai B'rith assured that McCloskley would have no peace, even as a private citizen. The group distributed a memorandum containing details of his actions and speeches to its chapters around the country. According to the memo, it was designed to "assist" local ADL groups with "counteraction guidance" whenever McCloskey appeared in public.

Trouble dogged him even on the campus. McCloskey accepted an invitation from the student governing council of Stanford University to teach a course on Congress at Stanford. Howard Goldberg—a council member and also director of the Hillel Center, the campus Jewish club—told the group that inviting McCloskey was "a slap in the face of the Jewish community." Student leader Seth Linfield held up preparation of class materials then demanded the right to choose the guest lecturers. McCloskey refused, asserting that the young director had earlier assured him he could choose these speakers himself.

Difficulties mounted as the semester went on. Guest speakers were not paid on time. McCloskey felt obliged to pay such expenses personally, then seek reimbursement. His own remuneration was scaled downward as the controversy developed. Instead of the $3,500 stipend originally promised, Linfield later reduced the amount to $2,000 and even that amount was in doubt. According to a report in the *San Jose Mercury News,* the $2,000 would be paid only if Linfield was satisfied with McCloskey's performance. One student, Jeffrey Au, complained to school authorities that the controversy impaired academic quality. Responding, Professor Hubert Marshall wrote that he viewed the student activities as "unprecedented and a violation of Mr. McCloskey's academic freedom."

McCloskey reacted sharply to his critics at Stanford:

It's a kind of reverse anti-Semitism. It is the Jewish community saying we don't want this person teaching at Stanford and, if he does teach, we don't want him using this material.

The *San Francisco Chronicle* observed that McCloskey's appointment had provoked interest beyond the university campus, noting that "Jewish leaders around the Bay Area expressed concern when Stanford's student government voted narrowly to hire McCloskey."

By mid-May, the controversy elicited action by the university provost, Albert H. Hastorf, who apologized in a letter that made news from coast to coast. He expressed the hope that McCloskey might derive "some small compensation" in knowing that his case "will cause us to revise our procedures so that future guest professors and other instructors at Stanford will enjoy the special protections that their positions warrant." With the apology came a payment which brought his stipend for the course to the $3,500 agreed to originally.

McCloskey told the *Peninsula Times-Tribune,* "Stanford doesn't owe me an apology." He said his satisfaction came when all but one of the fifty students rated his class "in the high range of excellence," but he warned that other schools might face trouble. He noted that the American Israel Public Affairs Committee "has instructed college students all over the country to take [similar] actions." (see chapters six and seven)

The end of the course did not terminate McCloskey's activities in foreign policy. Throughout 1983 and into 1984, while engaged in the practice of law, he filled frequent speaking dates on the Arab-Israel dispute in the United States, flew several times to Europe and the Middle East, and wrote numerous newspaper and journal articles.

While castigating Israeli policies, he also appealed to Palestinians and other Arabs to recognize the right of Israel to exist and on one occasion even traveled to Europe to make the appeal. In September 1983 he addressed the International Conference on the Question of Palestine at Geneva, urging the Conference to endorse all United Nations resolutions concerning the Middle East conflict. This, he explained, would put the group on record in support of Palestinian rights but also in support of Israel's right to exist on the land it occupied before the 1967 Arab-Israeli war. He offered amendments designed to lift a pending declaration from the level of "partisanship" to that of "fairness and truth," thus giving the conference effect beyond its membership and answering "the doubters and faint hearts" who had boycotted it.

McCloskey urged a call for the security of Israel, as well as justice for the Palestinians, and forecast that such action could "change American public opinion and ultimately the actions of the U.S. Congress." The conference rejected his advice.

"It Didn't Cripple Us" But—

While McCloskey, a leader in the white Republican establishment, battled for universal human rights and against further United States involvement in the Vietnam war, a black Baptist preacher from the District of Columbia, known nationally as a "street activist," pursued the same goals within Democratic ranks.

Both were members of the House of Representatives, good friends, and both undertook controversial journeys to Lebanon in behalf of peace. Both paid a price for their activism, but the preacher survived politically, while the ex-Marine did not. The preacher is the Reverend Walter Fauntroy. Working for justice in the Middle East—not their record of activism for civil rights at home or opposition to the Vietnam war—caused trouble for both of them.

In large measure, Fauntroy's problems began over another black leader's endeavors for justice in the Middle East. Andrew Young resigned under fire as the U.S. ambassador to the United Nations in August, 1979, after it was revealed that he had met with the PLO's U.N. observer, Zuhdi Labib Terzi. Many blacks were outraged by the resignation, blaming it on Israeli pressure and, like Young, found unreasonable the policy which prohibited our officials from talking even informally with PLO officials.

Relations between American blacks and Jews—long-time allies in the civil rights movement—had already been strained by disagreements over affirmative action programs intended to give blacks employment quotas and by Israel's close relations with the apartheid regime in South Africa. The resignation of Young, the most prominent black in the Carter Administration, intensified the strain. "This is the most tense moment in black and Jewish relations in my memory," said the Reverend Jesse Jackson shortly after the resignation.

During the civil rights movement of the 1960s, Fauntroy, one of the blacks most disturbed by the resignation, had worked with Young in the Southern Christian Leadership Conference (SCLC) under the Reverend Martin Luther King, Jr. They had acquired the nickname "The Brooks Brothers" because of their habit of wearing suits and neckties on civil rights marches while most of the others were dressed more casually.

To show support for Young and disagreement with United States policy, Fauntroy and SCLC President Joseph Lowery traveled to New York in the fall of 1979 to meet with Terzi. Fauntroy said he hoped to help establish communication between Arabs and Israelis and so promote a nonviolent solution to Middle East problems, adding, "Neither Andy Young nor I, nor other members of the SCLC, apologize for searching for the relevance of Martin Luther King's policies in the international political arena."

While Terzi said he was "happy and gratified" at the meeting with the black leaders and hoped "much more will be learned by the American people," prominent members of Washington's Jewish community were upset.

"I don't think a responsible Congressman should have any truck with terrorists," complained Rabbi Stanley Rabinowitz. Although most Jews echoed this sentiment, a few stood by Fauntroy. Prominent Jewish businessman Joseph B. Danzansky said Fauntroy "has a right to do what he thinks his position entitles him to do." Danzansky, a friend and political ally of Fauntroy, added, "I'd be very shocked if there were any trace of anti-Jewish feeling. I have confidence in him as a human being."

In an attempt to calm the critics and demonstrate their "fairness," Fauntroy, Lowery and other SCLC leaders met with U.S. Jewish leaders and with Israel's U.N. ambassador, Yehuda Blum. Afterwards, Fauntroy told reporters that the black leaders were "asking both parties [in the Middle East dispute] to recognize each other's human rights and the right of self-determination." But pro-Israel interests saw the outcome differently. Howard Squadron, president of the American Jewish Committee, emerged from the meeting to say that the SCLC contact with Terzi was "a grave error lending legitimacy to an organization committed to terrorism and violence."

Against this tense background, black leaders from across the United States convened in New York to express their concern over the Young resignation and to affirm their right to speak out on matters of foreign policy.

Some said they were making "a declaration of independence" in matters of foreign policy. Fauntroy said:

In every war since the founding of this nation, black citizens have borne arms and died for their country. Their blood was spilled from Bunker Hill to Vietnam. It is to be expected that should the United States become drawn into war in the Middle East black Americans once more will be called upon to sacrifice their lives. [His words were prophetic of the sacrifices blacks were soon to make in Lebanon. While blacks constitute only 10 percent of the total U.S. population, 20 percent of the Marines killed in the terrorist truck bombing at Beirut—47 of 246—were black.]

Even as they chafed at the criticism of their involvement in the Palestinian question, black leaders worried about how it would affect their efforts to advance civil rights in the United States. Jewish Americans had long been active in advocating civil rights and were often a major source of financial support for those efforts. Three of the four original organizers of the NAACP were Jewish. The *Washington Post* reported that during their meetings several black leaders "stressed the need to present a unified front on the self-determination issue, while at the same time acknowledging that some black organizations' heavy reliance on Jewish philanthropy might temper their views." The validity of this concern was borne out by reports that Jewish contributors had informed the NAACP and the Urban League that they would no longer be providing financial support.

"It didn't cripple us," says Fauntroy, who also serves as chairman of the board of the SCLC. "It just made us more resourceful and more sensitive to our need to put principle above politics on questions that bear on nonviolence and the quest for justice." It hurt fund raising for his personal campaign: "No question about that. Some of my former close supporters flatly stated to me that they were not going to contribute to my candidacy because I had taken the position that I did."

He demonstrated his persistence three weeks later when he joined Lowery on a controversial trip to the Mideast. As they departed, Lowery declared their determination to "preach the moral principles of peace, nonviolence, and human rights."

In a meeting with Yasser Arafat, they appealed for an end to violence, asking the PLO leader to agree to a six-month moratorium on violence. Arafat promised to present the proposal to the PLO's executive council.

Fauntroy recalls the dramatic moment, "We asked Dr. Harry Gibson of the United Methodist Church to pray. Then a Roman Catholic priest said a prayer in Arabic. We wept. At the end of the prayer, someone—I don't know who—started singing 'We Shall Overcome,' and Arafat just immediately crossed his arms and linked hands."

Jews in the United States, who had joined with blacks in singing the same hymn during the tense days of the civil rights movement in America, found this episode offensive and were alarmed at photos showing Fauntroy embracing Arafat. Some feared the emotional meeting symbolized a new black alliance with the PLO and a betrayal of their own support of blacks. They rejected the black leaders' insistence that they were impartial advocates of peace.

The controversy deepened when Fauntroy, on his return from the Middle East, announced that he had invited Arafat to speak in the United States at an "educational forum" to be sponsored by the SCLC. It would be the first in a series where opposing views could be considered.

He explained, "It would offer an opportunity for the American people to hear both sides of the conflict, to understand it and to influence our government." Predictably, the announcement sparked criticism. Rabbi Joshua Haberman of Washington Hebrew Congregation declared that the Arafat visit would "fuel the flames that have been festering."

At a news conference at his New Bethel Baptist Church, Fauntroy described his mission for peace and said he would persist: "I am first and foremost a minister of the gospel, called to preach every day that God is our father and all men are our brothers, right here from this pulpit." He added: "I could not be true to my highest calling if, when an opportunity to do so arose, I refused."

He challenged his critics: "So let anyone who wishes run against me. Let anyone who wishes withdraw his support. It doesn't matter to me."

Nor did Fauntroy budge when an issue close to his heart became threatened—the proposed Constitutional amendment to give full Congressional representation to the people of the District of Columbia. With the amendment pending before several state legislatures, Fauntroy's critics said his peacemaking efforts would jeopardize approval. He said he would not be moved by "people who are narrow and who want to protect our self-determination rights in the District of Columbia but refuse to see the right of other people who are also children of God."

Fauntroy's resolve was to be tested during the Maryland legislature's consideration of the issue. Before the vote on this wholly unrelated matter, two Jewish delegates, Steven Sklar and David Shapiro, who had supported the amendment the previous year put Fauntroy on notice. They warned Fauntroy that unless he condemned the PLO they would defeat the amendment by reversing their own votes and persuade others to join them. Fauntroy rejected the demand, but the news coverage got twisted. In an editorial entitled "Groveling for the DC Amendment," the *Washington Post* reported that Fauntroy had promised to issue the required statement and chided him accordingly: "a handful of Maryland delegates have got Walter Fauntroy jumping through a hoop." Fauntroy called the *Post* story "a total fabrication."

The amendment was subsequently approved by a single vote, but without the support of delegates Sklar and Shapiro.

Fauntroy's Middle East problems took on a new dimension in mid-October when Vernon Jordan, president of the National Urban League, delivered a speech denouncing contacts between black leaders and the PLO as "sideshows" that distracted attention from the "vital survival issues facing American blacks at home." Some black leaders, including civil rights activist Bayard Rustin of the A. Philip Randolph Institute and a number of NAACP representatives, aligned themselves with Jordan. Before leaving for Israel to express solidarity, Rustin said he wanted Israelis to know that "there are great numbers of black people who want the United States to give Israel whatever support it needs."

Other blacks supported Fauntroy and angrily denounced Jordan, accusing him of "selling out to the Jewish-Israeli lobby."

"Any civil rights organization that cannot take a stand without being worried about its white money being cut off doesn't deserve to be a civil rights organization," said the Reverend George Lawrence of the Progressive National Baptist Convention. "We understand where Vernon is coming from. . . . He doesn't want his bread cut off. We support the right of Israel to exist, too. But we also support justice for the Palestinian people."

Even before these exchanges among black leaders, Fauntroy announced that he had withdrawn his invitation to Arafat to visit the United States, citing the PLO failure to order a moratorium on violence. Even so, he said he would continue his peace efforts: "We think it is ludicrous to suggest that an appeal to the PLO to end its violence against Israeli men, women and children and to recognize the right of Israel to exist is tantamount to supporting terrorism and the destruction of Israel." Fauntroy added that he favored a 10 percent reduction in U.S. military aid to Israel, which, he said, would "send a message to Israel" not to use U.S.-supplied weaponry "on non-military targets."

While considered unbeatable in the District of Columbia, Fauntroy's Middle East stand provoked minor competition in his bid for re-election in 1982. Announcing her intention to seek Fauntroy's Congressional seat, Marie Bembery emphasized that she wanted "to protest Walter Fauntroy putting his arms around PLO leader Yasser Arafat and singing, 'We Shall Overcome.'" She declared that she would take no position on the Middle East conflict, stating that the District of Columbia's delegate should "take care of problems here first."

A month later, during the Israeli invasion of Lebanon, she raised the issue again at a candidates' forum at the Washington Hebrew Congregation. She baited Fauntroy: "I must say that I am shocked that Fauntroy would have the temerity, the gall to even show up at this forum, given his history of insensitivity to, and blatant misrepresentation of the Jewish community." Later in the evening, she said that if Washington's delegate were Jewish and hugged the Grand Dragon of the Ku Klux Klan, there was "no way he could come back to D.C. and tell me he represents me as a black resident and voter of the district."

Fauntroy, speaking later to the same tense audience, stated, "I am a supporter of Israel and Israel's right to exist, and I have the same sensitivity to the people in diaspora who are the people of Palestine. I continue to support the right of the Palestinian people to a homeland today."

Both candidates gave crisp responses when they were asked if they supported the Israeli invasion of Lebanon. Fauntroy responded, "No." When Bembery said, "Yes," the audience stood and applauded. The challenger's campaign fell far short on primary election day, with Fauntroy receiving 85 percent of the vote. In the heavily Democratic district, Fauntroy was unopposed in the November general election.

In the summer of 1983 Fauntroy found himself again embroiled in black-Jewish controversy. As chairman of the twentieth anniversary commemoration of the Rev. Martin Luther King's march on Washington, Fauntroy cooperated in a vain effort to win broad Jewish support for the celebration. He agreed with other leaders to revise a "foreign policy position" paper for the march to eliminate phrases offensive to Jewish leaders. The final version dropped a sentence saying there is general opposition to U.S. policy in the Middle East, as well as phrases referring to "Palestinian rights" and calling on both Israel and the United States to talk directly with the PLO. Despite these concessions, most national Jewish groups refused to participate.

Reflecting on the problems created by his quest for self-determination of people in the Middle East, as well as in the District of Columbia, Fauntroy calls it "a growing experience" and plans to push ahead on both fronts.

"Three Calls Within 13 Minutes"

Few members of the House of Representatives, besides McCloskey and Fauntroy, have criticized Israeli policy in recent years. To a great extent this results from the vigilance and skill of that government's lobby on Capitol Hill which reacts swiftly to any sign of discontent with Israel, especially by those assigned to the House Foreign Affairs Committee.

A young man working in 1981 in the office of the late Democratic

Congressman Benjamin S. Rosenthal of New York, who was then the leader of the House's "Jewish caucus," witnessed firsthand the efficiency of this monitoring.

Michael Neiditch, a staff consultant, was with Rosenthal in his office one morning when, just before 9 A.M., the phone rang. Morris Amitay, then executive director of AIPAC, had just read the Evans and Novak syndicated column that morning in the *Washington Post* and he didn't like what he read. The journalists reported that Rosenthal had recently told a group of Israeli visitors: "The Israeli occupation of the West Bank is like someone carrying a heavy pack on his back—the longer he carries it, the more he stoops over, but the less he is aware of the burden." Rosenthal had personally related the incident to Robert Novak. Although he used the descriptive image "ever so gently," according to Neiditch, it caused a stir.

Amitay chided Rosenthal for speaking "out of turn." About five minutes later, Ephraim "Eppie" Evron, the Israeli ambassador to the United States, called with the same message. Then, just a few minutes later, Yehuda Hellman of the Conference of Presidents of Major Jewish Organizations called. Again, the same message. Neiditch remembers that Rosenthal looked over and observed, "Young man, you've just seen the Jewish lobby's muscles flex." Neiditch recalls: "It was three calls within 13 minutes."

Another senior committee member, an Ohio Congressman who was more independent of Israel's interests than Rosenthal, nevertheless found his activities closely watched. Republican Charles Whalen felt the pressure of the lobby when he accepted a last-minute invitation to attend a February 1973 conference in London on the Middle East. It was held under the auspices of the Ford Foundation. No Israeli representative was present, but to his surprise, on his return to Washington, Whalen was called on by an Israeli lobby official who demanded all of the meeting's details—the agenda, those present, why Whalen went and why Ford had sponsored it.

Whalen recalls, "It was just amazing. They never let up." Whalen believes it was the last such conference Ford sponsored. "They got to them," Whalen speculates and adds that the experience was a turning point in his own attitude toward the lobby: "If I couldn't go to a conference to further my education, I began to wonder what's this all about."

A Minnesota Democrat had reason for similar wonderment after he left Congress. Richard Nolan, now a businessman in Minneapolis, discovered the reluctance of his former colleagues to identify themselves with a scholarly article on the Middle East. He individually approached fifteen Congressmen, asking each to insert in the *Congres-*

sional Record an article which discussed the potential for the development of profitable U.S. trade with Arab states. Written by Ghanim Al-Mazrui, an official of the United Arab Emirates, it proposed broadened dialogue and rejection of malicious stereotypes. Under House rules, when such items are entered in the *Record,* the name of the sponsoring member must be shown.

Nolan reports, "Each of the fifteen said it was a terrific article that should be published but added, 'Please understand, putting it in under my name would simply cause too much trouble.' I didn't encounter a single one who questioned the excellence of the article, and what made it especially sad was that I picked out the fifteen people I thought most likely to cooperate." The sixteenth Congressman he approached, Democrat David E. Bonior of Michigan agreed to Nolan's request. The article appeared on page E 4791 of the October 5, 1983, *Record.* It was one of those unusual occasions when the *Congressional Record* contained a statement that might be viewed as critical of policies or positions taken by Israel or, as in this case, promoting dialogue with the Arabs.

It was one of several brave steps by Bonior which may make him a future target of Israel's lobby. Speaking before the Association of Arab American University Graduates in Flint, Michigan, two months before the 1984 election, Bonior called for conditions on aid to Israel, declaring that the United States has been "rewarding the current government of Israel for undertaking policies that are contrary to our own," including Israel's disruption of "U.S. relations with long standing allies such as Jordan and Saudi Arabia."

"An Incredible Burst of Candor"

Even those high in House leadership who represent politically safe districts are not immune from lobby intimidation. They perceive lobby pressure back home and sometimes vote against their own conscience.

In October 1981 President Reagan's controversial proposal to sell AWACS (intelligence-gathering airplanes) and modifying equipment for F-15 fighter aircraft to Saudi Arabia was under consideration in the House. Congressman Daniel Rostenkowski, chairman of the Ways and Means Committee and one of the most influential legislators on Capitol Hill, got caught in the Israeli lobby counterattack. It was the first test of strength between the lobby and the newly-installed president. Under the law, the sale would go through unless both Houses rejected it. The lobby strategy was to have the initial test vote occur in the House, where its strength was greater, believing a lopsided House rejection might cause the Senate to follow suit.

Under heavy pressure from the lobby, Rostenkowski cooperated by voting "No." Afterwards he told a reporter for Chicago radio station WMAQ that he actually favored the sale but voted as he did because he feared the "Jewish lobby."

He contended that the House majority against the sale was so overwhelming that his own favorable vote "would not have mattered." Overwhelming it was, 301 to 111. Still, the Israeli lobby's goal was the highest possible number of negative votes in order to influence the Senate vote, and, to the lobby, Rostenkowski's vote did matter very much.

Columnist Carl Rowan called Rostenkowski's admission "an incredible burst of candor." While declaring "it is as American as apple pie for monied interests to use their dough to influence decisions" in Washington, Rowan added, "There are a lot of American Jews with lots of money who learned long ago that they can achieve influence far beyond their numbers by making strategic donations to candidates. . . . No Arab population here plays such a powerful role." Rostenkowski, however, was not a major recipient of contributions from pro-Israeli political action committees. In the following year, his campaign received only $1,000 from such groups.

While the lobby is watchful over the full membership of the House, particularly leaders like Rostenkoswki, it gives special emphasis to the members of the Foreign Affairs Committee, where the initial decisions are made on aid, both military and economic.

Allegiance to Israeli interests sometimes creates mystifying voting habits. Members who are "doves" on policy elsewhere in the world are unabashed "hawks" when Israel is concerned. As Stephen S. Rosenfeld, deputy editor of the editorial page of the *Washington Post,* wrote in May 1983:

A Martian looking at the way Congress treats the administration's aid requests for Israel and El Salvador might conclude that our political system makes potentially life-or-death decisions about dependent countries in truly inscrutable ways.

Rosenfeld was intrigued with the extraordinary performance of the Foreign Affairs Committee on one particular day, May 11, 1983. Scarcely taking time to catch its breath between acts, the panel required the vulnerable government of El Salvador to "jump a series of extremely high political hurdles" in order to get funding "barely adequate to keep its nose above water," while, a moment later, handing to Israel, clearly the dominant military power in the Middle East, "a third of a billion dollars more than the several billion dollars that the administration asked for it." One of Israel's leading partisans, Congressman

Stephen J. Solarz, spoke with enthusiasm for the El Salvador "hurdles" and for the massive increase to Israel.

"Nobody in the Leadership Will Say No"

Israel's lobby is especially attentive to the person occupying the position as chairman of the Foreign Affairs Committee and, because of his or her ability to control the agenda at legislative meetings, takes a close interest when a vacancy occurs in the chairmanship.

In January 1977, activists for the lobby found reason for concern when Clement J. Zablocki of Wisconsin, after waiting eighteen years as second-ranking Democrat on the Foreign Affairs Committee, was in line to take over after the retirement of Chairman Thomas E. Morgan. A group of younger Democrats, led by Benjamin S. Rosenthal of New York, tried to keep Zablocki from the chairmanship. They based their challenge on allegations contained in a closely-held 38-page report prepared by Rosenthal's staff which contended that Zablocki had voted against too many Democratic foreign policy initiatives and had dubious Korean connections.

Zablocki dismissed the Korean charges as "outright lies," and the *Congressional Quarterly* voting study reported that he had voted with his party 79 percent of the time in the previous Congress. Zablocki declared that the real complaint of Rosenthal and his associates was "a feeling that I was not friendly enough toward Israel." Yet, with the exception of one key vote, he had always supported aid to Israel. He told columnist Jack Anderson, who had publicized the Rosenthal report: "I'm not anti-Semitic, but I'm not as pro-Israel as Ben Rosenthal. Even [then Israeli Prime Minister] Rabin doesn't satisfy Rosenthal."

Despite the lobby's opposition, Zablocki was elected chairman, 182 to 72. But the experience may have dulled his enthusiasm for Middle East controversy, as he did not again issue statements or cast votes opposing lobby requests. An aide said Zablocki could hardly be blamed, since the House leadership, principally Speaker "Tip" O'Neill, discourages opposition to Israel: "Nobody in the leadership will say no to the Israeli lobby. Nobody."

"Outdoing the United Jewish Appeal"

Stephen J. Solarz, a hard-working Congressman who represents a heavily Jewish district in Brooklyn, prides himself on accomplishing many good things for Israel. Since his first election in 1974, Solarz established a reputation as an intelligent "eager beaver," widely-traveled, aggressive, and totally committed to Israel's interests. In committee, he seems always bursting with the next question before the witness responds to his first.

In a December 1980 newsletter to his constituents, he provided an unprecedented insight into how Israel—despite the budgetary restraints under which the U.S. government labors—is able to get ever-increasing aid. Early that year he had started his own quest for increased aid. He reported that he persuaded Secretary of State Cyrus Vance to come to his Capitol Hill office to talk it over. There he threatened Vance with a fight for the increase on the House floor if the administration opposed it in committee. Shortly thereafter, he said Vance sent word that the administration would recommend an increase—$200 million extra in military aid—although not as much as Solarz desired.

His next goal was to convince the Foreign Affairs Committee to increase the administration's levels. Solarz felt an increase approved by the committee could be maintained on the House floor. The first step was a private talk with Lee H. Hamilton, chairman of the subcommittee on Europe and the Middle East, the panel that would first deal with the request. Tall, thoughtful, scholarly and cautious, Hamilton prides himself on staying on the same "wavelength" as the majority—whether in committee or on the floor. Never abrasive, he usually works out differences ahead of time and avoids open wrangles. Representing a rural Indiana district with no significant Jewish population, he is troubled by Israel's military adventures but rarely voices criticism in public. He guards his role as a conciliator.

Solarz found Hamilton amenable: "He agreed to support our proposal to increase the amount of [military assistance] . . . by another $200 million." That would bring the total increase to $400 million. Even more important, Hamilton agreed to support a move to relieve Israel of its obligation to repay any of the $785 million in economic aid. The administration had wanted Israel to pay back one-third of the amount.

"As we anticipated," Solarz reported, "with the support of Congressman Hamilton, our proposal sailed through both his subcommittee and the full committee and was never challenged on the floor when the foreign aid bill came up for consideration." Democrat Frank Church of Idaho, the chairman of the Senate Foreign Relations Committee, and Jacob Javits, senior Republican—both strongly pro-Israeli—guided proposals at the same level smoothly through their chamber.

Solarz summed up: "Israel, as a result, will soon be receiving a grand total of $660 million more in military and economic aid than it received from the U.S. government last year." He reflected upon the magnitude of the achievement:

Through a combination of persistence and persuasion, we were able to provide Israel with an increase in military-economic aid in one year alone which is the equivalent of almost three years of contributions by the national UJA [United Jewish Appeal].

In his newsletter Solarz said that he sought membership on the Foreign Affairs Committee "because I wanted to be in a position to be helpful to Israel." He explained that, while "hundreds of members of Congress, Republicans as well as Democrats" support Israel, "it is the members of the Foreign Affairs Committee in the House, and the Foreign Relations Committee in the Senate, who are really in a position to make a difference where it counts—in the area of foreign aid, upon which Israel is now so dependent."

Solarz's zeal was unabated in September 1984 when, as a member of the House-Senate conference on Export Administration Act amendments, he demanded in a public meeting to know the legislation's implications for Israel. He asked Congressman Howard Wolpe, "Is there anything that the Israelis want from us, or could conceivably want from us that they weren't able to get?" Even when Wolpe responded with a clear "no," Solarz pressed, "Have you spoken to the [Israeli] embassy?" Wolpe responded, "I personally have not," but he admitted, "my office has." Then Solarz tried again, "You are giving me an absolute assurance that they [the Israelis] have no reservation at all about this?" Finally convinced that Israel was content with the legislation, Solarz relaxed, "If they have no problem with it, then there is no reason for us to."

A veteran Ohio Congressman observes:

When Solarz and others press for more money for Israel, nobody wants to say "No." You don't need many examples of intimidation for politicians to realize what the potential is. The Jewish lobby is terrific. Anything it wants, it gets. Jews are educated, often have a lot of money, and vote on the basis of a single issue—Israel. They are unique in that respect. For example, anti-abortion supporters are numerous but not that well educated, and don't have that much money. The Jewish lobbyists have it all, and they are political activists on top of it.

This Congressman divides his colleagues into four groups:

For the first group, it's rah, rah, give Israel anything it wants. The second group includes those with some misgivings, but they don't dare step out of line; they don't say anything. In the third group are Congressmen who have deep misgivings but who won't do more than try quietly to slow down the aid to Israel. Lee Hamilton is an example. The fourth group consists of those who openly question U.S. policy in the Middle East and challenge what Israel is doing. Since Findley and McCloskey left, this group really doesn't exist anymore.

He puts himself in the third group: "I may vote against the bill authorizing foreign aid this year for the first time. If I do, I will not state my reason."

Solarz has never wavered in his commitment to Israel. Another Congressman, although bringing much the same level of commitment when he first joined the committee, underwent a change.

"Bleeding a Little Inside"

Democratic Congressman Mervyn M. Dymally, former lieutenant-governor of California, came to Washington in 1980 with perfect credentials as a supporter of Israel. He says, "When you look at black America, I rank myself second only to Bayard Rustin in supporting Israel over the past twenty years." Short, handsome and articulate, Dymally was the first black American to go to Israel after both the 1967 and 1973 wars.

In his successful campaign for lieutenant-governor, he spoke up for Israel in all the statewide Democratic canvasses. He co-founded the Black Americans in Support of Israel Committee, organized pro-Israeli advertising in California newspapers and helped to rally other black officials to the cause. In Congress, he became a dependable vote for Israeli interests as a member of the Foreign Affairs Committee.

Nevertheless, in 1982 the pro-Israeli community withdrew its financial support, and the following year the AIPAC organization in California marked him for defeat and began seeking a credible opponent to run against him in 1984. Explaining this sudden turn of events, Dymally cites two "black marks" against his pro-Israeli record in Congress. First, he "occasionally asked challenging questions about aid to Israel in committee"; although his questions were mild and not frequent, he stood out because no one else was even that daring. Second—far more damning in the eyes of AIPAC—he met twice with PLO leader Yasser Arafat.

Both meetings were unplanned. The first encounter took place in 1981 during a visit to Abu Dhabi, where Dymally had stopped to meet the local minister of planning while on his way back from a foreign policy conference in southern India. The minister told him he had just met with Arafat and asked Dymally if he would like to see him. Dymally recalls, "I was too chicken to say 'no,' but I thought I was safe in doing it. I figured Arafat would not bother to see an obscure freshman Congressman, especially on such short notice."

To his surprise, Arafat invited him to an immediate appointment. This caused near panic on the part of Dymally's escort, an employee of the U.S. embassy, who was taking Dymally on his round of appointments in the ambassador's car, a vehicle bedecked with a U.S. flag on the front fender. Sensitive to the U.S. ban on contact between administration personnel and PLO officials, the flustered escort removed the flag, excused himself and then directed the driver to deliver Dymally to the Arafat appointment. "He was really in a sweat," Dymally recalls.

After a brief session with Arafat, he found a reporter for the Arab News Service waiting outside. Dymally told him Arafat expressed his desire for a dialogue with the United States. That night Peter Jennings reported to a nationwide American audience over ABC evening news from London that Dymally had become the first Congressman to meet Arafat since Ronald Reagan became president.

The news caused an uproar in the Jewish community, with many Jews doubting Dymally's statement that the meeting was unplanned. Stella Epstein, a Jewish member of Dymally's Congressional staff, quit in protest.

Dymally met the controversial PLO leader again in 1982 in a similarly coincidental way. He had gone to Lebanon with his colleagues, Democrats Mary Rose Oakar of Ohio, Nick Rahall of West Virginia and David E. Bonoir of Michigan, and Republican Paul N. "Pete" McCloskey to meet with Lebanese leaders, visit refugee camps and view the effects of the Israeli invasion.

Dymally was shocked by what he saw: "There's no way you can visit those [Palestinian] refugee camps without bleeding a little inside." After arrival they accepted an invitation to meet with Arafat, who was then under siege in Beirut.

His trouble with the Jewish community grew even worse. Dymally was wrongly accused of voting in 1981 for the sale of AWACS intelligence-gathering aircraft to Saudi Arabia. He actually voted the way the Israeli lobby wanted him to vote, against the sale. Moreover, to make his position explicit, during the House debate he stated his opposition in two separate speeches. He made the second speech, written for him by one of his supporters, Max Mont of the Jewish Labor Committee, Dymally explains, "because Mont complained that the first was not strong enough."

Still, the message did not get through or by this time was conveniently forgotten. Carmen Warshaw, long prominent in Jewish affairs and Democratic Party politics in California—and a financial supporter of his campaigns—accosted Dymally at a public dinner and said, "I want my money back." Dymally responded, "What did I do, Carmen?" She answered, "You voted for AWACS."

Dymally finds membership on the Foreign Affairs subcommittee on the Middle East a "no win" situation. He has alienated people on both sides. While one staff member quit in protest when he met Arafat, another, Peg McCormick, quit in protest when he voted for a large aid package that included money to build warplanes in Israel.

For a time Dymally stopped complaining and raising questions about Israel in committee. Asked why by the *Wall Street Journal,* he cited the lobby's role in my own loss in 1982 to Democrat Richard J. Durbin. He told the *Journal* reporter, "There is no question the Findley-Durbin race was intimidating."

Dymally found intimidation elsewhere as well. Whenever he complains, he says, he receives a prompt visit from an AIPAC lobbyist, usually accompanied by a Dymally constituent. He met one day with a group of Jewish constituents, "all of them old friends," and told them that, despite his grumbling, in the end he always voted for aid to Israel. He said: "Not once, I told them, have I ever strayed from the course." One of his constituents spoke up and said, "That's not quite right. Once you abstained." "They are that good," marveled Dymally. "The man was right."

"I Hear You"

After coming to Congress, Dymally waited two years before he complained publicly about aid to Israel. He first voiced his concern on a wintry day in 1983 in a Capitol Hill hearing room so crowded only those with sharp elbows could get inside the door. The newly-formed House subcommittee on Europe and the Middle East of the 98th Congress was meeting to hear testimony on how much economic aid should go to Israel. Those attending learned why such aid flows smoothly through Congress—and usually is increased en route.

Sitting at the witness table was Nicholas Veliotes, at that time the assistant secretary of state for Mideast and South Asia Affairs. The tall, dark-haired career diplomat of Greek ancestry had previously served in Israel and Jordan and was on Capitol Hill that day to explain why the Reagan Administration wanted Congress to approve $785 million for economic support of Israel as part of a $2.5 billion aid package for the coming fiscal year. The totals were exactly the same as those requested the year before, but the administration had decided, in a proposal helpful to the U.S. budget, to require that Israel pay back one-third of the amount it received for economic purposes.

Taking part in the discussion were seven Democrats and one Republican, freshman Congressman Ed Zschau of California.

The news media gave the event full coverage, with floodlights adding both heat and glare to the packed room. The lights weren't the only source of heat. For two sweltering hours Veliotes was roasted. Five of the Congressmen took turns pelting him with statements and questions which, in essence, castigated the administration for attempting to cut Israeli aid slightly from the amount approved the previous year. Only Dymally sided with the administration.

The nature, intensity and imbalance of the grilling might have led a stranger to assume that Veliotes was being examined—not by U.S. Congressmen—but by a committee of the Israeli parliament.

In two turns at questioning, Democrat Tom Lantos of California, a white-haired refugee from Hungary, sternly lectured Veliotes for being unresponsive to the new threats to Israel posed by the placement of new Soviet missiles in Syria as well as the expansion of Soviet arms sales to Libya. Lantos belittled as "skyhook policy" the insistence by the administration that all Israeli forces be removed from Lebanon.

Those who had followed Lantos' 1982 campaign for re-election were not surprised at his line of questioning. At fund-raising events Lantos hammered at the theme, "Israel needs a voice in Congress." He offered himself as that voice. In that subcommittee hearing "the voice" was tuning up.

A number of freshmen Democrats pursued similar questioning. Lawrence J. Smith of Florida saw Israeli military operations in Lebanon as a "substantial gain" toward "total peace" and wanted more money for Israel because aid dollars had been "eroded" by inflation.

Mel Levine, another Californian, chimed in, noting Israel's "loss" in revenue when it yielded control of the Sinai oilfields to Egypt in compliance with the Camp David agreement. Robert Torricelli of New Jersey suspected "coercion" because the administration did not increase its request for Israel.

Committee veteran Solarz reinforced the theme by recalling that over the last few years Congress had annually "adjusted upward" the level or "rearranged the terms" of aid in order to be "more helpful to Israel."

Only Dymally complained that aid to Israel was too high. "How can the United States afford to give so much money in view of our economic crisis . . . to a country that has rejected the President's peace initiatives and stepped up its settlements in the occupied territories?" he demanded.

Ed Zschau, a freshman Republican from California, provided the only other break from the pro-Israel questioning: "Do you think there should be conditions [on aid to Israel] that might hasten the objectives of the peace process?" Getting no response, he pressed on: "Given that we are giving aid in order to achieve progress in peace in the area, wouldn't it make sense to associate with the aid some modest conditions like a halt in the settlements policy?"

Veliotes gave only cautious responses to the challenges. When Zschau pressed for a direct answer, Veliotes answered simply, "I hear you." Whatever his private sentiments, he had no authority to encourage the conditions Zschau suggested.

Dymally spoke up again a month later when the Middle East subcommittee acted on the legislation to authorize aid to Israel and several other Middle East countries. Dymally offered an amendment increasing military aid to Egypt, half of it to be a loan and the other half a grant. He had logic behind his amendment: it would establish "parity" in the way the United States treated Israel and Egypt. Both were parties to the Camp David accords and considered friendly to the United States; and, Dymally argued, because Egypt's economic problems were more severe than Israel's, Egypt should receive U.S. generosity at least at the same level as that extended to Israel.

His amendment was defeated. Congressman Lantos spoke against it, citing "budgetary reasons." Only Dymally voted "yes." Its rejection came moments after the subcommittee had passed without opposition an amendment to increase military "forgiven direct credits" to Israel—a euphemism for outright grants—by $200 million, plus a hefty $65 million increase in economic aid. This time, the subcommittee was unmoved by "budgetary reasons," despite the increase in the federal budget deficit the amendment would cause. Only Dymally had the virtue of consistency that day: he voted in favor of both amendments.

During the same session the subcommittee voted to place legislative strings on the sale of jet fighters to Jordan. Before getting the aircraft, King Hussein would first be required to begin negotiations with Israel. This restriction reflected the expressed sentiments of the House of Representatives, as 170 of its members by then had signed a public letter to that effect. Although this public rebuke would undercut President Reagan's private efforts to win Hussein's cooperation, Robert Pelletreau, who as deputy assistant secretary of state was present to speak for the administration, sat silently in the crowded hearing room as the subcommittee adopted the restriction. Pelletreau's silence demonstrated the administration's unwillingness to confront the lobby.

"The Administration Can't Call the Tune"

Although administration officials often blame Congress for aid increases to Israel, they should save some of the blame for themselves. A month after Dymally's amendment was defeated in subcommittee—and Pelletreau's unbecoming silence—the full committee on Foreign

Affairs took up the same bill. This time the administration witness, Alvin Drischler, also a deputy assistant secretary of state, managed to land on both sides of the same question, destroying whatever influence his presence might have had.

Under consideration was an amendment offered by Congressman Joel Pritchard of Washington to rescind the $265 million additional grant aid approved for Israel by the subcommittee and to bring the total amount down to the level originally requested by the administration. Asked for comment, Drischler told the committee, "We support the administration's request." That is, he supported the Pritchard amendment, a position that was not surprising. However, Drischler quickly added: "But we do not oppose the add-on."

The committee room rocked with laughter when Chairman Clement J. Zablocki complained: "We're confused." Clearly, administration resolve, if it ever existed, had vanished. Pritchard was left fighting for the administration amendment without administration support. He warned that the administration would lose leverage in dealing with Israel if Congress approved the increase, but he added candidly: "There has always been the feeling that in Congress Israel has enough support to checkmate any administration initiative."

Democratic Congressman George Crockett of Michigan warned that the increase would "free additional capital for [Israeli Prime Minister] Begin to continue building settlements." But Kansas Republican Congressman Larry Winn countered by stating that increasing the grant money would "help" Israel meet its debt service obligation to the United States, which in 1983 would top $1 billion. Winn, in effect, was arguing that the United States should give Israel money to repay its debt to the United States. That sort of "logic" prevailed. The Pritchard amendment was defeated, 18 to 5. A lobbyist for the U.S. Agency for International Development later admitted that no fight was made for the Pritchard amendment because "the votes just aren't there."

Pritchard, witnessing Israel's influence on Congress, puts it differently: "The administration can't call the tune of American foreign policy."

"I Do Not Feel As Free"

Dymally's occasional independence in speaking and voting on Middle East questions predictably brought complaints from Israel's activists in his home district, and, although they did not succeed in finding a credible candidate to oppose him in 1984, he sees no likelihood that the breach will be closed. He says membership on the Foreign Affairs Committee is a "no win" situation.

"I must confess to you that I do not feel as free to criticize Israel as

I do to criticize Trinidad, the island on which I was born," Dymally declares. Noting that Trinidad was one of the islands supporting the U.S. invasion of Grenada in 1983, he says his own strong opposition to the invasion did not cause the islanders to turn against him. "Sure, some of Trinidad's leaders were unhappy with me. But they are not boycotting my campaign for re-election. In fact, people from that area are putting on a fundraiser in New York for me. They don't see me as anti-black, anti-Grenada, anti-West Indies. They just disagree with me on the invasion, but they don't fall out."

He contrasts this reaction with that of his Jewish critics in California. "What is tragic is that so many Jewish people misconstrue criticism of Israel as anti-Jewish or anti-Semitic." He speaks admiringly of the open criticism of Israeli policy that often occurs within Israel itself: "It is easier to criticize Israel in the Knesset [the Israeli parliament] than it is in the U.S. Congress, here in this land of free speech."

Dymally notes that 10 of the 37 members of the Foreign Affairs Committee are Jewish and finds it "so stacked there is no chance" for constructive dialogue." He names Republican Congressman Ed Zschau of California as the only member of the Subcommittee on Europe and the Middle East who "even shadow boxes." No one on the subcommittee, he says, is in there "punching."

Dymally believes the political scene in the United States would be improved "if citizens of Arab ancestry became more effective lobbyists themselves and became convinced of the need to give money to their cause." One of their problems, he says, is their lack of understanding of how to present their interests on Capitol Hill. "Foreign ethnics don't understand the importance of lobbying. Nor do they seem to have a sense of political philanthropy." Peter Spieller, a former student aide in his Congressional office, told him, "The word is out [in the Jewish community] that you have sold out for Arab money." Dymally chuckles. "I told him I wished the Arab Americans would give me some money." He says they have not helped, despite his need to pay some of his campaign debts from his 1980 campaign. Prior to that year, Dymally had been able to count on several thousand dollars in campaign contributions each time from Jewish sources. After he met Arafat and began to raise questions about Israeli policies, this money "dried up." In the 1982 campaign he says a Jewish friend bought two $100 tickets to a dinner. "That," he said, "was the extent of Jewish financial support that year."

Dymally's Committee on Foreign Affairs is easily dominated by the Israeli lobby partly because most Congressmen consider assignment there a political liability. With most Americans wanting foreign aid cut back, if not eliminated altogether, Congressmen representing politically marginal districts take a gamble when they support foreign aid and a still bigger gamble if they are assigned to the committee that handles it.

Donald J. Pease, a senior Democrat from Ohio, formerly a member of the Foreign Affairs Committee, explains why Congressmen with a special interest in Israel have no difficulty getting assigned to the committee: "It is one of the least sought after committees. If you ask for it, you are sure to get it. One year Democrats had to hunt for recruits just to fill their seats. The committee is looked on as a liability by most Democrats. It is an asset only to members with large Jewish constituencies." Republicans feel the same way.

Fourteen Freshmen Save the Day

Under the watchful eye of Israel's lobby, Congressmen will go to extreme measures to help move legislation providing aid to Israel. Just before Congress adjourned in December 1983, a group of freshmen Democrats helped the cause by taking the extraordinary step of changing their votes in the printed record of proceedings, a step Congressmen usually shun because it makes them look indecisive. This day, however, under heavy pressure from pro-Israel constituents, the first-term members buckled and agreed to switch in order to pass catch-all legislation known as a Continuing Resolution. The resolution provided funds for programs Congress had failed to authorize in the normal fashion, among them aid to Israel. Passage would prevent any interruption in this aid.

For once, both the House Democratic leadership and AIPAC were caught napping. Usually in complete control of all legislative activities which relate to Israel, AIPAC failed to detect the brewing rebellion. Concern over the budget deficit and controversial provisions in the bill for Central America led these freshman Democrats to oppose their own leadership. Unable to offer amendments, they quietly agreed among themselves to oppose the whole package.

When the roll was called the big electric board over the Speaker's desk showed defeat—the resolution was rejected, 206 to 203. Twenty-four first-term Democrats had deserted the leadership and voted no. Voting no did not mean they opposed Israeli aid. Some of them, concerned over the federal deficit, viewed it as a demand to the leadership to schedule a bill raising taxes. For others, it was simply a protest. But for Israel it was serious.

"The Jewish community went crazy," a Capitol Hill veteran recalls. AIPAC's professionals went to work. Placing calls from their offices just four blocks away, they activated key people in the districts of a selected list of the errant freshmen. They arranged for "quality calls" to individuals who had played a major role in the recent Congressional election. Each was to place an urgent call to his or her Congressman, insist on getting through personally and use this message:

Approval of the continuing resolution is very important. Without it, Israel will suffer. I am not criticizing your vote against it the first time. I am sure you had reasons. However, I have learned that the same question will come up for vote again, probably tomorrow. I speak for many of your friends and supporters in asking that you change your vote when the question comes up again.

Each person was instructed to report to AIPAC after making the calls. The calls were accordingly made and reported.

The House of Representatives took up the question at noon. It was the same language, word for word, which the House had rejected two days before. Silvio Conte, senior Republican on the Appropriations Committee, knowing the pressure that had been applied, during the debate challenged the freshmen Democrats to "stick to their guns" as "men of courage." Republican leader Bob Michel chided those unable to "take the heat from on high."

Some of the heat came, of course, from the embarrassed Democratic leadership, but AIPAC was the institution that brought about changes in votes. On critical issues, Congressmen respond to pressures from home, and, in such circumstances, House leaders have little leverage. To Republicans Conte and Michel, the main issue was the need for budgetary restraint. They argued that the measure should be rejected for that reason. During the debate, no one mentioned that day—or any other day—the influence of the Israeli lobby.

The urgent telephone messages from home carried the day. When the roll was called, 14 of the freshmen—a bit sheepishly—changed their votes. They were: C. Robin Britt of North Carolina, Jim Cooper of Tennessee, Richard J. Durbin of Illinois, Edward F. Feighan of Ohio, Sander M. Levin of Michigan, Frank McCloskey of Indiana, Bruce A. Morrison of Connecticut, James R. "Jim" Olin and Norman Sisisky of Virginia, Timothy J. Penny of Minnesota, Harry M. Reid of Nevada, Bill Richardson of New Mexico, John M. Spratt, Jr. of South Carolina and Harley O. Staggers, Jr., of West Virginia.

To give the freshmen an excuse they could use in explaining their embarrassing shift, the leadership promised to bring up a tax bill. Everyone knew it was just a ploy: the tax bill had no chance to become law. But the excuse was helpful, and the resolution was approved, 224 to 189. The flow of aid to Israel continued without interruption.

Subsidizing Foreign Competition

The final vote on the Continuing Resolution authorized a remarkable new form of aid to Israel. It included an amendment crafted by

AIPAC and sponsored by ardently pro-Israeli Congressmen Clarence Long of Maryland and Jack Kemp of New York that permitted $250 million of the military grant aid to be spent in Israel on the development of a new Israeli fighter aircraft, the Lavi. The new fighter would compete for international sales with the Northrop F-20 and the General Dynamics F-16—both specifically designed for export. The amendment authorized privileged treatment Uncle Sam had never before extended to a foreign competitor. It was extraordinary for another reason: it set aside a U.S. law that requires that all foreign aid procurement funds be spent in the United States.

During debate of the bill, Democrat Nick J. Rahall of West Virginia was the only Congressman who objected. He saw the provision as threatening U.S. jobs at a time of high unemployment:

Approximately 6,000 jobs would be lost as a direct result of taking the $250 million out of the U.S. economy and allowing Israel to spend it on defense articles and services which can just as easily be purchased here in the United States.

Americans are being stripped of their tax dollars to build up foreign industry. They should not have to sacrifice their jobs as well.

That day, Rahall was unable to offer an amendment to strike or change this provision because of restrictions the House had established before it began debate. All that he, or any other member, could do was to vote for or against the entire Long-Kemp amendment which included controversial provisions for El Salvador and international banks, as well as aid to Israel. The amendment was approved 262 to 150. Unlike Rahall's, most of the 150 negative votes reflected opposition to other features of the amendment, not to the $250 million subsidy to Israel's aircraft industry.

The following May, during the consideration of the bill appropriating funds for foreign aid, Rahall offered an amendment to eliminate the $250 million, but it was defeated 379 to 40. Despite the amendment's obvious appeal to constituents connected with the U.S. aircraft industry, fewer than 10 percent of House members voted for it. It was the first roll call vote on an amendment dealing exclusively with aid to Israel in more than four years, and the margin of defeat provided a measure of AIPAC power.

After the vote, AIPAC organized protests against the 40 legislators who had supported the amendment. Rahall recalls that AIPAC carried out a campaign "berating those brave 40 Congressmen." He adds, "Almost all of those who voted with me have told me they are still catching hell from their Jewish constituency. They are still moaning about the beating they are taking."

The "brave" Congressmen got little thanks. Two ethnic groups, the American-Arab Anti-Discrimination Committee and the National Association of Arab Americans, congratulated Rahall on his initiative and urged their members to send letters of congratulation to each of the 39 who supported his amendment. The results were meager. As the author, Rahall could expect to receive more supportive mail than the rest. He received "less than 10 letters" and speculates that the other 39 got still fewer.

"Don't Look to Congress to Act"

The reluctance of Congressmen to speak of Israel in critical vein was apparent in 1983 when the House gave President Reagan permission under the War Powers Act to keep U.S. Marines in Lebanon for 18 months. The vote took place a few days before the tragic truck-bombing killed over 240 Marines in Beirut. At the time the House acted, several Marines had already died. A number of Congressmen warned of more trouble ahead, opposing Reagan's request and strongly urging withdrawal of the U.S. military force. Five others took the other side, mentioning the importance of the Marine presence to the security of Israel's northern border.

In all, 91 Congressmen spoke, but they were silent on the military actions Israel had carried out in Lebanon during the previous year—its unrestricted bombing of Beirut, forcing the evacuation of the PLO fighters and then failing to provide security in the Palestine camps where the massacre occurred. These events had altered the Lebanese scene so radically that President Reagan felt impelled to return the Marines to Beirut. In other words, it was Israel's actions which made necessary the Marines' presence, yet none of these critical events was mentioned among the thousands of words expressed during the lengthy discussion.

A veteran Congressman, with the advantage of hindsight, explained it directly. Just after the terrorist attack which killed U.S. Marines who were asleep in their Beirut compound, Congressman Lee Hamilton was asked if Congress might soon initiate action on its own to get the Marines out of Lebanon. The query was posed by William Quandt, a Middle East specialist who had served in the Carter White House, at the close of a private discussion on Capitol Hill involving a small group of senior Congressmen. Hamilton, a close student of both the Congress and the Middle East, responded, "Don't look to Congress to act. All we know is how to increase aid to Israel."

The next year, discussions leading to the decisions on Israeli aid by Hamilton's subcommittee were less a public spectacle and Hamilton himself became less directly involved. In late February 1984 he was not consulted on aid levels, even privately, until the "Jewish caucus" led by freshman Democrat Larry Smith of Florida had worked out the details. Others in the caucus, all Democrats, were Mel Levine and Tom Lantos of California and Robert Torricelli of New Jersey. Torricelli, of Italian ancestry, represents one of the nation's most heavily Jewish districts. His colleagues often refer to him teasingly as "a non-Jewish Jew."

The group's four votes could always prevail in the ten-member subcommittee, since the other six members never voted against a pro-Israeli motion, and only Democrat Mervyn M. Dymally and Republican Ed Zschau even raised questions. Other Jewish Democrats on the full committee—Howard L. Berman of California, Ted Weiss and Gary L. Ackerman of New York, Sam Gejdenson of Connecticut, Howard Wolpe of Michigan and Stephen J. Solarz of New York—accepted the decisions of the "Jewish caucus." This established Smith as almost the de facto leader of the 29 Jews in the House, a remarkable role for a freshman. Asked to explain how a freshman could reach such influence, a Capitol Hill veteran said, "He's always there. He never misses a meeting. He never misses a lick."

Confronted by the caucus on the economic aid level, Hamilton agreed to support their recommendations with one modification. He insisted that the grant to Israel be increased by only $250 million above the administration's request for $850 million, rather than the $350 million increase the caucus wanted. With all of the items settled ahead of time, the subcommittee approved the unprecedented provisions for Israel without discussion, and then took up questions related to aid for other Middle East countries. The panel approved an amendment offered by Congressman Zschau stating that the funds were provided "with the expectation that the recipient countries shall pursue policies to enhance the peace process, including giving consideration to all peace initiatives by the president and others." By the time the amendment reached the full committee, AIPAC, without consulting Zschau, demonstrated its control over such things by arranging to have the language tied to the Camp David Accords rather than the Reagan recommendations. Written by AIPAC lobbyist Douglas Bloomfield, the substitute language was accepted on a voice vote.

In either form the amendment was innocuous, but that could not be said of two other amendments drafted by the lobby and passed overwhelmingly by the subcommittee. The first amendment, accepted without opposition, would prohibit all communications between the PLO and the U.S. government, even through third parties, until the PLO recognizes Israel. It was intended to bar the sort of informal contact with the Palestinian leadership maintained by both the Carter and Reagan administration. The other amendment, approved 7 to 2, would prohibit the sale of any advanced aircraft or weapons to Jordan until that country becomes "publicly committed" to recognizing Israel. When King Hussein of Jordan later criticized Israeli lobby influence in Washington in early 1984, he cited both of these amendments.

Meanwhile, Democratic Congressman Howard Berman of California secured hearings on a bill that would add an unprecedented new dimension to U.S. aid to Israel. Introduced in June 1984, it proposed granting $20 million to finance Israel's own foreign aid projects in Asia, Africa and Latin America. It would openly authorize activities similar to those that have been covertly financed by the CIA for 20 years (see chapter five).

Democrat Larry Smith of Florida applauded Berman's bill: "I think it will enhance the image of the U.S. in the Third World." Republican Larry Winn of Kansas gave it bipartisan support but noted that the initial $20 million would be "only a drop in the bucket; we're going to have to look further down the road at a lot more money." Although the bill remained in committee through the 1984 session, its supporters believe this type of aid to Israel will eventually be approved.

Clearly, the road Winn mentioned will slope upward. Aid to Israel—despite U.S. budget problems and Israel's defiant behavior toward the United States in its use of U.S.-supplied weapons and its construction of settlements on occupied territory—is still rising with no peak in sight.

Chapter 3

The Deliberative Body Fails to Deliberate

Just off the second-floor corridor connecting the central part of the U.S. Capitol building with the Senate wing is the restored old Senate chamber where visitors can look around and imagine the room echoing with great debates of the past. Action there first gave the Senate its reputation as the "world's greatest deliberative body" where no topic was too controversial for open debate.

In most respects, that reputation is deserved and honored. In fact, all five former Senators—John C. Calhoun, Daniel Webster, Henry Clay, Robert LaFollette and Robert Taft—who are pictured in the ornate reception room near the large chamber now used by the Senate, were distinguished by their independence and courage, not their conformity.

Today, on Middle East issues at least, independence and courage are almost unknown, and the Senate deliberates not at all. This phenomenon was the topic of discussion during a breakfast meeting in 1982 between Crown Prince Hassan of Jordan and Senator Claiborne Pell of Rhode Island, the senior Democrat on the Senate Foreign Relations Committee. Pell explained with candor his own record of consistent support for Israel and his failure to recognize Arab interests when he told the Jordanian leader, "I can be honest with you, but I can't be fair." Pell's record is typical of his colleagues.

Since the establishment of modern Israel in 1948, only a handful of Senators have said or done anything in opposition to the policies of the government of Israel. Those who break ranks find themselves in difficulty. The trouble can arise from a speech, an amendment, a vote, a published statement, or a combination of these. It may take the form of a challenge in the next primary or general election. Or the trouble may not surface until later—after service in the Senate has ended. Such was the destiny of a Senator from Illinois.

84

"Adlai, You Are Right, But—"

The cover of the October 1982 edition of the monthly magazine *Jewish Chicago* featured a portrait of Adlai E. Stevenson III, Democratic candidate for governor of Illinois. In the background, over the right shoulder of a smiling Stevenson, an Arab, rifle slung over his shoulder, glared ominously through a kaffiyeh that covered his head and most of his face. The headline announcing the issue's feature article read, "Looking at Adlai Through Jewish Eyes."

The illustration and article were part of an anti-Stevenson campaign conducted by some of the quarter-million people in Chicago's Jewish community who wanted Stevenson to fail in his challenge to Governor James R. Thompson, Jr.

Thompson, a Republican, was attempting a feat sometimes tried but never before accomplished in Illinois history: election to a third term as governor. Normally, a Republican in Illinois can expect only minimal Jewish support at the polls.

A crucial part of the anti-Stevenson campaign was a caricature of his Middle East record while he was a member of the United States Senate. Stevenson was presented as an enemy of Israel and an ally of the PLO.

Stevenson was attempting a political comeback after serving ten years in the Senate, where he had quickly established himself as an independent. During the oil shortage of the mid-1970s he alarmed corporate interests by suggesting the establishment of a government corporation to handle the marketing of all crude oil. He warned of the "seeds of destruction" inherent in nuclear proliferation and called for international safeguards to restrain other nations from using nuclear technology to manufacture weapons. Concerned about the country's weakening position in the international marketplace, he called for government-directed national economic strategies to meet the challenge of foreign competition.

Stevenson lacks the flamboyant extroverted character of many politicians. *Time* magazine described him as "a reflective man who seems a bit out of place in the political arena." Effective in committee, where most legislation is hammered out, he did not feel comfortable lining up votes. "I'm not a back slapper or logroller," he said. "I don't feel effective running about buttonholing Senators."

Chicago Daily News columnist Mike Royko wrote of Stevenson's lack of charisma in a tone of affectionate teasing:

The most dangerous element in politics is charisma. It makes people get glassy-eyed and jump and scream and clap without a thought in their heads. Adlai Stevenson never does that. He makes people drowsy. His hair is thinning. He has all the oratorical fire of an algebra teacher. His clothes look like something he bought from the coroner's office. When he feels good, he looks like he has a virus. We need more politicians who make our blood run tepid.

Royko could have added that Stevenson also has none of the self-righteousness often found on Capitol Hill. Although a "blue-blood," as close to aristocracy as an American can be, he displayed little interest in the cocktail circuit or the show business of politics. On a Congressional tour of China in 1975 he didn't seem to mind when the other three Senators received lace-curtained limousines and he and his wife, Nancy, were assigned a less showy sedan.

During his second Senate term, he became disillusioned with the Carter administration. He saw it as "embarrassingly weak" and more concerned with retaining its power than with exercising it effectively. In 1979, he announced he would not seek re-election to the Senate, but he mentioned a new interest: the presidency. He might run for the White House the next year. "I'm going to talk about ideas and see if an idea can still triumph, or even make a dent," he said. It didn't. Stevenson ultimately decided not to run. With Senator Edward Kennedy in the race, he felt he would get little media attention. By the time Kennedy pulled out Stevenson concluded it was too late to get organized.

After a year's breather, in 1981 he announced his interest in running for the governorship of Illinois. This time he followed through.

The make-up of his campaign organization, the character of his campaign, and the support he had received in the past in Jewish neighborhoods provided little hint of trouble ahead from pro-Israeli quarters.

Several of the most important members of his campaign team were Jewish: Philip Klutznick, president emeritus of B'nai B'rith and an organizer of the Conference of Presidents of Major Jewish Organizations, who agreed to organize Stevenson's main campaign dinner; Milton Fisher, prominent attorney and chairman of his finance committee; Rick Jasculca, a public relations executive who became Stevenson's fulltime press secretary.

Stevenson chose Grace Mary Stern as his running mate for the position of lieutenant governor. Her husband was prominent in Chicago Jewish affairs.

Stevenson himself had received several honors from Jewish groups in preceeding years. He had been selected by the Chicago Jewish community as 1974 Israel Bond "Man of the Year," commended by the American Jewish Committee for his legislative work against the Arab boycott of Israel in 1977, and honored by the government of Israel—which established the Adlai E. Stevenson III Chair at the Weizmann Institute of Science in Rehovot. Stevenson had every reason to expect that organized Illinois Jewry would overlook his occasional mild position critical of Israeli policy.

But trouble developed. A segment of the Jewish community quietly launched an attack that would cost him heavily. Stevenson's detractors were determined to defeat him in the governor's race and thus discourage a future Stevenson bid for the presidency. Their basic tool was a document provided by the AIPAC in Washington. It was presented as a summary of Stevenson's Senate actions on Middle East issues—though it made no mention of his almost unblemished record of support for Israel and the tributes the Jewish community had presented to him in testimony of this support. Like most AIPAC documents, it would win no prizes for balance and objectivity.

For example, AIPAC pulled from a 21-page report Stevenson prepared after a 1976 trip to the Middle East just this lonely phrase: "There is no organization other than the PLO with a broadly recognized claim to represent the Palestinians." This was a simple statement of fact. But the writer of the *Jewish Chicago* article, citing the AIPAC "summary," asserted that these words had helped to give Stevenson "a reputation as one of the harshest critics of both Israel policy and of U.S. support for the Jewish state." Stevenson's assessment of the PLO's standing in the Palestinian community was interpreted as an assault on Israel.

In fact, the full paragraph in the Stevenson report from which AIPAC took its brief excerpt is studied and reasonable:

The Palestinians are by general agreement the nub of the problem. Although badly divided, they have steadily increased in numbers, economic and military strength, and seriousness of purpose. They cannot be left out of any Middle East settlement. Their lack of unity is reflected in the lack of unity within the top ranks of the PLO, but there is no organization other than the PLO with a broadly recognized claim to represent the Palestinians.

The Stevenson report was critical of certain Israeli policies but hardly hostile to Israel. "The PLO," he wrote, "may be distrusted, disowned and despised, but it is a reality, if for no other reason than that it has no rival organization among Palestinians."

Stevenson went on to issue a challenge to the political leaders of America:

A new order of statesmanship is required from both the Executive and the Legislative Branches. For too long Congress has muddled or gone along without any real understanding of Middle Eastern politics. Neither the United

States, nor Israel, nor any of the Arab states will be served by continued ignorance or the expediencies of election year politics.

None of this positive comment found its way into the AIPAC report or into the *Jewish Chicago* article or into any of the anti-Stevenson literature which was distributed within the Jewish community during the 1982 campaign.

The anti-Stevenson activists noted with alarm that in 1980 Stevenson had sponsored an amendment to reduce aid to Israel and the year before had supported a similar amendment offered by Senator Mark O. Hatfield, Republican of Oregon. The Hatfield amendment proposed to cut by 10 per cent the amount of funds available to Israel for military credits.

Stevenson's amendment had focused on Israeli settlements in occupied territories, which President Carter and earlier administrations characterized as both illegal and an obstacle to peace but did nothing to discourage beyond occasional expressions of regret. Stevenson proposed withholding $150 million in aid until Israel halted both the building and planning of additional settlements. The amendment did not cut funds; it simply withheld a fraction of the $2.18 billion total aid authorized for Israel that year. In speaking for the amendment, Stevenson noted that the outlay for Israel amounted to 43 percent of all U.S. funds allocated for such purposes worldwide:

This preference for Israel diverts funds from the support of human life and vital American interests elsewhere in an interdependent and unstable world. . . . If it could produce stability in the Middle East or enhance Israel's security, it could be justified. But it reflects continued U.S. acquiescence in an Israeli policy which threatens more Middle East instability, more Israeli insecurity, and a continued decline of U.S. authority in the world. Our support for Israel is not the issue here. Israel's support for the ideals of peace and justice which gave it birth are at issue. It is, I submit, for the Israel government to recognize again that Israel's interests are in harmony with our own and, for that to happen, it is important that we do not undermine the voices for peace in Israel or justify those, like Mr. Begin, who claim U.S. assistance from the Congress can be taken for granted.

The amendment, like Hatfield's, was overwhelmingly defeated.

After the vote on his amendment, Stevenson recalls, he received apologetic comments. "Several Senators came up and said, 'Adlai, you are right, but you understand why I had to vote against you. Maybe next time.'" Stevenson did understand why: lobby intimidation produced the negative votes. He found intimidation at work on another front too, the news media. He offered the amendment, he explained, "because I thought the public was entitled to a debate on this critical issue," but news services gave it no attention.

That's another aspect of this problem. It's not only the intimidation of the American politician, it's also the intimidation of some American journalists. If it's not the journalists, then it's the editors and perhaps more so the publishers.

Anti-Stevenson campaigners also found it expedient to portray him as a supporter of Arab economic blackmail, despite his widely hailed legislative record to the contrary. Stevenson was actually the principal author of the 1977 legislation to prohibit American firms from cooperating with the Arab boycott of Israel. But in the smear campaign conducted against him in his gubernatorial bid his legislative history was rewritten. He was actually accused of trying to undermine the anti-boycott effort.

In fact, Stevenson, in a lonely and frustrating effort, saved the legislation from disaster. For this achievement, he received a plaque and praise from the American Jewish Committee. The chairman of the National Jewish Community Relations Council, Theodore R. Mann, wrote to Stevenson, expressing the organization's "deep appreciation for your invaluable contribution to the adoption of that landmark legislation." He added that the legislation "not only reassures the American Jewish community as to the commitment of America to fairness and nondiscrimination in international trade but, more fundamentally, stands as a reaffirmation of our nation's profound regard for principle and morality."

Jewish Chicago, making no mention of Stevenson's success in the anti-boycott effort or the unstinting praise he received from Jewish leaders, reported that he encountered "major conflicts" with "the American Jewish leadership" over the boycott legislation.

A flyer distributed by an unidentified "Informed Citizens Against Stevenson Committee," made the same charge. Captioned, "The Truth About Adlai Stevenson," it used half-truths to brand Stevenson as anti-Israel during his Senate years and concluded: "It is vitally important that Jewish voters be fully informed about Stevenson's record. Still dazzled by the Stevenson name, many Jews are totally unaware of his antagonism to Jewish interests." The "committee" provided no names or addresses of sponsoring individuals. Shirley Friedman, a free-lance writer in Chicago, later identified the flyer as her own. The message on the flyer concluded:

"Don't forget: It is well-known that Stevenson considers the governor's chair as a stepping-stone to the presidency. Spread the word— Let the truth be told!"

The word was indeed spread in the Chicago Jewish community throughout the summer and fall of 1982. The political editor of the Chicago *Sun-Times* reported in June that some activists for Thompson had been "working quietly for months to assemble a group to mobilize Jewish voters" against Stevenson.

The result of their efforts was "The Coalition for the Re-election of Jim Thompson" which included Jewish Democrats who had not backed Thompson previously. When Republican Senator Rudy Boschwitz of Minnesota, a strong supporter of Israel, came to Chicago in October to address a breakfast gathering sponsored by the Coalition, he declared that, as Senator, Stevenson was "a very steadfast foe of aid to Israel."

"Smear and Innuendo"

A major problem was the unprinted but widely whispered charge of anti-Semitism against Stevenson—a man, who, like his father, had spent his life championing civil rights for all Americans. "I learned after election day there was that intimation throughout the campaign," recalls Stevenson.

Phil Klutznick's daughter, Mrs. Bettylu Saltzman, who worked on Stevenson's campaign staff, remembers, "There was plenty of stuff going around about him being anti-Semitic. It got worse and worse. It was a much more difficult problem than anyone imagined."

Stevenson's running-mate, Grace Mary Stern, recalls: "There was a very vigorous [anti-Stevenson] telephone campaign in the Jewish community." She says leaflets charging Stevenson with being anti-Israel were distributed widely at local Jewish temples, and adds there was much discussion of the anti-Semitism accusation: "There was a very vigorous campaign, man to man, friend to friend, locker room to locker room. We never really came to grips with the problem."

Campaign fund raising suffered accordingly. The Jewish community had supported Stevenson strongly in both of his campaigns for the Senate. After his remarks in the last years of his Senate career, some of the Jewish support dried up. "Many of my most generous Jewish contributors stayed with me, but the organization types, the professionals did not," Stevenson recalls. He believes the withdrawal of organized Jewish support also cut into funds from out-of-state he otherwise would have received. In the end, Thompson was able to outspend Stevenson by better than two to one.

Fed up by early September with unfounded charges of anti-Semitism, Stevenson finally responded, charging that a "subterranean campaign of smear and innuendo" was being waged by supporters of

Thompson. His press secretary, Rick Jasculca, complained that the material distributed by the Coalition for the Re-election of Jim Thompson "tries to give the impression that Adlai is unquestionably anti-Israel." Thompson's political director, Philip O'Connor, denied there was a smear campaign and disavowed the Friedman flyer.

Thompson himself said of Stevenson, "I don't think he is an anti-Semite, [but he is] no particular friend of Israel." The Chicago *Sun-Times* published an editorial rebuke for this remark: "That's like saying, no, I don't think Stevenson beats his wife, but she did have a black eye last week." The editorial continued:

Far more important, the statement is not true; Stevenson as a Senator may have occasionally departed from positions advocated by the Israeli government, but out of well-reasoned motives and a genuine desire to secure a lasting peace for the area. Thompson's coy phrasing was a reprehensible appeal to the voter who measures a candidate's worth by a single, rubbery standard.

The only Jews who tried to counter the attack were those close to Stevenson. Philip Klutznick, prominent in Jewish affairs and chairman of the Stevenson Dinner Committee, said, "It is beneath the dignity of the Jewish community to introduce these issues into a gubernatorial campaign." Stevenson campaign treasurer Milton Fisher said: "Adlai's views are probably consistent with 40 percent of the Knesset [Israeli parliament]."

Stevenson was ultimately defeated in the closest gubernatorial election in the state's history. The margin was 5,074 votes—one-seventh of one percent of the total 3.5 million votes cast.

The election was marred by a series of mysterious irregularities which *Time* magazine described as "so improbable, so coincidental, so questionable that it could have happened only in Wonderland, or the Windy City." On election night ballot boxes from fifteen Chicago precincts inexplicably disappeared, and others turned up in the homes or cars of poll workers. Stevenson asked for a recount—past recounts had resulted in shifts of 5,000 to 7,000 votes—but the Illinois Supreme Court, by a 4-to-3 vote, denied his petition. Judge Seymour Simon, a Democrat, joined the three Republicans on the court in voting against Stevenson's request.

A post-election editorial in a suburban Chicago newspaper acknowledged the impact of the concerted smear campaign on the election outcome:

An intense last-minute effort among Chicago-area Jews to thwart Adlai Stevenson's attempt to unseat Illinois Gov. James Thompson in last Tuesday's election may have succeeded. The weekend before the election many Chicago and suburban rabbis spoke out against Stevenson and there were thousands of pamphlets and leaflets distributed in Jewish areas . . . , all attacking the former Senator.

After describing the attack, the editorial concluded,

The concentrated anti-Stevenson campaign, particularly since it went largely unanswered, almost surely cost him thousands of votes among the 248,000 Chicago-area Jews—266,000 throughout the state—who traditionally have leaned in his direction politically.

Campaign manager Joseph Novak agrees: "If that effort hadn't happened, Stevenson would be governor today." In the predominantly Jewish suburban Chicago precincts of Highland Park and Lake County "We just got killed, just absolutely devastated." Press secretary Rick Jasculca adds, "What bothers me is that hardly any rabbis, or Jewish leaders beyond Phil [Klutznick] were willing to speak up, and say this is nonsense to call Adlai anti-Israel."

Thomas A. Dine, executive director of the American Israel Public Affairs Committee, gloated, "The memory of Adlai Stevenson's hostility toward Israel during his Senate tenure lost him the Jewish vote in Illinois—and that cost him the gubernatorial election."

Stevenson too believes the effort to discredit him among Jews played a major role in his defeat: "In a race that close, it was more than enough to make the difference."

Asked about the impact of the Israeli lobby on the U.S. political scene, he responded without hesitation:

There is an intimidating, activist minority of American Jews that supports the decisions of the Israeli government, right or wrong. They do so very vocally and very aggressively in ways that intimidate others so that it's their voice— even though it's a minority—that is heard and felt in American politics. But it still is much louder in the United States than in Israel. In other words, you have a much stronger, more vocal dissent in Israel than within the Jewish community in the United States. The prime minister of Israel has far more influence over American foreign policy in the Middle East than over the policies of his own government generally.

The former Senator reports a profound change within the Jewish community in recent years:

The old passionate commitment of Jewish leaders to civil liberties, social welfare, in short, to liberalism has to a large extent dissipated. The issue now is much more Israel itself. If given a choice between the traditional liberal commitment and the imagined Israeli commitment, they'll opt now for the Israeli commitment.

Reflecting on his career and the price he has paid for challenging Israeli policies, Stevenson concluded:

I will have no hesitation about continuing. I wish I had started earlier and been more effective. I really don't understand the worth of public office if you can't serve the public. It's better to lose. It's better not to serve than to be mortgaged or compromised.

Stevenson followed the tradition of a colleague, a famous Senator from Arkansas who eloquently criticized Israeli policy and American foreign policy over a period of many years.

The Dissenter

"When all of us are dead, the only one they'll remember is Bill Fulbright." The tribute by Idaho Senator Frank Church, a fellow Democrat, was amply justified. As much as any man of his time, J. William Fulbright shaped this nation's attitudes on the proper exercise of its power in a world made acutely dangerous by nuclear weapons. Dissent was a hallmark of his career, but it was dissent with distinction. The fact was, Fulbright was usually right.

Fulbright first gained national attention by condemning the "swinish blight" of McCarthyism. In 1954 while many Americans cheered the crusade of the Wisconsin Senator's Permanent Investigations Subcommittee, Fulbright cast the lone vote against a measure to continue the subcommittee's funding. Because of this vote he was accused of being "a Communist, a fellow traveler, an atheist, [and] a man beneath contempt."

Fulbright opposed U.S. intervention in Cuba in 1961 and in the Dominican Republic four years later, and was ahead of his time in calling for detente with the Soviet Union and a diplomatic opening with China. When he proposed a different system for selecting presidents, Harry Truman was offended and called him "that over-educated Oxford s.o.b." Twenty-five years later, in 1974, the *New York Times* recognized him as "the most outspoken critic of American foreign policy of this generation."

His deepest and most abiding interest is the advancement of international understanding through education, and thousands of young people have broadened their vision through the scholarships that bear his name. But Fulbright also became well known for his outspoken opposition to the Vietnam War as "an endless, futile war . . . , debilitating and indecent"—a stand which put him at odds with a former colleague and close friend, President Lyndon B. Johnson. President

Johnson believed that America was embarked on a noble mission in Southeast Asia against an international Communist conspiracy. Fulbright put no stock in the conspiracy theory, feared the war might broaden into a showdown with China, and saw it as an exercise in "the arrogance of power."

In 1963 Fulbright chaired an investigation that brought to public attention the exceptional tax treatment of contributions to Israel and aroused the ire of the Jewish community. The investigation was managed by Walter Pincus, a journalist Fulbright hired after reading a Pincus study of lobbying. Pincus recalls that Fulbright gave him a free hand, letting him choose the ten prime lobbying activities to be examined and backing him throughout the controversial investigation. One of the groups chosen by Pincus, himself Jewish, was the Jewish Telegraph Agency—at that time a principal instrument of the Israeli lobby. Both Fulbright and Pincus were accused of trying to destroy the Jewish Telegraph Agency and of being anti-Semitic.

Pincus remembers, "Several Senators urged that the inquiry into the Jewish operation be dropped. Senators Hubert Humphrey and Bourke Hickenlooper [senior Republican on the Foreign Relations Committee] were among them. Fulbright refused."

The Fulbright hearings also exposed the massive funding illegally channelled into the American Zionist Council by Israel. More than five million dollars had been secretly poured into the Council for spending on public relations firms and pro-Israel propaganda before Fulbright's committee closed down the operation.

Despite his concern over the pro-Israeli lobby, Fulbright took the exceptional step of recommending that the United States guarantee Israeli's borders. In a major address in 1970 he proposed an American-Israeli treaty under which the United States would commit itself to intervene militarily if necessary to "guarantee the territory and independence of Israel" within the lands it held before the 1967 war. The treaty, he said, should be a supplement to a peace settlement arranged by the United Nations. The purpose of his proposal was to destroy the arguments of those who maintained that Israel needed the captured territory for its security.

Fulbright saw Israeli withdrawal from the Arab lands it occupied in the 1967 war as the key to peace: Israel could not occupy Arab territory and have peace too. He said Israeli policy in establishing settlements on the territories "has been characterized by lack of flexibility and foresight." Discounting early threats by some Arab leaders to destroy the state of Israel, Fulbright noted that both President Nasser of the United Arab Republic and King Hussein of Jordan had in effect repudiated such Draconian threats, "but the Israelis seem not to have noticed the disavowals."

During the 1970s Fulbright repeatedly took exception to the contention that the Middle East crisis was a test of American resolve against Soviet interventionism. In 1971, he accused Israel of "Communist-baiting humbuggery" and argued that continuing Middle East tension, in fact, only benefited Soviet interests.

Appearing on CBS television's "Face the Nation" in 1973, Fulbright declared that the Senate was "subservient" to Israeli policies which were inimical to American interests. He said the United States bears "a very great share of the responsibility" for the continuation of Middle East violence. "It's quite obvious [that] without the all-out support by the United States in money and weapons and so on, the Israelis couldn't do what they've been doing."

Fulbright said the United States failed to pressure Israel for a negotiated settlement, because

The great majority of the Senate of the United States—somewhere around 80 percent—are completely in support of Israel, anything Israel wants. This has been demonstrated time and time again, and this has made it difficult for our government.

The Senator claimed that "Israel controls the Senate" and warned, "We should be more concerned about the United States' interests." Six weeks after his "Face the Nation" appearance, Fulbright again expressed alarm over Israeli occupation of Arab territories. He charged that the U.S. had given Israel "unlimited support for unlimited expansion."

His criticism of Israeli policy caused stirrings back home. Jews who had supported him in the past became restless. After years of easy election victories trouble loomed for Fulbright in 1974. Encouraged, in part, by the growing Jewish disenchantment with Fulbright, on the eve of the deadline for filing petitions of candidacy in the Democratic primary Governor Dale Bumpers surprised the political world by becoming a challenger for Fulbright's Senate seat. Fulbright hadn't expected Bumpers to run, but recognized immediately that the popular young governor posed a serious challenge: "He had lots of hair [in contrast to Fulbright], he looked good on television and he'd never done anything to offend anyone."

There were other factors. Walter Pincus, who later became a *Washington Post* reporter, believed Fulbright's decision to take a golfing holiday in Bermuda just before the primary deadline may have helped to convince Bumpers that Fulbright would not work hard for the nomination. It was also the year of Watergate—a bad year for incumbents. In his campaign, Bumpers pointed with alarm to the "mess in Washington" and called for a change. The *New York Times* reported that he "skillfully exploited an old feeling that Mr. Fulbright . . . spent all his time dining with Henry Kissinger and fretting over the Middle East."

The attitude of Jewish voters, both inside Arkansas and beyond, was also a significant factor. "I don't think Bumpers would have run without that encouragement," says Fulbright. Following the election, a national Jewish organization actually claimed credit for the young governor's stunning upset victory. Fulbright has a copy of a memorandum circulated in May 1974 to the national board of directors of B'nai B'rith. Marked "confidential," the memo from Secretary-General Herman Edelsberg, announced that ". . . all of the indications suggest that our actions in support of Governor Bumpers will result in the ousting of Mr. Fulbright from his key position in the Senate." Edelsberg later rejected the memorandum as "phoney."

Since his defeat, Fulbright has continued to speak out, decrying Israeli stubbornness and warning of the Israeli lobby. In a speech just before the end of his Senate term, Fulbright warned, "Endlessly pressing the United States for money and arms—and invariably getting all and more than she asks—Israel makes bad use of a good friend." His central concern was that the Middle East conflict might flare into nuclear war. He warned somberly that "Israel's supporters in the United States . . . by underwriting intransigence, are encouraging a course which must lead toward her destruction—and just possibly ours as well."

Pondering the future from his office three blocks north of the White House, Fulbright sees little hope that Capitol Hill will effectively challenge the Israeli lobby:

It's suicide for politicians to oppose them. The only possibility would be someone like Eisenhower who already feels secure. Eisenhower had already made his reputation. He was already a great man in the eyes of the country, and he wasn't afraid of anybody. He said what he believed.

Then he adds a somewhat more optimistic note: "I believe a president could do this. He wouldn't have to be named Eisenhower." Fulbright cites a missed opportunity:

I went to Jerry Ford after he took office in 1975. I was out of office then. I had been to the Middle East and visited with some of the leading figures. I came back and told the president, 'Look, I think these [Arab] leaders are willing to accept Israel, but the Israelis have got to go back to the 1967 borders. The problem can be solved if you are willing to take a position on it.

Fulbright predicted that the American people would back Ford if he demanded that Israel cooperate. He reminded him that Eisenhower was re-elected by a large margin immediately after he forced Israel to withdraw after invading Egypt:

Taking a stand against Israel didn't hurt Eisenhower. He carried New York with its big Jewish population.

I told Ford I didn't think he would be defeated if he put it the right way. He should say Israel had to go back to the 1967 borders; if it didn't, no more arms or money. That's just the way Eisenhower did it. And Israel would have to cooperate. And politically, in the coming campaign, I told him he should say he was for Israel, but he was for America first.

Ford, Fulbright recalls, listened courteously but was non-committal: "Of course he didn't take my advice."

Yet the determination in the face of such disappointment echoes through one of his last statements as a U.S. Senator:

History casts no doubt at all on the ability of human beings to deal rationally with their problems, but the greatest doubt on their will to do so. The signals of the past are thus clouded and ambiguous, suggesting hope but not confidence in the triumph of reason. With nothing to lose in any event, it seems well worth a try.

Warning Against "Absolutism"

James G. Abourezk of South Dakota came to the Senate in 1973 after serving two years in the House of Representatives. The son of Lebanese immigrants—the first person of Arab ancestry elected to the Senate—he spoke up for Arab interests and quickly became a center of controversy.

Soon after he took office, Abourezk accepted an invitation to speak at Yeshiva University in New York, but anxious school officials called almost immediately to tell him of rising student protests against his appearance. A few days later, the chairman of the dinner committee asked Abourezk to make a public statement calling for face-to-face negotiations between Israel and its Arab neighbors, assuring Abourezk that this proposal, identical to the one being made by Israel's prime minister, Golda Meir, would ease student objections and end the protest. Although Abourezk favored such negotiations, he refused to make the requested statement. He explained, "I do not wish to be in the position of placating agitators." Rabbi Israel Miller, vice-president of the school, came to Washington to urge Abourezk to reconsider. When Abourezk again refused, the dinner chairman telephoned again, this time to report that students were beginning to picket. Sensing that school officials wanted the event cancelled, Abourezk offered to withdraw from the obligation. His offer was hastily accepted.

Soon after, Abourezk was announced as the principal speaker at a rally to be held in Rochester, New York, to raise money for victims of the Lebanese civil war. The rally's organizing committee was immediately showered with telephoned bomb threats. In all, 23 calls warned that the building would be blown up if Abourezk appeared on the program. With the help of the FBI, local police swept the building for bombs and, finding none, opened it for the program. A capacity crowd, unaware of the threats, heard the event proceed without incident.

After making a tour of Arab states in December 1973, Abourezk sympathized with Arab refugees in a speech at the National Press Club in Washington. Covering his speech for the AIPAC newsletter, *Near East Report,* Wolf Blitzer wrote, "If [Abourezk's] position were to prevail, Israel's life would be jeopardized." Blitzer's report was sent to Jews who had contributed to Abourezk's campaign, accompanied by a letter in which I. L. Kenen, AIPAC director, warned that Abourezk was "going to great lengths" to "undermine American friendship for Israel." The mailing, Abourezk recalls, began an "adversary relationship" with AIPAC. He adds, "I doubt that I would have spent so much time on the Middle East had it not been for that particular unfair personal attack." (In 1980, after retiring from the Senate, Abourezk founded the American-Arab Anti-Discrimination Committee, which now has 20,000 members and whose purpose, he says, "is to provide a countervailing force to the Israeli lobby.")

On one occasion in the Senate, Abourezk turned lobby pressure to his advantage. Wishing to be appointed in 1974 to fill a vacancy on the Senate Judiciary Committee, he warned David Brody, lobbyist for the B'nai B'rith's Anti-Defamation League, that if he did not secure the appointment he would seek a seat on the Foreign Relations Committee. He recalls, with a chuckle, "This warning had the desired effect. The last thing Brody wanted was to see me on Foreign Relations where aid to Israel is decided. Thanks to the help of the lobby I received the appointment to Judiciary, even though James Allen, a Senator with more seniority, also wanted the position." The appointment enabled Abourezk to chair hearings in 1977 on the legality of Israel's occupation of the West Bank and Gaza. "They were the first—and last hearings—on this subject," Abourezk recalls. "And not one of my colleagues attended. I was there alone."

In 1975, Abourezk invited the head of the PLO's Beirut office, Shafiq al-Hout, to lunch in the Senate and learned that PLO-related secrets are hard to keep. On Abourezk's assurance that the event would be kept entirely private, eleven other Senators, including Abraham Ribicoff of Connecticut, who is Jewish, attended and heard al-Hout relate the PLO side of Middle East issues. Within an hour after the event was concluded, Spencer Rich of the *Washington Post* telephoned Abourezk for comment. He had already learned the identity of all Senators who attended. The next day Israel's leading English language daily newspaper, the *Jerusalem Post,* reported that Ribicoff and the others had had lunch with "murderer" al-Hout.

A major storm erupted in 1977 when Abourezk agreed on short notice to fill in for Vice-President Walter Mondale as the principal speaker at the annual Jefferson-Jackson Day dinner sponsored in Denver by the Colorado Democratic Party. Jewish leaders protested his appearance, and John Mrozek, a labor leader in Denver, attacked Abourezk as "pro-Arab and anti-Israel." Betty Crist, a member of the dinner committee, moved that the invitation be withdrawn. When the Crist motion was narrowly rejected, the committee tried to find a pro-Israeli speaker to debate Abourezk, with the intention of cancelling the event if a debate could not be arranged. This gave the proceedings a comic twist, as Abourezk at no point had intended to mention the Middle East in his remarks. Unable to find someone to debate their guest, the committee reconsidered and let the invitation to Abourezk stand in its original form.

Arriving at the Denver airport, Abourezk told reporters, "As a United States Senator, I have sworn to uphold the government of the United States, but I never dreamed that I would be required to swear allegiance to any other government." In his remarks to the dinner audience of 700, he warned of the "extraordinary influence of the Zionist lobby." He said the United States "is likely to become, if it has not already, a captive of its client state."

He said, "The point of the controversy surrounding this dinner has been my refusal to take an absolutist position for Israel. There is extreme danger to all of us in this kind of absolutism. It implies that only one position—that of being unquestionably pro-Israel—is the only position."

The Rocky Mountain News reported that his speech received a standing ovation, "although there were pockets of people who sat on their hands." The Denver newspaper editorialized, "James Abourezk is not a fanatic screaming for the blood of Israel. Colorado Democratic leaders should be proud to have him as their speaker. He is better than they deserve."

"Sins of Omission"

The Israeli lobby's long string of Capitol Hill victories has been broken only twice during the past twenty-five years. Both setbacks occurred in the Senate and involved military sales to Saudi Arabia. In 1978 the Senate approved the sale of F-15 fighter planes by a vote of 54 to 44, and in 1981 the sale of AWACS (Airborne Warning and Control System) intelligence-gathering planes and special equipment for the F-15s by a vote of 52 to 48. Curiously, both controversies entangled the American Israel Public Affairs Committee in the politics of the state of Maine.

This involvement began on the Senate floor one afternoon in the spring of 1978 when Senator Edward "Ted" Kennedy received a whispered message which brought an angry flush to his face. AIPAC had forsaken a Senate Democrat with a consistently pro-Israeli record. Senator William Hathaway of Maine, who had, without exception, cast his vote in behalf of Israel's interests, was being "dropped" by the lobby in favor of William S. Cohen, his Republican challenger. Kennedy strode to the adjoining cloakroom and reached for a telephone.

Kennedy demanded an explanation from Morris J. Amitay, then executive director of AIPAC. Flustered, Amitay denied that AIPAC had taken a position against Hathaway. The organization, he insisted, provides information on candidates but makes no endorsements. Pressed by Kennedy, Amitay promised to issue a letter to Hathaway complimenting him on his support of Israel.

The letter was sent, but the damage had already been done. Though Amitay was technically correct—AIPAC does not formally endorse candidates for the House or Senate—the lobby has effective ways to show its colors, raise money and influence votes. In the Maine race, it was making calls for Cohen and against Hathaway. The shift, so astounding and unsettling to Kennedy, arose from a single "failing" on Hathaway's part. It was a sin of omission, but a cardinal sin nonetheless.

Over the years, Hathaway had sometimes refused to sign letters and resolutions which AIPAC sponsored. The resolutions were usually statements of opinion by the Senate—called "sense of the Senate" resolutions—and had no legislative effect. The letters were directed to the president or a cabinet officer, urging him to support Israel. In refusing to sign, Hathaway did not single out AIPAC projects; he often rejected such requests from other interest groups as well, preferring to write his own letters and introduce his own resolutions. Nor did he always refuse AIPAC. Sometimes, as a favor, he would set aside his usual reservations and sign.

Hathaway cooperated in 1975 when AIPAC sponsored its famous "spirit of 76" letter. It bore Hathaway's name and those of 75 of his colleagues and carried this message to President Gerald R. Ford: "We urge that you reiterate our nation's long-standing commitment to Israel's security by a policy of continued military supplies, and diplomatic and economic support." At another moment, this expression would cause no ripples. Since the administration of John F. Kennedy, the U.S. government had been following a policy of "continued military supplies." But when this letter was made public in January 1975, it shook the executive branch as have few Senate letters in history.

Ford, dissatisfied with Israeli behavior, had just issued a statement calling for a "reappraisal" of U.S. policies in the Middle East. His statement did not mention Israel by name as the offending party, but his message was clear: Ford wanted better cooperation in reaching a compromise with Arab interests, and "reappraisal" meant suspension of U.S. aid until Israel improved its behavior. It was a historic proposal, the first time since Eisenhower that a United States president even hinted publicly that he might suspend aid to Israel.

Israel's response came, not from its own capital, but from the United States Senate. Instead of relying on a direct protest to the White House, Jerusalem activated its lobby in the United States, which, in turn, signed up as supporters of Israel's position more than three-fourths of the members of the United States Senate.

A more devastating—and intimidating—response could scarcely be conceived. The seventy-six signatures effectively told Ford he could not carry out his threatened "reappraisal." Israel's loyalists in the Senate—Democrats and Republicans alike—were sufficient in number to reject any legislative proposal hostile to Israel that Ford might make, and perhaps even enact a pro-Israeli piece of legislation over a presidential veto.

The letter was a demonstration of impressive clout. Crafted and circulated by AIPAC, it had been endorsed overnight by a majority of the Senate membership. Several Senators who at first had said "No" quickly changed their positions. Senator John Culver admitted candidly, "The pressure was too great. I caved." So did President Ford. He backed down and never again challenged the lobby.

This wasn't the only time Hathaway answered AIPAC's call to oppose the White House on a major issue. Three years later, Ford's successor, Jimmy Carter, fought a similar battle with the Israeli lobby. At issue this time was a resolution to disapprove President Carter's proposal to sell F-15 fighters to Saudi Arabia. The White House needed the support of only one chamber to defeat the resolution. White House strategists felt that the House of Representatives would overwhelmingly vote to defeat the sale, so they decided to put all their resources into the Senate.

Lobbying on both sides was highly visible and aggressive. Frederick Dutton, chief lobbyist for Saudi Arabia, orchestrated the pro-sale forces on Capitol Hill. The *Washington Post* reported, "Almost every morning these days, the black limousines pull up to Washington's Madison Hotel to collect their Saudi Arabian passengers. Their destination, very often, is Capitol Hill, where the battle of the F-15s unfolds."

The Israeli lobby pulled out all the stops. It coordinated a nationwide public relations campaign which revived, as never before, memories of the genocidal Nazi campaign against European Jews during World War II. In the wake of the highly publicized television series, "Holocaust," Capitol Hill was flooded with complimentary copies of the novel on which the TV series was based. The books were accompanied by a letter from AIPAC saying, "This chilling account of the extermination of six million Jews underscores Israel's concerns during the current negotiations for security without reliance on outside guarantees." Concerning the book distribution, AIPAC's Aaron Rosenbaum told the *Washington Post:* "We think, frankly, that it will affect a few votes here and there, and simplify lobbying."

Senator Wendell Anderson of Minnesota at first agreed to support the proposed sale. He told an administration official: "Sure, I'll go for it. It sounds reasonable." But a few days before the vote he called back: "I can't vote for it. I'm up for election, and my Jewish cochairman refuses to go forward if I vote for the F-15s." Furthermore, he said, a Jewish group had met with him and showed him that 70 percent of the contributions to the Democratic Senatorial Campaign Committee the previous year came from Jewish sources.

The pressure was sustained and heavy. Major personalities in the Jewish community warned the fighter aircraft would constitute a serious threat to Israel. Nevertheless a prominent Jewish Senator, Abraham Ribicoff of Connecticut, lined up with Carter. This was a hard blow to Amitay, who had previously worked on Ribicoff's staff. Earlier in the year Ribicoff, while keeping his own counsel on the Saudi arms question, took the uncharacteristic step of criticizing sharply Israeli policies as well as the tactics of AIPAC. In an interview with the *Wall Street Journal,* Ribicoff described Israel's retention of occupied territory as "wrong" and unworthy of U.S. support. He said AIPAC does "a great disservice to the U.S., to Israel and to the Jewish community." He did not seek re-election in 1980.

The Senate approved the sale, 52 to 48, but in the process Carter was so bruised that he never again forced a showdown vote in Congress over Middle East policy.

Hathaway was one of the forty-four who stuck with AIPAC, but this was not sufficient when election time rolled around. AIPAC wanted a Senator whose signature—and vote—it could always count on. Searching for unswerving loyalty, the lobby switched to Cohen. Its decision came at the very time Hathaway was resisting pressures on the Saudi issue. The staff at the Democratic Senatorial Campaign Committee was outraged. One of them declared to a visitor: "AIPAC demands 100 percent. If a fine Senator like Hathaway fails to cooperate just once, they are ready to trade in his career." A staff member of a Senate committee declared: "To please AIPAC, you have to be more pure than Ivory soap—99.44 percent purity is not good enough." Lacking the purity AIPAC demanded, Hathaway was defeated in 1978.

Caught in the AWACS Dilemma

William S. Cohen was elected to the Senate but soon found himself in a storm similar to the one Hathaway, his predecessor, had encountered. Once again a proposal to sell military equipment to Saudi Arabia raised concerns among pro-Israeli forces about a Senator from Maine. It occurred soon after Ronald Reagan's inauguration, when the new president decided to approve the same request that the Carter administration had put off the year before. Saudi Arabia would be allowed to purchase its own AWACS planes, along with extra equipment to give Saudi F-15 fighters greater range and firepower. Israeli officials opposed the sale, because, they said, this technology would give Saudi Arabia the capacity to monitor Israeli air force operations.

As in 1978, the Senate became the main battleground, but the White House was slow to organize. Convinced that Jimmy Carter the year before had taken on too many diverse issues at once, the Reagan forces decided to concentrate on tax and budget questions in the early months of the new administration. This left a vacuum in the foreign policy realm which AIPAC filled skillfully. New director Thomas A. Dine orchestrated a bipartisan counter-attack against arms transfers to Saudi Arabia. Even before Reagan sent the AWACS proposal to Capitol Hill for consideration, the Associated Press reported that the Israeli lobby had lined up "veto-strength majorities."

AIPAC's campaign against AWACS began in the House of Representatives through a public letter attacking the sale sponsored by Republican Norman Lent in New York and Democrat Clarence Long of Maryland. Ultimately, in October, the House rejected the proposed sale by a vote of 301 to 111, but the real battleground was the Senate. Earlier in the year, before the Senate took up the question, Senator Bob Packwood of Oregon, always a dependable supporter of Israel, announced that fifty-four Senators, a majority, had signed a request that Reagan drop the idea. Needing time to persuade the Senators to change, the White House put off the showdown. By September, fifty

Senators had signed a resolution to veto the sale and six more promised to sign if needed. Once more, the White House had no choice but to delay.

This time the Saudis were testing their relationship with the new president and left more of the lobbying to the White House than was true in 1978. Their case relied heavily on personal efforts of Republican Senate leader Howard Baker, Senator John Tower, chairman of the Armed Services Committee, and Senator Charles Percy, chairman of the Foreign Relations Committee. Lobbyist Frederick Dutton was instructed to keep in the background, though David Sadd, executive director of the National Association of Arab Americans, helped organize the support of U.S. industries with a stake in the sale.

Meanwhile, Dine's team roamed the Senate corridors while AIPAC's grassroots contacts brought direct pressure from constituents. The *Post* reported that "AIPAC's fountain of research materials reaches a readership estimated at 200,000 people." Senator John Glenn of Ohio, said: "I've been getting calls from every Jewish organization in the country. They didn't want to talk about the issues. The big push was to get me to sign this letter and resolution." Glenn did not sign, largely because he hoped to broker a deal with the White House.

Syndicated columnist Carl T. Rowan wrote "there is strong evidence" that the AWACS struggle increased "public resentment against the 'Jewish lobby.' "

The issue was portrayed by some as a choice between President Reagan and Prime Minister Begin. Bumper stickers appeared around Washington which read, "Reagan or Begin?" When the Senate finally voted, Cohen, although announced in opposition, switched and provided one of the critical votes supporting the AWACS sale. He explained his reversal by declaring that Israel would have been branded the scapegoat for failure of the Middle East peace process if the proposal were defeated.

Aside from this "sin," one of "commission" in the eyes of AIPAC, his behavior was exemplary. Never once did he stray from the fold, and in 1984 AIPAC did not challenge his bid for re-election.

Standing Up for Civility

One of the most popular members of the Senate, Charles "Mac" Mathias of Maryland is something of a maverick—a role probably necessary for his political survival. He is a Republican in a state where Democrats outnumber Republicans by three to one.

During the Nixon administration especially, he frequently dissented from the Republican party line. His opposition to the war in

Vietnam and his staunch advocacy of civil rights and welfare initiatives earned him a place on the Nixon administration's "enemies list" of political opponents. In a December 1971 speech, before the Watergate break-in at Democratic headquarters that led to Nixon's downfall, and while the country was angrily divided by domestic tensions and the war in Vietnam, Mathias advised Nixon to work to "bind the nation's wounds." He urged the president to "take the high road" in the 1972 campaign and to disavow a campaign strategy "which now seems destined, unnecessarily, to polarize the country even more." In the same message Mathias criticized Nixon's advisers for "divisive exploitation of the so-called social issues [through] . . . the use of hard-line rhetoric on crime, civil rights, civil liberties and student unrest." Mathias was alarmed at what he saw as the Republican drift to the right.

In 1975 and 1976 he even considered running for president as an independent "third force" candidate in an effort to forge a "coalition of the center." The late Clarence Mitchell, director of the Washington office of the NAACP, said: "He's always arrived at his position in a reasoned way." In fact, early in his career he marked himself as a progressive and a champion of civil rights, and his constituency takes his liberalism on social issues in stride. A resident of Frederick, Mathias's home town, told the *Washington Post,* "Why, a lot of people around here think he's too liberal. But they seem to vote for him. The thing is, he's decent. He's got class."

He also has flashes of daring. In the spring of 1981, he wrote an article in the quarterly *Foreign Affairs* that he knew would put him in hot water with some of his Jewish constituents, criticizing the role played by ethnic lobbies—particularly the Israeli lobby—in the formation of U.S. foreign policy. The controversial article upset Maryland's influential Jewish community, which had consistently supported Mathias's campaigns for office. Mathias had voted to sell fighter planes to the Saudis in 1978 and his vote helped President Reagan get Senate clearance for the AWACS sale in 1981.

The same year the controversial article appeared, just after voters elected him to his third term in the Senate, Mathias took another step which appeared so politically inexpedient that many people assumed he had decided to retire from Congress in 1986. At the urging of Senators Howard Baker and Charles Percy, who wanted another moderate Republican on the Foreign Relations Committee, Mathias gave up a senior position on the Appropriations Committee in order to take the foreign policy committee assignment.

His committee decision shook the leadership of Baltimore, the largest city in the state and a competitor for federal grant assistance. As the *Baltimore Sun* noted in an article critical of the move, "Had he remained on the Appropriations Committee, Mr. Mathias almost certainly would have become chairman of the subcommittee that holds the purse strings for the Department of Housing and Urban Development, an agency of great importance to the 'renaissance' of Baltimore."

Contrary to the assumptions of Maryland political observers, Mathias was not planning to retire. Although he left a committee important to his constituents, the Senator welcomed the opportunity to help shape the issues that come before the Foreign Relations Committee. He was exhibiting a political philosophy admired by former Senator Mike Mansfield, who once called Mathias "the conscience of the Senate," and by former Secretary of State Henry Kissinger, who recognized Mathias as "one of the few statesmen I met in Washington."

These qualities led Mathias to write his controversial *Foreign Affairs* article calling for "the re-introduction of civility" into the discussion of "ethnic advocacy" in Congress. He acknowledged that ethnic groups have the right to lobby for legislation, but he warned, "The affirmation of a right, and of the dangers of suppressing it, does not . . . assure that the right will be exercised responsibly and for the general good."

Mathias cited the Israeli lobby as the most powerful ethnic pressure group, noting that it differs from others in that it focuses on vital national security interests and exerts "more constant pressure." Other lobbying groups "show up in a crisis and then disappear" and tend to deal with domestic matters. Mathias continued:

With the exception of the Eisenhower administration, which virtually compelled Israel's withdrawal from the Sinai after the 1956 war, American presidents, and to an even greater degree Senators and Representatives, have been subjected to recurrent pressures from what has come to be known as the Israel lobby.

He added an indictment of his colleagues: "For the most part they have been responsive [to pro-Israeli lobbying pressure], and for reasons not always related either to personal conviction or careful reflection on the national interest."

Mathias illustrated his concern by reviewing the "spectacular" success of AIPAC in 1975 when it promoted the "spirit of 76" letter: "Seventy-six of us promptly affixed our signatures although no hearings had been held, no debate conducted, nor had the administration been invited to present its views."

The Maryland Republican felt the independence of Congress was compromised by the intimidating effect of AIPAC's lobbying. He wrote that "Congressional conviction" in favor of Israel "has been immeasurably reinforced by the knowledge that political sanctions will be applied to any who fail to deliver" on votes to support high levels of economic and military aid to Israel.

Although he signed the 1975 AIPAC letter to President Ford, Mathias resisted AIPAC's 1978 lobbying against the Carter administration's proposal to sell 60 F-15 fighter planes to Saudi Arabia. In the Senate debate before the vote he said that both Israel and Saudi Arabia were important friends of the United States and that "both need our support."

Despite this attempt to balance American interests with Israel and the Saudi Arabia, Mathias said an "emotional, judgmental atmosphere" surrounded the arms sale issue. He quoted from a letter written to a Jewish newspaper in New York condemning his vote:

Mr. Mathias values the importance of oil over the well-being of Jews and the state of Israel. . . . The Jewish people cannot be fooled by such a person, no matter what he said, because his act proved who he was.

Yet Mathias had already responded to such criticism in his *Foreign Affairs* article:

Resistance to the pressures of a particular group in itself signals neither a sellout nor even a lack of sympathy with a foreign country or cause, but rather a sincere conviction about the national interest of the United States.

He appealed to both the president and the Congress to "help to reduce the fractiousness and strengthen our sense of common American purpose." The president's national constituency afford him a unique opportunity to work toward this end, but Congress, "although more vulnerable to group pressures," must also be active, he wrote.

Mathias asserted that it is not enough simply to follow public opinion: "An elected representative has other duties as well—to formulate and explain to the best of his or her ability the general interest, and to be prepared to accept the political consequences of having done so." He warned that ethnic advocacy tends to excessiveness and can thwart the higher good of national interests.

The Baltimore *Jewish Times* reported that Jewish leaders faced "a delicate dilemma" as they considered how to respond to the article:

Basically, they're damned if they do and damned if they don't. If they keep a low profile and do not challenge Mathias's assertions, they feel they will be shirking their duty and giving in. Yet if they "go after" the Senator, they will be falling into a trap by proving his point about excessive pressure.

Some Jews decided to take the latter course. Arnold Blumberg, a history professor at Towson State University, charged that Mathias "is in the mainstream of a tradition which urged Americans to pursue trade with Japan and Nazi Germany right up to the moment when scrap metal rained on the heads of American GIs from German and Japanese planes." A prominent Jewish community official charged that the article was "malicious" and expressed hurt that Mathias had the "poison in him to express these views." Congressman Benjamin S. Rosenthal, a Democrat from New York and a senior member of the House Foreign Affairs committee, charged that Mathias was "standing on the threshold of bigotry" and denying "to the ethnic lobbies alone the right to participate in shaping the American concensus on foreign policy." Other critics expressed the fear that the article would encourage anti-Semitism.

A spokesperson for the Maryland Jewish War Veterans organization said Mathias had "sold" himself "to the cause of the Saudis," while a letter to the *Baltimore Sun* chided, "I wish that [Mathias] had had the integrity to express those views one year prior to his re-election rather than one year after."

One critic, identified as "a former lobbyist," told the *Jewish Times* of Baltimore,

Mathias is a bright, well-respected legislator who's been effective on Soviet Jewry, but when it comes to Israel he was always the last to come on board. He was always reluctant, and was pressured by Jewish groups, and he resented the pressure. He sees himself as a statesman above the fray. Now he obviously feels he's in a position to say what he really believes.

The Jewish Community Relations Council in San Francisco criticized Mathias in its August 3, 1981, "Backgrounder" issue for raising the issue of "dual loyalty" within the "Jewish lobby." Mathias dismissed the charge as a false issue. In Maryland, the article was denounced by some rabbis, though Rabbi Jacob Angus of Baltimore publicly defended Mathias.

Two journalist friends, Frank Mankiewicz and William Safire, warned Mathias at the time that his article would "cause trouble." Two years later Mankiewicz assessed the Senator's future and said he felt the article had created serious problems.

Ethnic lobbying still worries Mathias. Pondering each word over a cup of tea one afternoon in the fall of 1983, he told me,

Ethnic ties enrich American life, but it must be understood they can't become so important that they obscure the primary duty to be an American citizen. Sometimes the very volume of this kind of activity can amount to an excessive zeal.

Some of his critics had not read his article, Mathias recalls with a smile. "In a way, they were saying, I haven't read it, but it's outrageous." At breakfasts sponsored by Jewish groups, Mathias was regularly challenged. "When this happened, I would ask how many had actually read my article. In a crowd of 200, maybe two hands would be raised."

Did the article close off communication with Jewish constituents? "I can't say it closed off access, but I have noticed that invitations have fallen off in the past two years." Mathias did not seek a fourth term in the Senate. He told a friend that controversy in the Jewish community was a factor in his decision.

$3.1 Million from Pro-Israel Sources

Boy wonder of industry, self-made millionaire, tireless Republican campaigner for progressive causes, Charles H. Percy was a bright prospect for the presidency for a time in the late sixties. He skyrocketed to prominence during his first term in the Senate, which began in 1967 after he won an upset victory over Paul Douglas, the popular but aging liberal Democrat.

In his first election 60 percent of Jewish votes—Illinois has the nation's fourth largest Jewish population—went to Douglas. But in the next six years Percy supported aid for Israel, urged the Soviet Union to permit emigration of Jews, criticized PLO terrorism, and supported social causes so forcefully that Jews rallied strongly to his side when he ran for re-election. In 1972 Percy accomplished something never before achieved by carrying every county in the state and, even more remarkable for an Illinois Protestant Republican, received 70 percent of the Jewish vote.

His honeymoon with Jews was interrupted in 1975 when he returned from a trip to the Middle East to declare, "Israel and its leadership, for whom I have a high regard, cannot count on the United States in the future just to write a blank check." He said Israel had missed some opportunities to negotiate and he described PLO leader Yasser Arafat as "more moderate, relatively speaking, than other extremists such as George Habash." He urged Israel to talk to the PLO if the organization would renounce terrorism and recognize Israel's right to exist behind secure defensible borders, noting that David Ben Gurion, Israel's first prime minister, had said that Israel must be willing to swap real estate for peace.

A week later Percy received this memorandum from his staff: "We have received 2,200 telegrams and 4,000 letters in response to your Mideast statements. . . . [They] run 95 percent against. As you might imagine, the majority of hostile mail comes from the Jewish community in Chicago. They threaten to withhold their votes and support for any future endeavors."

That same year Percy offended pro-Israel activists when he did not sign the famous "spirit of 76" letter through which seventy-six of his Senate colleagues effectively blocked President Gerald R. Ford's intended "reappraisal" of Middle East policy. This brought another flood of protest mail.

Despite these rumblings, the pro-Israel activists did not mount a serious campaign against Percy in 1978. With the Senator's unprecedented 1972 sweep of the state fresh in mind, they did not seek out a credible opponent either in the primary or the general election. In fact, when the Democratic nomination went largely by default to an unknown lawyer, Alex Seith, Jews took little interest. Even Percy's vote to approve the sale of F-15 planes to Saudi Arabia during the campaign year caused him no serious problem at that time.

In fact, only about one hundred Chicago Jews, few of them prominent, openly supported Seith. Seith's scheduler, who is Jewish, called every synagogue and every Jewish men's and women's organization in the state, but only one agreed to let the candidate speak. His campaign manager, Gary Ratner, concludes, "It was a ghetto mentality. Most Jews felt there was no way Percy would lose, so why get him mad at us." Of the $1 million Seith spent, less than $20,000 came from Jews. Encouraged by Philip Klutznick, a prominent Chicago Jewish leader, Illinois Jews contributed several times that amount to Percy. Of 70 Jewish leaders asked to sign an advertisement supporting the Senator, 65 gave their approval. On election day, Jewish support figured heavily in Percy's victory. He received only 53 percent of the statewide total but an impressive 61 percent of the Jewish vote.

The 1984 campaign was dramatically different. Pro-Israel forces targeted him for defeat early and never let up. Percy upset Jews by voting to support the Reagan administration sale of AWACS radar planes to Saudi Arabia (a sale also supported by the Carter administration). These developments provided new ammunition for the attack already underway against Percy. Percy's decision was made after staff members who had visited Israel said they had been told by an Israeli military official that the strategic military balance would not be affected, but that they did not want the symbolism of the United States doing business with Saudi Arabia.

Early in 1984, AIPAC decided to mobilize the full national resources of the pro-Israel campaign against Percy. In the March primary, it encouraged the candidacy of Congressman Tom Corcoran, Percy's challenger for the nomination. One of Corcoran's chief advisers and fundraisers was Morris Amitay, former executive director of AIPAC. Corcoran's high-decibel attacks portrayed the Senator as anti-Israel. His fund-raising appeals to Jews cited Percy as "Israel's worst adversary in Congress." A full-page newspaper advertisement, sponsored by the Corcoran campaign, featured a picture of Arafat and headlined, "Chuck Percy says this man is a moderate." A letter to Jewish voters defending Percy and signed by fifty-eight leading Illinois Jews made almost no impact.

Although Percy overcame the primary challenge, Corcoran's attacks damaged his position with Jewish voters and provided a strong base for AIPAC's continuing assault. Thomas A. Dine, executive director of AIPAC, set the tone early in the summer by attacking Percy's record at a campaign workshop in Chicago. AIPAC encouraged fundraising for Paul Simon and mobilized its political resources heavily against Percy. It assigned several student interns fulltime to the task of anti-Percy research and brought more than one hundred university students from out-of-state to campaign for Simon.

Midway in the campaign, AIPAC took a devious step to make Percy look bad. The key votes selected by AIPAC and used to rate all Senators showed Percy supporting Israel 89 percent of the time during his career. This put him only a few points below Simon's 99 percent rating in the House of Representatives and was hardly the contrast AIPAC wanted to cite in its anti-Percy campaign. The lobby solved the problem by changing its own rulebook in the middle of the game. It added to the selected list a number of obscure votes Percy had cast in the subcommittee and letters and resolutions that Percy had not signed. The expanded list dropped the Senator's rating to only 51 percent, a mark useful to Simon when he addressed Jewish audiences.

While most financial support from pro-Israel activists came to Simon from individuals, political action committees figured heavily. By mid-August these committees had contributed $145,870 to Simon, more than to any other Senate candidate. By election day, the total had risen to $235,000, with fifty-five committees participating.

In addition, a California Jewish activist, Michael Goland, using a loophole in federal law, spent $1.6 million for billboard, radio and television advertising which urged Illinoisans to "dump Percy" and called him a "chameleon."

Percy undertook vigorous countermeasures. Former Senator Jacob Javits of New York, one of the nation's most prominent and respected Jews, and Senator Rudy Boschwitz, chairman of the Senate Foreign Relations Committee subcommittee concerning the Middle East, made personal appearances for Percy in Chicago, and one hundred Illinois Jews led by former Attorney General Edward H. Levi sponsored a full-page advertisement which declared that Percy "has delivered for Illinois, delivered for America and delivered for Israel." The advertisement, in an unstated reference to Goland's attacks, warned, "Don't let our U.S. Senate race be bought by a Californian."

Except for charging in one news conference that Simon proclaimed that he had a 100 percent voting record for the pro-Israel lobby, Percy tried to avoid the Israel-Jewish controversy in the campaign.

These precautions proved futile, as did his strong legislative endeavors. His initiatives as chairman of the Senate Foreign Relations Committee brought Israel $425 million more in grant aid than Reagan had requested in 1983 and $325 million more in 1984, but these successes for Israel seemed to make no difference. A poll taken a month before the election showed a large majority of Jews supporting Simon. The Percy campaign found no way to stem the tide.

When the votes were counted, Percy had lost statewide by 89,000 votes. One exit poll indicated that Percy won 35 percent of the Jewish vote. In the same balloting Illinois Jews cast only 30 percent of their votes for the re-election of President Ronald Reagan, despite their unhappiness with the chief executive's views on the separation of church and state, abortion, and other social issues—not to mention his insistence on selling AWACS planes to Saudi Arabia.

In an election decided by so few votes, any major influence could be cited as crucial. Although broadly supportive of Reagan's program, Percy was remembered by many voters mainly as a moderate, progressive, Republican. Some conservative Republicans rejoiced at his defeat. The "new right," symbolized by the National Conservative Political Action Committee, withheld its support from Percy and early in the campaign indicated its preference for Simon, despite the latter's extremely liberal record in Congress.

Yet the Middle East controversy alone may have been sufficient to cost Percy his Senate seat. Thousands of Jews who had voted for Percy in 1978 left him for the Democratic candidate six years later. And these votes fled to Simon mainly because Israel's lobby worked effectively throughout the campaign year to portray the Senator as basically anti-Israel. Percy's long record of support for Israel's needs amounted to a repudiation of the accusation, but too few Jews spoke up publicly in his defense. The Senator found that once a candidate is labeled anti-Israel the poison sinks so swiftly and deeply it is almost impossible to remove.

The Middle East figured heavily in campaign financing as well as voting. Simon's outlay for the year was $5.3 million and Percy's about $6 million. With Goland spending $1.6 million in his own independent attack on Percy, total expenditures in behalf of the Simon candidacy came to $6.9 million.

Forty percent—$3.1 million—came from Jews disgruntled over Percy's position on Arab-Israel relations. Indeed, Simon was promised half this sum before he became a candidate. While he was still pondering whether to vacate his safe seat in the House of Representatives in order to make the race, he was assured $1.5 million from Jewish sources. The promise came from Robert Schrayer, Chicago area businessman and leader in the Jewish community, whose daughter, Elizabeth, was helping to organize anti-Percy forces in her job as assistant director of political affairs for AIPAC.

Reviewing the impact of the Middle East controversy on his defeat, Percy says, "Did it make the difference? I don't know. But this I believe: I believe Paul Simon would not have run had he not been assured by Bob Schrayer that he would receive the $1.5 million." Simon acknowledges, "This assurance was a factor in my decision."

AIPAC's Dine told a Canadian audience: "All the Jews in America, from coast to coast, gathered to oust Percy. And American politicians—those who hold public positions now, and those who aspire—got the message."

Chapter 4

The Lobby and the Oval Office

On a Sunday afternoon, just a few days before the presidential election in 1960, John F. Kennedy, the Democratic candidate, parked his car in front of the residence at 4615 W Street, just off Foxhall Road in a fashionable section of Washington. He was alone, unencumbered by the Secret Service officers soon to be a part of his life.

He wanted to get away from campaign pressures and have a chat with Charles Bartlett, a journalist and a close friend of many years. Their friendship had remained firm since they became acquainted in Florida immediately after World War II, and it was Bartlett who first introduced Kennedy to his future bride, Jacqueline Bouvier.

The night before, Kennedy had gone to dinner with a small group of wealthy and prominent Jews in New York. An episode of the evening troubled him deeply. Describing it to Bartlett as an "amazing experience," he said one of those at the dinner party—he did not identify him by name—told him he knew his campaign was in financial difficulty and, speaking for the group, offered "to help and help significantly" if Kennedy as president "would allow them to set the course of Middle East policy over the next four years." It was an astounding proposition.

Kennedy told Bartlett he reacted less as a presidential candidate than as a citizen. "He said he felt insulted," Bartlett recalls, "that anybody would make that offer, particularly to a man who even had a slim chance to be president. He said if he ever did get to be president he would push for a law that would subsidize presidential campaigns out of the U.S. Treasury. He added that whatever the cost of this subsidy, it would insulate presidential candidates in the future from this kind of pressure and save the country a lot of grief in the long run."

Just what Kennedy said in response to the proposition, Barlett did not know. "Knowing his style, he probably made a general comment and changed the subject."

114

After learning of the event from Bartlett, I talked with one of the people attending the dinner, Myer Feldman, a Washington attorney who worked closely in the Kennedy campaign in 1960 and later became assistant to the president with special responsibilities for liaison with the Jewish community. I hoped he could supply further details. As a freshman Congressman in 1961–62, I had had several friendly encounters with Feldman over wheat sales to the Soviet Union.

He recalled the gathering which, he said, was held at the apartment of Abraham Feinberg, chairman of the American Bank and Trust Company in New York and influential in national Jewish affairs and the Democratic Party. Those attending, Feldman recalled, were "ambiguous about Kennedy." They weren't sure "which way he would go" on Middle East policy and therefore not sure they would support him. The candidate was "peppered with tough and embarrassing questions." Asked for his opinion about moving the U.S. embassy in Israel from Tel Aviv to Jerusalem, Kennedy had replied, "Not under present circumstances." He said Kennedy answered all questions directly and made a good impression on his hosts. Feldman said he was unaware of the proposition that "insulted" the future president.

It was not the first time Middle East politics intruded forcibly into presidential campaigns. Bartlett says that when he related the episode to Roger L. Stevens, head of the John F. Kennedy Center for the Performing Arts in Washington, D.C., Stevens responded, "That's very interesting, because exactly the same thing happened to Adlai [former U.N. Ambassador Adlai E. Stevenson] in Los Angeles in 1956." Stevenson was then the Democratic candidate for president, opposing the re-election of Dwight D. Eisenhower.

Ethnic group pressure is an ever-present part of U.S. partisan politics, and because the president of the United States is the executor of all foreign policy, and the formulator of most of it, pressures naturally center on the people who hold or seek the presidency. When the pressure is from friends of Israel, presidents—and presidential candidates—often yield.

Lobby pressure on the White House is applied at several different levels. The most direct—person-to-person—varies greatly, depending on the inclinations of the person who is president at the time.

Some of those applying pressure are close personal friends whose influence is limited to just one presidency, an example being Harry S. Truman's close friendship with Ed Jacobson, his former haberdashery partner and an ardent Zionist. Mr. and Mrs. Arthur Krim, Jewish leaders from New York, maintained a close relationship with Lyndon B. Johnson. A White House official of the period recalls: "Arthur Krim stayed at the LBJ Ranch during crucial moments before the 1967 war and his wife, Mathilde, was a guest in the White House during the war." White House logs show that Mrs. Krim talked frequently by telephone with Johnson.

Other Jewish leaders maintain a relationship from one administration to another. Abraham Feinberg of New York, who hosted the dinner for Kennedy in October 1960, kept close White House ties over a period of years. He was a frequent visitor at the White House during the Johnson years, and as late as 1984, during the pre-convention presidential campaigning, brought the leading Democratic contenders, Walter Mondale and Gary Hart, together for a private discussion at his New York apartment. Philip Klutznick of Chicago, former president of B'nai B'rith, kept close relations throughout the Truman, Eisenhower, Kennedy, Johnson and Carter administrations.

Sometimes Israeli diplomats have a personal relationship which gives them direct access to the president. Ephraim Evron, then deputy chief in the Israeli embassy and a friend since Senate days, sometimes talked privately with Johnson in the Oval Office.

The second level of pressure comes through officials close to the president—his adviser on relations with the Jewish community or others among his top aides. President Kennedy told a friend, with a chuckle, that he learned that when he was away from Washington, Myer Feldman, his adviser on Jewish matters, would occasionally invite Jewish leaders to the White House for a discussion in the Cabinet Room.

The third level for pressing the presidency is within the top levels of the departments—the State Department, Defense Department and National Security Council—where Israeli officials and groups of U.S. citizens who are pro-Israeli activists frequently call to present their agendas to cabinet officers or their chief deputies (see chapter five).

"The Votes Are Against You"

Zionists began pressing their case early in the administration of Harry S. Truman and intensified their efforts in 1947 when Truman initially expressed opposition to the establishment of a Jewish state in Palestine. Jewish leaders bought newspaper advertising designed to transform public shame and outrage over the Holocaust into popular support for the idea of a Jewish national homeland. Both Houses of Congress passed resolutions urging presidential support.

When Truman continued to resist and publicly urged citizens to avoid inflaming "the passions of the inhabitants of Palestine," a group of New Jersey Jews wired: "Your policy on Palestine . . . has cost you our support in 1948." With election day approaching, it was a reminder of the grim political facts of life. Two-thirds of American Jews lived in

New York, Pennsylvania and Illinois, and these states would cast 110 electoral votes in the presidential voting. Considered the underdog in the upcoming election despite his incumbency, Truman knew he must have those votes to win.

With a proclamation announcing the new state of Israel expected soon, Truman assembled his Middle East ambassadors to get their views. Their spokesman, ambassador to Egypt Pinkerton "Pinky" Tuck, advised against immediate recognition. He told Truman the decision should be delayed long enough to carry out the consultation with Arab states that Truman's predecessor, Franklin D. Roosevelt, had promised the king of Saudi Arabia.

Truman replied, "Mr. Tuck, you may be right, but the votes are against you." In deciding to recognize Israel immediately, Truman rejected not just Tuck's advice but that of all his military and diplomatic advisers. He chose instead the recommendation of his close friend and former associate in the haberdashery trade, Ed Jacobson. In fact, pro-Israeli partisans today generally view Truman's immediate recognition of Israel as a prime example of effective lobbying through a "key contact" rather than the usual pressure tactics. Jacobson's pro-Zionist view was shared by Truman's political advisers, particularly Clark Clifford.

Secretary of State George C. Marshall opposed the decision so strongly that he bluntly told Truman soon after his recognition announcement that if the election were held the next day he would not vote for him. Sentiments were of course much different in Israel. During a 1949 White House visit, the chief rabbi of Israel told the president, "God put you in your mother's womb so you would be the instrument to bring about the rebirth of Israel after 2000 years."

In partisan political terms, Truman's decision paid off. On election day he received 75 percent of the Jewish vote nationally, which helped him win a razor-thin upset victory—and a permanent place of honor on the face of Israeli postage stamps, as well as in the hearts of Zionists.

"Dismayed by 'Partisan Considerations' "

Presidential behavior toward the state of Israel took a turn in the opposite direction when Truman's successor, Dwight D. Eisenhower, assumed office. He resisted pressures from the Israeli lobby and on three occasions forced Israel to abandon major policies to which it was publicly and strongly committed.

In September 1953, he ordered a cancellation of all aid—amounting to $26 million—until Israel stopped work on a diversion canal being constructed on the Jordan River in violation of the 1949 ceasefire agreements, a project which would help assure Israeli control of water resources which were important to all nations in the region. It was the first time a president actually cut off all aid to Israel. He also instructed the Treasury Department to draft an order removing the tax-deductible status of contributions made to the United Jewish Appeal and other organizations raising funds for Israel in the U.S.

Predictably, Eisenhower's decision kicked up a major storm. Dr. Israel Goldstein told an audience of 20,000 celebrating Jerusalem's 3,000th birthday at New York's Madison Square Garden: "Peace will not be helped by withholding aid as an instrument of unwarranted duress." New York members of Congress joined the bandwagon. Senator Robert Wagner called the decision "cruel and intemperate," and Congressman Emanuel Celler denounced it as a "snap judgment." All major Jewish organizations condemned the action.

Eisenhower stood firm in withholding aid, and less than two months later Israel announced it was ceasing work on the river diversion project. The president had won a first round, the confrontation was postponed, aid to Israel was resumed, and the order ending the privileged tax status enjoyed by Zionist groups was not issued.

Eisenhower faced the lobby again in October 1956, just days before his re-election as president. Israel had negotiated a secret deal with Britain and France under which the three nations would coordinate a military attack on the Nasser regime in Egypt, which had just taken over the Suez Canal. Israel would strike across the Sinai Desert and move against the canal, while British and French forces, after an air bombardment, would invade from the north.

The allied governments assumed that the United States would not interfere; France and Britain believed that Eisenhower would avoid a public showdown with his wartime allies. Israel, with the U.S. presidential election just days away, counted on partisan pressures from its American lobby to keep candidate Eisenhower on the sidelines. All miscalculated.

When Israel's invasion of Egypt began on October 29, Eisenhower immediately cancelled all aid to Israel. He permitted only the delivery of food already in transit, stopping all other forms of assistance, both economic and military. These measures created such pressure that Israel halted its attack. The British and French, also under heavy U.S. pressure, abandoned their invasion from the north.

Despite partisan assaults on his Middle East policy, the president was, of course, easily re-elected. In fact, more American Jews voted for Eisenhower in 1956 (40 percent) than those who had supported him in 1952 (36 percent).

But Eisenhower's problems with Israel were far from over. Even after the invasion was halted, Israel decided to keep occupying forces in the Egyptian-administered Gaza Strip, as well as the strategic village of Sharm el-Sheik at the access to the Gulf of Aqaba. Despite protests by the United States and six resolutions by the United Nations, Israel refused to withdraw. As weeks passed, lobby pressure against Eisenhower's position received support from Eleanor Roosevelt, former President Truman, and leaders of both parties in the Senate, Democrat Lyndon Johnson of Texas and Republican William Knowland of California.

Informed that the United States might support U.N. sanctions against Israel, Knowland threatened to resign as a member of the U.N. delegation and warned Secretary of State John Foster Dulles, "This will mean a parting of the ways." Dulles was firm: "I think you should study this. We cannot have all our policies made in Jerusalem." Dulles told Henry Luce, owner of Time, Inc. and a supporter of Israel's position, "I am aware how almost impossible it is in this country to carry out a foreign policy not approved by the Jews. [But] I am going to try to have one. This does not mean I am anti-Jewish, but I believe in what George Washington said in his farewell address, that an emotional attachment to another country should not interfere."

Eisenhower considered the issue vital. He summoned the bipartisan leadership of Congress to the White House to request their support. Unwilling to tangle with pro-Israeli activists, the group refused. That night the president wrote in his diary: "As I reflected on the pettiness of the discussion of the morning, I found it somewhat dismaying that partisan considerations should enter so much into life-or-death, peace-or-war decisions."

A determined president took his case to the American people in a televised address in the spring of 1957:

Should a nation which attacks and occupies foreign territory in the face of the United Nations disapproval be allowed to impose conditions on its own withdrawal? If we agreed that armed attack can properly achieve the purposes of the assailant, then I fear we will have turned back the clock of international order.

Letters and telegrams poured into the White House, but almost all of the communications came from Jews, 90 percent supporting Israel's position. Dulles complained, "It is impossible to hold the line because we get no support from the Protestant elements in the country. All we get is a battering from the Jews."

Eisenhower persisted, declaring that the United States would support a U.N. resolution imposing sanctions if Israel did not withdraw from all of the Sinai peninsula and from Gaza and threatening to take away the tax privilege enjoyed by donors to Israeli causes. Faced with that prospect, Israel finally capitulated and withdrew from the occupied territory.

"Armed Shipments Are . . . Ready to Go"

Israel fared better at the hands of the next occupants of the White House. Presidents John F. Kennedy and Lyndon B. Johnson began to help Israel in its military activities, not hold it back.

Although there is no evidence to suggest that Kennedy accepted the dinner party proposition—to exchange control of Middle East policy for campaign contributions—he fared well on election day in 1960, receiving 82 percent of the Jewish vote, topping even Harry Truman's 75 percent, and, as president, he made a decision vital to Israel's military plans. He approved for the first time the U.S. sale of weapons to Israel.

But Israel's military fortunes received a still greater boost with the arrival in the Oval Office of President Lyndon B. Johnson. Johnson's sympathy for the underdog—in his view, Israel—made him responsive to the demands of Israel and its lobby in the United States. Friends of Israel with special influence included Arthur Goldberg, U.S. ambassador to the United Nations, Philip Klutznick of Chicago, and three New Yorkers, Abraham Feinberg and Arthur and Mathilde Krim. The latter often worked through the Rostow brothers, Walt Rostow, Johnson's national security adviser, and Eugene Rostow, assistant secretary of state for political affairs.

In a September 1966 letter to Feinberg, Klutznick called for an improved relationship between Johnson and the American Jewish community. He did not want Jewish differences with Johnson over the Vietnam war and aid to private schools, for example, to complicate American support for Israel. He called on Feinberg to help establish a "sense of participation." The elements of a deal were present. At the time, Johnson desperately wanted public support for the war in Southeast Asia, and the Jewish leaders wanted assurance that the U.S. would stand by Israel in a crisis.

Aid levels were increased, clearances issued for almost any military item, and extensive credit extended.

Lobby pressure may not have been needed to persuade Johnson to support Israel, but the pressure came nevertheless. Harold Saunders, a member of the National Security Council staff and later Carter's assistant secretary of state for the Near East and South Asia, recalls the avalanche of telegrams and letters that urged President Johnson to stand behind Israel when Egypt's President Nasser closed the Strait of Tiran in May 1967: "I had 150,000 telegrams and letters from the Jewish community in boxes in my office. I do not exaggerate. There were 150,000 pieces of paper sitting there. They all said the same thing. And Johnson decreed that every one of them should be answered."

In early June, on the day that Israel attacked Egypt, the president received this urgent message from Rostow: "Arthur Krim reports that many armed shipments are packed and ready to go to Israel, but are being held up. He thinks it would be most helpful if these could be released."

Israel was at war, and this time the president of the United States would cause no problems. Aid would go forward without interruption, and calls for sanctions against Israel in the United Nations would face adamant U.S. opposition. The United States would actively support Israel's military endeavors. Powerful new ties with Israel would lead the president of the United States to cover up the facts concerning one of the most astonishing disasters in the history of the United States Navy, the Israeli attack on the USS *Liberty* (see chapter five).

Saunders recalls that after the Arab-Israeli war, pro-Israeli interests blanketed the White House with the basic demand that Israel not be forced to withdraw from territory it occupied until the Arab states agreed to a "just and lasting peace" with Israel. Under this demand, Israel could use occupied Arab territory as a bargaining "chip" in seeking Arab recognition, an option that President Eisenhower refused to permit Israel to use after the Suez crisis in 1957.

Saunders adds, "This Israeli demand was accepted by President Johnson without discussion in the National Security Council or other policy institutions. It has had a profound impact on the course of events in the Middle East since that time." According to another high official of that period, the policy was adopted because the lobby succeeded in "pervading the very atmosphere of the White House."

Nixon's Order Ignored

Although Johnson's successor, Richard M. Nixon, came to office with little Jewish help, he supported Israel so heavily in his first term as president that in 1972 re-election campaign Israel's ambassador to Washington, Yitzhak Rabin, openly campaigned for him. Nixon won 35 percent of the Jewish vote in 1972, up 20 points from four years before.

In 1973 he came powerfully to Israel's defense when Arab states tried to recover territory seized in 1967 by the Israelis. During the conflict, the weapons and supplies Nixon ordered airlifted to Israel proved to be Israel's lifeline. His decision to order forces on a high state of alert worldwide may have kept the Soviet Union from undertaking a larger role.

Privately, Nixon criticized Israel for failing to cooperate in a comprehensive settlement of issues with its Arab neighbors. On several occasions, he ordered Henry Kissinger, national security adviser and later secretary of state, to suspend aid to Israel until it became more cooperative. Three days before he resigned the presidency, Nixon instructed Kissinger to disapprove an Israeli request for "long-term military assistance." Kissinger writes in his memoirs: "He would cut off all military deliveries to Israel until it agreed to a comprehensive peace. He regretted not having done so earlier; he would make up for it now. His successor would thank him for it. I should prepare the necessary papers." Kissinger adds that Nixon did not return to the subject. Although "the relevant papers were prepared," according to Kissinger, they were "never signed." Nor did Kissinger see fit to carry out the orders. (In July 1984, Nixon verified the Kissinger account, saying it was accurate and adding that he "still believes that aid to Israel should be tied to cooperation in a comprehensive settlement.")

Assuming the presidency in 1975, Ford took no action on the cutoff papers prepared for Nixon, but confronted Rabin, who by then had become the Israeli prime minister, over the same comprehensive peace settlement issue. In an effort to elicit greater Israeli cooperation, Ford announced in 1975 that he would "reassess" U.S. policy in the Middle East (see chapter three). Under lobby-organized pressure from the Senate, Ford dropped the reassessment, but this retreat did not win him votes when he sought a full term as president the next year. In 1976, 68 percent of the Jewish vote went to Democrat Jimmy Carter.

Uncritical Support Is No Favor to Israel

During the period between Carter's election in 1976 and his inauguration in January 1977, the Israeli lobby played a role in his decision on who would manage foreign policy. Carter decided to nominate as Secretary of State Cyrus Vance, a man of decency and fairness and possessing the right impulses on Middle East policy, but in doing so he passed over George W. Ball, a man who had all these same important qualities but who also possessed the experience, personal force and worldwide prestige Carter would need in upcoming crises in the Middle East and elsewhere.

When I visited him at his Princeton, N.J., residence during the summer of 1983—seeking background facts on this period—Ball was well into writing his fourth major book. I found him at the end of a narrow corridor lined with cartoons and photographs of the political past, in a large high-ceilinged room bustling with the activity of a city newsroom just before presstime. Once a private art gallery, it is now filled with computers, papers, books and busy people.

At the center of it all, pecking away at a word processor keyboard and surrounded by papers stacked high on a U-shaped table sat the former deputy secretary of state under two presidents, former U.S. ambassador to the United Nations, and former executive with one of Manhattan's largest investment banking firms. At 73, he was still busy trying to bring order out of a world in disarray. The *Manchester Guardian* characterized him as "an idealist facing chaos with dignity."

I was armed with questions. What price had Ball paid for speaking out on Middle East issues? Had it hurt his law practice, spoiled his chances to serve in higher office? Ball took time to talk, but he was busy. He had just addressed the cadets at West Point and was midway in preparing an editorial piece for the *Washington Post* in which he would warn the Reagan administration of immense pitfalls ahead in its Lebanese policy. He was one of my heroes, especially for his courage on Vietnam policy, and I admired his brilliance as a writer. Eloquent and witty, he reminded me more of his colleague in the Johnson administration, former Secretary of State Dean Rusk, but their views on Vietnam were sharply at odds.

"I'll be with you in a minute," Ball said, glancing up from the keyboard. He gave the computer keys a few more whacks, stood up, whipped out a diskette and told his assistant, Lee Hurford, "Print it all." His six-foot two-inch frame exuded confidence and power. Making his way through the array of books and papers, he explained, "I'm addicted to this machine. I would never go back to a typewriter. I quit commuting to Manhattan," he added, gesturing down the corridor, "because I can slip down here evenings if I have some ideas to put down."

Put them down he has. Over the years many diplomats have firmly criticized Israeli policies, but most have confined their advice to private circles. Those who have spoken out publicly usually have done so in muted tones. Close friends doubt that Ball has any muted tones. He has never pulled any punches. But while on government assignments Ball dutifully kept his advice private.

Ball has paid a price for such candor on Israeli policy. He was one of only three people considered for appointment as secretary of state under President Carter, and except for his outspoken views on Middle East affairs, his nomination would have seemed inevitable.

His political and professional credentials were immaculate. A lifelong Democrat, he twice campaigned vigorously for Adlai E. Stevenson for president. In 1959 he became a supporter of John F. Kennedy's presidential ambitions. His diplomatic experience and prestige were diverse and unmatched. He had served as number two man in the State Department under Presidents John F. Kennedy and Lyndon Johnson. In those assignments he dealt intimately with the Cuban missile crisis and most other major issues in foreign policy for six years. He took the job as ambassador to the U.N., a job he did not want, because, in his words, "L.B.J. had surrounded me."

Ball challenged military policies forcefully within administration circles. On a proposed policy question Johnson would frequently go around the cabinet room for advice, then say, "Now let's hear what Ball has to say against it."

Ball consistently argued against the buildup in Vietnam. The *Washington Post* described him as "the consistent dove in a hawkish administration." Journalist Walter Lippman, a close friend, urged him to resign in protest: "Feeling as you do, you should resign and make your opposition public." Ball declined, believing it important that criticism of the war be heard directly from within the administration, though Johnson usually rejected his advice.

Ball was one of America's best-known and most admired diplomats, but he probably spiked his prospects of becoming Carter's secretary of state when he wrote an article entitled "The Coming Crisis in Israeli-American Relations" for the Winter 1975/76 issue of *Foreign Affairs* quarterly. It provoked a storm of protest from the Jewish community.

In the article, Ball cited President Eisenhower's demand that Israel withdraw from the Sinai as "the last time the United States ever took, and persisted in, forceful action against the strong wishes of an Israeli government." He saw the event as as watershed. "American Jewish leaders thereafter set out to build one of Washington's most effective lobbies, which now works in close cooperation with the Israeli embassy."

He lamented the routine leakage of classified information:

Not only do Israel's American supporters have powerful influence with many members of the Congress, but practically no actions touching Israel's interests can be taken, or even discussed, within the executive branch without it being quickly known to the Israeli government.

He bemoaned Israel's rejection of U.S. advice at a time when Israel's dependence on U.S. aid had "reached the point of totality."

Yet he was not surprised that Israel pursued an independent course:

Israelis have been so long conditioned to expect that Americans will support their country, no matter how often it disregards American advice and protests and America's own interests.

Despite such sharp criticism, candidate Carter for a time considered Ball his principal foreign policy adviser and selected him as one of three finalists for secretary of state when, as the president-elect, he took up the process of selecting his cabinet. The other two finalists were Paul Warnke, former assistant secretary of defense and, of course, Cyrus Vance.

Zbigniew Brzezinski, Carter's national security adviser, wrote in his book *Power and Principle* that Ball was his preference for secretary of state during the period preceding election day although he later shifted to Vance. Asked for his views during the postelection process at Plains, Georgia, Brzezinski told Carter that Ball would be "a strong conceptualizer but probably a poor organizer, an assertive individual but probably somewhat handicapped by his controversial position on the Middle East." He said Ball's appointment as secretary of state would be received "extremely well in Western Europe and Japan, probably somewhat less so in the developing countries, and negatively in Israel."

A number of Jewish leaders urged Carter not to name Ball to any significant role in his administration. The characteristic which made Ball unacceptable to the Israeli lobby was his candor; he wasn't afraid to speak up and criticize Israeli policy. Carter dropped Ball from consideration.

With Carter's cabinet selection process completed, Ball continued to speak out. Early in 1977 he wrote another article in *Foreign Affairs,* "How to Save Israel in Spite of Herself," urging the new administration to take the lead in formulating a comprehensive settlement that would be fair to the Palestinians as well as Israel. For a time Carter moved in this direction, even trying to communicate with the Palestine Liberation Organization through Saudi Arabia. When this approach floundered, Carter shifted his focus on attempting to reach a settlement between Egypt and Israel at Camp David, where Ball believes Carter was double-crossed by Begin. "I talked with Carter just before Camp David. We had a long dinner together. He told me he was going to try to get a full settlement on Middle East issues, and he seemed to understand the significance of the Palestinian issue. On this I have no doubt, and I think he desperately wanted to settle it." After Camp David, Israel frustrated Carter's goals, continuing to build settlements in occupied territory and blocking progress toward autonomy for Palestinians in the West Bank.

Although not a part of the Carter Administration, Ball continued to be an all-time favorite on television interview shows. One of these appearances led to a public exchange with a Jewish leader. On a panel interview in late 1977 Ball said he felt the Jewish community in the United States had put United States interests "rather secondary in many cases."

To Morris B. Abram, Manhattan lawyer and former president of the American Jewish Committee, these were fighting words. Enlisted the year before in support of the effort to make Ball the secretary of state, Abram wrote him a public letter, published in the *Washington Post,* charging that these comments established Ball "as one who is willing to accept and spread age-old calumnies about Jews."

Responding in the *Washington Post,* Ball denied that he was suggesting that "even the most ardent Zionist consciously choose Israel over America." He explained, "I suggest rather that the effect of their uncritical encouragement of Israel's most excessive actions is not wholly consistent with the United States' interests." His correspondence with Abram was published in the *Washington Post.* Ball concluded,

When leading members of the American Jewish community give [Israel's] government uncritical and unqualified approbation and encouragement for whatever it chooses to do, while striving so far as possible to overwhelm any criticism of its actions in Congress and in the public media, they are, in my view, doing neither themselves nor the United States a favor.

During the Reagan administration, Ball became one of the few Democrats trying to take his party back to the Middle East morality of Eisenhower. Of Reagan, he said,

He did not demand, as he should have done under the law, that we would exact the penalties provided unless the Israelis stopped murdering civilians with the weapons we had provided them solely for self-defense. Instead he bought them off by committing our own Marines to maintain order while we persuaded the PLO leaders to leave rather than face martyrdom.

Ball did not let his business career, any more than his public career, soften his public expressions. He admitted that his plain talk about the Middle East "certainly hasn't helped" his business career:

I'm sure that my partners at Lehman Brothers had to absorb a certain amount of punishment. But they were tolerant and understanding people. I never felt I lost anything very much by speaking out. I'm politically untouchable, but I am sure certain groups would rather shoot me than deal with me.

While never shot at for his views, his encounters with the Israeli lobby were numerous and began early in his career. He recalls the day, during the 1952 presidential race, when a pro-Israel emissary visited Adlai Stevenson's presidential campaign headquarters in Springfield, Illinois. The emissary told Ball that his friends had gathered a "lot of money" but wanted to "discuss the Israeli question" before turning it over. Ball says Stevenson met with the group—"He met with any group"—but he "never made any of the promises expected."

In more recent presidential campaigns, Ball experienced lobby pressure of a different kind. In early 1979, impressed with the early pronouncements of John B. Anderson, Ball announced that he planned to vote for the maverick Republican who was running for president as an independent. Upon hearing the news, an elated Anderson called Ball and promised to visit him at Princeton "soon." Anderson changed his mind. He never came. Convinced by his campaign staff that he had to cultivate the pro-Israeli community if he hoped to make progress as a candidate, Anderson made a ritual visit to Israel. He issued statements fully supporting Israel. He shunned Ball.

The elder statesman had a similar experience in 1983. After testifying to the Senate Foreign Relations Committee one morning, Ball was approached by Senator John Glenn, who was already testing the presidential waters. Glenn invited Ball to call because he wanted his advice on foreign policy issues. After trying unsuccessfully to get calls through, Ball wrote him. He stated his willingness to help Glenn set up a panel of scholars and former diplomats who could help the candidate with ideas, statements and speeches during the hectic days of campaigning. Ball had done the same thing for Adlai Stevenson in 1956. Several weeks later a letter arrived from Glenn stating that he would take up the suggestions with his campaign staff. That was the end of Ball's relationship with Glenn.

Despite the intimidating factors that led candidates Carter, Anderson and Glenn to avoid his help, Ball feels the lobby is overrated in the power it can deliver. While it controls many votes in strategically important states and provides generous financial support to candidates, he contends these are not the principal factors of influence.

Ball believes the lobby's instrument of greatest power is its willingness to make broad use of the charge of anti-Semitism: "They've got one great thing going for them. Most people are terribly concerned not to be accused of being anti-Semitic, and the lobby so often equates criticism of Israel with anti-Semitism. They keep pounding away at that theme, and people are deterred from speaking out."

In Ball's view, many Americans feel a "sense of guilt" over the extermination of Jews by Nazi Germany. The result of this guilt is that the fear of being called anti-Semitic is "much more effective in silencing candidates and public officials than threats about campaign money or votes."

He Was Not Consistent

Although proceeding without the services of George Ball, Jimmy Carter, for a fleeting moment, gave every indication of being a president who would stand up to Israel and pursue policies based on U.S. interests in the Middle East. He came to the presidency determined to be fair to Arab interests, as well as Israel, and once in office even advocated a homeland with secure borders for the Palestinians (see introduction).

While this endeavor soon faded, Carter made great strides in foreign policy elsewhere. In addition to organizing the Camp David Accords, his administration marked the consummation of the treaty with Panama, normalization of diplomatic relations with China, a major reform in international trade policy, and the initial agreement with the Soviet Union on strategic arms limitation, But in overall Middle East policy he lacked consistent purpose and commitment.

Carter was dismayed when Jews in the United States remained disgruntled with his administration despite his major role in achieving a long-sought Israeli goal, the peace treaty between Egypt and Israel. A senior diplomat whose career stretches back over twenty years, remembers the pressures Jewish groups brought to bear following the joint U.S.-Soviet communiqué of October 1977. Carter was trying to revive the Geneva conference on the Middle East in order to get a comprehensive settlement of the Arab-Israeli dispute. The American Jewish community strongly objected. The diplomat recalls, "I remember I really had my hands full meeting with protesting Jewish groups. I figured up one day, totaling just the people the groups said they represented, that I must have met with representatives of half the entire U.S. Jewish community."

The groups came well briefed. All, he says, used the same theme:

What a terrible unpatriotic act it was to invite the Russians back into the Middle East; it was anti-Israel, almost anti-Semitic. I would spend part of my time meeting Jewish groups on Capitol Hill in the offices of Senators and Congressmen.

Other times I would meet with groups of 20 to 40 in my conference room at State Department. Meanwhile Secretary of State Vance would be meeting with other groups, and the President with still others.

The pressure was too much. Carter yielded to lobby pressures and quickly dropped the proposal. Carter also learned, like Ford before him, that yielding to the lobby on relations with Israel did not pay dividends on election day. Many Jews deserted him when he sought re-election in 1980.

"They Wouldn't Give Him a Dime"

The same year, the pressures of pro-Israeli activists became decisive in the fortunes of a renegade Texas Democrat who turned Republican because he wanted to succeed Jimmy Carter as president.

In October 1979, John Connally, who had been Democratic governor of Texas, came to Washington to give the first major foreign policy speech of his campaign for the presidency. The field of Republican aspirants to the White House was already crowded. Although Ronald Reagan had not yet formally entered the race, seven other Republicans had announced their candidacy.

Connally's campaign theme was "leadership for America," and television advertisements showed him the "candidate of the forgotten American who goes to church on Sunday." This American, Connally believed, was looking for leadership. His speech to the Washington Press Club contained a section outlining a plan to resolve the Arab-Israeli conflict. It was part of a campaign strategy designed to present the former governor of Texas and secretary of the treasury as a decisive leader capable of talking man to man with powerful foreigners. He had served in several cabinet positions under President Nixon. From this wide-ranging political experience, he should have known the sensitivity of the Arab-Israeli question.

Several Middle East peace plans had been advanced by sitting presidents, but the plan Connally outlined in his speech was the most ambitious ever presented by a candidate for the office. He argued that the Carter initiative at Camp David had stalled because of failed diplomatic leadership and that it was time for the United States to pursue a new Middle East policy, one "based not on individual Arab or Israeli interests, but on American interests."

American interests demanded peace and stability in the region, Connally said, and this could best be achieved by a program whereby the Israelis withdrew from occupied Arab territories in return for Arab acceptance of Israeli sovereignty and territorial integrity. The Arabs would be obligated to "renounce forever all hostile actions toward Jews and give up the use of oil supply and prices to force political change." This would ensure an uninterrupted supply of Middle Eastern oil, which, Connally said, "is and will continue to be the lifeblood of Western civilization for decades to come." The United States would guarantee the stability of the region by greatly expanding its military presence there.

Connally became the first prominent presidential candidate to declare his support for Palestinian self-determination. He said the Palestinians should have the option of establishing an independent state on the West Bank and Gaza or an autonomous area within Jordan. Palestinian leaders willing to work for a compromise peace settlement with Israel should be welcomed to discussions, he added, but "those extremists who refuse to cooperate and continue to indulge in terrorism should be treated as international outlaws by the international community."

Connally also suggested that future American aid be conditioned on Israeli willingness to adopt a more reasonable policy on the West Bank. Noting the strain imposed upon the Israeli economy by the need for constant military preparedness, he said, "Without billions of dollars in American economic and military aid, Israel simply could not survive. Yet it is only candid to say that support for this level of aid, in the absence of greater willingness by Israeli leadership to compromise with their neighbors, is eroding." He criticized the Begin government's "policy of creeping annexation of the West Bank," quoting a group of American Jewish leaders who earlier in the year had denounced Israeli policy on the West Bank as "morally unacceptable and perilous for the democratic character of the Jewish state."

Connally knew his speech would stir controversy, and indeed the criticism came quick and hard. Rabbi Alexander Schindler, president of the Union of American Hebrew Congregations, said Connally's call for withdrawal from the territories "is a formula for Israel's liquidation." The *Washington Star* quoted unnamed Israeli officials in Washington as calling his plan "a total surrender to blackmail by Arab oil-producing countries." Henry Siegman, executive director of the American Jewish Congress, said Connally's criticism of the Camp David peace process "gives encouragement to the Arab confrontation states who urge a violent solution to the Arab-Israeli conflict. It is disappointing, although perhaps not surprising, that Mr. Connally should emerge as the candidate of the oil interests." Connally's campaign manager later accused the Israeli embassy of orchestrating the attack.

Few news commentators praised his speech. *Christian Science Monitor* columnist Joseph C. Harsch found Connally's peace plan remarkable for its candor. Harsch wrote that Connally "broke with and, indeed, defined the pro-Israel lobby." He "said things about Israel which no prominent American politician has dared to say for a long time, with the exception of Senator J. William Fulbright." Agreeing that the peace plan was really nothing new, Harsch pointed out that it "comes out of the book of official American foreign policy as stated since the 1967 war." What was unusual, Harsch wrote, was that this policy should be articulated by a candidate for president:

The immediate question is whether Mr. Connally can demonstrate that it is possible to take the official government position on Middle East policy and still survive in the present political climate.

Writing in the *Nation,* Arthur Samuelson called Connally's plan "both wrong and dangerous," but went on to say that "Connally's candor is praiseworthy":

For all too long, public debate over the Middle East has been characterized by a marked dishonesty on the part of aspirants for public office. Rather than put forward how they plan to break the impasse in American-Israeli relations that has remained constant since 1967, they fall over one another in praise of Israel's virtues.

The *Washington Post* called Connally's speech "a telling measure of how American debate on this central issue is developing":

No previous candidate for a major party's presidential nomination has staked out a position so opposed to the traditional line. Mr. Connally offers no deference to the 'Jewish lobby,' attacking the current Israeli government's policies head on.

Within a few days of the speech, however, less friendly voices were heard. A Jewish Republican running for mayor of Philadelphia snubbed Connally by refusing to be photographed with him. Two Jewish members of Connally's national campaign committee resigned in protest. One of them, Rita Hauser, chairman of the Foreign Affairs Council of the American Jewish Committee, called the speech "inexcusable" and said it represented "the straight Saudi line." The second, attorney Arthur Mason, said he was fearful that Connally's speech might stir anti-Semitism.

The bad news kept coming. The New York Republican Committee withdrew its invitation for Connally to speak at its annual Lincoln Day dinner, and traditional big givers boycotted a fundraiser in New York that was to feature Connally. The *Washington Post* quoted an unnamed source who said the speech had robbed Connally of support which his pro-business positions had won among some Jews: "Now they wouldn't give him a dime."

Certainly the Connally candidacy suffered problems unrelated to his positions on the Middle East. The campaign experienced organizational difficulties, the forceful Texan came across to some as too "hot" on the "cool" medium of television, and he was undoubtedly hurt by his switch from the Democratic to the Republican party in 1973.

But Winton Blount, Connally's campaign chairman, believes that

none of these factors equalled the "devastating" effect of the controversial speech. Connally himself says there is "no question" that the
speech hurt. Columnist William Safire, an admirer of Connally but also
a pro-Israeli hard-liner, made a pained assessment of the speech's effect on the presidential race:

Supporters of Israel—along with many others concerned with noisy U.S.
weakness in the face of Soviet military and Arab economic threats—made a
reassessment of Ronald Reagan and decided he looked ten years younger.

Succumbing to Israeli Dictates

In 1984, it was no contest at all on the Republican side of the
presidential race, either for the nomination or in respect to policy
toward Israel. Ronald Reagan had the field to himself and was not
about to risk a confrontation like the one fatal to the candidacy of John
Connally four years before.

In late 1983, certain to be a candidate for re-election, Reagan was
in a position to deliver, not just promise. He had encountered Israeli
pressures in opposition to his September 1982 peace plan and his delay
in delivering fighter aircraft in the wake of Israel's bombing of the Iraq
nuclear plant. But he had avoided a major showdown with Israel, and,
beginning in 1983, Reagan went all-out for the Jewish vote, pandering
to the Israeli lobby while trying to keep the Middle East crisis on hold
until after the election.

Polls showed the need for repair work. In 1980 Reagan had received 40 percent of the Jewish vote—the largest ever by a Republican—but half of this support had since drifted away. In April 1983
Albert A. Spiegel, a longtime Reagan supporter, had quit as a special
adviser to Reagan on Jewish affairs. Spiegel was upset over a newspaper story which said Reagan intended to press his Middle East peace
plan despite Jewish opposition and felt he could be re-elected without
Jewish votes.

In December Reagan launched a broad bid for Jewish support. The
first action was upgrading the position of White House liaison with the
Jewish community, but his changes on the policy front were even more
significant. After meeting with Israeli Prime Minister Yitzhak Shamir
in December 1983, Reagan announced a dramatic increase in the level
of aid. Instead of the old formula, under which Israel was required to
pay back some of the funds advanced, the administration requested
that in the future all aid be in the form of a grant. In addition, in a
gesture to Israel's sagging industry, he agreed that $250 million in U.S.
aid funds could be spent in Israel to help finance the manufacture of a

new Israeli warplane. United States aircraft firms were dismayed, because they receive no similar government aid. (See chapter two.)

Reagan proposed a new higher level of "strategic cooperation" in the military field and a free trade relationship which would make Israel the only nation with tariff-free access to both the European community and the United States.

All of this won applause from the Israeli lobby. *Near East Report,* the AIPAC newsletter, declared editorially: "[Reagan] has earned the gratitude of all supporters of a strong U.S.–Israel relationship."

In March, Reagan made further concessions to the lobby. He refused to intercede with Israel at the request of King Hussein of Jordan, whom he had been pressing to join the peace process. Aiming both to strengthen Yasser Arafat against more radical elements within the Palestine Liberation Organization, and to improve his own influence over the Palestinian cause, Hussein asked the president for help. He wanted Reagan to press Israel to permit Palestinians living on the West Bank and Gaza to attend the upcoming session of the Palestine National Council. In another message, Hussein asked the United States to support a U.N. resolution declaring illegal the settlements Israel has built in Arab territory it occupies, a position maintained for years by previous presidents. Reagan rejected both requests. Hussein told a reporter for the *New York Times* that "the United States is succumbing to Israeli dictates," and he saw no hope for future improvement.

The leading contenders for the Democratic nomination, like Reagan, never missed an opportunity to pledge allegiance to Israel.

"Conscience of the Democrats"

The 1984 presidential contest often focused on the competition between former Vice-President Walter Mondale and Senator Gary Hart on the question of who was more loyal to Israel. Mondale accused Hart of being weak in supporting the removal of the U.S. embassy from Tel Aviv to Jerusalem. Hart accused Mondale of trying to "intimidate and coerce Israel into taking unacceptable risks" while he was vice-president under President Carter.

Actually, Mondale was the principal pro-Israel force within the Carter Administration. During the 1980 campaign he responded to lobby pressure by helping to engineer a diplomatic maneuver that proved costly to the United States. When Donald McHenry, the U.S. ambassador to the United Nations, cast a vote March 1 rebuking Israel publicly for its settlements policy—the first such rebuke of an Israeli action since the Eisenhower administration—Jewish circles were furious, and so was Mondale. McHenry's vote supported a resolution which offended the pro-Israel lobby on two points: it was critical of Israeli settlements on the West Bank, and it referred to East Jerusalem as "occupied territory."

Mondale organized an immediate counterattack within White House circles. He persuaded Carter that the State Department had wrongly advised him. Late in the evening of the controversial vote the White House announced a "failure in communications" between Washington and New York. It explained that McHenry had misunderstood his instructions and should have abstained. Three days later, Secretary of State Cyrus Vance personally took the blame for the "failure." Few believed him.

Both the nation and the Carter-Mondale ticket would have been better off if Carter had ignored Mondale's demand for a vote reversal. For Carter the episode was an unrelieved diplomatic disaster. Arabs were outraged at what they viewed as a shameless withdrawal in the face of Jewish pressure. American Jews, urged to action by Israeli Defense Minister Ariel Sharon, doubted the honesty of the explanation and felt betrayed. Sharon told Jews in New York, "I do not like to interfere with internal United States affairs, but the question of Israeli security is a question for Jews anywhere in the world." To the world, the administration appeared out of control.

Senator Edward Kennedy was the main beneficiary of Carter's embarrassment. Calling the U.N. vote a "betrayal" of Israel, he won the Massachusetts primary 2-to-1 over Carter and also carried New York and Connecticut, where earlier polls had shown Carter ahead. In New York, Jews voted 4-to-1 for Kennedy. A member of the Israeli parliament said: "The American Jewish community showed itself to have the leverage to swing a vote over the issue of whether the president is good to Israel."

Mondale's measures did not placate the Jewish vote. In November Carter-Mondale became the first Democratic presidential ticket that failed to win a majority of the Jewish votes cast, exit polls showing it receiving, at the most, 47 percent.

After losing on the Carter ticket to Reagan-Bush, Mondale devoted himself full-time to campaigning for the presidency, with uncritical support of Israel becoming a principal plank in his platform. Early in the campaign, he dismissed the idea that Saudi Arabia would "become a strong assertive force for moderation" and urged the prepositioning of high-technology U.S. military equipment in the custody of Israeli "technicians, an arrangement that would eliminate any possibility that the equipment could be used for purposes independent of Israeli wishes."

Later, Mondale and his campaign team carefully avoided any relationship with Arab interests, or even Arab American interests. In June 1984, this zeal led Thomas Rosenberg, Mondale's finance director in Illinois, to return five $1,000 checks to Chicagoans of Arab ancestry who had presented them as campaign donations. He explained that some of the comments they had made in a personal meeting with Mondale amounted to "an anti-Israeli, anti-Semitic diatribe," but one of the five, Albert Joseph, a lifelong Democrat and owner of Hunter Publishing company, denied the accusation, recalling, "We passed 45 minutes with [Mondale] in the utmost friendliness and respect."

Joseph said that when the checks were returned he was informed by Joseph Gomez, at the time a member of the Mondale finance committee in Illinois, that Mondale's organization had decided to "take no more money from Arab Americans in the future." The Chicago publisher said he felt "insulted, betrayed and shocked." He told a reporter that Mondale was "disenfranchising a whole group of Americans." Upset by the decision to return the funds, Gomez, a Chicago banker and Hispanic leader, withdrew from the Mondale campaign. Gomez said the Mondale campaign decision confirmed his view that "people of Arab ancestry are the most persecuted group in America today."

Candidate Gary Hart's record of support for Israel was as unblemished as Mondale's, and his campaign organization displayed a similar indifference to Arab American sensibilities. Upon learning that the First American Bank in Washington—where he had done personal banking for years—had been purchased by a group of Middle East investors in 1982, Hart immediately closed out a campaign loan of $700,000 and severed all ties with the bank. His special counsel explained, "We didn't know it was an Arab bank. We got [Hart] out of it as soon as we knew." Hart's competitor for the nomination, Jesse Jackson, denounced the act as a "serious act of racism."

As a Senator, Hart voted for every pro-Israeli measure, opposed every initiative intended to provide arms to Arab states, and put his signature on every major letter and resolution helpful to the Israeli cause. When a few colleagues, like Senator John Glenn, condemned Israel's raid on the Iraqi nuclear installation, he deplored the condemnation.

Senators Ernest Hollings of South Carolina and Alan Cranston of California and former Florida governor Reuben Askew—early dropouts in the Democratic competition—were similarly uncritical in their support of Israel. So was Senator John Glenn of Ohio, who had been expected by many observers to take a middle road position on Mideast policy. In the past he had criticized Israeli military actions, supported the sale of F-15 aircraft to Saudi Arabia, and even suggested talks with the PLO: "I don't think we should reject talking with the PLO. . . . PLO terrorism is not unique in that area."

Bitten by the presidential bug, Glenn shifted ground in 1983, effectively ruling out such talks and excusing his vote for F-15 sale on the grounds that Saudi Arabia would otherwise have bought planes from France with "no strings attached."

In a speech to the Foreign Policy Association in New York, Glenn went much further, saying that the United States should recognize Jerusalem as the official capital of Israel once the terms of Camp David are completed or if negotiations break down completely. He characterized the PLO as "little more than a gang of thugs" and said the biggest obstacle to peace in the Middle East was Arab refusal to accept the legitimacy of Israel.

Although the speech did not allay Jewish suspicion, it cost him the support of citizens who felt the next president must respond to Arab as well as Israeli concerns. One of Glenn's closest colleagues, an Ohio Congressman, reacted with alarm and distress: "Glenn caved in, and he didn't have to do it. I was so demoralized by that statement I delayed making some calls to labor people in his behalf." The speech caused a veteran diplomat of the Johnson administration, former Ambassador Lucius Battle, to refuse to serve as a Glenn foreign policy adviser.

Only two candidates spoke up for a balanced policy in the Middle East: black civil rights activist Jesse L. Jackson and George McGovern, the 1972 Democratic presidential nominee. McGovern called for the creation of an independent Palestinian state and criticized Israeli military and settlement actions. His proposals were even more precise than those that brought John Connally's campaign to an end four years before.

In a speech at a Massachusetts synagogue in February, McGovern asked, "Is it not both bad politics and bad ethics to brand as anti-Israel an American politician who is willing to apply the same critical standards to Israeli policies that are applied to United States policies?" McGovern said that even though during his 22 years in Congress he had voted "100 percent" for measures providing economic and military aid to Israel, he nevertheless opposed Israel's invasion of Lebanon: "I don't think one sovereign nation has the right to invade another."

Neither McGovern nor Jackson had a serious prospect for nomination. In different ways, each presented himself in the role of "party conscience." The "Super Tuesday" primaries in March eliminated McGovern, and only Jackson's conscience remained in the campaign.

Jackson became controversial with U.S. Jews four years before his presidential bid when he carried his human rights activism abroad to Lebanon and there met PLO leader Yasser Arafat. Until then the former disciple of the Reverend Martin Luther King had worked mainly for black rights through his organization, People United to Save Humanity (PUSH), a Chicago-based group that received substantial Jewish financial support. In Lebanon, he came face-to-face with the misery of Palestinians, describing them as "the niggers of the Middle East."

Early in 1983, Jackson began traveling the country as a "noncandidate" but already drumming up interest in a "rainbow coalition" of interest groups. At a time when prospective candidates often try to blur controversial statements made in the past, Jackson reiterated his recommendation that the United States open a dialogue with the Palestine Liberation Organization. In a statement over New York television he said the United States can best help Israel by supporting the creation of a Palestinian homeland. Until that happens, he said, Palestinians will engage in "more acts of terrorism, more acts of desperation." He urged direct U.S. talks with the PLO to get the peace process moving, but he said our diplomats cannot even discuss this option, because "intimidation is so great" in the United States. These statements put him at odds with most Jewish leaders.

By the time he became a candidate in October 1983, *Washington Post* editorial editor Meg Greenfield called Jackson one of the nation's two greatest political orators (sharing the honor with President Reagan). He immediately enlivened the political scene by flying to Syria where he negotiated the release of a U.S. Navy pilot held captive there. He proclaimed, "The temperature has been lowered somewhat between Syria and America. The cycle of pain has been broken."

In the critical primaries beginning in March, he received impressive support in Illinois, New York and Pennsylvania, as well as southern states. In televised debates with Mondale and Hart, Jackson called for compassion in dealing with all people in the Middle East and rejected the "terrorist" labels so often attached to all Palestinians. While Mondale and Hart rejected Jackson's plea for a comprehensive Middle East peace involving a Palestinian homeland in the West Bank, the exchange was moderate in terms and expression, the first time that Palestinian rights had been discussed with civility in a presidential campaign.

Jackson found himself on the defensive when a reporter disclosed that in private conversation he had referred to Jews as "Hymies" and New York as "Hymietown," a slip that led many to charge him with being anti-Semitic. He was encumbered by the endorsement of controversial black leader Louis Farrakhan, who called Judaism a "dirty religion" and Hitler a "wickedly great man." Inspired by attacks from

Jewish leaders, the press never let up in pressing him concerning allegations of anti-Semitism and his relationship with Farrakhan. Even in his press conference in Cuba, where his endeavors brought the release of several U.S. citizens, the anti-Semitic theme dominated the questioning. In advance of the Democratic convention, the American Jewish Committee organized a campaign to keep Jackson from attaining prominence in the campaign of the expected nominee, Walter Mondale.

Despite these problems, he rallied support broadly enough to remain a major factor through the convention.

While no one expected Jackson to be on the presidential ticket, he emerged a winner even before the convention. He proved that a black man could be a credible candidate for the nation's highest office, even while supporting positions strongly opposed by the Israeli lobby. In doing so, he lifted the self-esteem of two ethnic groups often abused or neglected in U.S. society: blacks and Arab Americans.

The winner of the presidential sweepstakes, Ronald Reagan, was left to wonder if his heroic endeavors for Israel had paid off at the polls. He received 31 percent of the Jewish vote, down from the 40 percent he received in 1980.

Chapter 5

Penetrating the Defenses at Defense—and State

The Pentagon, that enormous, sprawling building on the banks of the Potomac, houses most of the Department of Defense's central headquarters. It is the top command for the forces and measures which provide Americans with security in a troubled world. Across the Potomac is the Department of State, a massive eight-story building on Washington's Foggy Bottom, the nerve center of our nation's worldwide diplomatic network. These buildings are channels through which flow each day thousands of messages dealing with the nation's top secrets. No one can enter either building without special identification or advance clearance. Armed guards seem to be everywhere, and in late 1983 concrete emplacements were added and heavy trucks strategically parked to provide extra buffers if a fanatic should launch an attack. These buildings are fortresses where the nation's most precious secrets are carefully guarded by the most advanced technology.

But how secure are the secrets?

"The leaks to Israel are fantastic. If I have something I want the secretary of state to know but don't want Israel to know, I must wait till I have a chance to see him personally."

This declaration comes from an ambassador still on active duty in a top assignment, reviewing his long career in numerous posts in the Middle East. Although hardly a household name in the United States, his is one of America's best-known abroad. Interviewed in the State Department, he speaks deliberately, choosing his words carefully.

"It is a fact of life that everyone in authority is reluctant to put anything on paper that concerns Israel if it is to be withheld from Israel's knowledge," says the veteran. "Nor do such people even feel free to speak in a crowded room of such things."

The diplomat offers an example from his own experience. "I received a call from a friend of mine in the Jewish community who wanted to warn me, as a friend, that all details of a lengthy document on Middle East policy that I had just dispatched overseas were 'out.'" The document was classified "top secret," the diplomat recalls. "I didn't believe what he said, so my friend read me every word of it over the phone."

His comments will upset pro-Israel activists, many of whom contend that both the State Department and Defense Departments are dominated by anti-Israeli "Arabists." Such domination, if it ever existed, occurs no longer. In the view of my diplomat source, leaks to pro-Israeli activists are not only pervasive throughout the two departments but "are intimidating and very harmful to our national interest." He says that because of "the ever-present Xerox machine" diplomats proceed on the assumption that even messages they send by the most secure means will be copied and passed on to eager hands. "We just don't dare put sensitive items on paper." A factor making the pervasive insecurity even greater is the knowledge that leaks of secrets to Israel, even when noticed—which is rare—are never investigated.

Whatever intelligence the Israelis want, whether political or technical, they obtain promptly and without cost at the source. Officials who normally would work vigilantly to protect our national interest by identifying leaks and bringing charges against the offenders are demoralized. In fact, they are disinclined even to question Israel's tactics for fear this activity will cause the Israeli lobby to mark them as trouble-makers and take measures to nullify their efforts, or even harm their careers.

The lobby's intelligence network, having numerous volunteer "friendlies" to tap, reaches all parts of the executive branch where matters concerning Israel are handled. Awareness of this seepage keeps officials—whatever rung of the ladder they occupy—from making or even proposing decisions that are in the U.S. interest.

If, for example, an official should state opposition to an Israeli request during a private interdepartmental meeting—or worse still, put it in an intraoffice memorandum—he or she must assume that this information will soon reach the Israeli embassy, either directly or through AIPAC. Soon after, the official should expect to be mentioned by name critically when the Israeli ambassador visits the secretary of state or other prominent U.S. official.

The penetration is all the more remarkable because much of it is carried out by U.S. citizens in behalf of a foreign government. The practical effect is to give Israel its own network of sources through which it is able to learn almost anything it wishes about decisions or resources of the U.S. government. When making procurement demands, Israel can display better knowledge of Defense Department inventories than the Pentagon itself.

Israel Finds the Ammunition—in Hawaii!

In its 1973 Yom Kippur war against Egypt and Syria, Israel sustained heavy losses in weapons of all kinds, especially tanks. It looked to the United States for the quickest possible resupply. Henry Kissinger was their avenue. Richard Nixon was entangled in the Watergate controversy and soon to leave the presidency, but under his authority the government agreed to deliver substantial quantities of tanks to Israel.

Tanks were to be taken from the inventory of U.S. military units on active duty, reserve units, even straight off production lines. Nothing was held back in the effort to bring Israeli forces back to desired strength as quickly as possible.

Israel wanted only the latest-model tanks equipped with 105 millimeter guns. But a sufficient number could not be found even by stripping U.S. forces. The Pentagon met the problem by filling part of the order with an earlier model fitted with 90-millimeter guns. When these arrived, the Israelis grumbled about having to take "second-hand junk." Then they discovered they had no ammunition of the right size and sent an urgent appeal for a supply of 90-millimeter rounds.

The Pentagon made a search and found none. Thomas Pianka, an officer then serving at the Pentagon with the International Security Agency, recalls: "We made an honest effort to find the ammunition. We checked everywhere. We checked through all the services—Army, Navy, Marines. We couldn't find any 90-millimeter ammunition at all." Pianka says the Pentagon sent Israel the bad news: "In so many words, we said: 'Sorry, we don't have any of the ammunition you need. We've combed all depots and warehouses, and we simply have none.' "

A few days later the Israelis came back with a surprising message: "Yes, you do. There are 15,000 rounds in the Marine Corps supply depot in Hawaii." Pianka recalls, "We looked in Hawaii and, sure enough, there they were. The Israelis had found a U.S. supply of 90-millimeter ammunition we couldn't find ourselves."

Richard Helms, director of the CIA during the 1967 Arab-Israel war, recalls an occasion when an Israeli arms request had been filled with the wrong items. Israeli officials resubmitted the request complete with all the supposedly top-secret code numbers and a note to Helms that said the Pentagon perhaps had not understood exactly which items were needed. "It was a way for them to show me that they knew exactly what they wanted," Helms says. Helms believes that during this period no important secret was kept from Israel.

Not only are the Israelis adept at getting the information they want—they are masters at the weapons procurement game. Les Janka, a former deputy assistant secretary of defense who is a specialist in Middle East policy, recalls Israeli persistence:

They would never take no for an answer. They never gave up. These emissaries of a foreign government always had a shopping list of wanted military items, some of them high technology that no other nation possessed, some of it secret devices that gave the United States an edge over any adversary. Such items were not for sale, not even to the nations with whom we have our closest, most formal military alliance—like those linked to us through the North Atlantic Treaty Organization.

Yet Janka learned that military sales to Israel were not bound by the guidelines and limitations which govern U.S. arms supply policy elsewhere. He says, "Sales to Israel were different. Very different."

Janka has vivid memories of a military liaison officer from the Israeli embassy who called at the Defense Department and requested approval to purchase a military item which was on the prohibited list because of its highly secret advanced technology: "He came to me, and I gave him the official Pentagon reply. I said, 'I'm sorry, sir, but the answer is no. We will not release that technology.' "

The Israeli officer took pains to observe the bureaucratic courtesies and not antagonize lower officials who might devise ways to block the sale. He said, "Thank you very much, if that's your official position. We understand that you are not in a position to do what we want done. Please don't feel bad, but we're going over your head." And that of course meant he was going to Janka's superiors in the office of the secretary of defense, or perhaps even to the White House.

Asked if he could remember an instance in which Israel failed to get what it wanted from the Pentagon, Janka pauses to reflect, then answers, "No, not in the long run."

Janka has high respect for the efficiency of Israeli procurement officers:

You have to understand that the Israelis operate in the Pentagon very professionally, and in an omnipresent way. They have enough of their people who understand our system well, and they have made friends at all levels, from top to bottom. They just interact with the system in a constant, continuous way that keeps the pressure on.

The Carter White House tried to establish a policy of restraint. Zbigniew Brzezinski, Carter's assistant for national security, remembers in an interview Defense Secretary Harold Brown's efforts to hold the line on technology transfer. "He was very tough with Israel on its requests for weapons and weapons systems. He often turned them down." But that was not the final word. For example, Brzezinski cites as the most notable example Brown's refusal to sell Israel the controversial antipersonnel weapon known as the cluster bomb. Despite written agreements restricting the use of these bombs, Israel used them twice against populated areas in Lebanon, causing death and injury to civilians. Brown responded by refusing to sell the deadly replacements. But even on that request, Israel eventually prevailed. President Reagan reversed the Carter administration policy, and cluster bombs were returned to the approved list.

Others who have occupied high positions in the executive branch were willing to speak candidly, but, unlike Janka, they did so with the understanding that their names would not be published. As one explains, "My career is not over. At least, I don't want it to be. Quoting me by name would bring it to an end." With the promise of anonymity, he and others gave details on the astounding process through which the Israeli lobby is able to penetrate the defenses at the Defense Department—and elsewhere.

Sometimes the act is simple theft. One official says, "Israelis were caught in the Pentagon with unauthorized documents, sometimes scooping up the contents of 'in boxes' on desk tops." He recalls that because of such activity a number of Israeli officials were told to leave the country. No formal charges of espionage have ever been filed, and Israel covered each such exit with an excuse such as family illness or some other personal reason: "Our government never made a public issue of it." He adds, "There is a much higher level of espionage by Israel against our government than has ever been publicly admitted."

The official recalls one day receiving a list of military equipment Israel wanted to purchase. Noting that "the Pentagon is Israel's 'stop-and-shop,'" he took it for granted that the Israelis had obtained clearances. So he followed usual procedure by circulating it to various Pentagon offices for routine review and evaluation:

One office instantly returned the list to me with a note: 'One of these items is so highly classified you have no right to know that it even exists.' I was instructed to destroy all copies of the request and all references to the particular code numbers. I didn't know what it was. It was some kind of electronic jamming equipment, top secret. Somehow the Israelis knew about it and acquired its precise specifications, cost and top secret code number. This meant they had penetrated our research and development labs, our most sensitive facilities.

Despite that somber revelation, no official effort was launched to discover who had revealed the sensitive information.

"They Always Get What They Want"

Israel's agents are close students of the U.S. system and work it to their advantage. Besides obtaining secret information by clandestine operations they apply open pressure on executive branch offices thoroughly and effectively. A weapons expert explains their technique:

If promised an answer on a weapons request in 30 days, they show up on the 31st day and announce: 'We made this request. It hasn't been approved. Why not? We've waited 30 days.' With most foreign governments, you can finesse a problem. You can leave it in the box on the desk. With Israel, you can't leave anything in the box.

He says the embassy knows exactly when things are scheduled for action:

It stays on top of things as does no other embassy in town. They know your agenda, what was on your schedule yesterday, and what's on it today and tomorrow. They know what you have been doing and saying. They know the law and regulations backwards and forwards. They know when the deadlines are.

He admires the resourcefulness of the Israelis in applying pressure:

They may leak to Israeli newspapers details of their difficulty in getting an approval. A reporter will come in to State or Defense and ask a series of questions so detailed they could be motivated only by Israeli officials. Sometimes the pressure will come, not from reporters, but from AIPAC.

If things are really hung up, it isn't long before letters or calls start coming from Capitol Hill. They'll ask, 'Why is the Pentagon not approving this item?' Usually, the letter is from the Congressman in whose district the item is manufactured. He will argue that the requested item is essential to Israel's security. He probably will also ask, 'Who is this bad guy in the Pentagon—or State—who is blocking this approval? I want his name. Congress would like to know.'

The American defense expert pauses to emphasize his point: "No bureaucrat, no military officer likes to be singled out by anybody from Congress and required to explain his professional duty."

He recalls an episode involving President Carter's secretary of defense, Harold Brown:

I remember once Israel requested an item on the prohibited list. Before I answered, I checked with Secretary Brown and he said, 'No, absolutely no. We're not going to give in to the bastards on this one.' So I said no.

Lo and behold, a few days later I got a call from Brown. He said, "The Israelis are raising hell. I got a call from [Senator Henry] 'Scoop' Jackson, asking why we aren't cooperating with Israel. It isn't worth it. Let it go."

When Jimmy Carter became president, the Israelis were trying to get large quantities of the AIM 9-L, the most advanced U.S. air-to-air missile. The Pentagon kept saying, "No, no, no. It isn't yet deployed to U.S. troops. The production rate is not enough to supply even U.S. needs. It is much too sensitive to risk being lost." Yet, early in his administration, Carter overruled the Pentagon, and Israel got the missiles.

A former administration official recalls a remarkable example of Israeli ingenuity:

Israel requested an item of technology, a machine for producing bullets. It was a big piece of machinery, weighed a lot, and it was exclusive. We didn't want other countries to have it, not even Israel. We knew if we said 'no,' the Israelis would go over our heads and somehow get approval. So, we kept saying we were studying the request. Then, to our astonishment, we discovered that the Israelis had already bought the machinery and had it in a warehouse in New York.

The Israelis did not have a license to ship the equipment, but they had nonetheless been able to make the purchase. When they were confronted by the Defense official, they said, "We slipped up. We were sure you'd say 'yes,' so we went ahead and bought it. And if you say no, here's the bill for storage, and here's what it will cost to ship it back to the factory." Soon after, the official recalled, someone in the State Department called and said, "Aw, give it to them," adding an earthy expletive.

This sense of futility sometimes reaches all the way to the top. Unrestricted supplies to Israel were especially debilitating in the 1974–77 period when U.S. military services were trying to recover from the 1973 Arab-Israeli war. In that conflict the United States stripped its own army and air forces in order to supply Israel.

During this period of U.S. shortage, Israel kept bringing in its shopping lists. The official recalls that the Pentagon would insist, "No, we can't provide what you want now. Come back in a year or so." In almost every one of those cases, he said, the Pentagon position was overruled by a political decision out of the White House. This demoralized the professionals in the Pentagon but, still worse, handicapped national security: "Defense Department decisions made according to the highest professional standards went by the board in order to satisfy Israeli requests."

"Exchanges" That Work Only in One Direction

The Israelis are particularly adept at exploiting sympathetic officials, as a former Pentagon officer explains:

We have people sympathizing with Israel in about every office in the Pentagon. A lot of military personnel have been in Israel, and some served there, making friends and, of course, a number of Israeli personnel study in U.S. military schools.

The guts, the energy, the skill of the Israelis are much admired in the Pentagon. Israelis are very good at passing back to us their performance records using our equipment. Throughout our military schools are always a large number of Israeli students. They develop great professional rapport with our people.

For years, the United States and Israel have exchanged military personnel. On paper, it works both ways. In practice, Israel is the major beneficiary. The process is more one of national character than anything clandestine. Israeli officers generally speak English, so it's no problem for them to come to America and quickly establish rapport with U.S. officers. On the other hand, hardly any U.S. officers speak Hebrew.

Language disparity is not the only problem. One of equal gravity is the American laxity in enforcing its security regulations. Many Israeli officers spend a year in a sensitive area—one of the U.S. training commands, or a research and development laboratory. At the start they are told they cannot enter certain restricted areas. Then, little by little, the rules are relaxed. A former Defense Department official explains:

The young Israeli speaks good English. He is likeable. You know how Americans are: they take him in, and he's their buddy. First thing you know, the restrictions are forgotten, and the Israeli officers are admitted to everything in our laboratories, our training facilities, our operational bases.

The former official quickly adds that rules are seldom relaxed at the other end:

This means that the officer training exchange is really a one-way street. Israel does not permit our officers, whether they speak Hebrew or not, to serve in sensitive military facilities in Israel. Many areas are totally off limits. They are very strict about that. Our officers cannot be present even when U.S.-supplied equipment and weapons are being delivered for the first time.

U.S. officers on exchange programs in Israel are, more often than not, given a desk in an office down the hall, and assigned just enough to do to keep them busy and prevent them from being too frustrated. Without knowledge of Hebrew, they have almost no way to know what is going on.

Camaraderie is also an element. Many employees in the executive branch, Jewish and non-Jewish, feel that the United States and Israel are somehow "in this together" and therefore cooperate without limit. Many also believe that Israel is a strategic asset and that weapons and other technology provided to Israel serve U.S. purposes. These feelings sometimes cause official restrictions on sharing of information to be modified or conveniently forgotten. As one Defense official puts it, the rules get "placed deeper and deeper into the file":

A sensitive document is picked up by an Israeli officer while his friend, a Defense Department official, deliberately looks the other way. Nothing is said. Nothing is written. And the U.S. official probably does not feel he has done anything wrong. Meanwhile the Israelis ask for more and more.

Despite such openhanded generosity, Israel does not hesitate to try to get classified information by espionage, a process that the United States years ago tried unsuccessfully to halt.

Mossad's Role in the Network

On one occasion—and only one—an employee of the U.S. government was punished for leaking classified information to Israel, and that was thirty years ago. In 1954, Fred Waller, a career foreign service officer in charge of the Israel-Jordan desk at the State Department, read in a classified document that a friend on the staff of the Israeli embassy—under suspicion for espionage—was being recommended by the FBI for expulsion from the United States.

Waller told associates that he considered the charges "unjustified" and, according to allegations, tipped off his friend at the Israeli embassy. For this, Waller was first marked for dismissal but later permitted simply to retire. "They wanted to throw him out without a nickel," states Don Bergus, who succeeded Waller in the State Department assignment. During those years of "McCarthyism," Bergus recalls, "the FBI was recommending that a lot of people be declared persona non grata. They were so happy with themselves in doing this. They knew damned well their recommendations wouldn't be acted upon."

Bergus recalls that Israel got a lot of information without espionage activity: "A lot of the information was volunteered. The apples were put on the table, and I don't blame Israel for taking them."

The investigation of Waller occurred during the high point of our government's concern over Israeli intelligence activities in the United States. Because the Eisenhower administration was trying to withhold weapons from Israel, as well as other states in the Middle East, a major attempt was made to bring leaks of classified information under control. A veteran diplomat recalls the crisis: "Employees in State and Defense were being suborned and bribed on a wide scale, and our government went to Israel and demanded that it stop."

After high-level negotiations following the Waller affair, the

United States and Israel entered into an unwritten agreement to share a larger volume of classified information and at the same time to restrict sharply the clandestine operations each conducted in the other's territory. The diplomat explains that it was supposed to be a two-way street: "The deal provided that we would get more from them too, and it was hoped the arrangement would end the thievery and payoff of U.S. employees."

The understanding with Israel did not end the problem, however, as the Israelis were not content to let the U.S. decide what classified information it would receive. Israel did not live up to the terms of the agreement and continued to engage broadly in espionage activities throughout the United States.

This was still true more than twenty years after the Waller episode, during the tenure of Atlanta mayor Andrew Young as U.S. ambassador to the United Nations during the Carter administration. Young recalls, "I operated on the assumption that the Israelis would learn just about everything instantly. I just always assumed that everything was monitored, and that there was a pretty formal network."

Young resigned as ambassador in August 1979 after it was revealed that he had met with Zuhdi Terzi, the PLO's UN observer, in violation of the U.S. pledge to Israel not to talk to the PLO. Press reports on Young's episode said Israeli intelligence learned of the meeting and that Israeli officials then leaked the information to the press, precipitating the diplomatic wrangle which led to Young's resignation.

Israel denied that its agents had learned of the Young-Terzi meeting. The press counselor at the Israeli embassy went so far as to tell the *Washington Star,* "We do not conduct any kind of intelligence activities in the United States." This denial must have been amusing to U.S. intelligence experts, one of whom talked with *Newsweek* magazine about Mossad's activities here: "They have penetrations all through the U.S. government. They do better than the KGB," said the expert, whom the magazine did not identify.

The *Newsweek* article continued:

With the help of American Jews in and out of government, Mossad looks for any softening in U.S. support and tries to get any technical intelligence the administration is unwilling to give to Israel.

'Mossad can go to any distinguished American Jew and ask for his help,' says a former CIA agent. The appeal is a simple one: 'When the call went out and no one heeded it, the Holocaust resulted.'

The U.S. tolerates Mossad's operations on American soil partly because of reluctance to anger the American Jewish community.

Another reason cited: Mossad is often a valuable source of information for U.S. intelligence.

Penetration by Israel continued at such a high level that a senior State Department official who has held the highest career positions related to the Middle East confides, "I urged several times that the U.S. quit trying to keep secrets from Israel. Let them have everything. They always get what they want anyway. When we try to keep secrets, it always backfires."

An analysis prepared by the CIA in 1979, 25 years after the U.S.-Israeli espionage agreement, gives no hint that Mossad had in any way restricted its operations within the United States. According to the 48-page secret document, entitled, *Israel: Foreign Intelligence and Security Services,* the United States continues to be a focus of Mossad operations:

In carrying out its mission to collect positive intelligence, the principal function of Mossad is to conduct agent operations against the Arab nations and their official representatives and installations throughout the world, particularly in Western Europe and the United States. . . .

Objectives in Western countries are equally important (as in the U.S.S.R. and East Europe) to the Israeli intelligence service. Mossad collects intelligence regarding Western, Vatican and UN policies toward the Near East; promotes arms deals for the benefit of the IDF; and *acquires data for silencing anti-Israel factions in the West.* [emphasis added]

Under "methods of operation," the CIA booklet describes the way in which Mossad makes use of domestic pro-Israeli groups. It states that "Mossad over the years has enjoyed some rapport with highly-placed persons and government offices in every country of importance to Israel." It adds, "Within Jewish communities in almost every country of the world, there are Zionists and other sympathizers, who render strong support to the Israeli intelligence effort." It explains,

Such contacts are carefully nurtured and serve as channels for information, deception material, propaganda and other purposes. . . . Mossad activities are generally conducted through Israeli official and semiofficial establishments; deep cover enterprises in the form of firms and organizations, some especially created for, or adaptable to, a specific objective, and penetrations effected within non-Zionist national and international Jewish organizations. . . .

Official organizations used for cover are: Israeli Purchasing Missions and Israeli Government Tourist, El Al and Zim offices. Israeli construction firms, industrial groups and international trade organizations also provide nonofficial cover. Individuals working under deep or illegal cover are normally charged with penetrating objectives that require a long-range, more subtle approach, or with activities in which the Israeli government can never admit complicity. . . .

The Israeli intelligence service depends heavily on the various Jewish communities and organizations abroad for recruiting agents and eliciting general information. The aggressively ideological nature of Zionism, which emphasizes that all Jews belong to Israel and must return to Israel, had had its drawbacks in enlisting support for intelligence operations, however, since there is considerable opposition to Zionism among Jews throughout the world.

Aware of this fact, Israeli intelligence representatives usually operate discreetly within Jewish communities and are under instructions to handle their missions with utmost tact to avoid embarrassment to Israel. They also attempt to penetrate anti-Zionist elements in order to neutralize the opposition.

The theft of scientific data is a major objective of Mossad operations, which is often attempted by trying to recruit local agents:

In addition to the large-scale acquisition of published scientific papers and technical journals from all over the world through overt channels, the Israelis devote a considerable portion of their covert operations to obtaining scientific and technical intelligence. This had included attempts to penetrate certain classified defense projects in the United States and other Western nations.

The Israeli security authorities (in Israel) also seek evidence of illicit love affairs which can be used as leverage to enlist cooperation. In one instance, Shin Beth (the domestic Israeli intelligence agency) tried to penetrate the U.S. Consulate General in Jerusalem through a clerical employee who was having an affair with a Jerusalem girl. They rigged a fake abortion case against the employee in an unsuccessful effort to recruit him. Before this attempt at blackmail, they had tried to get the Israeli girl to elicit information from her boyfriend.

Israel's espionage activities, according to the CIA, even included "crude efforts to recruit Marine guards [at the United States Embassy at Tel Aviv] for monetary reward." It reports that a hidden microphone "planted by the Israelis" was found in the office of the U.S. ambassador in 1954, and two years later telephone taps were found connected to two telephones in the residence of the United States military attaché. Retired diplomat Don Bergus recalls the episode: "Our ambassador, Ed Lawson, reported the bug in a telegram to Washington that went something like this: 'Department must assume that all conversations in my office as well as texts of my telegrams over the last six months are known to the Israelis.' Ed had dictated all telegrams to his secretary."

During the Iranian hostage crisis in 1980, columnist Jack Anderson quoted "U.S. intelligence reports," actually supplied by the Israeli embassy, by way of the American Israel Public Affairs Committee, that the PLO had mined the embassy to frustrate any rescue attempt by the United States. The intelligence reports proved to be bogus.

Asked about the present activities of Mossad in the United States, a senior official in the Department of State, is candid:

We have to assume that they have wire taps all over town. In my work I frequently pick up highly-sensitive information coming back to me in conversations with people who have no right to have these secrets. I will ask, 'I wonder who has the wiretaps out to pick that up,' and usually the answer is, 'I don't know, but it sure isn't us.'

The same official says he never gives any highly sensitive information over his office phone. "You have to respect their ingenuity. The Mossad people know how to get into a system."

"No One Needs Trouble Like That"

Leaks of classified information remain a major problem for policy-makers. An official whose identity I promised to withhold says that during the Carter administration his colleagues feared even to speak up even in small private meetings. When Israeli requests were turned down at interagency meetings attended at most by fifteen people—all of whom knew the discussions were to be considered top secret—within hours "the Israeli military attaché, the political officer, or the ambassador—or all of them at once—were lodging protests. They knew exactly who said what, even though nothing had been put on paper." He adds, "No one needs trouble like that."

He says David McGiffert, assistant secretary of defense for international security affairs, was often subjected to pressure. Frequently the Israeli embassy would demand copies of documents that were still in the draft stage and had not reached his desk.

To counteract these kinds of leaks some officials have taken their own precautions.

Although no charges are ever brought against those suspected of leaking information to Israel, they are sometimes bypassed when classified documents are handed out. The word is forwarded discreetly to drop their names from the distribution list. One such official served during both the Carter and Reagan administrations and remains today in a sensitive foreign policy position. When he occupied a senior position in the Carter administration, his superiors were instructed to "clear nothing" in the way of classified documents related to the Middle East through his office and used extreme caution when discussing such matters in his presence. One of his colleagues says, admiringly,

"He is brilliant. He belongs in government, but he has a blind spot where Israel is concerned."

To strike back at government officials considered to be unsympathetic to Israeli needs the pro-Israel lobby singles them out for personal attack and even the wrecking of their careers. In January 1977 a broad-scale purge was attempted immediately after the inauguration of President Carter. The perpetrator was Senator Richard Stone of Florida, a Democrat, a passionate supporter of Israel. When he was newly installed as chairman of the Senate Subcommittee on the Middle East, he brought along with him a "hit list" on a call at the White House. In his view fifteen officials were not sufficiently supportive of Israel and its weapons needs, and he wanted them transferred to positions where their views would create no problems for Israel. Marked for removal were William Quandt, Brzezinski's assistant for Middle East matters, and Les Janka, who had served on the National Security Council under Ford. The others were career military officers, most of them colonels. Stone's demands were rejected by Brzezinski and, according to a senior White House official, "after pressing reasonably hard for several days," the Senator gave up. Although unsuccessful, his demands caused a stir. One officer says, "I find it very ironic that a U.S. Senator goes to a U.S. President's National Security Adviser and tells him to fire Americans for insufficient loyalty to another country."

Leaks Disrupt American Foreign Policy

Four times in recent years, major leaks of information to Israel caused serious setbacks in our relations with Israel's neighbors. The first destroyed an arrangement with Jordan that had been serving U.S. security interests successfully for years.

Under a long-standing secret agreement, Jordan's King Hussein received secret financial support from the CIA. It was a carry-over of a normal support system developed by the British. Under it, moderate leaders like Hussein received payments in exchange for helpful services which enabled them to maintain their political base without having to account to anyone locally.

Early in the Carter administration, a White House review was ordered of all covert operations, including, of course, the CIA payments in the Middle East. Nineteen people attended the review meeting in early February 1977, and one of the senior officials who attended recalls: "I feared at the time that leaks were certain to occur." A few days later, the *Washington Post* headlined a story, "CIA Paid Millions to Jordan's King Hussein." Written by Bob Woodward, the article said that over a period of twenty years the CIA had made "secret annual payments totaling millions of dollars" to Hussein. It said the payment in 1976 was $750,000, and the disclosure provoked wide international controversy.

When he read Woodward's *Washington Post* article, Senator James G. Abourezk of South Dakota called in Harold Saunders, then an official of the National Security Council, and received confirmation that Israel, as well as Jordan, was receiving secret payments from the CIA. Abourezk recalls that Saunders estimated that during the same period that Hussein received about $10 million, over $70 million went to Israel. The payments helped Israel support its own burgeoning foreign aid program in Africa, payments which Abourezk believes still continue. Hussein used the funds to maintain a strong relationship with the Bedouin tribes of his desert kingdom.

After confirming the information, Abourezk called Woodward and asked if he was aware of the CIA aid to Israel when he wrote about the payments to Jordan. Abourezk recalls, "Woodward admitted knowledge of the payments to Israel but said he thought the circumstances were different and that was why he did not write about them." Abourezk recalls being so outraged at this explanation and Woodward's "selective" coverage of the news that he shouted over the phone, "It seems to me that sort of judgment is better left up to the readers of the *Post.*"

Abourezk tried unsuccessfully for several months to interest Washington journalists in the news that Israel too received CIA payments. Months later, after the furor over Jordan had died down, Jack Anderson mentioned the payments to Israel in his syndicated column. There was no public outcry.

The CIA arrangement with Jordan was viewed by Zbigniew Brzezinski, Carter's National Security Adviser, as "very valuable" to the United States. But as a result of the publicity, he recalls, the arrangement had to be cancelled, Hussein was embarrassed, and the United States suffered a setback in its relations with the Arab world.

The next leak so embarrassed U.S.-Saudi relations that a career intelligence officer was ordered out of Saudi Arabia. After the fall of the Shah of Iran in 1979, there was speculation that the Saudi regime also might fall. The CIA station chief in Saudi Arabia reported this information to Washington in a secret cable, citing it as only a rumor, not a forecast. On the basis of this and other reports and analysis in Washington, the CIA produced a paper given restricted circulation in the official policy community. That paper discussed the stability of the Saudi regime. A report was leaked to news services, which erroneously stated that the CIA station chief in Saudi Arabia predicted the fall of the Saudi government within six months.

John C. West, former governor of South Carolina, was the U.S. ambassador to Saudi Arabia at the time. West recalls the CIA story: "Of course, there was no such prediction that the Saudi government would fall, but that's the way it was printed." The episode caused deep resentment in the Saudi capital and the station chief was asked to leave.

West had other problems with leaks. On another occasion, this time in 1980, a government employee's leak of secret information destroyed a sensitive mission to Saudi Arabia and, in West's opinion, led to a costly confrontation between the president and the Senate. The leak came from a secret White House meeting where West and a small group of high officials decided several Saudi requests to buy military equipment. "The arms package was of very, very great concern to the Saudis," West recalls:

It was essential that they, as serious customers, not be embarrassed. As we went over the items, I said, 'Whatever we do, we must not say 'no' to the Saudis on any of these. It's very important that we avoid a flat turn down.'

The group agreed to approve four of the requests, but found the other two highly controversial. The Saudis wanted to buy high-technology AWACS intelligence-gathering aircraft and special bomb racks for F-15 fighter planes they already owned. These sales would cause an uproar in neighboring Israel, and the Carter administration did not want to offend either government.

West worked out solutions to both problems. "Let's do this," he advised the group:

The bomb racks haven't yet been adopted as a part of the U.S. system. There are still some bugs that need to be worked out. Let's explain that we won't make a decision until we decide the bomb racks are right and meet our own requirements. Given that explanation, the Saudis will go along.

On the AWACS dilemma, West predicted the Saudis would withdraw their request to buy the planes if the United States would resume a practice initiated during the tense period following the fall of the Shah of Iran. At that time, he says, "The U.S. met Saudi intelligence needs by operating AWACS planes from Saudi bases and supplying to the Saudi government the information accumulated on these flights." West told the group, "I will explain to the Saudis that the U.S. can't deliver the new planes until 1985, and by then the technology will probably be outdated."

West's recommendations were accepted. The Saudis would be permitted to buy the four non-controversial items, and the other two requests would be set aside in a way that would cause no offense. West says, "I was instructed to explain the decisions personally when I returned to Saudi Arabia."

But once again, sensitive information was leaked in a twisted form. West recalls,

The very day I left for Saudi Arabia, the *New York Times* published a story headlined: 'Carter Is Said to Refuse Saudi Request for Arms.' Other news services reported that at a high level meeting the White House decided to turn down the Saudi request, and after debating several days how to break the news, instructed West simply to tell them 'no.'

I knew nothing of the leak until I landed in Saudi Arabia ready to meet Saudi officials in appointments already scheduled. The news story hit me in the face when I got off the plane. It was terrible.

The *Times* story delivered the blunt negative answer that West had warned must be avoided at all cost. "It destroyed all chance of success in my diplomatic mission."

West does not know how the newspapers got the damaging report. Only a few had attended the meeting in the White House, but notes were taken, memos prepared. He speculates that the story, with deliberate inaccuracies, was leaked by "someone determined to worsen relations between the U.S. and Saudi Arabia."

A few months later, the Carter administration resumed AWACS operations based in Saudi Arabia. Nonetheless, embarrassed by the earlier headlines, Saudi officials decided to insist on buying their own AWACS planes and launched a public relations campaign in the United States that culminated in a costly, bruising showdown two years later in the U.S. Senate. Without the leak, West feels, the Saudis would have accepted the Carter administration decision and the AWACS controversy would never have surfaced. If so, the U.S. taxpayers might have been spared an extra $1.2 billion in aid to Israel—the price Israel's lobby demanded as compensation when it lost the AWACS vote in the Senate.

West recalls that leaks to Israel were so frequent that he imposed strict rules on communications:

I would never put anything in any cable that was critical of Israel. Still, because of the grapevine, there was never any secret from the government of Israel. The Israelis knew everything, usually by the time it got to Washington. I can say that without qualification.

West adds that if he wanted to communicate any information that was in any way critical of Israel, he felt more confident using an open telephone line than a top-secret cable.

West's problems with the lobby did not end with his departure from diplomatic service. Before leaving his post in 1981, in an interview in Jeddah, he told a reporter the "most difficult question" he encountered during his work as ambassador was trying to explain why talks between the U.S. and the PLO were not permitted.

This mild comment caused trouble when West returned to private life. His appointment as distinguished professor of Middle East studies at the University of South Carolina brought a strong protest from a group of South Carolina Jews led by State Senator Hyman Rubin. "The group charged bias," West recalls, "and the protest so disturbed the university administration that public announcement of my appointment was delayed for more than a year." When he learned of the protest, West asked Rubin to arrange a meeting with his group. The result was a candid two-hour discussion between twenty critics and the ambassador-turned-professor. In its wake, West says, "The controversy subsided," and he assumed his post.

In 1983 the Israeli embassy itself directly arranged a news leak which effectively blocked U.S. support for a Jordanian rapid deployment force, though it concealed its own role. The White House was privately considering a proposal under which the U.S. would help Jordan establish an airborne unit able to provide swift help if nearby Arab states were threatened. A White House official explains,

When the Bahrainis asked for help during the Iranian crisis, Jordan wanted to help but had no way to get there. The Jordanian force idea is sound. Arabs need to be able to defend their own territory. Instead of having an American rapid deployment force going to the Persian Gulf, it would be better for Arabs to do the job themselves. Better to have Muslims defending Muslim territory than American boys.

L. Dean Brown, former ambassador to Jordan, says the proposal would have been a "godsend" to the small countries of the gulf. "What Jordan needed were C-130 transport planes in order to move light weapons by air."

At first, Israel raised no objection. Told of the plan while he was still Israel's ambassador to the United States, Moshe Arens simply listened. A White House official close to the project recalls, "We told Arens that we were going to have Israeli interests in mind, but we were going ahead. We would proceed in a way that would not harm Israel."

The non-committal Israeli reaction was mistaken as a green light, and, after getting clearance from the intelligence committees of Congress, the Reagan administration proceeded with secret negotiations.

After Arens left to become Israel's defense minister, the proposal ran into trouble. Briefed on the progress of the project by Secretary of State Shultz, Meir Rosenne, Israel's new ambassador, suddenly raised objections. The Israeli embassy tipped off a reporter for an Israeli radio station about the issue, suggesting he go to Congressman Clarence Long, chairman of the House Appropriations Subcommittee that handles aid to Israel, and "he will tell you the whole story." Long cooperated, Israeli radio broke the story, and with controversy swirling in Israel, AIPAC joined the fray with its own salvos.

A White House official recalls the effect. "Once this became public," he says, "King Hussein of Jordan backed away too. He didn't want to be seen as a tool of the Americans." The official says his colleagues at the White House were convinced that the whole thing was a carefully engineered leak by the Israeli embassy. It was delayed only until Arens left Washington. "It was a carom shot, bounced through Doc Long and Israeli radio in such a way that it would not be traced back to the embassy." Former U.S. Ambassador Brown describes the leak by the Israelis as "purposeful."

"The State Department Leaks Like a Sieve"

A leak got Talcott Seelye, ambassador to Syria, in hot water in 1981 when he sent a classified cable from Syria to the State Department protesting a resolution just introduced in the House of Representatives by Stephen Solarz, a member of the Foreign Affairs Committee. Solarz represents a New York district in which Jews of Syrian origin are numerous, and his resolution criticized Syria for not permitting more Jews to leave that country.

In the cable Seelye warned that approval of the resolution would make Syria less cooperative, not more. Seelye explains, "My cable said that if Solarz is sincere and serious about getting the Jews out of Syria, he will not go ahead with this resolution; on the other hand, if he merely wants to make points with the voters, he should do something else." The cable was leaked to Solarz, who called Secretary of State Vance and demanded: "Look, you've got to get Seelye out of there." Vance was furious over the leak.

Seelye kept his job, but the State Department did little to defeat the resolution. When the resolution was taken up in the House, only one no vote was heard.

The employee guilty of leaking the cable to Solarz worked under Ed Sanders, Carter's official liaison with the Jewish community, who then had an office in the State Department as well as the White House. No punishment was imposed; the employee was simply transferred to a different job.

The leak confirmed the fears of diplomats who had strongly opposed locating a Jewish liaison office in the State Department. One diplomat of the period describes Sanders as "a very decent human being, and he was there to do his job at the request of the president. At the same time, some of the stuff we were doing should not get out of the building to anybody."

Harold Saunders, a scholarly career Middle East specialist who occasionally got in hot water by noting Arab concerns, was then assistant secretary of state and voiced his feelings to Vance: "How would you like having somebody from U.S. Steel sitting in our Economic Bureau's tariff office?" Vance too opposed the arrangement, but Sanders's State Department office was not closed for months.

Seelye pinpoints a very mundane reason for the wave of leaks: the prevalence of copying machines. He says that as ambassador to Syria he operated on the assumption that the Israelis would learn everything he sent to Washington. He says, "The trouble with our system of classification is that even when we limit distribution, say, to just twenty copies for the whole government, one of the offices on the list will make a dozen extra copies for their own use, and so on. It's hard to control."

Veterans in government lay the blame for much of the leaking on political appointees holding important positions in the State Department and not on career diplomats. In the early months of the Reagan Administration, National Security Adviser Richard Allen was viewed as highly sympathetic to Israeli interests and, in fact, as the de facto clearance officer, encouraging the placement of personnel acceptable to the state of Israel in key positions. After Allen's departure from government, a senior officer of the State Department recalls, "No one was needed to replace him, as people with pro-Israeli interests—we call them mail carriers—are spotted in every important office."

A senior diplomat, now on leave, says: "The leaks are almost never traced to professional foreign service officers. In my experience, leaks are normally by staff members brought in by political appointees, and every administration brings in a lot of them. They seem to be all over the place." He says these "loose-tongued amateurs" are prominent on the seventh floor, where offices of senior State Department officials are located, and on the staff for policy planning, as well as in the White House. This gives them ready access to sensitive material. "Unfortunately," he adds, "they do not have the same idea of discipline and sense of loyalty as the professionals."

Some leaks originate from a few members of Congress and their staff. A former Defense Department official recalls,

There were individuals on Capitol Hill that the Pentagon viewed as conduits to Israel. No question about it. A number of times we would get requests from

Congressmen or Senators for intelligence materials. We knew damn well that these materials were not for their own edification. The information would be passed to Israel.

For example, we would get a letter from a Congressman, stating he had heard the Pentagon had done a study on the military balance between Israel and its Arab neighbors. He would like to have a copy of it. We would respond, 'We can't give you a copy, but we can give you an oral briefing.' The usual answer is, 'Sorry, we are not interested in an oral briefing.'

The Case of Stephen Bryen

In the opinion of all these sources, Israeli penetration of State and Defense has reached an all-time high during the Reagan administration. In 1984 people known to have intimate links with Israel were employed in offices throughout the bureaucracy and particularly in the Defense Department, where top-secret weapons technology and other sensitive matters are routinely handled.

The bureaucracy is headed by Fred Ikle, undersecretary of defense for international security. The three personalities of greatest importance in his area are Richard Perle, Ikle's assistant for international security policy; Stephen Bryen, Perle's principal deputy, whose assigned speciality was technology transfer; and Noel Koch, principal deputy to Richard Armitage, assistant secretary for international security affairs. Koch was formerly employed by the Zionist Organization of America. Perle previously served on the staff of Democratic Senator Henry Jackson of Washington, one of Israel's most ardent boosters, and had the reputation of being a conduit of information to the Israeli government. Stephen Bryen came to the administration under the darkest cloud of all.

Bryen's office is represented on the inter-agency unit, known as the National Disclosure Policy Commission, which approves technology transfers related to weapons systems. The commission includes representatives of State, National Security Council and the intelligence services, as well as Defense. Bryen was publicly accused in 1978 of offering a top-secret document on Saudi air bases to a group of visiting Israeli officials.

The accusation arose from an incident reported by Michael Saba, a journalist and former employee of the National Association of Arab Americans. Saba, who readily agreed to a lie detector test by the FBI, said he overheard Bryen make the offer while having breakfast in a Washington restaurant. At the time, Bryen was on the staff of the Senate Foreign Relations Committee. A senior career diplomat expresses the problem State Department officials encountered during that period: "Whenever Bryen was in the room we always had to use extreme caution." During the controversy, Bryen was suspended from the committee staff but later reinstated. He later left the committee position and became executive director of the Jewish Institute for National Security Affairs (JINSA), an organization founded—according to *The Jewish Week*—to "convince people that the security of Israel and the United States is interlinked." When Bryen moved to a position in the Defense Department, his wife, Shoshona, replaced him at JINSA.

After nine months the investigating attorneys recommended that a grand jury be empanelled to consider the evidence against Bryen. According to the Justice Department, other witnesses testified to Bryen's Israeli contacts. Indeed, a Justice Department memorandum dated January 26, 1979, discussed "unresolved questions thus far, which suggest that Bryen is (a) gathering classified informations for the Israelis, (b) acting as their unregistered agent and (c) lying about it. . . ." The Justice Department studied the complaint for two years. Although it found that Bryen had an "unusually close relationship with Israel," it made no charges and in late 1979 closed the file. Early in 1981 Bryen was hired as Richard Perle's chief deputy in the Pentagon. He remains in this highly responsible position today.

Perle himself was also the subject of an Israel-related controversy. An FBI summary of a 1970 wiretap recorded Perle discussing classified information with someone at the Israeli embassy. He came under fire in 1983 when newspapers reported he received substantial payments to represent the interests of an Israeli weapons company. Perle denied conflict of interest, insisting that, although he received payment for these services after he had assumed his position in the Defense Department, he was between government jobs when he worked for the Israeli firm.

Because of these controversies both Perle and Bryen were given assignments in the Reagan administration which—it was expected— would keep them isolated from issues relating to Israel. But, observes a State Department official, it has not worked out that way. Sensitive questions of technology transfer which affect Israeli interests are often settled in the offices of Perle and Bryen.

Despite the investigation, Bryen holds one of the highest possible security classifications at the Department of Defense. It is a top secret/ code word classification, which gives him access to documents and data anywhere in the government, almost without limit. A high official in the Department of State explains the significance of his access: "With this classification, Bryen can keep up to date not only on what the United States has in the way of technology, but on what we hope to have in the future as the result of secret research and development."

"I'll Take Care of the Congress"

Admiral Thomas Moorer recalls a dramatic example of Israeli lobby power from his days as chairman of the Joint Chiefs of Staff. At the time of the 1973 Arab-Israeli war Mordecai Gur, the defense attaché at the Israeli embassy who later became commander-in-chief of Israeli forces, came to Moorer demanding that the U.S. provide Israel with aircraft equipped with a high technology air-to-surface anti-tank missile called the Maverick. At the time, the U.S. had only one squadron so equipped. Moorer recalls telling Gur:

I can't let you have those aircraft. We have just one squadron. Besides, we've been testifying before the Congress convincing them we need this equipment. If we gave you our only squadron, Congress would raise hell with us.

Moorer looks at me with a steady piercing gaze that must have kept a generation of ensigns trembling in their boots: "And do you know what he said? Gur told me, 'You get us the airplanes; I'll take care of the Congress.'" Moorer pauses, then adds, "And he did." America's only squadron equipped with Mavericks went to Israel.

Moorer, speaking in his office in Washington as a senior counselor at the Georgetown University Center for Strategic and International Studies, says he strongly opposed the transfer but was overruled by "political expediency at the presidential level." He notes President Richard Nixon was then in the throes of Watergate. "But," he adds,

I've never seen a President—I don't care who he is—stand up to them [the Israelis]. It just boggles your mind.

They always get what they want. The Israelis know what is going on all the time. I got to the point where I wasn't writing anything down.

If the American people understood what a grip those people have got on our government, they would rise up in arms. Our citizens don't have any idea what goes on.

On another occasion, fear of lobby pressure caused a fundamental decision on further military sales to Israel to be deliberately pigeonholed. It involved the general consensus of professionals in the Pentagon that Israel had enough military power for any need as of 1975. By then it had reached a level of regional superiority that was overwhelming. In December 1976 the Middle East Arms Transfer Panel wrote a report to Secretary of Defense Donald Rumsfeld, concluding that no additional arms sales to Israel were necessary. However, Rumsfeld did not send the report to the State Department. It was the closing days of the Ford administration, and its transmission as an official document and subsequent leakage would have given the Democrats a partisan edge with the Israeli lobby.

Jewish groups in the United States are often pressed into service to soften up the secretary of state and other officials, especially in advance of a visit to the United States by the Israeli prime minister. A senior Defense official explains, "Israel would always have a long shopping list for the prime minister to take up. We would decide which items were worth making into an issue and which were not. We would try to work things out in advance." There was the constant threat that the prime minister might take an arms issue straight to the president, and the tendency was to clear the agenda of everything possible. "We might decide that we don't want this chicken shit electronic black box to be an issue between the president and prime minister, we would approve it in advance."

On one such occasion, Ed Sanders, President Carter's adviser on Jewish affairs, brought a complaint to the National Security Council offices: "I'm getting a lot of flack from Jewish Congressmen on the ALQ 95-J. What is this thing? And why are we being so nasty about it? Shouldn't we let Israel have it? The president is getting a lot of abuse because the Pentagon won't turn it loose." It was a high technology radar jamming device, and soon it was approved for shipment to Israel.

In advance of Carter's decision to provide a high technology missile to Israel, a procession of Jewish groups came, one after another, to say:

Please explain to us why the Pentagon is refusing to sell AIM 9-L missiles to Israel? Don't you know what this means? This missile is necessary so the Israelis will be able to shoot down the counterpart missile on the Mig 21 which carries the Eight Ball 935.

A former high-ranking official in security affairs cites the intimidating effect of this procession on career specialists:

When you have to explain your position day after day, week after week to American Jewish groups—first, say, from Kansas City, then Chicago, then East Overshoe—you see what you are up against. These are people from different parts of the country, but they come in with the very same information, the same set of questions, the same criticism.

They know what you have done even in private meetings. They will say, 'Mr. Smith, we understand that in interagency meetings, you frequently take a hard line against technology transfers to Israel. We'd like you to explain yourself.'

They keep you on the defensive. They treat you as if you are the long pole in the anti-Israeli tent no matter how modest the position you have taken.

Jewish groups in turn press Capitol Hill into action:

We'll get letters from Congressmen: 'We need an explanation. We're hearing from constituents that Israel's security is threatened by the refusal of the Pentagon to release the AIM 9-L missile. Please, Mr. Secretary, can you give me your rationale for the refusal?'

The certainty of such lobby pressure can be costly to taxpayers. In one instance it kept the U.S. from trying to recover U.S.-supplied arms which Israel captured from Lebanon. During Israel's invasion of Lebanon in 1982, its forces overran and captured tons of equipment of all sorts, including weapons supplied by the United States to the government forces in that country. Knowledge of this came to light in an unusual way a year later.

During a visit to Lebanon, the Reverend George Crossley, of Deltona, Florida, was shown cases of U.S.-made M-16 rifles which Israeli officials said were captured from Palestinian forces. Crossley noted they carried a Saudi insignia and wrote down the serial numbers. Saudi Arabia, of course, had no forces involved in the fighting in Lebanon, and the clergyman jumped to the conclusion that rifles the U.S. had sold to Saudi Arabia were turned over to PLO forces in Lebanon, then captured by the Israelis. If true, this would have been a violation of a U.S. law which prohibits transfer of U.S.-supplied weapons to another country without permission.

Crossley wrote to his Congressman, Bill Chappell, Jr., who asked the State Department to explain. A check of records showed the U.S. had never sold M-16 rifles to the Saudis, who prefer a German make. The rifles in question were provided directly to forces of the Lebanese government.

The episode got public attention at a time when the U.S. government, at great expense, was once again equipping Lebanese forces. A White House official, reading accounts of the Crossley affair, asked the desk officer at the Pentagon why the U.S. didn't demand that the Israelis give back these rifles and all other equipment they had taken from the Lebanese army. The Pentagon had an accurate list of what the U.S. had supplied. Surely, he argued, the Israeli government could be forced to cooperate, and this would ease U.S. costs substantially.

The desk officer exploded: "Are you kidding? No way in hell! Who needs that? I answer maybe one hundred letters a month for the secretary of defense in reply to Congressmen who bitch and complain about our mistreatment of Israel. Do you think that I want to increase my work load answering more shitty letters? Do you think I am going to recommend action that will increase the flow of problem letters to my boss? Be serious."

Every official of prominence in the State and Defense Departments proceeds on the assumption—and certainty—that at least once a week he will have to deal with a group from the Jewish community. One of them summarizes,

One has to keep in mind the constant character of this pressure. The public affairs staff of the Near East Bureau in the State Department figures it will spend about 75 percent of its time dealing with Jewish groups. Hundreds of such groups get appointments in the executive branch each year.

In acting to influence U.S. policy in the Middle East, the Israeli lobby has the field virtually to itself. Other interest groups and individuals who might provide some measure of counterbalancing pressure have only begun to get organized.

Americans of Arab ancestry, for example, remain divided. A diplomat who formerly served in a high position in the State Department gives this example:

When a group concerned about U.S. bias favoring Israel would come in for an appointment, more often than not those in the group start arguing among themselves. One person will object to a heavy focus on Palestinian problems. Another will want Lebanon's problems to be central to the discussion. I would just sit back and listen. They had not worked out in advance what they wanted to say.

Les Janka had similar experiences. In a commentary at a gathering sponsored by the American Enterprise Institute, he recalled visits by groups sympathetic to Arab problems:

Their complaints tended to be fairly general. They would say, 'We want the U.S. to be more even-handed, more balanced,' or 'We want you to be more interested in the Palestinians.' Nothing specific. In contrast the Jewish groups come in with a very specific list of demands.

On all kinds of foreign policy issues the American people just don't make their voices heard. Jewish groups are the exceptions. They are prepared, superbly briefed. They have their act together. It is hard for bureaucrats not to respond.

Chapter 6

The Assault on "Assault"

Although Israel's lobby seems able at will to penetrate our nation's strongest defenses in order to gain the secret information it wishes, when the lobby's objective is keeping such information secret, our defenses suddenly become impenetrable.

After seventeen years, James M. Ennes Jr., a retired officer of the U.S. Navy, is still having difficulty prying loose documents which shed light on the worst peacetime disaster in the history of our Navy. In this quest, he has encountered resistance by the Department of Defense, the Anti-Defamation League of B'nai B'rith, the American Israel Public Affairs Committee, the book publishing industry, the news media, and the Israeli Foreign Ministry. The resistance, seemingly coordinated on an international scale, is especially perplexing because Ennes' goal is public awareness of an episode of heroism and tragedy at sea which is without precedent in American history.

As the result of a program of concealment supported by successive governments in both Israel and the United States, hardly anyone remembers the miraculous survival of the USS *Liberty* after a devastating assault by Israeli forces on June 8, 1967, left 34 sailors dead, 171 injured, and the damaged ship adrift with no power, rudder or means of communication.

The sustained courage of Captain William L. McGonagle and his crew in these desperate circumstances earned the *Liberty* a place of honor in the annals of the U.S. Navy. But, despite energetic endeavors, including those of Ennes, McGonagle's officer of the deck that day, the entries remain dim and obscure. Ennes's stirring book-length account of the attack, *Assault on the Liberty*, itself continues to be under heavy assault five years after publication.

The episode and its aftermath were so incredible that Admiral Thomas L. Moorer, who became chairman of the Joint Chiefs of Staff a month after the attack, observes, "If it was written as fiction, nobody would believe it."

Certain facts are clear. The attack was no accident. The *Liberty* was assaulted in broad daylight by Israeli forces who knew the ship's identity. The *Liberty,* an intelligence-gathering ship, had no combat capability and carried only light machine guns for defense. A steady breeze made its U.S. flag easily visible. The assault occurred over a period of nearly two hours—first by air, then torpedo boat. The ferocity of the attacks left no doubt: the Israeli forces wanted the ship and its crew destroyed.

The public, however, was kept in the dark. Even before the American public learned of the attack, U.S. government officials began to promote an account satisfactory to Israel. The American Israel Public Affairs Committee worked through Congressmen to keep the story under control. The President of the United States, Lyndon B. Johnson, ordered and led a cover-up so thorough that sixteen years after he left office, the episode was still largely unknown to the public—and the men who suffered and died have gone largely unhonored.

The day of the attack began in routine fashion, with the ship first proceeding slowly in an easterly direction in the eastern Mediterranean, later following the contour of the coastline westerly about fifteen miles off the Sinai Peninsula. On the mainland, Israeli forces were winning smashing victories in the third Arab-Israeli war in nineteen years. Israeli Chief of Staff Yitzhak Rabin, announcing that the Israelis had taken the entire Sinai and broken the blockade on the Strait of Tiran, declared: "The Egyptians are defeated." On the eastern front the Israelis had overcome Jordanian forces and captured most of the West Bank.

At 6 A.M. an airplane, identified by the *Liberty* crew as an Israeli Noratlas, circled the ship slowly and departed. This procedure was repeated periodically over an eight-hour period. At 9 A.M. a jet appeared at a distance, then left. At 10 A.M., two rocket-armed jets circled the ship three times. They were close enough for their pilots to be observed through binoculars. The planes were unmarked. An hour later the Israeli Noraltas returned, flying not more than 200 feet directly above the *Liberty* and clearly marked with the Star of David. The ship's crew members and the pilot waved at each other. This plane returned every few minutes until 1 P.M. By then, the ship had changed course and was proceeding almost due west.

At 2:00 P.M. all hell broke loose. Three Mirage fighter planes headed straight for the *Liberty,* their rockets taking out the forward machine guns and wrecking the ship's antennae. The Mirages were joined by Mystère fighters, which dropped napalm on the bridge and deck and repeatedly strafed the ship. The attack continued for over 20 minutes. In all, the ship sustained 821 holes in her sides and decks. Of these, more than 100 were rocket size.

As the aircraft departed, three torpedo boats took over the attack, firing five torpedoes, one of which tore a 40-foot hole in the hull, killing 25 sailors. The ship was in flames, dead in the water, listing precariously, and taking water. The crew was ordered to prepare to abandon ship. As life-rafts were lowered into the water, the torpedo boats moved closer and shot them to pieces. One boat concentrated machine-gun fire on rafts still on deck as crew members there tried to extinguish the napalm fires. Petty Officer Charles Rowley declares, "They didn't want anyone to live."

At 3:15 P.M. the last shot was fired, leaving the vessel a combination morgue and hospital. The ship had no engines, no power, no rudder. Fearing further attack, Captain McGonagle, despite severe leg injuries, stayed at the bridge. An Israeli helicopter, its open bay door showing troops in battle gear and a machine gun mounted in an open doorway, passed close to the deck, then left. Other aircraft came and went during the next hour.

Although U.S. air support never arrived, within fifteen minutes of the first attack and more than an hour before the assault ended, fighter planes from the USS *Saratoga* were in the air ready for a rescue mission under orders "to destroy or drive off any attackers." The carrier was only 30 minutes away, and, with a squadron of fighter planes on deck ready for a routine operation, it was prepared to respond almost instantly.

But the rescue never occurred. Without approval by Washington, the planes could not take aggressive action, even to rescue a U.S. ship confirmed to be under attack. Admiral Donald Engen, then captain of the *America,* the second U.S. carrier in the vicinity, later explained: "President Johnson had very strict control. Even though we knew the *Liberty* was under attack, I couldn't just go and order a rescue." The planes were hardly in the air when the voice of Secretary of Defense Robert S. McNamara was heard over Sixth Fleet radios: "Tell the Sixth Fleet to get those aircraft back immediately." They were to have no part in destroying or driving off the attackers.

Shortly after 3 P.M., nearly an hour after the *Liberty*'s plea was first heard, the White House gave momentary approval to a rescue mission and planes from both carriers were launched. At almost precisely the same instant, the Israeli government informed the U.S. naval attaché in Tel Aviv that its forces had "erroneously attacked a U.S.

ship" after mistaking it for an Egyptian vessel, and offered "abject apologies." With apology in hand, Johnson once again ordered U.S. aircraft back to their carriers.

When the second launch occurred, there were no Israeli forces to "destroy or drive away." Ahead for the *Liberty* and its ravaged crew were 15 hours of lonely struggle to keep the wounded alive and the vessel afloat. Not until dawn of the next day would the *Liberty* see a U.S. plane or ship. The only friendly visit was from a small Soviet warship. Its offer of help was declined, but the Soviets said they would stand by in case need should arise.

The next morning two U.S. destroyers arrived with medical and repair assistance. Soon the wounded were transferred to the carrier hospital by helicopter. The battered ship then proceeded to Malta, where a Navy court of inquiry was to be held. The inquiry itself was destined to be a part of an elaborate program to keep the public from knowing what really had happened.

In fact, the cover-up began almost at the precise moment that the Israeli assault ended. The apology from Israeli officials reached the White House moments after the last gun fired at the *Liberty*. President Johnson accepted and publicized the condolences of Israeli Prime Minister Levi Eshkol, even though information readily available showed the Israeli account to be false. The CIA had learned a day before the attack that the Israelis planned to sink the ship. Congressional comments largely echoed the president's interpretation of the assault, and the nation was caught up in euphoria over Israel's stunning victories over the Arabs. The casualties on the *Liberty* got scant attention. Smith Hempstone, foreign correspondent for the *Washington Star*, wrote from Tel Aviv, "In a week since the Israeli attack on the USS *Liberty* not one single Israeli of the type which this correspondent encounters many times daily—cab drivers, censors, bartenders, soldiers—has bothered to express sorrow for the deaths of these Americans."

The Pentagon staved off reporters' inquiries with the promise of a "comprehensive statement" once the official inquiry, conducted by Admiral Isaac Kidd, was finished. Kidd gave explicit orders to the crew: "Answer no questions. If somehow you are backed into a corner, then you may say that it was an accident and that Israel has apologized. You may say nothing else." Crew members were assured they could talk freely to reporters once the summary of the court of inquiry was made public. This was later modified; they were then ordered not to provide information beyond the precise words of the published summary.

The court was still taking testimony when a charge that the attack had been deliberate appeared in the U.S. press. An Associated Press story filed from Malta reported that "senior crewmen" on the ship were convinced the Israelis knew the ship was American before they attacked. "We were flying the Stars and Stripes and it's absolutely impossible that they shouldn't know who we were," a crew member said. The Navy disputed the story, saying the U.S. "thoroughly accepted the Israeli apology."

Testimony completed, Admiral Kidd handcuffed himself to a huge box of records and flew to Washington to be examined by the Chief of Naval Operations, Admiral McDonald, as well as by Congressional leaders before the long-awaited summary statement was issued. When finally released, it was far from comprehensive. It made no attempt to fix blame, focusing almost entirely on the actions of the crew.

The censored summary did not reveal that the ship had been under close aerial surveillance by Israel for hours before the attack and that during the preceding 24 hours Israel had repeatedly warned U.S. authorities to move the *Liberty*. It contained nothing to dispute the notion of mistaken identity. The Navy reported erroneously that the attack lasted only 6 minutes instead of 70 minutes and asserted falsely that all firing stopped when the torpedo boats came close enough to identify the U.S. flag. The Navy made no mention of napalm or of life-rafts being shot up. It even suppressed records of the strong breeze which made the ship's U.S. flag plainly visible.

The report did make one painful revelation: Before the attack the Joint Chiefs of Staff had ordered the *Liberty* to move further from the coast, but the message "was misrouted, delayed and not received until after the attack."

Several newspapers criticized the Pentagon's summary. The *New York Times* said it "leaves a good many questions unanswered." The *Washington Star* used the word "cover-up," called the summary an "affront" and demanded a deeper and wider probe. Senator J. William Fulbright, chairman of the Senate Foreign Relations committee, after a closed briefing by Secretary of State Dean Rusk, called the episode "very embarrassing." The *Star* concluded: "Whatever the meaning of this, embarrassment is no excuse for disingenuousness."

In early July, the Associated Press quoted Micha Limor, identified as an Israeli reservist who had served on one of the torpedo boats, as saying that Israeli sailors noticed three numbers as they circled the *Liberty* but insisted the numbers meant nothing to them.

Lieutenant James M. Ennes, Jr., a cypher officer recovering in a hospital from shrapnel wounds, was incredulous when he read the Limor story. He had been officer of the deck. He knew the ship's name appeared in large letters on the stern and the hull number on the bow. He knew also that a breeze made the Stars and Stripes easily visible during the day. He had ordered a new 5-by-8 foot flag displayed early on the day of the attack. By the time the torpedo boats arrived, the original flag had been shot down but an even larger 7-by-13 foot flag was mounted in plain view from a yardarm. He knew that the attackers, whether by air or surface, could not avoid knowing it was a U.S. ship. Above all else, he knew that *Liberty*'s intercept operators had heard the Israeli reconnaissance pilots correctly reporting to Israeli headquarters that the ship was American.

Disturbed by the Limor story and the exchange of public messages concerning the assault, Ennes determined to unravel the story. During the four months he was behidden at Portsmouth, Virginia, he collected information from his shipmates. Later, while stationed in Germany, he recorded the recollections of other crew members. Transferred to Washington, D.C., he secured government reports under the Freedom of Information Act and also obtained the full Court of Inquiry report, which was finally, after nine years, declassified in 1976 from being top secret.

The result was Ennes's book, *Assault on the Liberty,* published in 1980, two years after he retired from the Navy. Ennes discovered "shallowness" in the court's questioning, its failure to "follow up on evidence that the attack was planned in advance"—including evidence that radio interceptions from two stations heard an Israeli pilot identify the ship as American. He said the court, ignoring the ship's log, which recorded a steady breeze blowing and confirming testimony from crewmen, concluded erroneously that attackers may not have been able to identify the flag's nationality, because the flag, according to the court, "hung limp at the mast on a windless day."

Concerning Israeli motives for the attack, Ennes wrote that Israeli officials may have decided to destroy the ship because they feared its sensitive listening devices would detect Israeli plans to invade Syria's Golan Heights. (Israel invaded Syria the day after the *Liberty* attack, despite Israel's earlier acceptance of a ceasefire with its Arab foes.)

Ennes learned that crewmen sensed a cover-up even while the court was taking testimony at Malta. He identified George Golden, the *Liberty*'s engineering officer and acting commanding officer, as the source of the Associated Press story charging that the attack was deliberate. Golden, who is Jewish, was so outraged at the prohibition against talking with reporters that he ignored it—risking his future career in the Navy to rescue a vestige of his country's honor.

The American embassy at Tel Aviv relayed to Washington the only fully detailed Israeli account of the attack—the Israeli court of inquiry report known as "Israeli Preliminary Inquiry 1/67." The embassy message also contained the recommendation that, at the request of the Israeli government, it not be released to the American people. Ennes believes this is probably because both governments knew the mistaken identity excuse was too transparent to believe.

Another request for secrecy was delivered by hand to Eugene Rostow, undersecretary of state for political affairs. It paralleled the message from the embassy at Tel Aviv imploring the Department of State to keep the Israeli court of inquiry secret because "the circumstances of the attack [if the version outlined in the file is to be believed] strip the Israeli Navy naked." Although Ennes saw that message in an official file in 1977, by 1984 it had vanished from all known official files. Ennes believes Israeli officials decided to make the Israeli Navy the scapegoat in the controversy. With the blame piled on its Navy, the orphan service that has the least clout in Israel's military hierarchy, Israel then asked the U.S. to keep the humiliation quiet. United States officials agreed not to release the text of the Israeli report.

Legal Adviser's Report Becomes Top Secret

During this same period—the weeks immediately following the assault on the *Liberty,* an assessment of the "Israeli Preliminary Inquiry 1/67" was prepared by Carl F. Salans, legal adviser to the secretary of state. It was prepared for the consideration of Eugene Rostow. The report, kept top secret until 1983 and apparently given only cursory examination by Secretary of State Dean Rusk, examines the credibility of the Israeli study and reveals as has no other single document the real attitude of the U.S. government toward the Israeli attack on the USS *Liberty.* It was a document too explosive to release.

Item by item, Salans demonstrated that the Israeli excuse could not be believed. Preparing the report immediately after the attack, he relied mainly on the limited information in Admiral Isaac Kidd's court of inquiry file. He never heard Ennes, Golden, nor any of the principal witnesses. He found enough there to discredit the Israeli document thoroughly. The items Salans examined were the speed and direction of the *Liberty,* aircraft surveillance, identification by Israeli aircraft, identification by torpedo boats, flag and identification markings, and time sequence of attacks. In each instance, eyewitness testimony or known facts disputed the Israeli claims of innocent error.

For example, the Israeli report contended that the *Liberty* was traveling at a speed of 28 to 30 knots, hence behaving suspiciously. Its actual speed was five knots. Israeli reconnaissance aircraft claimed to have carried out only two overflight missions, at 6:00 and 9:00 A.M.

Aircraft actually overflew the *Liberty* eight times, the first at 5:15 A.M. and the last at 12:45 P.M.

The Israeli report charged that the *Liberty*, after refusing to identify itself, opened fire. Captain McGonagle testified that the only signals by the torpedo boats came from a distance of 2,000 yards when the attack run was already launched and torpedoes on their way. The blinker signals could not be read because of intermittent smoke and flames. Not seeing them, the *Liberty* could not reply. Immediately thereafter it was hit by a torpedo and 25 sailors died instantly.

The Israeli report contended that the *Liberty* did not display a flag or identifying marks. Five crewmen testified that they saw the naval ensign flying the entire morning and until the attack. When the flag was shot away during the air attack, another larger flag was hoisted before the torpedo onslaught began. Hull markings were clear and freshly painted. The Israelis tried to shift responsibility by asserting that the attack originated through reports that the coastal area was being shelled from the sea. Salans said it should be clear to any trained observer that the small guns aboard the *Liberty* were incapable of shore bombardment.

The Salans report was forwarded September 21, 1967, to Under Secretary of State Rostow. This means that high officials of the administration knew the falsity of Israeli claims about the *Liberty* soon after the assault itself.

With a document in hand so thoroughly refuting the Israeli claims, the next logical step obviously would be its presentation to the Israeli government for comment, followed by publication of the findings.

Instead, it was stamped "top secret" and hidden from public view, as well as the attention of other officials of our government and its military services, along with the still-hidden Israeli report. Dean Rusk, secretary of state at the time, says that he has "no current recollection" of seeing the Salans report. He adds, however, that he "was never satisfied with the Israeli purported explanation of the USS *Liberty* affair."

The cover-up of the Salans report and other aspects of the episode soon had agonizing implications for United States security.

If the Navy had been candid about the *Liberty* episode even within its own ranks, the nation might have been spared the subsequent humiliation of an ordeal that began five months later when North Korean forces killed a U.S. sailor and captured the USS *Pueblo* and its entire crew. The agony ended when the crew was released after experiencing a year of captivity under brutal conditions.

Pueblo commander Lloyd M. Bucher later concluded that if he had been armed with facts of the disaster in the Mediterranean, he might have prevented the *Pueblo* episode.

In the late summer of 1967, still ashore but preparing to take command of the ill-fated ship, Bucher learned of the *Liberty*'s misfortune. Headed for hostile waters near North Korea, he believed his mission would profit from the experience and asked for details. Bucher recalls how his request was brushed aside: "I asked my superiors about the disaster and was told it was all just a big mistake, that there was nothing we could learn from it." When he later read the Ennes book, Bucher discovered that the *Liberty* crew had encountered many of the same problems his ship faced just before its capture. Both ships had inadequate means for destroying secret documents and equipment, and, in a crisis, even the ship itself. Both had serious shortcomings in control procedures. Bucher blames "incompetency at the top" and "lack of response to desperate calls for assistance during the attack." He speaks bitterly of the *Pueblo*'s ordeal:

We had a man killed and 14 wounded. Then a year of pretty damned severe brutality which could have been prevented had I been told what happened to the *Liberty*. It's only because that damned incident was covered up as thoroughly as it was.

The cover-up of the attack on the *Liberty* had other, more personal consequences. On recommendation of the Navy Department, William L. McGonagle, captain of the *Liberty,* was approved by President Johnson for the nation's highest award, the Congressional Medal of Honor. According to Ennes, the captain "defied bullets, shrapnel and napalm" during the attack and, despite injuries, stayed on the bridge throughout the night. Under his leadership, the 82 crewmen who had survived death and injury had kept the ship afloat despite a 40-foot hole in the side and managed to bring the crippled vessel to safe harbor.

McGonagle was an authentic hero, but he was not to get the award with the customary style, honor, ceremony and publicity. It would not be presented personally by the president, nor would the event be at the White House. The Navy Department got instructions to arrange the ceremony elsewhere. The president would not take part. It was up to the Navy to find a suitable place. Admiral Thomas L. Moorer, who had become chief of naval operations shortly before the order arrived, was upset. It was the only Congressional Medal in his experience not presented at the White House. He protested to the Secretary of Defense Robert S. McNamara, but the order stood. From the two houses of the legislature for which the medal is named came not a voice of protest.

The admiral would have been even more upset had he known at the time that the White House delayed approving the medal until it was cleared by Israel. Ennes quoted a naval officer as saying: "The government is pretty jumpy about Israel. The State Department even asked the Israeli ambassador if his government had any objection to McGonagle getting the medal. 'Certainly not,' Israel said." The text of the accompanying citation gave no offense: it did not mention Israel.

The secretary of the Navy presented the medal in a small, quiet ceremony at the Navy Yard in Washington. Admiral Moorer said later he was not surprised at the extraordinary arrangements. "They had been trying to hush it up all the way through." Moorer added, "The way they did things I'm surprised they didn't just hand it to him under the 14th Street Bridge."

Even tombstone inscriptions at the Arlington National Cemetery perpetuated the cover-up. As with McGonagle's citation, Israel was not mentioned. For fifteen years the marker over the graves of six *Liberty* crewmen read simply, "died in the Eastern Mediterranean." No mention of the ship, the circumstances, or Israel. Visitors might conclude they died of natural causes. Finally, survivors of the ship banded together into the USS *Liberty* Veterans Association and launched a protest that produced a modest improvement. The cover-up was lifted ever so slightly in 1982 when the cemetery marker was changed to read, "Killed USS *Liberty*." The dedication event at gravesite was as quiet as the McGonagle ceremony years before. The only civilian official of the U.S. government attending, Senator Larry Pressler, promised further investigation of the *Liberty* episode but two years later had done nothing.

The national cover-up even dictated the phrasing of letters of condolence to the survivors of those killed in the assault. In such circumstances, next of kin normally receive a letter from the president setting forth the facts of the tragedy and expressing profound feelings over the hardship, sacrifice and bravery involved in the death. In fact, letters by the hundreds were then being sent to next of kin as the toll in Vietnam mounted.

To senior White House officials, however, death by Israeli fire was different from death at the hands of the Vietcong. A few days after the assault on the *Liberty,* the senior official in charge of President Johnson's liaison with the Jewish community, Harry McPherson, received this message from White House aide James Cross:

Thirty-one [sic] Navy personnel were killed aboard the USS *Liberty* as the result of the accidental [sic] attack by Israeli forces. The attached condolence letters, which have been prepared using basic formats approved for Vietnam war casualties, strike me as inappropriate in this case.

Due to the very sensitive nature of the whole Arab-Israeli situation and the circumstances under which these people died, I would ask that you review these drafts and provide me with nine or ten different responses which will adequately deal with this special situation.

The "special situation" led McPherson to agree that many of the usual paragraphs of condolence were "inappropriate." He suggested phrases that de-emphasized combat, ignored the Israeli role and even the sacrifice involved.

Responding to the "very sensitive nature" of relations with Israel, the president's staff set aside time-honored traditions in recognizing those killed in combat. McPherson suggested that the letters express the president's gratitude for the "contribution to the cause of peace" made by the victims and state that Johnson had tried to avert the Israeli-Arab war.

While Washington engaged in this strange program of coverup, *Liberty* crewmen could remember with satisfaction a moment of personal pride, however brief. On the afternoon of June 10, 1967, as the battered ship and its crew prepared to part company with the USS *America* for their journey to Malta and the court of inquiry, carrier Captain Donald Engen ordered a memorial service for those who had died during the assault. Held on the deck of the *America* where more than 2,000 sailors were gathered, the service was an emotional moment. Afterwards, as the ships parted, Engen called for three cheers for the *Liberty* crew. Petty Officer Jeffery Carpenter, weakened from loss of blood, occupied a stretcher on the Liberty's main deck. Crewman Stan White lifted one end of the stretcher so Carpenter could see as well as hear the tribute being paid by the carrier. "Such cheers!" Engen told me. "Boy, you could hear the cheers echo back and forth across the water. It was a very moving thing."

It was the only "moving thing" that would be officially bestowed in tribute to the heroic crew.

"This Is Pure Murder"

Books have perpetuated myths about the *Liberty*. Yitzhak Rabin, military commander of Israeli forces at the time, declared in his memoirs published in 1979 that the *Liberty* was mistaken for an Egyptian ship: "I must admit I had mixed feelings about the news [that it was actually a U.S. ship]—profound regret at having attacked our friends and a tremendous sense of relief [that the ship was not Soviet]." He wrote that Israel, while compensating victims of the assault, refused to pay for the damage to the ship "since we did not consider ourselves responsible for the train of errors."

Lyndon Johnson's own memoirs, *Vantage Point,* continued the fiction that the ship had been "attacked in error." Although his signature had appeared on letters of condolence to 34 next of kin, his memoirs reported the death toll at only ten. He cited 100 wounded; the actual count was 171. He added, "This heartbreaking episode grieved the Israelis deeply, as it did us."

Johnson wrote of the message he had sent on the hotline to Moscow in which he assured the Soviets that carrier aircraft were on their way to the scene and that "investigation was the sole purpose of these flights." He did not pretend that protection and rescue of the ship and its crew were among his objectives, nor did he record that the carrier aircraft were never permitted to proceed to the *Liberty* even for "investigation." The commander-in-chief devoted only sixteen lines to one of the worst peacetime naval disasters in history.

Moshe Dayan, identified in a CIA report as the officer who personally ordered the attack, made no mention of the *Liberty* in his lengthy autobiography. According to the CIA document, Dayan had issued the order over the protests of another Israeli general who said, "This is pure murder."

The cover-up also dogged Ennes in the marketing of his book. Despite high praise in reviews, book orders routinely got "lost," wholesale listings disappeared mysteriously, and the Israeli lobby launched a far-flung campaign to discredit the text. The naval base in San Diego returned a supply of books when a chaplain filed a complaint. Military writer George Wilson told Ennes that when the *Washington Post* printed a review, "It seemed that every phone in the building had someone calling to complain about our mention of the book."

The *Atlanta Journal* called Ennes's *Assault on the Liberty* a "disquieting story of Navy bungling, government cover-up and Israeli duplicity that is well worth reading." The *Columbus Dispatch* called it "an inquest of cover-up in the area of international political intrigue." Journalist Seymour Hersh praised it as "an insider's book by an honest participant," and the prestigious Naval Institute at Annapolis called it "probably the most important naval book of the year."

Israel took swift measures to warn U.S. readers to ignore the reviews. The Israeli Foreign Office charged, "Ennes allows his very evident rancor and subjectivity to override objective analysis," and that his "conclusions fly in the face of logic and military facts." These charges, Ennes later said, were "adopted by the Anti-Defamation League of B'nai B'rith for distribution to Israeli supporters throughout the United States." A caller to the American Israel Public Affairs Committee was told that the book was "a put-up job, all lies and financed by the National Association of Arab Americans." Ennes said the "emotional rhetoric" caused "serious damage to sales and a marked reluctance of media executives to allow discussion of this story."

As the result of radio talk shows and lecture platforms on which Ennes appeared, he heard from people "all over the country" who had been frustrated in efforts to buy his book. Several retail book stores, seeking to order the book from the publisher, Random House, were given false information—they were told the book did not exist, or that it had not been published, or that it was out of print, or that it was withdrawn to avoid a law suit.

Talk show host Ray Taliaferro caused a stir one Sunday night in 1980 when he announced over San Francisco radio station KGO that he would interview Ennes the following Sunday. Over 500 protest letters poured into the station, but the program went on as scheduled. Public response was overwhelming, as listener calls continued to stream in for a full hour after the two-hour show with Ennes had ended. Two phone calls arrived threatening Taliaferro's life—one on a supposedly private line.

At the invitation of Paul Backus, editor of the *Journal of Electronic Defense,* Ennes wrote a guest editorial in 1981 on the implications of the *Liberty* incident, stating that friendly nations sometimes feel compelled to take hostile actions. In the case of the *Liberty,* he added,

Because the friendly nation . . . is the nation of Israel, and because the nation of Israel is widely, passionately and expensively supported in the United States, and perhaps also because a proper inquiry would reveal a humiliating failure of command, control and communications, an adequate investigation . . . has yet to be politically palatable.

Backus was stunned when the owners of the magazine, an organization of military and defense-related executives known as the Association of Old Crows, ordered him not to publish the Ennes editorial. Association spokesman Gus Slayton wrote to Backus that the article was "excellent" but said "it would not be appropriate to publish it now in view of the heightened tension in the Middle East." Backus, a retired Navy officer, resigned: "I want nothing more to do with organizations which would further suppress the information." The Ennes piece was later given prominent play in a rival magazine, *Defense Electronics,* which later found it a popular reprint at $3 a copy.

As Ennes lectured at universities in the midwest and west in 1981 and 1982, he encountered protests in different form. Although most reaction was highly favorable, hecklers called him a liar and an anti-Semite and protested to administrators against his appearance on campus. Posters announcing his lectures were routinely ripped down. Wording identical with that used by the Israeli Foreign Office and B'nai B'rith in attacks on the book appeared in flyers distributed by local "Jewish Student Unions" as Ennes spoke to college audiences.

Criticism of the Ennes book seemed to be coordinated on a national—even international—scale. After National Public Radio read the full text of the book over its book-reading network, alert local Anti-Defamation League spokesmen demanded and received the opportunity for a 10-minute rebuttal at the end of the series. The rebuttal in Seattle was almost identical with a document attacking the book issued by the Israeli Foreign Office in Jerusalem. Both rebuttals matched verbatim a letter criticizing Ennes that had appeared in the Jacksonville (Florida) *Times-Union.*

Ennes's misfortunes took an ironic turn in June 1982 when ABC's Nightline cancelled the broadcast of a segment it had prepared on the 15-year reunion of the *Liberty* crew. The show was pre-empted by crisis coverage of Israel's invasion of Lebanon, which had begun the day before. In early 1983, Nightline rescheduled the segment, but once again Israel intruded; this time an interview with its new U.S. ambassador, Moshe Arens, took the allotted time. Meanwhile, the edited tape and 15 reels of unedited film had disappeared from the studio library. (Ennes's book may have cost the former captain of the ill-fated *Pueblo* an appearance on ABC's "Good Morning America" television show in 1980. Bucher had been invited to New York for a post-captivity interview. Suddenly the interview was withdrawn. A studio official told Bucher only that he had heard there were problems "upstairs," but then he asked Bucher, "Did you have a book review published recently in the *Washington Post?*" He had indeed, a review which heaped praise on the Ennes book).

Later in 1983, the Jewish War Veterans organization protested when the Veterans of Foreign Wars quoted Ennes to support its call for "proper honors" for those killed on the *Liberty* and again when James R. Currieo, national commander of the Veterans of Foreign Wars, referred to the "murderous Israeli attack." Currieo excited Jewish wrath even more when he published in the VFW magazine a letter to President Reagan inviting the White House to send a representative to the cemetery to help honor the men who died. There was no reply.

Four years after publication of *Assault on the Liberty,* Ennes is still receiving a steady flow of mail and telephone calls about the episode. Elected by his shipmates as their official historian, he became editor of *The USS Liberty Newsletter.* Meanwhile, not wishing to be fettered to an endless struggle of conscience, he is writing another book on an unrelated subject and trying to leave the *Liberty* matter behind. He finds it cannot be left behind. The book continues to generate a swirl of controversy that will not go away.

Another retired officer, Admiral Thomas L. Moorer, applauds Ennes's activities and still wants an investigation. He scoffs at the mistaken identity theory, and says he hopes Congress will investigate and if it does not, he favors reopening the Navy's court of inquiry. He adds, "I would like to see it done, but I doubt seriously that it will be allowed."

Asked why the Johnson administration ordered the cover-up, Moorer is blunt: "The clampdown was not actually for security reasons but for domestic political reasons. I don't think there is any question about it. What other reasons could there have been? President Johnson was worried about the reaction of Jewish voters."

Moorer says the attack was "absolutely deliberate" and adds, "The American people would be goddam mad if they knew what goes on."

"Like Sending a Weather Report"

The publication in September 1990 of Victor Ostrovsky's *By Way of Deception* is certain to broaden awareness of what goes on in the realm of Israeli perfidy.

The shocking exposé, written by a former Israeli spy, reports that the Mossad, Israel's intelligence agency, failed to relay to the United States early data about the 1983 suicide bombing that killed 241 U.S. marines asleep in a barracks at the Beirut airport.

An informant had told the Mossad that a large truck was being fitted by Shi'ite Muslims with spaces that could hold bombs of exceptional size. Local agents concluded that the marine barracks was among the most likely targets, but, according to Ostrovsky, the Mossad chief in Tel Aviv made a conscious decision not to warn the U.S. government, declaring: "We're not there to protect Americans." Accordingly, only a routine notice went to the CIA, which, Ostrovsky writes, "was like sending a weather report."

In equally foolish acts, the government of Israel requested and a New York judge ordered that the book be banned in the United States. The *New York Post* headlined: "Israelis muzzle spy author." *The New York Times* summed up the book's allegation: the Mossad failed to warn the CIA because it wanted "to poison American relations with Arab countries."

When the ban was overturned by a higher court the next day, the book enjoyed a second round of nationwide publicity. Overnight it was a bestseller.

Chapter 7

Challenges to Academic Freedom

The Israeli lobby pays special attention to the crucial role played by American colleges and universities in disseminating information and molding opinion on the Middle East. Lobby organizations are concerned not only with academic programs dealing with the Middle East but also with the editorial policies of student newspapers and with the appearance on campus of speakers critical of Israel. In all three of these areas of legitimate lobby interest and activity, as in its dealings on Capitol Hill, pro-Israeli organizations and activists frequently employ smear tactics, harassment and intimidation to inhibit the free exchange of ideas and views.

As government, academic and public awareness of the Middle East increased following the 1973 OPEC oil price hike, such organizations as the American Israel Public Affairs Committee and the American Jewish Committee developed specific programs and policies for countering criticism of Israel on college campuses.

Making It "Hot Enough" on Campus

In 1979 AIPAC established its Political Leadership Development Program, which trains student activists on how to increase pro-Israeli influence on campus. Coordinator Jonathan Kessler recently reported that in just four years "AIPAC's program has affiliated over 5,000 students on 350 campuses in all 50 states":

They are systematically monitoring and comprehensively responding to anti-Israeli groups on campus. They are involved in pro-Israel legislative efforts, in electoral campaign politics as well.

However self-serving and perhaps exaggerated such statements may be, AIPAC works closely with the B'nai B'rith Hillel Foundation on campuses. When Kessler is introduced to campus audiences, it is as one who has "trained literally thousands of students." His campus contacts send him tapes or notes from talks that are considered to be "pro-Palestinian" or "anti-Israeli" and alert him to upcoming speaking engagements. Kessler keeps the notes on file and when he hears that a particular speaker is coming to a campus, he sends summaries of the speaker's usual points and arguments, his question-answer style, and potentially damaging quotes—or purported quotes—from other talks. Kessler specializes in concocting questions with which the speaker will have difficulty and in warning the campus organizers away from questions the speaker answers well.

If the student union or academic senate controls what groups may be allowed to reserve halls, Kessler works to get friends of Israel into those bodies. If the control is with the administration, speakers are accused of advocating violence, either by "quoting" earlier speeches or by characterizing them as pro-PLO. AIPAC students also argue that certain forums, such as memorial lectures should not be "politicized." While this may not always bar the speaker, Kessler advises that "if you make it hot enough" for the administrators, future events will be discouraged and even turned down rather than scheduled.

Kessler's students receive training—through role-playing and "propaganda response exercises"—in how to counter anti-Israel arguments. These exercises simulate confrontations at pro- and anti-Israel information tables and public forums.

Once a solid AIPAC contingent is formed, it takes part in student conferences and tries to forge coalitions with other student groups. AIPAC then has pro-Israeli resolutions passed in these bodies and can run pro-Israel advertisements signed by the (liberal) Americans for Democratic Action and (conservative) Young Americans for Freedom, for example, rather than just by AIPAC. The workshop handout says: "Use coalitions effectively. Try finding non-Jewish individuals and groups to sign letters to the editor, for it is far more effective and credible."

In 1983 AIPAC distributed to students and faculty around the country a ten-page questionnaire on political activism on their campuses. Its instructions include: "Please name any individual faculty who assist anti-Israel groups. How is this assistance offered? What are the propaganda themes . . . ?" The survey results form the body of the *AIPAC College Guide: Exposing the Anti-Israel Campaign on Campus,* published in April 1984.

While AIPAC claims to respect the right of all to free speech, number eight on its list of 10 suggested "modes of response" to pro-Palestinian events or speakers on campus reads: "Attempt to prevent."

Number 10 on the same list reads "Creative packaging." Edward Said, a professor of comparative literature at Columbia University who frequently speaks on campuses in support of the Palestinian cause, described a case of "creative packaging" at the University of Washington where he spoke in early 1983:

They stood at the door of the auditorium and distributed a blue leaflet which seemed like a program but it was in fact a denunciation of me as a 'terrorist.' There were quotations from the PLO, and things that I had said were mixed in with things they claimed the PLO had said about murdering Jews. The idea was to intimidate me and to intimidate the audience from attending.

Said reports another experience at the University of Florida, where the group protesting Said's talk was led by a professor of philosophy:

They tried to disrupt the meeting and [the professor] finally had to be taken out by the police. It was one of the ugliest things, not just heckling but interrupting and standing up and shouting. It's pure fascism, outright hooliganism.

Another episode involving Said occurred at Trinity College in Hartford, Connecticut. In the fall of 1982 Said spoke, at the invitation of the college's Department of Religion, on the subject of Palestine and its significance to Christians and Muslims as well as Jews. As the day of the talk approached, the department began to get letters of protest from prominent members of the Hartford Jewish community and from Jewish faculty members. Said, said the protesters, was pro-Palestinian and had made "anti-Israel" statements. One writer asked the organizers of the talk: "How could you do this, given the fact that there are two Holocaust survivors on the faculty?"

After Said spoke, more letters of protest arrived at the religion department, and a move was made to deny the department a new $1 million chair in Jewish Studies. The uproar died down after several months, but the protests had their effect. Asked whether the department would feel free, given the reaction of the Jewish community, to invite Edward Said again, a department spokesperson responded, "No, I don't think we would."

The *AIPAC College Guide* also includes profiles of 100 U.S. campuses and the anti-Israel campaign "unprecedented in scope and magnitude" which supposedly pervades them. Anti-Semitism is also cited as a major influence on some campuses. For example, Colorado State University's campus newspaper, the *Collegian,* is said to have printed anti-Semitic letters to the editor; but only a letter which "sought to draw attention to the 'Jewish lobby and the true extent of its influence over the U.S. media' " is cited as evidence.

An example of how the lobby works on campus came in the spring of 1982 when the American Indian Law Students Association (AILSA) at Harvard Law School hosted a conference on the rights of indigenous peoples in domestic and international law. They invited Deena Abu Lughod, an American of Palestinian origin who worked as a researcher at the PLO mission to the United Nations, to participate in the conference. The Harvard Jewish Law Students Association (HJLSA), which according to one source has an active membership of only about twenty, first asked AILSA to remove Abu-Lughod from the program.

When this failed, the Jewish group protested vehemently to the dean of the law school and also asked the dean of students to consider withdrawing all funding for the conference. The latter refused, saying she was "not in the business of censoring student conferences." But the dean of the law school, who was slated to give the opening address at the conference, backed out. Several members of the Indian Law Students Association and the director of the Harvard Foundation (which co-sponsored the conference), received telephoned death threats. One came from callers who identified themselves as Jewish Harvard students. Told of these, a member of the HJLSA said, "We were contacted by the JDL [Jewish Defense League], but we didn't want to have anything to do with any disruption of the conference."

The conference took place as scheduled, but one organizer recalls:

The atmosphere was incredibly tense. We were really very concerned about Deena's physical safety and about our own physical safety. We had seven policemen there. We had many, many marshals and very elaborate security. We had searches at the door, and we confiscated weapons, knives—not pocket knives—but butcher knives. We also had dogs sniff the room for explosives. The point is that the event did occur, but in a very threatening atmosphere.

The following spring, a group of Third World student organizations at Harvard invited the director of the PLO Information Office in Washington, Hassan Abdul-Rahman, to speak on the theme "Palestine: Road to Peace in the Middle East." Again the Harvard Jewish Law Students Association organized a demonstration, but this time the protesters packed the hall and actively disrupted the meeting. "It was just an absolute madhouse inside," recalls one student who was present. "Abdul-Rahman spoke for probably an hour and a half to virtually constant taunting, jeering, insults, screams, shouts, cursing."

According to the *Harvard Law Record,* a representative of the Harvard Arab Students Society "struggled" simply to relate a biographical sketch of the speaker and to provide an introduction to his talk. "It was an extremely intimidating atmosphere," recalls the student:

We just barely kept the lid on things. I think the fact that these events occurred is a testimony to our perseverence, not to the lack of intimidation. Because the intimidation is really very overt and very strong.

In both cases the protesters used material provided by the Anti-Defamation League of B'nai B'rith.

In still another incident at Harvard, a member of the Harvard law faculty who had visited the Israeli-occupied West Bank on a tour organized by North American Friends of Palestinian Universities gave a talk on campus after his return. Prior to the talk, a group of students from the Harvard Jewish Law Students Association came to the professor's office. They told him that they just wanted to make sure that he knew "all the facts" before giving his talk, and if he wasn't going to give a "balanced" picture, they intended to picket his address.

Recently asked if he altered his talk in any way as a response to the visit by the students, the professor said, "No, but that's because I knew what was going on whether or not they came to my office. I knew they were going to be there and I knew what the situation was." He added that "the presence of a highly charged group of Jewish law students" changed the nature of his talk "from one that was more directed at what was actually going on for the Palestinians into one that was more abstract and about the relationship between power and knowledge here and there and in a lot of other places." After the talk, the representatives of the HJLSA sent the professor a letter saying they were "very satisfied with the balanced nature" of his presentation. "Which made me think," he said, "it had been a little too balanced."

He said the Israeli-Palestinian conflict was "an issue about which we've never had a successful, open discussion at this school." The professor said that, while he didn't feel intimidated, "I felt that I was operating in a place in which there were limits on what I could say."

AIPAC is not the only pro-Israel organization to keep files on speakers. The Anti-Defamation League of B'nai B'rith keeps its own files. Noam Chomsky, world renowned professor of linguistics at MIT and author of two books on the Middle East, was leaked a copy of his ADL file, containing about a hundred pages of material. Says Chomsky: "Virtually every talk I give is monitored and reports of their alleged contents (sometimes ludicrously, even comically distorted) are sent on to the [Anti-Defamation] League, to be incorporated in my file."

Says Chomsky:

When I give a talk at a university or elsewhere, it is common for a group to distribute literature, invariably unsigned, containing a collection of attacks on me spiced with "quotes" (generally fabricated) from what I am alleged to have said here and there.

I have no doubt that the source is the ADL, and often the people distributing the unsigned literature acknowledge the fact. These practices are vicious and serve to intimidate many people. They are of course not illegal. If the ADL chooses to behave in this fashion, it has a right to do so; but this should also be exposed.

Student publications are also monitored. When the monthly *Berkeley Graduate,* a magazine of news and opinion intended for graduate students at the University of California at Berkeley, published in its April 1982 issue several articles critical of Israeli Prime Minister Menachem Begin and his government's policies, the office of the magazine began to receive anonymous phone calls, generally expressing in crude terms the callers' opinion of the magazine. One caller suggested that the editor, James Schamus, "take the next train to Auschwitz." According to Schamus, these calls continued for several weeks.

The campus Jewish Student Board circulated a petition protesting the content of the April issue and characterized the *Graduate* as anti-Semitic—until it discovered that editor James Schamus was himself Jewish. Schamus met with Jewish Student Board members and agreed to furnish space in the following issue of the magazine for a 4,000-word rebuttal, but they were not satisfied.

The following week, members of the Jewish Student Board introduced a bill in the Graduate Assembly expressing "regret" at the content of the April issue and stipulating that if an oversight committee were not formed "to review each issue's content before it goes to press," steps would be taken to eliminate the *Graduate.* The assembly voted down the resolution but agreed to revive a moribund editorial oversight committee to set editorial policy. Opponents of the bill, including editors of several campus publications, defended the right of the *Graduate* to print "without prior censorship."

The next day, the Student Senate narrowly defeated a bill that would have expressed "dissatisfaction" with the *Graduate* magazine. An earlier draft of the bill, amended by the Senate, would have asked the Senate to "condemn" the publication. An editorial in *The Daily Californian,* the university's main student newspaper, said that such "meaningless censures" came not out of intelligent consideration of an issue, but out of "irrational urgings to punish the progenitor of an idea with which one disagrees."

The May issue of the *Graduate* did contain a response to Schamus's original article. The author concluded his piece by calling the April issue of the *Graduate* "simple, unvarnished anti-Semitism in both meaning and intent."

Later in May, Schamus left for a two-month vacation. While he was gone, the Graduate Assembly leadership decided by administrative fiat to cut the amount of student funds allocated to the *Graduate* by 55 percent and to change the accounting rules in such a way that the magazine could no longer survive. Schamus resigned, along with his editorial and advertising staffs. In an interview with the *San Francisco Examiner,* Schamus said that the series on Begin "directly precipitated our silencing." He told the *Daily Californian:* "This whole situation was a plan by student government censors to get rid of the magazine and create a new one in its own image next year." The chairman of the Graduate Assembly denied any conspiracy. "The Israel issue had absolutely nothing to do with it," he said. He acknowledged, however, that the controversy over the issue "brought up the question of content in the *Graduate.*" The *Graduate* is today little more than a calendar of events that comes out four or five times a year.

Student Editor Under Fire

Another student newspaper editor who learned to think twice before criticizing Israel is John D'Anna, editor of the *Arizona Daily Wildcat* at the University of Arizona in Tucson during the 1982–83 academic year. In February of 1983, 22-year-old D'Anna wrote an editorial entitled "Butcher of Beirut Is Also a War Criminal," in which he decried the fact that former Israeli Defense Minister Ariel Sharon was permitted to remain a member of the Israeli Cabinet after being found "indirectly responsible" for the massacre of Palestinian civilians at the Sabra and Shatila camps in Lebanon. If Nazi war criminal Klaus Barbie, the infamous "butcher of Lyon" was to be tried for his crimes against humanity, asked D'Anna, "shouldn't those responsible for the Beirut massacre be tried for theirs?"

D'Anna was shocked at the reaction to his editorial:

My grandparents were the only John D'Annas listed in the phone book, and they were harassed with late night phone calls. I personally got a couple of the type 'If we ever catch you alone. . . .' There were threats on my life. I also got hate mail. Some of the letters were so vitriolic it makes me shudder.

There followed a series of letters to the newspaper accusing D'Anna of "irresponsible polemic," "fanning hatred" and "inciting violence." The director of the local B'nai B'rith Hillel Foundation wrote that D'Anna's editorial "merely inflames passions, draws conclusions on half-truths and misleads."

The uproar prompted D'Anna to write an apology in a subsequent issue. He said that while he stood by his beliefs, "I just wish I had expressed those beliefs differently." He agreed with some of his critics that it was a bad editorial and that he could have made the same points "without arousing passions and without polemic."

Nevertheless, the day after D'Anna's apology appeared, members of twenty local Jewish groups wrote to the university president demanding that the *Wildcat* editor resign or be fired for his "anti-Semitic" and "anti-Israel" editorial. If he was not fired by noon the following Monday, said the letter, the group would tell *Wildcat* advertisers that the newspaper was "spreading hatred," in the hope that the advertisers would cancel their ads. The group's spokesman was Edward Tennen, head of the local Jewish Defense League, a group founded by Meir Kahane, who advocates the forcible expulsion of Arabs from Israel. The JDL is shunned by AIPAC and other Jewish groups.

When the deadline passed without D'Anna's removal, the group calling for a boycott, having dubbed itself "United Zionist Institutions," distributed a letter to local businesses and ad agencies urging them to stop supporting the *Wildcat*'s "anti-Semitic editor" and his "consciously orchestrated bigotry." Calling D'Anna "an accomplice to PLO aims," the letter asked the advertisers to "search your consciences and do what you know must be done." D'Anna noted that the group's acronym was UZI, the name of the standard issue Israeli machine gun.

Meanwhile, about twenty-five members of local Jewish groups, mostly from the campus Hillel organization, attended a meeting of the university's Board of Publications during which they confronted D'Anna with their complaints. As the former editor recalls it:

I was on the hot seat for about two hours. And I tried to deal with all their questions and they kept demanding that steps be taken. I asked them what steps, and they said they wanted a review board. And I said 'That's fine, you can review anything you want after it comes out in the paper,' and they said 'No, we want to review it before it comes out in the paper,' and I said that was totally unacceptable.

In the end the boycott effort was ineffective, as only two businesses cancelled their advertising. Moreover, D'Anna received firm support from the newspaper staff and from the head of the university's journalism department, himself Jewish. Yet the former editor recalls that the campaign against him had an impact: "It was effective to a certain extent. I was gun-shy and it was quite a while before I touched any international issue."

"It Seemed to Be Politics"

The Hartford Seminary in Hartford, Connecticut, has the oldest Islamic studies program in the United States. Beginning in the early 1970s, the president of the seminary began to receive complaints from members of the Hartford Jewish community that the program was anti-

Jewish. One person said the program was in fact an "al-Fatah support group." More recently, Willem A. Bijlefeld, director of the seminary's Center for the Study of Islam and Christian-Muslim Relations, was asked by the local daily *Hartford Courant* to write a piece about PLO leader Yasser Arafat. On New Year's Eve, 1983, the day following publication of his article, Bijlefeld received a phone call from a man who identified himself only as Jewish. The caller said that the seminary had a long tradition of "anti-Jewish propaganda" and accused Bijlefeld of supporting "the killing of Jews and the destruction of Israel." He then expressed his joy at the "extremely painful death" of NBC news anchorwoman Jessica Savitch, killed in an automobile accident, which he said was a "manifestation of divine justice" since she had "lied" about the number of Lebanese forced out of their homes during the 1982 Israeli invasion. The caller said that he was fully confident that this kind of punishment awaited "any enemy of Israel." Said Bijlefeld, "The implications for me were clear."

Ostracism is another weapon of the lobby. Eqbal Ahmad is an American scholar of Pakistani origin who holds two Ph.D. degrees from Princeton University, one in political science and one in Islamic studies. He is also a fellow at Washington's Institute for Policy Studies. Ahmad has written widely on the Middle East and has had a number of articles published on the op-ed page of the *New York Times*. Ahmad says that as a critic of Israeli policies and a supporter of the rights of the Palestinians, he has been ostracized by the academic community:

It is not only the material punishments that people encounter, but the extraordinary environment of conformity that is imposed upon you and the price in isolation that individuals have to pay for not conforming on this issue.

Ahmad joined the faculty of Cornell University in 1965. "I was a young assistant professor, generally liked by my colleagues," recalls Ahmad. "And they continued to be very warm and civil to me despite the fact that many of them were conservative people and I had already become fairly prominent in the anti-Vietnam war movement."

After the Arab-Israeli war of June 1967, Ahmad made a speech at Cornell criticizing Israel's conquest and retention of Arab territory and also signed petitions supporting the right of the Palestinians to self-determination. Throughout his two remaining years at Cornell, says Ahmad, no more than four of the entire faculty spoke to him. "I would often sit at the lunch table in the faculty lounge, which is generally very crowded, and I would have a table for six to myself." Ahmad says that of the four who remained his friends, three were Jewish:

The issue is not one of Jew versus gentile. There is a silent covenant within the academic community concerning Israel. The interesting thing is that the number of prominent Jews who have broken the covenant is much larger than the number of gentiles.

In 1983, Ahmad's name appeared in the B'nai B'rith publication *Pro-Arab Propaganda in America: Vehicles and Voices.* "This they are doing to somebody who has not to date received any form of support from an Arab government or an Arab organization," says Ahmad. Ahmad says that about a quarter of his income comes from speaking engagements, mainly university endowed lectures. Since the publication of the B'nai B'rith "enemies list," his speaking invitations have dropped by about 50 percent. "These invitations come from my reputation as an objective, independent scholar," says Ahmad. "By putting me under the rubric of propagandist they have put into question my position as an objective scholar."

Since Ahmad left Cornell in 1969 he has not been able to obtain a regular teaching appointment. He has been a visiting professor at one college or another every year. Towards the end of his 1982–83 term at Rutgers University College in Newark, New Jersey, he was considered for a regular appointment, but at the last minute it fell through. Says Ahmad,

I have been told privately that it was because Zionist professors objected to my appointment. The dean was told that I would not get the vote of the faculty because accusations had been made that I was anti-Semitic and had created an anti-Semitic atmosphere on the campus while I was teaching there. All this was told to me in private; I have nothing in writing. . . .

S. C. Whittaker, former chairman of the Political Science Department at Rutgers University College and the man who originally hired Ahmad as a visiting professor, was away when the question of a full professorship for Ahmad came up. "When I got back," said Whittaker, "I was told that he'd been a great smash as a teacher and that his enrollments were terrific. But when the proposal to have him stay on permanently came up, it was shot down, and it seemed to be politics."

Arab Funding Too Hot to Handle

In 1977, three of America's most prestigious small colleges, Swarthmore, Haverford and Bryn Mawr, proposed to seek funds from a private Arab foundation for a joint Middle East studies program. The three "sister schools," located in the affluent "mainline" suburbs of Philadelphia, already shared a Russian studies program.

The idea for the joint program originated in conversations between college officials and Swarthmore alumnus Willis Armstrong, a former assistant secretary of state who had recently become secretary-treasurer of the Triad Foundation. The Washington-based foundation had been established by wealthy Saudi entrepreneur Adnan Khashoggi to finance, in his words, "programs with long-range goals for building bridges of understanding between countries." Khashoggi is a flamboyant multimillionaire who made his fortune by serving as a middleman to foreign companies, including several major defense contractors, seeking business in Saudi Arabia.

The three-year $590,000 program worked out by Armstrong and the colleges was exemplary by everyone's account. The plan would provide foreign student scholarships to needy Arab students, expand the colleges' collections of books and periodicals dealing with the Middle East and strengthen existing Middle East-related courses. In addition, about one-fourth of the grant would be used to finance a rotating professorship. The visiting professors would teach courses on the Middle East and its relation to disciplines including anthropology, art history, economics, history, political science and religion.

"It was as innocuous and rich as a proposal could be," recalled Swarthmore Vice-President Kendall Landis five years later. Haverford President Stephen Cary had described it at the time as "promising in terms of academic enrichment." The program would serve to "raise the consciousness of students about the Middle East situation," commented Haverford's associate director of development, John Gilbert.

Perhaps the most enthusiastic supporter of the plan was Bryn Mawr President Harris Wofford. A former Peace Corps director, Wofford was known for his long interest in promoting international understanding. He called the Middle East studies proposal "a good prospect for something we badly want."

The grant proposal included a guarantee of absolute academic freedom. "This was to be done in accordance with the highest academic standards," explained Armstrong. "The colleges would choose the visiting professors, *they'd* buy the books and *they'd* pick out the students to whom to give scholarships."

Moreover, the rotating professorship meant that no one professor would be around long enough to develop roots. "We really bent over backwards to be completely fair," said Landis. "Jewish professors would be employed as well as others."

"There was never any pressure from Triad in any discussions we had with them," said Haverford's Cary, "nor any indication from them that it couldn't be a study that would include Israel. So I never had any criticism of the Triad Foundation people at all."

The agreement with Triad was all but concluded by the three colleges. All that remained was to present the grant proposal formally to the Triad Foundation which, Armstrong assured the college officials, would accept it and write out the check.

Some, however, like Ira Silverman of the American Jewish Committee, saw dangers in the plan. Silverman had received a telephone call from Swarthmore political science professor James Kurth alerting the AJC to the grant proposal. In a confidential memorandum he prepared for the AJC's National Committee on Arab Influence in the United States, Silverman wrote:

Professor Kurth, who is not Jewish, believed that the proposed program should be of concern to the AJC inasmuch as it would not only expand study of the contemporary Arab world but would explicitly seek to bring the Arab political message to those campuses.

Professor Kurth brought these facts to our attention and asked for AJC help in blocking the implementation of the program. We discussed the matter and agreed that it would make most sense to try to kill the program through quiet, behind-the-scenes talks with college officials, before 'going public'; and that protests against the program need not be based solely or particularly on Jewish opposition to Arab influence. Instead, we thought it should be possible to generate concern about the program based on its sponsorship by Khashoggi and its evident public relations aims, not appropriate for colleges of the stature of these three schools.

Silverman went right to work orchestrating a campaign to discredit Khashoggi and Triad:

I immediately sent Professor Kurth a folder of information on Khashoggi, the Triad Corporation and Triad Foundation which was compiled by the AJC Trends Analysis Division.

I also notified the AJC Philadelphia chapter of these developments so that they could be in touch with Professor Kurth to assist in getting some local Philadelphia Jewish community leaders, alumni of the schools or otherwise associated with them, to raise questions about the proposed grant."

The effect of the AJC's efforts to "kill the program" was stunning. Using material provided by Silverman, the Swarthmore student newspaper, *The Phoenix,* published an article which falsely stated that Khashoggi was "under indictment by a federal grand jury" in connection with certain payments to Lockheed. Asked later about the role this article played in the controversy, James Platt, who had edited the student newspaper, said: "The *Phoenix* got things out there publicly, at least for students and certain alums who probably hadn't heard about it beforehand, to make their phone calls and be upset and so forth." Where had he gotten his information? He refused to say. "I'd prefer to talk to the people first just to make sure they have no problem with that. At the time, it was to remain confidential."

Before the *Phoenix* article appeared, Swarthmore President Theodore Friend called a meeting of department representatives to obtain the concurrence of faculty on the tentative grant proposal. Some of the faculty were reported to have objected to the plan. On the evening after the *Phoenix* article appeared, a petition was circulated in the college dining hall calling Khashoggi a "munitions monger" and referring to "kickbacks" in the Middle East. The petition, which called on the administration to drop the proposal, was signed by 230 students and faculty. Almost at the same time, the Philadelphia Jewish Federation had a letter on the president's desk.

"Speaking from memory," says one observer close to the Swarthmore scene, "it all happened in about eighteen and a half minutes. It was like the Great Fear sweeping across France during the French Revolution."

On November 3, 1977, articles appeared in *The Philadelphia Inquirer* and in another Philadelphia paper, *The Evening Bulletin*. The latter was headlined: "Colleges Hesitate in Scandal." By November 4, the student newspaper published jointly by Bryn Mawr and Haverford had also published an article detailing both the grant proposal and Khashoggi's background. The same issue included an editorial entitled "Say No to Triad."

The Jewish Community Relations Council, the American Jewish Committee and the Anti-Defamation League of B'nai B'rith also issued a joint statement: "It is altogether appropriate that the schools should seriously question the wisdom of accepting any grant from such a tainted source and one which is dominated by a figure like Adnan Khashoggi."

Finally, the Washington office of the AJC put Professor Kurth in touch with Congressman James Scheuer, who is Jewish and a Swarthmore alumnus. According to Armstrong, Scheuer called President Friend and requested the telephone numbers of the members of the college's Board of Managers "so he could call them at once and get them to put a stop to this outrageous thing."

Various groups tried to enlist faculty intervention. Harrison Wright, a professor of history at Swarthmore, recalled later that there were "memos to the whole faculty and to the department chairmen by different groups. It was a fairly short but quite sharp exchange of different points of view."

The first of the three colleges to publicly withdraw from the joint effort was Haverford. In a prepared statement, Haverford President Cary said the college was "grateful to Triad for its willingness to consider an application," but "because of Haverford's Quaker background it has decided it shouldn't apply for funds derived so directly from arms traffic which it deplores."

Swarthmore's withdrawal followed immediately. President Friend announced the college's decision in these words:

At a time of rigorous financial planning and examination of curriculum, our lack of a significant existing base in Middle Eastern studies at Swarthmore does not in our view warrant what at present could only be a temporary experiment.

Peter Cohan, a leader of student protest against the Triad grant, complained later to a *Phoenix* reporter that the statement "did not establish principles, but spoke only to the immediate situation." In the same *Phoenix* article, Swarthmore Vice-President Landis pointed out that the decision on the Triad grant was made "amid a whirlwind of protest which arose from 'more than just Khashoggi.'" According to Landis, "There were other concerns within the protest."

In a letter to the *Phoenix,* Ben Rockefeller, another student, agreed with Landis:

Jewish students are not disturbed about the Rockefellers' business conduct because they aren't truly contesting anybody's business conduct: the alleged concern about Mr. Khashoggi's professional character is a ruse to conceal an anti-Arab prejudice.

Only Bryn Mawr continued to pursue the grant. "I think the question of judging the source of money is not a simplistic one," said President Wofford. Wofford defended the college's decision in an article published in the Bryn Mawr/Haverford student newspaper, *The News,* which was on record as opposing the grant:

No one at Bryn Mawr has suggested that Mr. Khashoggi's record is irrelevant or that we don't care about it. We explored that record in the three-college discussions last summer and circulated information we found. If there is new information we should consider it carefully. But instead of simply saying 'No' to Triad, as *The News* proposes, I think we should examine all the facts and together think about the issues raised.

In deciding our next steps, we need to guard against prejudice, against misinformation, and against the politics of purely personal psychic satisfaction. Wouldn't it be prejudice to accept a donation from Lockheed, for example, which *was* found guilty of improper practices, while refusing it from Triad, whose donor (contrary to the Swarthmore *Phoenix's* allegation) has not been indicted let alone convicted of anything?

The Philadelphia Inquirer supported Bryn Mawr's position. In an editorial entitled ". . . But Money Has No Smell," the newspaper said it did not believe it necessary that Haverford, Swarthmore and Bryn

Mawr "look with revulsion" at the source of the $590,000 grant. "We believe they would do well to follow the counsel of the celebrated American philosopher, Woody Allen, and take the money and run." Like Wofford, the newspaper pointed out that "quite a few sources of donations to higher education would not bear close scrutiny."

The American Jewish Committee memo notes with satisfaction that, though Bryn Mawr pursued the grant proposal, it did so "on a substantially reduced scale."

In fact, Bryn Mawr's request for funds ultimately went unanswered. Khashoggi had been badly burned. He gave up the foundation and with it the offer to the three colleges.

Reflecting on the controversy and on Bryn Mawr's decision to stay with the proposal, Wofford said: "We were in a relatively strong position because that same year we had started a program of inviting people who wanted to contribute to Bryn Mawr's Judaic Studies program to donate Israel bonds." The Jewish community was pleased by this. "In fact," said Wofford, "I was awarded the Eleanor Roosevelt award of the Israel Bonds Organization." Asked how he felt about the withdrawal of the other colleges, Wofford said,

We felt sort of run out on by both of them. In the first place they publicly withdrew without any real consultation. And secondly, it was something we had thought through and it seemed an unfair flap at a potential donor.

In a letter to President Friend, Willis Armstrong said:

Swarthmore seems to me to have taken leave of its principles and to have yielded all too quickly to partisan and xenophobic pressure from a group skilled in the manipulation of public opinion. I am at a loss to think how the United States can promote peace in the Middle East unless we can gain Arab confidence in our understanding and objectivity. For a Quaker institution to turn its back on an opportunity to contribute to this understanding is profoundly depressing.

Haverford President Cary, like Swarthmore's President Friend, denies that his decision to withdraw from the grant proposal was influenced by pressures from the Jewish community. Said Cary:

I did have some letters from some of our Jewish alumnae who thought that we should have no part of such a thing. But that had nothing to do with my decision.

Haverford's provost at the time, Tom D'Andrea, assesses the importance of Jewish opposition differently:

One of the big issues, of course, had to do with very strong opposition from Jewish organizations. I think a lot of it had to do with Arab influence and the whole Middle East situation. But then, of course, you get into really serious questions about academic freedom. The freedom of expression. Well, one way you can avoid that is to find another peg to hang the protest on and the arms one is a little cleaner given the Quaker factor.

In concluding his memo describing the success of the American Jewish Committee's efforts to foil the Middle East studies program at the three colleges, Ira Silverman wrote:

Our participation was not widely known on the campuses and not reported in the public press, as we wished. This is a good case history of how we can be effective in working with colleges to limit Arab influence on campuses—although in view of the schools' Quaker background and Khashoggi's cloudy reputation as an arms merchant, its happy ending is not likely to be replicated easily in other cases.

Swarthmore, Haverford and Bryn Mawr have done little since the 1977–78 events to improve their offerings in a field that has become too hot for many colleges to handle.

Another college about a hundred miles away showed more courage, although it too nearly faltered.

Returning Solicited Gifts

Georgetown University's Center for Contemporary Arab Studies (CCAS) was the first academic program in the United States devoted exclusively to the study of the modern Arab world. Established in 1975, the center is a functional part of the Georgetown University School of Foreign Service. As such, CCAS not only offers an academic program leading to a master's degree in Arab studies but also provides opportunities for students with other international interests to learn about the 22 political systems and 170 million people in North Africa, the Nile valley, the Fertile Crescent, and the Arabian Peninsula.

Since federal funding for a traditional Middle East center at Georgetown had twice been sought and denied, the directors of the new center decided early on to seek support from private sources. They hoped to obtain about half the needed funds from Arab governments. The dean of Georgetown's School of Foreign Service, Peter F. Krogh, explained the original plan: "It was our view that we should not play favorites among the Arab states and seek support from some but not from others. This would then suggest that the academic program would also play favorites."

After obtaining approval for the plan from the university's development office and from Georgetown's president at the time, the Reverend R. J. Henle, Dean Krogh visited all the Arab embassies and missions in Washington. He told them about the center's plans and asked for their assistance. "I went to all of them," says Krogh, "whether they had diplomatic relations with the United States or not, whether they were moderate or radical, whatever their stripe." John Ruedy, chairman of the center's program of studies, recalls the fund raising philosophy in similar terms: "We were going to be sure that we weren't labeled as being in anybody's pocket."

The first country to contribute was Oman, soon followed by grants from United Arab Emirates, Egypt, and Saudi Arabia. Then, in May 1977, Libya committed $750,000, payable over five years, to endow a professorial chair in Arab culture.

The Libyan gift aroused controversy. According to one faculty member, there was "considerable consternation" among faculty, students and some administrators and trustees. The protest included a letter to the student newspaper, the *Georgetown Voice,* from columnist Art Buchwald. Buchwald calling the gift "blood money from one of the most notorious regimes in the world today." But Georgetown's executive vice-president for academic affairs, the Reverend Aloysius P. Kelley, told the *Washington Post* at the time that the Libyan gift "contributes to the fulfillment of the main purpose of the center . . . which is to increase knowledge of the Arab world in the United States." Says Dean Krogh, "Libya was responding to the blanket request to all Arab countries to take an interest in our work and to help us where they could. It was an endowment. They sent the check; we deposited it. They never inquired, never asked for an accounting. They didn't even ask for a stewardship report." Center Director Michael Hudson stressed in press interviews that no conditions were attached to the gift regarding who could occupy the chair or what the chosen professor could teach. "We don't mix politics and education," Hudson told the *Washington Post.*

The next governmental contributors were Jordan, Qatar and Iraq. The Iraqi gift of $50,000 came in the spring of 1978. It was an unrestricted contribution which the center subsequently decided to use to hire a specialist in Islamic ethics.

In the meantime, Henle had been replaced as president of Georgetown by the Reverend Timothy S. Healy. In July of 1978, Healy took the unusual step of returning Iraq's $50,000 gift without advising the center of his intentions. The official reason given for the action was that another donor had come forward to provide funds for the same purpose. In his letter to the director general of Iraq's Center for Research and Information, Healy wrote:

I feel obliged in conscience to return to Your Excellency the generous check which you have sent us. I hope that in doing this, we can continue our conversations and that it will be possible for the university to return to the generosity of the Iraqi government in the future and ask for a gift for which full credit can be given to the government which gave it. I am sure you will understand the delicacy of the university's position in this matter.

But faculty members at the Center for Contemporary Arab Studies said they did not understand "the delicacy of the university's position." Arab Studies Director John Ruedy commented at the time: "Acting as agents of the university, we solicited money from Iraq. The president of this university returned it without ever seeking our approval. His intervention into this is really extraordinary." Dean Krogh told the press: "This is the first time we've given back a grant as long as I've been here," adding that the issue had been "taken out of my hands."

According to the *Washington Star,* both supporters and opponents of the Iraqi grant agreed that "the decision was politically motivated." Ruedy told the *Star:* "I don't know what other basis there would be for refusing the money." CCAS faculty members charged that Father Healy's own support for Israel, combined with pressure from pro-Israeli members of the university's community and from influential Jewish leaders, led him to return the gift.

John Ruedy recalls the incident:

The timing was appalling. We were just shocked. We had been arguing with [Healy] over that for a couple of months. He said he didn't like it. We knew he was distressed about it. But we thought that we had convinced him that he must quietly accept the gift because we had asked for it under the mandate given to us by his predecessor.

According to one member of the CCAS faculty, the center's problems really began with the arrival of Healy:

His whole political socialization regarding the Middle East took place within the context of New York City [where Healy grew up]. He told us early on that if he had been here in our formative days, we wouldn't exist. He was a vulnerable instrument for these people and they kept pushing and pushing and pushing. He was under enormous pressure.

Father Healy refused to comment to the press on his decision to return the gift, saying that to do so "would only harm the institution." The university's executive vice-president for academic affairs and provost, the Reverend Aloysius P. Kelley, declined to comment directly on whether the university had considered any other use for the general purpose grant.

Despite Healy's return of the Iraqi gift, Georgetown's new Arab studies center came under attack. In June 1979 *The New Republic,* a liberal weekly that has become a staunchly pro-Israeli magazine under owner Martin Peretz, ran an article by Nicholas Lemann on Georgetown's Center for Contemporary Arab Studies insinuating that the center was "nothing but a propagandist for the Arabs." Wrote Lemann, "Unlike the older Middle Eastern studies centers at other universities, the Georgetown center makes no attempt to achieve balance by studying Israel along with the Arab nations or by hiring Israeli scholars." Center Director Michael Hudson and Dean Peter Krogh answered this charge in a reply which was prepared but never published:

Since when was it required, for example, that a center for Chinese studies study the Soviet Union and employ Soviet scholars?. . . . The center studies the Arabs and it employs scholars recruited through normal University Departmental and School procedures which provide for appointments without discrimination of any kind. If this country is not allowed by particular interest groups to pursue the study of the Arabs by the same standards applied to the study of other major peoples and cultures, this country's knowledge of, and international relations with, a significant group of countries is going to be deeply, perhaps tragically, flawed.

The *New Republic* article added that the Georgetown Center "is constantly charged with violating standards of scholarly objectivity" but did not say by whom. Author Lemann referred to the center's critics, "who, in the cloak-and-dagger spirit, like to remain anonymous."

Hudson and Krogh, in their unpublished reply, wrote:

Detective Lemann, to his credit, discovers "an informal network of people" operating in the "cloak and dagger spirit" who are busy trying to embarrass the center in some way. To his discredit, he associates himself with this undercover group by borrowing upon these anonymous accusations in criticizing an open, legitimately constituted academic program. A more worthy approach would have been to investigate and reveal the composition, operations, and motivations of this "informal network." We think the public should be deeply concerned about an underground group which seeks to undermine the imparting of knowledge and understanding about the Arab world; certainly we would be interested in any findings Mr. Lemann (or his publisher, Mr. Martin Peretz) could provide on this question.

Despite the return of the Iraqi grant, Georgetown continued to receive Arab funds, including grants of $1 million each from Kuwait and Oman in the fall of 1980. An article in the *Washington Post* reporting the Kuwaiti gift quoted Ira Silverman of the American Jewish Committee as saying that Georgetown's Arab studies center "has a clearly marked pro-Arab, anti-Israel bias in its selection of curriculum material, its faculty appointments, and speakers." By accepting money from "political sponsors of one point of view," said Silverman, Georgetown might be "selling something very precious to Americans—the integrity of its universities."

Georgetown officials rejected criticism of the Arab gifts, pointing out that if it had pro-Arab scholars in the Arab studies center, it had pro-Israel scholars elsewhere on its faculty, particularly in its Center for Strategic and International Studies.

Then, in February 1981 President Healy again returned an Arab donation which had been solicited and received by the Arab studies center. This time it was the grant from Libya received four years earlier. Of the $750,000 pledged over five years, $600,000 had been received. Healy personally took a check for that amount, plus about $42,000 in interest earned, to the Libyan embassy. Healy said Libya's "accent on violence as a normal method of international policy and its growing support of terrorism made [keeping the money] . . . incompatible with everything Georgetown stands for."

Once again, many doubted the official reason given. As one professor in the Arab studies program put it: "If it was strictly an ethical judgment, it certainly was a long time in coming." John Ruedy added:

If you ask around here, you'll probably find nobody in our center who approves of the policies of [Iraqi President] Saddam Hussein. But we have tried to maintain cooperative relationships with the government and, to the extent that we can, with the Iraqi people. We think that this is our mission. And I feel the same way about Libya. I find [Libyan President] Kaddafi very objectionable in most instances. This was a gift, as far as I'm concerned, from the Libyan people.

"This whole thing is something out of the blue," Professor Hisham Sharabi told the *Washington Post*. "It's very strange."

Dean Peter Krogh opposed returning the money but did not make an issue of it. He declined to comment to the press, except to say, "We never felt any pressure from the Libyan government" on how the money was to be spent. But, he observes: "Deans are deans and presidents are presidents. Presidents do pretty much what they please."

Ira Silverman of the American Jewish Committee was "delighted that Georgetown has made this decision." Moreover, the day after the return of the Libyan money, the New York City investment banking firm, Bear, Stearns & Co., donated $100,000 to Georgetown. Said senior managing partner Alan Greenberg, "We admire them, and this is our little way of saying thank you."

Healy told the *Post* that in returning the money to Libya, "I was under absolutely no heat and pressure, but it worried me. I guess I'm just kind of slow to move, but I came to a growing realization that what Libya is up to is incompatible with Georgetown."

In an interview with the *Washingtonian* magazine, however, he was more candid. Originally, he had approved the Libyan gift despite some misgivings. He told the magazine the Libyan money "had been a huge nuisance and had kept him entangled in a verbal version of the Arab-Israeli war." Reported the *Washingtonian:*

His Jewish friends screamed at him privately, and the American Jewish Committee issued a statement publicly condemning the university. Even his gestures of appeasement and balance—a goodwill trip to Israel, an honorary degree for the Israeli ambassador to the United States, refusal of a gift from Iraq, wearing a yarmulke at a Jewish service on campus—did little to offset Jewish anger over the Libyan money.

In fact, pressure on Healy had been intense before his return of the Libyan grant. One expression of Jewish anger took the form of a visit to Healy's office by a delegation of rabbis. Max Kampelman, an influential Jewish member of Georgetown University's Board of Trustees, also interceded with Healy directly. As a former ambassador to the Helsinki Accords, Kampelman was "a major factor," observes Dean Krogh. Former ambassador to the United Nations Arthur Goldberg reportedly added his weight to the combined pressure. In addition, Healy received, according to John Ruedy, "loads of letters." Another Georgetown professor called it "hate mail."

Indeed, controversy over the Arab studies program largely subsided after the return of the Libyan grant. As one professor at the center put it, "If returning the Libyan money has brought us some breathing space and gotten the monkey off our backs, maybe it was worth it." But since then Arab governments have been less forthcoming with contributions. Says Ruedy, "We know that in some cases it has specifically to do with a sense of affront. Returning a gift in one donor's face is seen as an attack on all of them."

On the other hand, Georgetown University has now committed itself and its own financial resources to Arab studies. In the spring of 1983, Arab studies was one of nine graduate programs which the university "designated for excellence." "I feel that this may mean we have crossed the Rubicon," said Ruedy.

One reason Georgetown's Arab studies center has been able to survive, and even prosper despite the controversy, is that it is affiliated with a private university. Says Ruedy,

You could probably not have an Arab studies program in a public institution. You can have a Jewish studies program, of course. In fact, that is politically very advantageous. . . . Georgetown and the Jesuits are as far from dependency on Jewish support as you could be.

"That Was the Buzzword, 'Arab' "

The second U.S. university to create an Arab studies program, Villanova University in Pennsylvania, is also Catholic. In 1983, Villanova set up the Institute for Contemporary Arab and Islamic Studies. The director, Father Kail Ellis, is an Augustinian priest of Lebanese origin. Villanova's is a modest program, involving as yet no outside funds, which offers certificates in Arab studies to undergraduates majoring in other fields. The institution also sponsors conferences, lectures and cultural events. Says Father Ellis: "Our goal is to familiarize the students with the history, language, politics and culture of the Arab Islamic world."

Despite the program's modest scope and the absence of Arab funding, there was considerable opposition to it from within the university, mainly from the political science department. "The pressure wasn't really overt as such," says Ellis. "It was always behind the scenes. There are a couple of faculty people who were the most vocal against it and they organized the opposition."

The political science department was originally asked to comment on the proposal for establishing the institute. In a minority report attached to the department's comments, one professor warned about the effect of such a program on the Jewish community:

Villanova exists in a larger community on which it depends for both financial and political support. This larger community is made up of Protestants, Catholics and Jews and very few Muslims. If Villanova creates an Islamic Studies Institute, it will have no effect, positive or negative, on its Catholic and Protestant constituencies. But because this issue has high emotional content, it will in my view have strong negative effects on the Jewish community in the Villanova area who though relatively few in number are financially and politically influential.

Such an institute might reflect on Villanova University's president in such a way as to affect his ability to function on the Holocaust Committee where his efforts have provided great credibility for Villanova among the Jewish Committee. It is my opinion that the existence of such an institute might dry up possible Jewish financial and political support.

Another professor commented:

Israel is the single most important United States ally in the Middle East politically, it has extensive and close economic and business ties with the U.S., it is the cultural and religious homeland of millions of Americans. To exclude the study of Israel from the proposed program is a mistake and may affect potential enrollment.

Ellis explains: "The idea was to broaden the program from Arab studies. That was the buzzword, 'Arab.'"

Georgetown's John Ruedy was invited to Villanova as a consultant to participate in the preparations for the Arab studies proposal. "The opposition was very interesting," said Ruedy:

It was the Zionist issue but nobody said it. I could just tell, because I'd been there before. The first line of opposition is on academic grounds. But when you get around all these and answer all the questions, then they bare their fangs and say, "This is anti-Israel, this is anti-Semitic, and it will be against the interests of the university. And we have to relate to Jewish donors and so on." This is precisely what happened at Villanova.

After the institute opened, Father Ellis received a letter from American Professors for Peace in the Middle East, a national pro-Israeli organization. The executive director, George Cohen, took issue with a map that appeared in the brochure. The map, clearly labeled "The Arab and Islamic World," shows only the Arab countries of the Middle East and Africa in dark green and the non-Arab Islamic countries, namely, Turkey, Afghanistan and Pakistan in light green. Cohen noted that the map did not identify Israel. "Is this an error," he asked, "or is it intended to make a political statement, excluding Israel?"

Ellis wrote back that the purpose of the map was to identify the Arab and Islamic countries with which the program dealt:

It was not our intention to make a political statement about Israel or any other country, such as Ethiopia, Cyprus, Mali, Chad or even the Turkmen, Uzbek and Tajik Republics of the Soviet Union, all of which are located in the area and have substantial Moslem populations but which were excluded from the map.

Cohen was not satisfied and wrote another letter, saying he did not accept Ellis's response and asking him to "present this issue to your department before I take it further."

Cohen did not specify what measures he might employ in "taking it further," and Ellis did not respond to his second letter. Meanwhile the Institute for Contemporary Arab and Islamic Studies has continued to gain acceptance within the Villanova scholarly community.

Meanwhile, the attacks against the academic community in Middle East studies are, in the view of a leading scholar, continuing and "perhaps getting even stronger." He adds, "They are not directed just at one or two institutions but appear to have a nationwide basis."

Think Tank Under Pressure

Of the many "think tanks" that have sprung up around the country in the last two decades, Georgetown University's Center for Strategic and International Studies is one of the most prestigious. Established in 1965, CSIS has grown to comprise a staff of 150, with a budget of $6 million and a publications list of nearly 200 titles. Among the eminent names on the Center's roster are Henry Kissinger, Howard K. Smith, Lane Kirkland and John Glenn. CSIS is a non-profit, tax-exempt organization which, though known to be conservative in outlook, includes both Democrats and Republicans on its advisory board.

Based in Washington, the center views the provision of expert research and analysis to government leaders as one of its most vital functions. As part of Georgetown University, CSIS considers itself an "integral part of the academic community." Scholarly participation in all center activities "insures that the widest and most rigorous thinking is brought to bear on issues."

The center, says its brochure, is "well-equipped to function in a true interdisciplinary, nonpartisan fashion." Yet, a report completed in 1981 by the director of the center's Oil Field Security Studies Project was suppressed on the eve of Congressional action on the sale of AWACS planes to Saudi Arabia. Supporters of Israel from outside the center were opposed to the sale and did not want the contents of the report known because they feared it could be used effectively in winning Congressional approval. Six months later, the author of the offending study was fired by the center and urged to leave town.

The victim was Mazher Hameed—a native of Saudi Arabia, a graduate of the Fletcher School of Law and Diplomacy and a specialist on international security affairs. Former U.S. ambassador to Saudi Arabia James Akins wrote of Hameed in 1983, "I know of no one else in this country with his insight, his honesty, his analytical ability and his profound knowledge of the Middle East, particularly the Arabian Peninsula." Hameed was hired by the center in November of 1980 as a research fellow "with responsibilities for research on a project on Saudi oil field security." In the letter of appointment, CSIS Executive Director Amos Jordan wrote: "This letter also constitutes a formal approval of the oil field security project."

The scope of the project was outlined in a memorandum to Jordan prepared a month earlier by Wayne Berman, responsible to Jordan for fund raising. That memo stated that the project would focus on the political and military analysis of oil field vulnerabilities in the Middle East, the likelihood of attacks from various sources, an examination of security planning, and technical defense profiles.

Amos Jordan himself brought up with Hameed the need to evaluate the AWACS/F-15 enhancement package before it became an issue on Capitol Hill.

For the next nine months, Hameed carried out his research and wrote a series of drafts of a report on his results. These drafts were shown to Amos Jordan, who had become vice chairman of the center, and to David Abshire, the chairman, as well as to several experts outside the center. The final report was to be published by CSIS.

Jordan told Hameed after reading one of the earlier drafts that his work was "brilliant" and that he wanted to see more work of that caliber emerging from the center. Abshire concurred with this view. Jordan personally gave copies of one of the earlier drafts to William Clark, at that time deputy secretary of state and subsequently President Reagan's national security advisor. Other Middle East experts who praised the report were Anthony Cordesman, international editor of the *Armed Forces Journal,* and William Quandt, director of the Energy and National Security Project of the Brookings Institution.

In August 1981, Abshire and Jordan left together for a trip to Tokyo. They took Hameed's final draft with them. Jordan sent back a telex praising the study: "On plane I read Hameed's Saudi security paper," read the telex, "which is informative and beautifully written." The telex went on to suggest that the report should be edited to tone down its strong advocacy of the AWACS/F-15 package. "Paper makes strong case without overkill," wrote Jordan. "Careful edit to meet above point needed before CSIS publishes in house by about 10 or 15 September. Suggest 300 copies."

In accordance with these instructions, Hameed met with Jean Newsom, a senior editor at the center, and William Taylor, director of political and military studies, and the three of them set to work on the final editing. At the same time, Newsom initiated talks with McGraw-Hill concerning publication of the report.

Jean Newsom, when asked to confirm that the center had negotiated publication of the report with McGraw-Hill, demurred. She said in a telephone interview: "We were not negotiating with McGraw-Hill, just seeing whether they were interested." But Trish Wilson, a research assistant for Hameed at the time, said, "They were talking about what the price was. They gave McGraw-Hill an estimate of how much they could sell the book for."

The editing proceeded simultaneously with the negotiations through September and into October when, without warning, the center's comptroller, David Wendt, told Hameed that David Abshire had called from California where he was vacationing on his way back from

Japan. The message from Abshire was that the report was not to be released.

Upset, Hameed pursued the matter with Jordan and others at the center: "They told me that many very large contributors to the center would be upset if they saw a report that was, as they described it, 'lacking in objectivity.'" Research assistant Paul Sutphin recalls:

I remember that it came as quite a surprise that suddenly there was going to be a problem with the center's putting out the report. Everything fell apart at the last moment. Hameed said that suddenly the "powers on high" had decided to nix the center's support of the publication.

Trish Wilson also remembers the incident: "They didn't want him to publish it at all, even privately."

Another of Hameed's research assistants, George Smalley, who had been hired at the beginning of October on a salary basis was told before the month was out that his status would be changed. "Due to budget problems," he was to work on a fee basis and would no longer be granted any of the benefits initially agreed upon. These included social security, a paid vacation, sick leave, and free tuition at Georgetown University after one year. Smalley is convinced there was a direct link between the fate of Hameed's report and the fate of his own position with the center.

At that stage Hameed decided to take the initiative:

I wanted the report out before the AWACS issue came up in Congress. Because this was a document that was relevant to what was being discussed on the Hill and I want my work to be looked at.

Hameed sent copies of the 85-page report to major corporations that contributed to the center. He told them: "I understand you people would be upset if you saw this report coming out of the center." Until that time, says Hameed, he had no relationship with these companies. The center had asked him specifically not to go to any of these corporations for funding because it had long-standing relationships with most of them and didn't want these disturbed.

"These people," says Hameed, "for the first time heard about me, saw the report, got excited and started calling the center to ask what was going on. They said that not only was the document interesting, not only did it have a unique point of view, but it had something very timely to say." Some of these companies, acknowledged Hameed, were engaged in the lobbying effort on behalf of the AWACS sale. "They found something that they liked very much," he recalls, "and they wanted to use it. So I used some influence of that sort to get a compromise." The compromise was that the center permitted Hameed to release the report as a private document. "But they didn't want me to indicate my designation at the center. I could just say I was a research fellow and program director without mentioning the name of the project." Naming the project would have given the report additional credibility. "They didn't want him to say that it was under the research auspices of the center," confirms Paul Sutphin.

Hameed complied with the request. "For me the primary interest was to get the document out and to get it read. What the document had to say was more important than these other matters." So Hameed had the report printed at his own expense and released it himself.

The response to the report in government circles was immediate. Recalls Hameed: "People at the State Department asked for copies, people on the Hill asked for copies, NSC [the National Security Council] asked for copies." After Egyptian President Anwar Sadat was assassinated the following month, William Clark gave copies of Hameed's report to former Presidents Nixon, Ford and Carter to help update themselves on the Middle East while en route to Cairo for Sadat's funeral. Clark called CSIS Vice-Chairman Amos Jordan specifically to tell him about it. Jordan conveyed this information to Hameed and assured him that the center's chairman, David Abshire, concurred in praising the report.

On October 28, the U.S. Senate voted 52 to 48 against a resolution that would have blocked the AWACS sale to Saudi Arabia. Although the House had passed such a resolution two weeks earlier, a majority in both chambers was required to prevent the sale from going through. The Senate vote represented a rare defeat for the pro-Israeli lobby and one it was not about to forget.

In November Amos Jordan received a visit from Steve Emerson, an aide in former Senator Frank Church's law firm, who had earlier assisted Church on the Senate Foreign Relations Committee. Emerson asked Jordan probing questions about the center's activities, some of them concerning Hameed's project. He told Jordan he was writing an article for *The New Republic* about the influence of "petro-dollars." Emerson said he was interested in Hameed's report and wanted to know who had funded it. After the interview, Jordan called Hameed, cautioned him that there might be some "turbulence" and advised him to "fasten your seatbelt." To Jordan, the interview was "something threatening." He later told Hameed: "It was clear that Emerson's questions were hostile, and we were concerned that we would be subject to some unwarranted charges."

In early December, Emerson and his associates returned to the center and brought with them the draft of the Emerson article for *The*

New Republic. It was part of a series Emerson was writing for the magazine on alleged Arab attempts to manipulate U.S. public opinion. The suggestion was that policy "think tanks" receiving money from oil corporations with Arab business were under obligation to serve the political interests of those companies. But the draft fell short of singling out CSIS, and center officials continued to feel they could safely weather the storm caused by Hameed's report.

Hameed, exhausted physically and emotionally, left in December for a vacation, but only, he said, after receiving assurance from Jordan that there was "nothing to worry about."

"I came back in January," said Hameed, "to learn that these gentlemen had returned once more to the center with another draft of the *New Republic* article. This time the draft appeared to compromise the center in a more specific way."

Nevertheless, another member of the center's senior staff, Jon Vondracek, had been in touch with the publisher of *The New Republic,* Martin Peretz. He told Hameed that he thought the center had enough clout to prevent the magazine from doing any harm.

During the same period, Emerson phoned Hameed's office, asking questions about the report and, more specifically, about how Hameed's project was funded. When Hameed declined to reveal his sources of funding, Emerson threatened to expose an alleged "petro-dollar" connection at CSIS. Hameed wished him luck. In addition to calling Hameed and his staff, Emerson had also contacted several corporations trying to find out who had funded the research.

"What was funny," says Hameed, "was that my project had some funding but not from any of the companies you would expect. I felt I shouldn't go to companies that had an obvious interest in influencing my work. What I had to say didn't need influence from other groups, particularly those that were funding it. But beyond that I didn't want the appearance of such influence. Having been meticulous about all this, I was especially irked to have this problem at the end."

On February 17, 1982, the first of Steve Emerson's promised series of articles appeared in *The New Republic.* Entitled "The Petro-dollar Connection," the article was to be followed, according to the magazine, by future articles dealing with "strings-attached donations to policy think tanks, universities, and research institutions."

The very next day, the center found itself under the spotlight from another sources. *Platt's Oilgram News,* a respected newsletter owned by McGraw-Hill, published an article on February 18 about Hameed's report, saying the document had been "kept under wraps" by CSIS. Entitled "Georgetown Study: Israel Could 'Create' a Saudi Oil Embargo to Pressure U.S.," the article quoted from the section of the report which discussed threats to Saudi Arabia from its neighbors. This was one of the sections that the CSIS directors were most nervous about, because it made the point that since Israel considered Saudi Arabia a "confrontation state" in the Arab-Israeli conflict, the Israelis might make pre-emptive strikes against Saudi military and economic assets.

"The study notes," said the *Oilgram* article, "that Israel already occupies Saudi territory (the islands of Tiran and Sanafir) and that since 1976, Israeli aircraft have been making practice bombing runs over the Saudi airbase of Tabuk, dropping empty fuel tanks on several occasions. In addition, Israel has pointed out that its air force has the capability to create an 'oil embargo' of its own by destroying Saudi oil installations."

The editor of *Platt's Oilgram News*, Onnik Maraschian, did not know who had written the report or that it had been released privately months earlier. "All we knew was that there was a report," says Maraschian. "It was distributed as a draft, as a CSIS report, and then it got pulled back, but we ran it nevertheless because it started as a project of CSIS."

After the *Platt's* article appeared, CSIS began to receive phone calls from people wanting copies of the study. This created an embarrassing situation for the center. Should they admit that they had suppressed the report? How could they explain the fact that they had never published it? Vice-Chairman Amos Jordan attempted a solution in the form of a memorandum to "Concerned Staff" that deserves a prize for obfuscation. The memo called the staff's attention to the publication of the *Platt's* article and suggested they use the following paragraph to answer all inquiries:

The center has not 'completed last fall' a study entitled 'Saudi Security and the Evolving Threat to U.S. Interests.' We have had underway for over a year a project on oil field security and research and that study continues. The project has produced several research fragments, including a partial draft with the title cited, but that does not represent a center study—rather it is only a small piece of the problem; and that at an early stage. When the study is completed later this year and becomes a CSIS report, it will be made public.

"They were quite taken aback when they saw that we used the story," recalls Maraschian. "Obviously when they commissioned the man to do this study they knew what his qualifications were. So why did they go with it for a year and then pull it back?" Maraschian had an idea: "You see, what they got mad at was the possibility of a pre-emptive strike by Israel."

Interestingly, Hameed was not the only one who thought that Is-

rael might make a pre-emptive strike against Saudi Arabia. In the secret version of a government report entitled "U.S. Assistance to the
State of Israel," and leaked to the press in June 1983, the CIA is cited
as warning that in reaction to the modernization of Arab armies, Israel
might launch "pre-emptive attacks in future crises." In fact, over the
years Israeli military officials have talked openly about such strikes
against Saudi Arabia.

Embarrassed by the *Platt's* article and worried about efforts by
the Israeli lobby to discredit the center, Jordan and Abshire—despite
their own inclination to support the sale of AWACS to Saudi Arabia—
apparently finally decided that Hameed was too great a liability. A
week later, the center's comptroller, David Wendt, told Hameed he
would have to pay an additional surcharge on his office space amounting to $1,570 a month. As project director, Hameed was already paying
24 percent of his project funds to cover office overhead costs and
another 20 percent to help cover the center's general operations. The
new charge would come on top of what he was already paying.

"I grumbled a bit but finally agreed," recalls Hameed. "Then came
the bombshell. They made it retroactive back 18 months!" Wendt told
Hameed that, with the new charges, his project was $40,000 in deficit.
Wendt said he would have to report the deficit and that it was likely that
Hameed's project would be terminated.

The stunned Hameed called John Shaw, a member of the senior
staff. Shaw confided to Hameed that David Abshire was furious,
though Shaw wouldn't say why. Committee meetings were held
throughout that day in order, Hameed believes, to discuss how to deal
with the "problem." The answer reached, says Hameed, was to offer
up his head.

In April Hameed met with Jordan, whom he found uncharacterist-
ically cold and distant. Jordan said he was concerned about the
"deficit" and warned that Hameed's project was in an unsustainable
financial position.

A few days later, Jordan sent Hameed a letter stating that the
project would have to be terminated by the end of the following month.
Jordan added that he would be happy to review his decision and that
Hameed might be hired back if he could raise "especially large amounts
of money."

After receiving the letter, Hameed met again with Jordan. He still
hoped there was something he could do to prevent the imminent col-
lapse of his project. He still saw Jordan as a friend, a man who had
supported him personally and professionally. He thought that Jordan
had been given a distorted picture of his project's finances. But Jordan
was unmoved. He responded to Hameed that the new surcharge had

been decided formally and that the matter was beyond his control. Hameed pleaded with Jordan to give him at least three or four months in which to wind things up, but to no avail.

Hameed spoke to other prominent people at the center in a desperate attempt to save his project. One told him, "Just lie low and once this thing blows over, we can probably arrange to have you come back." But, recalls Hameed with some bitterness, "Basically, no one stood up for me. They all looked the other way. They let it happen. The knives were out."

Then, on March 5, shortly after learning that his job was to be terminated, Hameed arrived at his office to find that it had been burgled during the night. Someone had managed to penetrate three locked doors and had then pried open the file cabinet next to Hameed's desk. The burglar had first to enter the office building, which was equipped with an electronic surveillance system using card readers. Then he had to enter the locked door to the office suite and finally the locked door to Hameed's office. There were no signs of forced entry. But the file cabinet was bent and the drawer had been wrenched open. Adds Paul Sutphin: "This bore no signs of a common burglary. There were other valuable things that were not taken." In fact, nothing was taken at all. "It was such a lousy job, so obvious," says Trish Wilson, "that we concluded it was there to scare us."

The next day Hameed found that the post office box he used for some of his correspondence had been broken open. A few days later, the mailbox at his home was broken open. "Other weird things started to happen as well," recalls Hameed. "For example, I'd leave for the weekend and come back and find things in my house that didn't belong there . . . like contact lenses."

These incidents were particularly frightening to Hameed—and the contact lens prank needlessly cruel—because he is blind.

Hameed left the center at the end of March. In May and June, *The New Republic* published the second and third parts of its series on petrodollar influence in the United States. The promised exposé of "strings-attached donations to policy think tanks" was missing from the series.

The last episode in Hameed's relations with CSIS occurred in May 1982, some weeks after he had left the center. Officers of the center contacted a number of Hameed's friends as well as corporate executives in an effort to discredit him. In one case, a senior administration official's help was sought to encourage Hameed to "leave town."

Several corporations, after learning that Hameed had been fired, cut back their contributions to Georgetown University and made it clear that the reason was the treatment accorded Mazher Hameed.

Amos Jordan, asked to comment on Hameed's charges, insisted that these various circumstances were coincidental and that Hameed's departure related only to his performance. He denied that the center responded to lobby pressure: "I went out of my way to protect and sponsor Hameed despite the deficits. I am concerned that the center not have a reputation for being a Zionist foil."

It was an unsettling, traumatic time for the scholar. In a short space of weeks, people from the pro-Israel magazine descended on the center—threatening an expose of petrodollar influence, warning about the center's tax status under IRS regulations, questioning the funding of Hameed's project. Preceding and following these events were the center's suppression of the report, the personal harassment of Hameed, his associates and his friends—and his dismissal. If the coincidence of these events was pure happenstance, it was a remarkable coming together.

Recalling what he knew of Hameed's tenure at CSIS, William Quandt, senior fellow at the Brookings Institution and a personal friend of Hameed's said: "The way they terminated his whole relationship there was rather strange. He was very shabbily treated, to say the least." Les Janka, former special assistant in the White House for Middle East affairs, said: "CSIS did not have the courage to put out under its own name a paper that made a significant contribution to public debate."

Chapter 8

Tucson: Case Study in Intimidation

In November 1980, Sheila Scoville, outreach coordinator at the University of Arizona's Near Eastern Center, was visited in her office by a short, balding man in his late forties. His immediate purpose was to borrow a book, but as he left he remarked: "I understand you are running a pro-Arab propaganda network."

The man was Boris Kozolchyk, a law professor at the University of Arizona and vice-chair of the Community Relations Committee of the Tucson Jewish Community Council. Kozolchyk's remark signalled the beginning of a three-year attack against the Near Eastern Center that would culminate in the barring of outreach materials from local public schools and the resignation of the center's director. The attack, orchestrated by local Jewish community leaders, succeeded despite the finding of a panel of nationally known Middle East scholars that charges of anti-Israel bias in the program were groundless.

The details of Tucson's long ordeal constitute a noteworthy case study of the unrelenting commitment and resourcefulness of pro-Israel activists at the community level.

The Near Eastern Center, devoted to increasing knowledge and understanding of the Middle East, is one of only eleven such facilities in the United States which receive federal funding. To qualify for federal support, each of these centers must devote a portion of its resources to "outreach" and educational programs for the local community. These may take the form of films, public lectures, information and consultation services, seminars for businessmen, or curriculum development for the public schools.

Sheila Scoville had been coordinating these outreach activities for the University of Arizona for four years when the Tucson Jewish Community Council began making its complaints. With a Ph.D. in Middle

East history from UCLA, she was well qualified for the job and had made the Tucson outreach program one of the most active programs in the country. Scoville, a petite blond in her late thirties, had also co-founded the Middle East Outreach Council, the coordinating body for the eleven Middle East outreach programs in the United States.

In February 1981, Kozolchyk and three other representatives of the Tucson Jewish Community Council (TJCC) contacted William Dever, chairman of the Oriental Studies Department of which the Near Eastern Center is a part. They told Dever that in their opinion both Scoville and Near Eastern Center Director Ludwig Adamec had an "anti-Israeli bias which called into question their objectivity about the Middle East." Dever said that the authority for the outreach program rested with the federal government, which provided most of the funds. He suggested that the group form an official committee and gave them, in his own words, "carte blanche" to check out any of the Near Eastern Center's outreach materials. He even said that he would "personally remove" from the library shelves any materials which the Tucson Jewish Community Council found offensive. In a later meeting which Adamec attended, the director of the Near Eastern Center responded: "We do not have anything inflammatory or propagandistic. You tell me which books you find that way. I'll look at them, and if I agree I'll tell Sheila to throw them in the wastepaper basket." But Kozolchyk and the others rejected this offer. Their aims were more ambitious.

Following Dever's advice, the TJCC formed a committee of four women who called themselves "concerned teachers." (Only two of them were actually teachers, both at the private Tucson Hebrew Academy.) Dever then introduced the group to Sheila Scoville and told her to provide them whatever help they required in conducting their investigation.

Among the four women were Carol Karsch, co-chair of the TJCC Community Relations Committee and wife of the president of Tucson's largest conservative synagogue. Karsch was to join Kozolchyk as a major figure in the attack against the outreach program. The group first met with Scoville and "grilled" her, as she recalls it, about her activities. They asked for a copy of her mailing list and for the names of teachers who had checked out materials from the library. Then the group, permitted to enter the Near Eastern Center after hours, set to work collecting and reviewing library materials. By May, the four women had prepared a "preliminary report."

Instead of returning to Dever with their findings, the TJCC committee complained directly to the U.S. Department of Education. Carol Karsch wrote the letter to Washington, attaching to it the group's report. The report questioned the use of federal funds to promote outreach "in an area so inherently complex and conflictive [sic] as Middle East studies."

The report strongly suggested that the ultimate aim of the TJCC was to shut down the outreach program altogether:

Even if numerous materials were added objectively portraying Israel and her interests, coupled with the removal of objectionable and propagandistic material regarding the Arab viewpoint, the problem would still exist.

It is the outreach function *per se* (and not the implementation by any specific institution) which ought to be addressed.

The Department of Education replied to the TJCC that it was not responsible for the content or scholarly quality of the outreach material, which was the responsibility of the university.

Accordingly, the TJCC again focused on the university. A delegation from the council visited the office of university president John Schaefer and complained to him of the anti-Israeli bias they perceived in the outreach materials. After assuring the group that all such materials must conform to university standards, Schaefer referred the matter to Dean Paul Rosenblatt of the Liberal Arts College. Rosenblatt arranged a meeting on October 5, 1981, between representatives of the TJCC and members of the Oriental Studies Department faculty. Sheila Scoville was not invited. At that meeting the new head of the Oriental Studies Department, Robert Gimello, suggested that the TJCC "document more specifically" its concerns so that his department could provide a response. At the same time, Gimello agreed to set up an ad hoc committee within the Oriental Studies Department to review the outreach program.

The TJCC seized this opportunity and, armed with additional library materials, set to work on its report. None of those who reviewed the materials had any academic credentials in the Middle East field. On March 19, 1982, it presented a document of nearly one hundred pages to the university. It included reviews of fifteen Near Eastern Center publications, eight books, five pamphlets and bibliographies, and two teachers' guides. The report objected to one book's reference to Palestine as "the traditional homeland of the Arabs" and another description of the Palestine Liberation Organization as "the only legitimate representative of the Palestinian people." It faulted a map for failing to designate Jerusalem as the capital of Israel—even though, of course, not even the United States recognizes it as such—and cited "the pervasive theme throughout most materials that Jews are interlopers in an area that rightfully belongs to the Arabs."

Among the twelve appendices to the report was a "memorandum

of law" prepared by a Tucson attorney, Paul Bartlett. He contended that the outreach center violated the First Amendment to the Constitution as well as eligibility guidelines for federal funds by trying to "eliminate the Israeli point of view from the spectrum of views presented to the public schools and the press regarding the Arab-Israeli conflict." The memorandum contended further that the program violated the constitutional separation of church and state by showing "a religious preference with respect to the Middle East" since it "advances the religion of Islam and consciously belittles the connection between the Jewish religion and the Middle East."

The report was co-authored by Boris Kozolchyk and Carol Karsch, with the help of four volunteers: a rabbi, an agricultural economist who had studied in Israel, and a non-Jewish couple (the husband a lawyer and the wife an elementary school teacher).

Gimello welcomed the report as a "thoughtful, well-intentioned community response." The ad hoc committee within Gimello's Oriental Studies Department was itself ill-equipped to make a scholarly review of the outreach program, as its five members included a Japanese linguist, an Indian rural anthropologist and Gimello himself, an expert on Buddhism. Of the five committee members, only two had a Middle East background: one a specialist in Arabic literature, and one in Jewish history. Adamec did not participate in the committee's work because he had gone on a six-month sabbatical to Pakistan in January. Sheila Scoville was not consulted.

After receiving the TJCC report in March, the ad hoc committee met regularly for two months to review the materials it criticized and to try to decide what to do about it. In May, 1982, as the academic year drew to a close with the work still unfinished and several members of the committee due to leave for the summer, the committee adopted an interim response that shocked many: "Pending, and without prejudice to, the final resolution of our deliberations, the Near East Center's outreach program will suspend its distribution of materials to elementary and secondary schools."

The suspension of the outreach program was an unexpected victory for the TJCC, which named Kozolchyk and Karsch "Man and Woman of the Year" at its annual awards dinner in June. The four volunteers who had helped them were also presented with "Special Recognition" awards for their "scholarly and objective analyses."

But the victory celebration proved to be premature. When Near East Center Director Ludwig Adamec returned from Pakistan in mid-August, he was incensed at the action of the Oriental Studies Department. He dispatched a memo to all department faculty drawing their attention to the TJCC campaign against the outreach program and to the ad hoc committee's action. The TJCC report, he said, was not scholarly and was replete with ad hominem attacks, false issues and innuendo. Adamec said the closing of the outreach program was ill-advised, premature and done without the committee's consulting expert opinion: "It is utterly inappropriate that a committee of scholars without expertise in the field" judge the matter.

Adamec's annoyance increased when he saw the headlines in an early September issue of the student newspaper: "Interim Report: Department Drops Anti-Israel Materials." In a statement to the editor of the student newspaper, Adamec wrote:

Our center does not contain any "anti-Israeli" materials; it contains books and other items which discuss the Middle East, including Israel. . . . Our books have been selected on the basis of expert recommendation and it would not be feasible to proceed in a manner different from, let's say, the university library, which does not endorse the material contained on its shelves.

Naturally, we want to enjoy the friendship and support of all segments of the community in Arizona and therefore we give serious consideration to the concerns of all. I do not think there is any need to make sensational copy about an issue which has now been resolved.

But the issue was far from resolved. With strong encouragement from Adamec, Gimello prepared a memo reversing the suspension of the Outreach Center and containing the ad hoc committee's "Final Response" to the TJCC report. After acknowledging the right of community groups to comment on and criticize the university's outreach program, the memo stated that the members of the Department of Oriental Studies reserved to themselves the final authority to evaluate the academic merit of any of their programs. The memo took "strong exception" to TJCC personal criticism of Sheila Scoville and Ludwig Adamec and, in particular, "the attribution to them of certain political biases":

It happens that both scholars deny the accusations in question, but more important than the truth or falsity of the accusations is the fact that they are irrelevant and out of order. Members of our department are entitled to whatever political views they may choose to hold. . . . The university in any free and open society is by design an arena of dispute and contention, and it does not cease to be such an arena when it engages in community outreach. . . . For all of these reasons, we have resolved not to close our outreach program. Neither will we discard any of the books we use in that program, or keep them under lock and key, or burn them.

The memo stressed the need to offer the community a variety of opinions on the Middle East, "a variety with which any citizen must be familiar before he can responsibly, intelligently and freely formulate his own opinions." The ad hoc committee found, however, "in the whole array of the program's holdings, no general pattern of political discrimination and no evidence that political palatability, to any group, has ever been used as a criterion in the selection of materials."

The TJCC had contended that the materials used in the outreach program, while suitable for use within the university, were inappropriate for use in elementary and secondary schools because younger students lacked the sophistication to understand them. Gimello's memo pointed out that the immediate clientele of the Outreach Center was not the students but their teachers and that the final decisions as to which materials were suitable for their younger charges should be left up to the teachers.

Carol Karsch then launched a personal attack on William Dever, Gimello's predecessor as head of the Oriental Studies Department. Dever was an archaeologist who had done much digging in Israel. He had returned in August from a year's sabbatical in Israel and was dependent on Israeli goodwill for much of his archaeological research. In late October, three weeks after receiving the department's "Final Response," Karsch told Shalom Paul, a visiting Israeli professor about to return to Tel Aviv, that Dever was no longer a friend of Israel. Karsch told Paul to go back and spread the word so that Dever would "never again dig in Israel." Karsch did not realize that Professor Paul was a close friend of Dever's and had no intention of carrying such a message back to Israel. Instead, he got word back to Dever of his conversation with Karsch before leaving Tucson.

With this information, Dever sent Mrs. Karsch an angry letter saying, in part:

I have reason to believe that you (and perhaps others) have attempted to implicate me in charges of: (1) obstructing the Jewish Community Council's "investigation" of this department's outreach program while I was Head; (2) threatening to undermine the Judaic Studies Program if you pursued your investigation; (3) instigating the reopening of the outreach program when I returned from Israel last August; and (4) participating in a deliberate arrangement to keep Jewish faculty from serving on the department's newly-appointed committee to oversee the Near East Center and its outreach program. I have also learned from more than one recent, direct source that I have now been labeled publicly in the Jewish Community as 'anti-Zionist' and even 'anti-Semitic.'

Dever denied all of the charges and said that "far from obstructing your investigation, the record will show that I was both candid and cooperative—which neither you nor other members of your group have been." Noting that his research, professional standing and livelihood had been jeopardized, Dever told Karsch that he considered the attack grounds for legal action and signed his letter: "Awaiting your response, William Dever."

There was no response. Instead, Carol Karsch and Boris Kozolchyk sent to the university a scathing "Reply to the Department of Oriental Studies' Final Response," calling that document a "smokescreen" and demanding that the department rebut the TJCC charges point by point. Once again, the department agreed to accommodate the TJCC. From December 10 to December 29, 1982, Middle East area faculty drafted a 330-page "Extended and Detailed Response to the Tucson Jewish Community Council's Report on Middle East Outreach at the University of Arizona." The document was presented to the new university president, Henry Koffler, who had succeeded Schaefer in September.

Outside Experts Get Sidetracked

President Koffler was new to Tucson and was desirous of integrating himself with the community. He had addressed a meeting of Haddasah, the women's Zionist organization, within a few months of his arrival. Instead of endorsing the Oriental Studies Department's report, he decided to bring to Tuscon a panel of Middle East scholars from around the country who would investigate the TJCC charges, review the outreach materials, and serve as arbiters of the dispute.

Koffler asked the TJCC and the Oriental Studies Department each to present a list of eight scholars. Each side could then veto half of the other side's choices. From the final list of eight scholars Koffler selected four: Richard Frye of Harvard, Carl Brown of Princeton, William Brinner of Berkeley and Nahum Glatzer of Boston University. It was agreed that the four scholars would meet in Tucson from July 29 to August 1, 1983 to examine the charges against the outreach program and to decide whether each item of material contested by the TJCC was "essentially scholarly or essentially propagandistic."

In the meantime, Koffler ordered the faculty and staff of the Department of Oriental Studies not to speak to the press or to take the matter outside the university. The TJCC, not content to await the decision of the scholars, observed no such discretion.

First, with the help of the National Jewish Community Relations Advisory Council in New York, the TJCC again brought the matter to the attention of the U.S. Department of Education in Washington. The associate director of the New York organization sent a letter to Edward Elmendorf, assistant secretary for post secondary education, repeating the TJCC's objections to the outreach program. The TJCC sent a copy of its report attacking the program to Elmendorf and to U.S. Representative James McNulty and U.S. Senator Dennis DeConcini, both of Arizona. In a letter to the DOE, DeConcini said that if the TJCC's charges were correct, "then the federal funding from the Department of Education for this type of project should be terminated immediately." The Senator from Arizona asked in his letter for a complete federal investigation of the charges.

Responding to the two Congressmen, the Department of Education pointed out that it was federal policy to leave the evaluation of publications and other academic materials to "normal academic channels" and that the impending meeting of the panel of experts "should lead to a mutually satisfactory resolution of this matter."

When Adamec learned of the steps the TJCC had taken, he sent a letter to President Koffler in which he suggested that Koffler ask the TJCC why it carried its complaint outside the university after agreeing to Koffler's arbitration efforts. Adamec also questioned the motivation for the TJCC action "at a time when our application for [renewal of federal] funding in national competition is being decided." He suggested that "our accusers want to hurt our chances of being selected."

When, despite these efforts, the center received its federal funding for the following academic year, Senator DeConcini and Representative McNulty wrote jointly to U.S. Secretary of Education Terrence Bell complaining that the "funding cycle had been completed" without the peer review group's being provided with the TJCC report documenting "possible propagandizing through the outreach program." They appealed to Bell, "as the only official who can temporarily halt the funding," to do so and to order the complete investigation that DeConcini had earlier requested.

Secretary Bell responded to the two Congressmen with a letter stating that "Federal interference would be unwarranted and illegal." Wrote Bell: "Questions of academic freedom as well as of state and local control of education also enter in here." Despite his generally firm position on the matter, Bell did seek to appease the indignant Congressmen by informing them that he would "encourage the university to suspend its dissemination of the contested materials pending the outcome of the local committee proceedings."

While the TJCC was enlisting the aid of Congress, Ludwig Adamec learned that he was being attacked by Boris Kozolchyk. In a letter to university President Koffler, Adamec charged that Kozolchyk had made "untrue statements about my background and personal life." In particular, he wrote, Kozolchyk had told members of the university's Department of Judaic Studies that Adamec was "a member of the German Wehrmacht during World War II." He had also told Professor Dever that Adamec had been "arrested as a Nazi." Finally, Kozolchyk claimed that Adamec had, at a public gathering, characterized Israel as a "pirate state." Adamec had in fact been arrested as a teenager by the Nazis for trying to escape into Switzerland from his native Austria. After a year and a half in jail, he was sent to a concentration camp where he remained until the end of the war. In his letter, he simply said that all of the charges were ridiculous and wrote:

I do not know Dr. Kozolchyk and cannot imagine what is the purpose of these slanderous remarks other than to make me appear unfit to carry out my duties as a professor of Middle East studies and as director of the Near East Center, which I have founded and managed since 1975.

He asked that the university's grievance committee reprimand Kozolchyk and require him to desist from his defamatory campaign.

But Kozolchyk and the TJCC were not to be deterred. Having failed to get satisfaction from Washington, they turned their attention to the local community and, in particular, the local school district. In May 1983, the TJCC delivered a copy of its attack on the outreach program to Jack Murrieta, assistant superintendent of the Tucson Unified School District. In addition, the TJCC made fresh allegations to Murrieta about a new course that Sheila Scoville had taught during the spring semester called "Survey of the Middle East." Without giving the university a chance to respond to the charges, Murrieta sent out a memorandum to the eight high school teachers and librarians who had taken Scoville's course. The memorandum notified the teachers that the school district would not offer salary increase credits for the course "pending investigation" and would not allow textbooks or teaching aids from the course in district classrooms without approval from each teacher's supervisor.

One of those who received a copy of Murrieta's memorandum was Robert Gimello. The head of the Oriental Studies Department was angered that the school district should take such an action without consulting his department. First of all, the course was new, and had not been included in the original TJCC attack of 1982. Moreover, in a deliberate attempt not to exacerbate the ongoing controversy, Sheila Scoville had avoided the modern period of Middle East history altogether, ending her course with the establishment of Israel in 1948. In a letter to Murrieta, Gimello defended Scoville and refuted the new TJCC allegations:

There has, in fact, been no discrimination in enrollment; neither the materials used in the course nor the manner of their presentation has been propagandistic in nature; and we are confident that the course violates no federal guidelines. Claims to the contrary are profoundly offensive to us not only because they are untrue but also because they would appear to be part of a concerted attempt to interfere with the free dissemination of information and legitimate scholarly opinion.

But Murrieta maintained his "lock-out" of the outreach program. The teachers, who had received his memorandum the day after completing the final exam for the course, were enraged and a group of them took the matter to the Arizona Civil Liberties Union. The ACLU agreed with the teachers that the school district action represented "a potential violation of academic freedom rights" and consented to represent them. ACLU Associate Director Helen Mautner met with Murietta and another school district official to discuss the issue. In a letter sent later to the president and other members of the school board, she said she had had the distinct impression that much of her conversation with the school district officials was "full of either deliberate obfuscation on their part or evasiveness." Mautner wrote that she was "dismayed" that the district had taken such action after the employees had finished the course and with what appeared to be "very little attempt to ascertain some facts" or to discuss the matter "with both sides of the controversy." The ACLU decided, nevertheless, to await the judgment of the blue ribbon panel concerning the charges of bias before pressing suit against the district.

Meanwhile, arrangements for the blue ribbon panel proceeded, growing more complex with each letter exchanged between President Koffler and the TJCC. The list of items which the TJCC wanted the panel to cover incuded: the outreach materials themselves and their "networking" among outreach coordinators, the choice of emphasis in their presentation and distribution, their effect on children, foreign government and oil company sponsorship, the perception of university endorsement, Scoville's workshop for teachers and her new survey course, the funding, administration and supervision of the outreach program, and the Department of Oriental Studies' defense of the program.

Koffler decided, with the agreement of the TJCC, that the panel would deal only with some of the items. The university would then carry out a separate investigation of the others.

On July 15, the University of Arizona controversy finally broke into the public domain. Once again, breaking its word of keeping the matter private, the TJCC had given copies of its report to the local press. Articles appeared simultaneously in the two major Tucson dailies, while a local television program carried interviews with Carol Karsch of the TJCC, Sylvia Campoy of the Tucson Unified School District, and ACLU official Helen Mautner. Meanwhile, the department's response to the now public charges against it remained, as ever, under virtual lock and key. Moreover, under orders from President

Koffler not to speak to the press, Gimello, Adamec and Scoville could neither answer reporters' questions nor appear on television programs.

The newspapers quoted liberally from the TJCC report, including its contention that "a national effort linking corporate and Arab interests was promoting the dissemination of [outreach] materials" and that "the vast majority of materials evinced, to varying degrees, an unmistakable bias and inaccuracy." Carol Karsch informed television viewers of the program's "systematic exclusion of materials on Israel" and said that the outreach program and Department of Oriental Studies were "in the position of being an advocate for one side of a difficult, complex political issue."

The morning the story hit the press, Sheila Scoville received a number of phone calls from newspaper and television reporters, all wanting the department's side of the controversy. "But I couldn't say anything," recalled Scoville later, lamenting the gag rule imposed by President Koffler. Robert Gimello felt similarly frustrated and finally wrote a long letter to Koffler. He said that one of the several reporters whom he had dodged throughout the day had finally managed to reach him late at night. "It was clear from what the reporter told me—as it is from the article in this morning's *Star*—that he had in his possession documents of TJCC authorship," wrote Gimello. The chairman of the Oriental Studies Department had fended off the reporter's questions "even to the point of not answering when he asked about whether or not we had ever formally replied to the TJCC's report." Wrote Gimello:

I did feel it necessary, however, to make the one brief and entirely unelaborated observation that the Department of Oriental Studies does not believe that its Middle East Outreach Program reflects the anti-Israeli, pro-Arab bias that has been alleged . . . particularly in view of the fact that the reporter had at his disposal the whole array of TJCC charges and arguments.

Gimello said that his department had sought to abide by the ground rules relating to the adjudication panel and had refrained from public argument with the TJCC. "The TJCC, however, has not done the same," he wrote. ". . . This latest press flap seems to me to be only the most recent in a series of bad-faith actions."

Gimello said the situation was developing to the considerable disadvantage of his department. "The charges against us have been made public in all their detail and in all their scurrilousness. As a result, I suspect that it will be henceforth very difficult for my colleagues and myself to refrain from making statements in our own defense." The fairness and success of the adjudication process, said Gimello, depended on "both sides playing by the rules." Gimello then stated that the TJCC's charges were not only "untrue and profoundly offensive" but that "they threaten to do us real harm." He ended his anguished letter by suggesting that the mere announcement of the panel procedure was not enough and that something had to be said in the department's behalf. Gimello told the university president: "I now think we stand in need of your support."

While the "gag order" prevented representatives of the Oriental Studies Department from providing some balance to the press coverage, Tucson's two daily papers did find teachers who had taken Scoville's course and were willing to speak in her defense. One teacher said the TJCC charges "smacked of almost an open insult." Another said that the suggestion that the teachers were being given propaganda that later would be distributed to students "sort of made us out to be a bunch of dummies." She said she was "mystified" by the charges. "I keep thinking maybe we're talking about completely different programs. I haven't seen anything like what they're talking about." Describing herself as "pro-Israeli," the teacher said that Scoville's course had concluded with a short video presentation about the forming of Israel which was "very fair, very balanced."

One of the TJCC's complaints was that maps handed out during the course did not include Israel. Said the teacher: "Of course the map didn't have Israel on it, because the map was of the Ottoman Empire and Israel was not part of the Ottoman Empire." A librarian who had been enrolled in the Middle East course commented: "If somebody can get to the district and get them to do this without even asking a question, that's what I find frightening."

With the exception of the article reflecting these comments, however, the press coverage of the controversy just two weeks before the panel of experts was to meet presented the Near Eastern Center in a damaging light. Moreover, the interviews with Carol Karsch made it clear that the TJCC had now totally gone back on its promise to abide by the decision of the blue ribbon panel. In a statement published in the *Arizona Star,* Karsch said of the committee of scholars: "We absolutely have not agreed to a committee, period."

Gimello was stunned by Karsch's statement. He told reporters: "I thought we had the agreement with the president of the council some months ago, and if they say there has been no agreement, that comes as something of a surprise to me." In fact, Karsch's statement contradicted assurances given earlier to President Koffler and documented in a letter Koffler wrote to Representative McNulty on April 18: "I persuaded both the department and the council to agree to the rulings of an outside panel of experts," said the letter.

By July 19, it was clear that the TJCC had managed to persuade

Koffler to redefine the panel's mandate. In a joint statement with TJCC President Sol Tobin, Koffler said that the panel was simply one "part of a thorough fact-finding process," and would not make a binding decision but would merely "advise the university concerning the work of the outreach program."

The four scholars finally met in closed-door sessions from July 29 to August 1. The panel members heard representatives of the TJCC present their charges and then, in a separate hearing, members of the Near Eastern Center defended the outreach program. The scholars drafted their report and transmitted it to President Koffler. They were not allowed to keep copies of it themselves, nor were any copies distributed.

Then came the bombshell: President Koffler refused to release the panel's report. Instead he appointed, with the approval of the Tucson Jewish Community Council, a University of Arizona law professor named Charles Ares to conduct the "second phase" of the university's investigation. The panel's report would not be released, said the president, until the second phase of the review was completed.

Scoville, Adamec and Gimello, prevented from seeing the panel's report which they expected would vindicate them, were now asked to cooperate in Ares's wide-ranging investigation of all the TJCC charges not covered by the panel. These included the funding, administration and supervision of the outreach program; allegations of bias and enrollment irregularities surrounding Sheila Scoville's Middle East survey course; and the question of whether the "Extended Response" of the Department of Oriental Studies had been fully endorsed by all department faculty.

According to Scoville, Ares asked her for copies of her correspondence as outreach coordinator and for copies of financial reports, including the accounts of the national Middle East Outreach Council of which she was treasurer. "He also probed into my personal life and moral character," she said, not wishing to elaborate. From Gimello, Ares attempted to discover which professors had written each section of the Oriental Studies Department's written defense. Gimello refused to give Ares the names. But the last straw for Gimello came when Ares began asking questions about the Middle East Studies Association, an international association of Middle East scholars which has been headquartered at the University of Arizona since 1981. Ares's probings into MESA's financing prompted Gimello to set down in a letter his strong reservations about the scope of Ares's investigation. Gimello wrote to Ares that he could not in good conscience respond to his questions about MESA and wished to explain his reasons, since "I suspect that, through no fault of your own, you do not fully appreciate what it is you are asking." The letter went on:

Since the inception of this controversy my colleagues and I have been convinced that our critics' charges against the outreach program were a pretext, merely an opening move in an elaborate effort to control and/or stifle other aspects of our Department's and this University's work in Middle East Studies. Kozolchyk and company have repeatedly denied this, but, frankly, we have not believed them.

Your questions today about MESA serve only to confirm our disbelief. . . . Questions regarding the presence of MESA at the University of Arizona, including questions about its finances, are entirely outside the legitimate scope of your investigation and even further afield of the proper interests of the TJCC. I really cannot participate in or abet any effort by our critics to expand their calumny beyond what even they themselves had said were its limits.

Gimello said that he considered the TJCC request for the inclusion of MESA in the investigation to constitute "an absolutely unjustifiable attempt both to interfere in university affairs and to abridge academic freedom."

After learning that an attempt had been made to investigate MESA, the organization's executive secretary, Michael Bonine, wrote a letter to President Koffler which contained even stronger language:

I am very disturbed at the mere fact that Professor Ares has asked about MESA. . . . I can only surmise that Professor Ares is asking about MESA due to the urging and pressure of his colleague, Dr. Kozolchyk. Certainly, the TJCC would not mind damaging the reputation of MESA and its position at the University of Arizona. . . .

The charges of the TJCC are irresponsible and its tactics reprehensible: secret tape recordings; vicious slander and innuendos against the director and outreach coordinator; leaks to the press when it serves its purpose; planting of "spies" in classes; . . . slander against the previous head of the Department of Oriental Studies; . . . and agreeing to an arbitration panel, but then . . . putting sufficient pressure on the administration to extend the scope of the inquiry. . . .

What is most disturbing about the last point is the fact that the TJCC evidently has sufficient influence and power not only to dictate the agenda but to change the 'rules' as well.

Adamec cooperated with Ares at first, but balked when the investigation was extended to MESA and to Sheila Scoville's private life. He wrote to Ares, "It has now become nationally known that the TJCC demanded that Dr. Scoville be fired and the Near Eastern Center be closed because of its purported anti-Israel bias." He said that having failed to make the anti-Israel accusations stick, the TJCC was now resorting to a "fishing expedition":

It seems not to have occurred to you or to the administration of this university that workshops, classes, conferences, seminars and similar academic endeavors are not subject to political scrutiny. . . . The blue ribbon panel has met, and we know we are vindicated. A continuation of this investigation is harassment and political persecution.

Meanwhile, the Tucson Unified School District had launched its own investigation of the University of Arizona outreach program. TUSD Compliance Officer Sylvia Campoy, who had been assigned the task, explained to the press: "We have to adhere to Title VI [of the Civil Rights Act]—that we will not allow bias or discrimination on the basis of race, creed or color." Not waiting for the release of the panel's report, the TUSD came out on September 13 with its own findings. Its 11-page report, backed up by appendices taken verbatim from the original TJCC attack, stated: "There appears to be a significant bias in the operation of the Near East Center Outreach Program of a decisively anti-Israel and pro-Arab character." The report charged Sheila Scoville with deliberately avoiding the Arab-Israeli conflict by ending her Middle East survey course with the year 1948: "The choice of dates and texts are [sic] indicative of the tendency of the outreach program's intent to exclude information about Israel as compared to the Arab countries."

The report claimed that

In general, the outreach program appears to constitute unauthorized activities within the district which are of a highly political nature. . . . The danger posed to otherwise harmonious religious or racial relations among teachers, students, and even parents is serious and altogether unnecessary. . . . TUSD does not tolerate the presentation of biased materials promoting defamation of a culture, race, sex or religion in order to rectify the image of another culture, race, sex or religion.

While the panel's findings remained a closely-guarded secret, the TUSD report, like the TJCC report which inspired it, was widely quoted in the press. The *Arizona Daily Star,* ran the headline "Teaching Tools from UA Near Eastern Center 'Pro-Arab,' TUSD says." The article quoted the report's author, Sylvia Campoy, as saying that Scoville's Middle East survey course was "blatant pro-Arab, subtle anti-Israel," and that "the Israeli government apparently was not contacted for materials" (on the period 600 to 1948, before Israel existed). The *Daily Star* reporter did not contact the Oriental Studies Department for comment on the TUSD report, mentioning in the 700-word article only that "officials in the Oriental Studies Department have denied charges of bias and propaganda."

Adamec again wrote an angry letter, this time to the editor of the *Daily Star.* "I am astonished that you would print these charges without trying to get the 'other side' of the story," he wrote. He asked how a course which dealt with a period prior to the foundation of Israel could be "biased against Israel." He said the texts used in the course were not "oil company or Arab government sources, as implied in your article" and that there was nothing "improper" in reimbursing the teacher's tuition, a common practice at the university's College of Education. Adamec ended his letter with this:

We realize that at present Middle Eastern studies is a controversial field, and that people with emotional attachment to one or another faction in Israel may try to influence our activities. As an educational institution we cannot allow this to happen.

These last lines were edited out of the printed version which appeared nine days later.

The *Tucson Citizen* wrote a more balanced article a few days later entitled "Charges of Bias in UA Class Called Groundless." The article quoted Gimello as saying he was "astounded" by the TUSD report, while former Oriental Studies Department head William Dever pointed out that Campoy was not qualified to evaluate the program for any sort of bias. Noting the similarities between the TUSD and TJCC reports, Dever said: "It is the same groundless charges repeated word for word with no hard evidence."

"No Systematic Pattern of Bias"

On September 23, after nearly two months of suspense, Koffler released the blue ribbon panel's report. The scholars completely vindicated the outreach program.

The report found "no systematic pattern of bias" in the outreach materials and "no overt policy bias" in their selection, presentation or distribution. On the contrary, "the selection of the material generally showed skill and good will on the part of the coordinator." The scholars said they were convinced that "the outreach activity at the University of Arizona does not attempt to advance the interests of any political group, state, or states. Nor do we see in the Outreach Library evidence of any effort to detract from any political group, state or states."

As for the use of some foreign government publications and corporation-sponsored material in the outreach program, the panel found that "these materials are appropriate for use with accompanying explanations" of their nature. In reference to the TJCC's claim that the program improperly attempted to rectify the image of Arabs, the panel found that "there is nothing intrinsically wrong with this approach or activity, nor does the panel find anything sinister in efforts to eliminate stereotyping." Charges that books used or statements made in the outreach program were "related to the effort . . . of certain Arab states to delegitimize Israel in the family of nations" were, in the panel's view, "completely groundless."

The panel refuted virtually every charge that the TJCC had made against the outreach program, conceding only that the materials used in the workshop "struck us as being generally superficial and uninspired." They added, "This was because the outreach library from which the selection was made is unfortunately quite limited." The panel, which had been asked to look into the supervision and structure of the outreach program, also said that "better supervision of the selection and presentation of the outreach materials would enhance the program. Responsibility for the program would better rest on a committee than on one individual." The panel's report contained specific recommendations as to how the outreach program might be restructured so as to become a more interdisciplinary program involving more of the faculty.

Having responded to the issues put before them, the four scholars then turned to the general matter of academic freedom. This section of the report, some five and a half pages long, was a diplomatically-worded denunciation of the tactics of the TJCC. It reads in part:

The TJCC has exercised its right to question the university and the university has responded fully and adequately. The TJCC is entitled to disagree with the university position and to make that disagreement known. To insist, however, that the case can be closed only after the university takes action in line with the TJCC demands is to cross a clearly demarcated line. It is to go beyond the legitimate right to question and to be informed, moving into the illegitimate demand to control and to censor.

The TJCC has now reached this line. Pressing its demands further can only be seen as an effort to erode university autonomy, as an attack on academic freedom.

We accept that members of the TJCC do not wish to attack academic freedom, but in our judgment new challenges will be viewed by the public as harassment. And, alas, for all of us—university and community—the public image will be correct.

The panel report then defended outreach coordinator Sheila Scoville. In another implicit condemnation of the TJCC, the report said that Scoville had been allowed to become "the issue."

This should not have been permitted to happen, and the damage cannot now be easily repaired. An individual possessing the requisite academic credentials and acting as an acknowledged member of the university community has had her integrity called into question. Not her competence but her integrity. We trust all the parties concerned—even if they cannot agree on anything else—will accept that this unfortunate situation must be redressed. Academic freedom is meaningless unless it protects the individual whose ideas or whose chosen field of activity may be unpopular in certain quarters.

Ares's report, to the surprise of those who believed that Ares sided with the TJCC, supported the findings of the blue ribbon panel. It was released the same day as the panel report. First, in Sheila Scoville's Middle East survey course, Ares could find "no evidence that a specific point of view was advocated or that the instructor sought to shape the participants' lesson plans to fit such a point of view." Ares found nothing wrong with reimbursing teachers for the course and no evidence of discrimination in enrollment. Nor did Scoville, as the TJCC had charged, seek to "replace the curricular processes of a School District." Wrote Ares: "On all the evidence available there is no ground to believe that there were any irregularities in the way the course was arranged or taught."

Nor did Ares find any irregularities in the funding or sponsorship of the outreach program. While some of the center's funding came from oil corporations such as Mobil and Exxon, Ares found nothing untoward in these general purpose grants. As for the question of whether the extended response had been endorsed by all members of the Oriental Studies Department, this aspect of Ares's investigation had been thwarted by Gimello's refusal to release the names of the authors of individual sections of the response. Ares appears to have realized himself the impropriety involved. He wrote:

There seems no room for doubt that the response has the full support of the Department Faculty. It has been urged that individual members of the faculty be interviewed, presumably to determine whether they agree with every statement of every book review in it. This seems unreasonable. These are mature scholars of natural independence. Without some evidence that the response is not approved at least by a substantial majority of the Department, an effort to cross question them now would be quite destructive.

Ares then turned his attention to tapes of Scoville'e classroom remarks that had been surreptitiously made by a TJCC "plant" who attended her 1982 teachers' workshop. The TJCC had made a partial transcript of the tapes which they claimed showed evidence of Scoville's bias. They were made available to Ares but not to the panel. Ares wrote:

I discuss these [cassette tapes] for several reasons. (1) The partial transcript has been circulated but was not considered by the panel. (2) A partial transcript is necessarily selective and would not permit an impression of the overall tone of the proceedings. (3) The tapes were made without the prior consent or knowledge of the teacher of the workshop and this implicates academic freedom even in its most minimal dimension. . . . Despite grave misgivings about listening to tapes made under such circumstances, I ultimately concluded that the harm that would be done to the credibility of the fact-finding process by refusing to listen, would be greater than the increased harm to academic freedom, much of which had already been inflicted in any event.

Therefore, I listened to the tapes and read the partial transcript after advising Dr. Scoville that she would also have the opportunity to do the same. She has not done so.

Ares then pronounced his finding: "Listening to the tapes and reading the partial transcript does not undermine the panel's finding that there was no discernible policy bias."

Despite the refutation of the TJCC's claims in two separate reports, President Koffler's cover letter summarizing their findings seemed calculated to present the TJCC defeat in the best possible light. In the section of his summary entitled "Findings," Koffler leads off as follows: "The Tucson Jewish Community Council was justified in its concern that the outreach program had not had appropriate supervision." In the next sentence, Koffler actually manages to subordinate the major and critical finding of the investigations to what was in effect a crumb thrown out to the TJCC: "Further, while the selection of the material has not been biased, the panel notes that the printed materials are generally superficial and uninspired." Koffler ended his cover letter with a muffled criticism of the TJCC's attack on Scoville:

Considerable concern by the [Tucson Jewish Community] Council has been expressed about the integrity of the outreach coordinator. The professional reputation of individuals who work in sensitive areas is always subject to an increased risk of criticism. Hence it is incumbent on any critic to take extra care to ensure fairness in rendering judgments which could be both professionally and personally destructive. I therefore believe it is important that I draw special attention to the fact that the panel concluded that no overt policy bias is discernible in the selection and distribution of the materials by the Coordinator.

The panel's report and Ares's findings together represented a clear vindication of the Near Eastern center and its outreach program. Of all the many and various changes made by the TJCC, only one was sustained. The program would benefit from restructuring and greater supervision. In fact, the Department of Oriental Studies had already reached that conclusion in the spring of 1983 and was only awaiting the panel's recommendations before implementing its own reforms. Beyond these reforms, Koffler wrote, the university proposed to take no further action.

Interviewed on television after the release of the two reports, Gimello and Adamec expressed their belief that they had been vindicated and that the affair had now been resolved. Carol Karsch also claimed victory in her appearance before the cameras:

Oh, the report far from vindicates the Near Eastern Center. As a matter of fact, if you read it carefully, it confirms our concern that it was not managed properly. . . . The presentation of the Middle East, including Israel, must be accurate; it must be fair; and it must be consistent with our American ideals. This has not been the case. It would remain to be seen how the university would prepare to deal with this.

Another spokesman for the TJCC, Mark Kobernic, was quoted on a radio news report as saying: "We certainly don't believe that there's been any sort of vindication of the program in that it should go on in its present form."

Carol Karsch also wrote a self-congratulatory "analysis" piece for the Jewish weekly *Arizona Post.* Asserting that "a grave issue has faced the Tucson Jewish community for the past two years, she argued that

Our research and that of the Anti-Defamation League and American Jewish Committee evaluated the materials on Arab-Israeli conflict as biased, propagandistic and having a strong pro-Arab anti-Israel slant. The panel found that the materials were not scholarly and characterized them as "superficial and uninspired," "lacking in depth," and most importantly, often containing a "point of view."

This was apparently Karsch's interpretation of the panel's statement which said: "Although certain passages in the works reviewed might be seen as expressing particular points of view, we find no systematic pattern of bias in the works." Karsch continued:

We must not let ourselves get bogged down in a battle of semantics. Whether to call pro-Arab materials 'biased' or to say that they demonstrate a "point of view," the effect remains the same.

Then came this startling claim: "The major thrust of Dr. Koffler's report was the admission of an overriding need for radical changes in the program." Karsch concluded by again raising the spectre of a national anti-Israel conspiracy:

Our responsibility in Tucson is part of a national challenge to counter a powerful, well-financed effort to promote the Arab cause while attempting to undermine the legitimacy of Israel. The price of Jewish security has always been vigilance.

Obviously, the battle wasn't over, although by now it had gone on for two years.

"It Came as a Terrible Surprise"

Despite the findings of Ares and the blue ribbon panel, the administration of the Tucson Unified School District met on October 14, 1983, and officially adopted the recommendations contained in Sylvia Campoy's anti-outreach report. Interviewed by telephone after the meeting, Campoy said: "We have totally disassociated ourselves from the outreach program." She said that teachers would be denied salary increment credit not only for Scoville's Middle East survey course but also for any future course offered by the outreach program. No materials from the outreach program would be permitted in the classrooms.

At a TUSD school board meeting a few days later, both Robert Gimello and William Dever criticized Campoy's report, calling it "shoddy, hasty and one-sided." Gimello told the board: "I hope that district policies are not decided on because of uncritical submission to pressure-group tactics." The school board voted to reinstate salary increment credits to the teachers who had taken Sheila Scoville's Middle East survey course on the grounds that taking the credits away retroactively had been unfair. There was no discussion of future policy, however, or of the TUSD administrative decision to ban the outreach materials from classrooms. Merrill Grant, district superintendent, stood behind the decision and so did the school board.

Nor were the program's continuing headaches confined to the school district. At a faculty senate meeting, also in early October, President Koffler said that while no bias had been found in the outreach program, the panel did find cause for the TJCC allegation that the program had not been properly supervised. In particular, the panel found that the quality of the program had not benefitted from faculty participation. For this reason it had been decided to create a board of governors to oversee the center's operations. Koffler repeated the panel's finding that materials used in the outreach program were "superficial and uninspired" and said: "A report which points to defects in the quality of the work is scarcely a vindication of the center."

Adamec was enraged. In a letter to all members of the faculty senate, he said he found the accusation that the outreach program had not been properly supervised "insulting":

I am an expert in Middle East studies with fifteen books to my name and thirty years of experience in the field. . . . Dr. Scoville's outreach activities have been praised by officials of the Department of Education as being a 'model program' and it is in good part due to the excellent evaluation of our outreach program that we have won funding for ten years in spite of keen national competition.

Do we need to be supervised, directed, and governed by a board? As long as the board is a consultative body I welcome its creation, even though the Near Eastern Center is the only center at this University for which such 'guidance' is deemed necessary.

But it soon became clear that the board was to be more than "advisory." In a memo from the university's acting dean, it was specified that the board would give approval for funding requests and expenditures, select and review personnel in the center, "including the director," review the quality of the center's programs and, in particular, the quality of the outreach materials. It would review and even initiate future plans for the center and "oversee and be involved in all policy matters affecting the center."

The board of governors set up to supervise the center had only one faculty member from the Middle East area core. Meanwhile, the roster of "center faculty" was augmented, in order to increase faculty involvement, to include professors from the South Asia, Near Eastern archaeology, arid lands, anthropology and Judaic studies departments—and all were given equal voting power.

In Adamec's view, these measures deprived the Near Eastern Center of the autonomy it had previously enjoyed and were indicative of an attempt to nudge him out of his position. On December 5, 1983, Adamec sent to the university's acting dean his letter of resignation. Announcing that he would leave his position at the end of the fall 1984 semester, he wrote: "After almost three years of political attacks from which we were eventually vindicated, the most urgent task you have assigned to your board of governors is yet another review of center 'personnel,' namely the director and the outreach coordinator." After summing up the measures that had been taken, Adamec said,

There is no need to further detail instances of what may or may not have been intentional harassment and discrimination against the center and its personnel. My work as center director was a labor of love for which I did not receive any compensation; those who want to see someone else in my position will not have long to wait.

Sheila Scoville stated that under the changed circumstances she would not work for a new director and so would resign as outreach coordinator when Adamec left. It was doubtful whether, with the departure of Adamec and Scoville, the Near Eastern Center would continue to obtain federal funds. Adamec himself predicted its ultimate demise: "I have a pretty good idea that a year from now there may not be any money for the center," he said.

And so, the Tucson Jewish community was to have its way. Not only had it effectively crippled the outreach program by getting its materials banned from the classrooms of Arizona's largest school district; it had, with the help of President Koffler, brought about the resignation of the two individuals it had targeted from the outset.

In an interview, William Dever said that when he heard about the TUSD decision,

I realized we'd been had. [The TJCC] has endless time and devotion and resources and we don't. We're just a few individuals, acting on our own, taking time from our real work to fight this hopeless battle. . . . What bothers us is we know that is not an isolated case in this community. The local people have been forced into admitting this is part of a much larger national campaign and we know that other Near Eastern centers have been under pressure. They can say 'We did it in Tucson; we can do it to you, too.'

Robert Gimello commented: "This has been an education in disillusionment for me. I had been very suspicious of claims that there was interference by a pro-Isareli lobby in many areas of our public life. But having gone through the last two years, I'm now less suspicious. It came as a terrible surprise to me."

It was no surprise, however, when the Tucson Jewish community singled out for recognition several of the people prominent in the school district's decision. Six months after Sylvia Campoy issued the directive dissociating the school district from the program, she and two members of the board, Eva Bacal and Raul Grijalva, were honored by the Jewish Community Relations Committees. Bacal, like Superintendent Merrill Grant, is prominent in the Jewish community. At the dinner Campoy was recognized for "leadership in ensuring compliance and equal opportunity." Chairing the event was Carol Karsch, who the previous year had been cited as Tucson's Jewish "woman of the year" for her attack on the same program.

For Campoy the best was yet to come. A month later, the Jewish weekly announced that she would be the guest of the Jewish community in a week-long, expense-paid tour of Israel organized by Karsch with the support of the American Jewish Committee and the local Jewish Community Foundation.

It is interesting to note that Karsch and others in the Tucson Jewish community became "vigilant" only in 1981, six years after the Near East Center was founded. That was the same year in which the American Jewish Committee, whose assistance to the TJCC Karsch acknowledges, came out with its report entitled "Middle East Centers at Selected American Universities." Written by Gary Schiff, project director for the "Academy for Educational Development," the report asserts that funding by Arab governments or "pro-Arab corporations" exercises "at least a subliminal influence" on students and faculty in

Middle East centers "as well as on the nature, content, and outcome of the programs."

The Schiff report recommends that universities should exercise "close oversight" of outreach programs. For its part, the American Jewish Committee stated in a press release that it intended to follow up the Schiff report by "continuing to monitor the Middle East centers" around the country, by "collecting and evaluating outreach materials in cooperation with local community groups, teachers, professors, etc.," and by "meeting with university officials to discuss oversight mechanisms and review procedures in case problems arise." The Schiff report refers ominously to the "overall attempt to delegitimize the state [of Israel] . . . as prelude to its destruction."

Observers of events in Tucson saw the TJCC campaign as a test case in preparation for similar attacks on other Middle East centers in the United States. The Schiff report and the cooperation between the TJCC and such national organizations as the American Jewish Committee and the Anti-Defamation League of B'nai B'rith lend credence to this hypothesis. Other federally-funded Middle East area studies centers are at Harvard, Columbia, UCLA, Berkeley, Princeton and New York University (the latter two share a joint program), and at the Universities of Texas, Michigan, Pennsylvania, Utah and Washington.

The success of the Tucson attack soon served to encourage moves against another outreach program. During the summer of 1982, Charlotte Albright, Middle East outreach coordinator at the University of Washington in Seattle, was visited by Arthur Abramson of the American Jewish Committee. Abramson asked Albright for a report on the activities of the center over the preceding five years. When she refused, he said that similar reports had been requested from the Middle East Outreach Centers in Tucson and Los Angeles and reminded Albright that the Tucson center had been closed down (this was during the four months of the program's suspension). Abramson further claimed that Jonathan Friedlander, the coordinator of the center at UCLA, had provided him with a requested report. When Albright called Friedlander about this, however, he said that no such report had been either requested or provided. Confronted with this information, Abramson said he had Friedlander's report in his files and would show it to Albright. He never did so.

After attending a 1984 conference for outreach coordinators, Sheila Scoville, her own future clouded by the controversy that had swirled around her, was pessimistic: "The other coordinators think they can work with these pressure groups. My experience is you simply cannot. I fear that in the future outreach programs inevitably will take on a political bias and cease to serve educational purposes."

One striking aspect of the Tucson controversy was the absence of public opposition to the TJCC campaign within the Jewish community. The comments of one Jewish professor at the university throw some light on the reason for the general reluctance of Jews to speak out.

This professor told Richard Frye, one of the four scholars brought to Tucson to review the TJCC charges, that Karsch and Kozolchyk had the Jewish community "almost in a stranglehold" and "anyone who speaks against them is speaking against the national organization, the policy." The professor said the pressures on him were "terrible." "After all," he told Frye, "we get our funds, our grants, from various Jewish communities. . . . What I am telling you is branding me a quisling."

Another Jewish professor at the university, Jerrold Levy, was interviewed shortly after the school board meeting and asked about the lack of protest from the more liberal elements within Tucson's Jewish community. He said, "I think everybody's a little frightened." Levy had himself sent letters deploring the TJCC attacks to the editors of three newspapers, but none was printed. He explained his daring:

I don't depend on Jewish funds for my academic work or for my livelihood. It's the people in the professional classes, doctors, lawyers, who feel intimidated. The friends I have within the [Reform] congregation are very, very close to the chest on political matters. I know a professional man who is very liberal, but now that he's got a well-established business, he's not coming out against the TJCC. There are some concerned people who are not saying anything. We're up against a very well-organized group of co-religionists here. There's some fairly good blackballing going on.

While Levy said that a lot of people privately disagreed with the TJCC, he also gave another reason for the lack of Jewish voices raised in protest: misinformation.

I called two older members of the Jewish community whom I really respect and I said, 'What do we do?' And their answer was pretty generally: 'Where there's smoke there's fire. They [the TJCC] wouldn't have started this attack if there hadn't been something going on.' I asked them what they had read. Well, they'd only read the editorials in the [Jewish] *Arizona Post*. Nothing else. There's a lack of awareness, a lack of facts. The *Arizona Post* has published some pretty slanted things.

Levy said he had tried to reason with both Kozolchyk and Karsch. They responded by inviting him to an "educational series" they were holding on why Jews should support Israeli Prime Minister Begin.

It was a series of evening lectures which were strictly brainwashing. And at the second one I got up during the discussion and told them the facts that they'd got wrong. They had manipulated maps and all kinds of funny things. And they disinvited me from the group. It's that simple. This is not a group that's open to discussion.

Levy describes the general atmosphere of Tucson in similar terms:

It's an awful lot like the McCarthy period. And I include not only the Near Eastern Center [controversy] but the whole line taken on Israel. It's an awful lot like Germany in the thirties, too. It's a lot like what we Jews have been yelling about, that we want to be free from. And then who starts doing it again? It's a very scary business.

Chapter 9

Church and State

Dwight Campbell, the youthful clerk of Shelby County, Illinois, sat quietly through the meeting in a Shelbyville restaurant. It was fall 1982, the campaign season in Illinois, and during the session I discussed foreign policy issues with a group of constituents. Only when the gathering had begun to break up did Campbell call me aside to voice his deep concern over remarks I had made criticizing Israeli policy in Lebanon.

He identified himself as a Christian and, speaking very personally and without hostility, warned me that my approach to the Middle East was both wrong from a political standpoint and, more importantly, in conflict with God's plan. He concluded with a heartfelt injunction: "I would not advocate anything to interfere with the destiny of Israel as set forth in the Bible."

The urgency in his voice was striking. It seemed clear that this public official, well-respected in his community, was not compelled to support Israel by external pressure. Nor was he motivated by a desire for professional or social advancement. As with many evangelical Christians, his support came from deep conviction.

Americans like Dwight Campbell comprise a natural constituency for Israel and add enormous strength to the manipulations of the Israeli lobby. Democratic Congressman Lee H. Hamilton, chairman of the Middle East Subcommittee, hears similar comments when he visits his district in rural Indiana. At "town meetings" which Hamilton conducts, constituents frequently speak up, beginning by identifying themselves as Christians, and then urge that he support Israel's needs completely and without reservation.

Many U.S. Christians, both conservative and mainline, support Israel due to shared cultural and political values and in response to the horror of the Holocaust. Many convervatives feel, as did the young

238

official in Shelbyville, that the creation of Israel in 1948 came in fulfillment of biblical prophecy, and that the Jewish state will continue to play a central role in the divine plan.

Religious affiliation also tends to influence members of the mainstream denominations, particularly Protestant, toward a pro-Israeli stance. An exclusive focus on biblical tradition causes many Christians to see the Middle East as a reflection of events portrayed in the Bible: twentieth century Israelis become biblical Israelites, Palestinians become Philistines, and so on in a dangerous, though most often unconscious, chain of historical misassociation. The distinction between Jewish settlers on the occupied West Bank and the Hebrew nation which conquered the land of Canaan under Moses and Joshua becomes obscured.

Virtually all Christians approach the Middle East with at least a subtle affinity to Israel and an inclination to oppose or mistrust any suggestion that questions Israeli policy. The lobby has drawn widely upon this support in pressing its national programs. More important, fresh perspectives which challenge shibboleths and established prejudices regarding the Middle East are often denounced by both the lobby and many of its Christian allies as politically extremist, anti-Semitic, or even anti-Christian.

The religious convictions of many Americans have made them susceptible to the appeals of the Israeli lobby, with the result that free speech concerning the Middle East and U.S. policy in the region is frequently restricted before it begins. The combination of religious tradition and overt lobby activity tends to confine legitimate discussion within artificially narrow bounds.

Conservative Christians Rally to the Cause

Fundamentalist and evangelical groups have been active in this campaign to narrow the bounds of free speech. Jerry Falwell and Pat Robertson proselytize tirelessly for ever-increasing U.S. backing of Israel, citing scriptural passages as the basis for their arguments. As the membership of conservative Protestant churches and organizations has expanded over the last decade, this "Christian Zionist" approach to the Middle East has been espoused from an increasing variety of "pulpits": local churches, the broadcast media and even the halls of Congress.

Senator Roger W. Jepsen, a first-term legislator from Iowa, told the 1981 annual policy conference of AIPAC that one of the reasons for his "spirited and unfailing support" for Israel was his Christian faith. He declared that "Christians, particularly Evangelical Christians, have been among Israel's best friends since its rebirth in 1948." His views are hardly unique, even among members of Congress, but his statement on this occasion aptly expressed the nearly mystical identification some Christians feel toward Israel:

I believe one of the reasons America has been blessed over the years is because we have been hospitable to those Jews who have sought a home in this country. We have been blessed because we have come to Israel's defense regularly, and we have been blessed because we have recognized Israel's right to the Land. . . .

Jepsen cited his fundamentalist views in explaining his early opposition to the sale of AWACS to Saudi Arabia but then credited divine intervention as the reason he switched position the day before the Senate voted on the proposal. On election day, November 6, 1984, Iowans—spurred by the Israeli lobby— did their own switching, rejecting Jepson's bid for a second term.

Jerry Falwell, leader of the Moral Majority and a personal friend of Menachem Begin and Yitzhak Shamir, has been described by *The Economist* of London as "the silk-voiced ayatollah of Christian revivalism." Acclaimed in a *Conservative Digest* annual poll as the most-admired conservative outside of Congress (with President Reagan the runner-up), Falwell embodies the growing Christian-Zionist connection. He has declared: "I don't think America could turn its back on the people of Israel and survive. God deals with nations in relation to how those nations deal with the Jew." He has testified before Congressional committees in favor of moving the U.S. embassy from Tel Aviv to Jerusalem. Falwell is perhaps the best known of the pro-Israel fundamentalist spokesmen, but he is by no means the only one.

In the summer of 1983, Mike Evans Ministries of Bedford, Texas, broadcast an hour-long television special called "Israel, America's Key to Survival." Evangelist Evans used the program to describe the "crucial" role played by Israel in the political—and spiritual—fate of the United States. Since the show was presented as "religious programming," it was given free broadcast time on local television stations in at least 25 states, in addition to the Christian Broadcasting Network cable system. Yet the message of the program was by no means entirely spiritual.

Interspersing scripture quotations with interviews of public and military figures and other evangelists, including Pat Robertson, Oral Roberts and Jimmy Swaggart, Evans made a number of political assertions about Israel. These included the wild contention that if Israel gave up control of the West Bank and other territories occupied after the 1967 war, the destruction of Israel and the United States would follow; and the implication that Israel is a special victim of Soviet pressure in the form of "international terrorism," which would otherwise be brought to bear directly against the United States and Latin America.

Evans concluded the broadcast with a climactic appeal for Christians to come to the support of "America's best friend in that part of the world" by signing a "Proclamation of Blessing for Israel." Stating that "God distinctly told me to produce this television special pertaining to the nation of Israel," Evans argued that the proclamation was particularly important since "war is coming, and we must let our President and Prime Minister Begin know how we, as Americans, feel about Israel." He has since presented the proclamation to both Prime Minister Shamir and President Reagan, and in a recent publication he congratulated his supporters: "You never thought you would be having such an effect upon the two most powerful leaders in the entire world! But, yes, you are!"

Still, Evans was dissatisfied with Reagan's response. In an August 1984 fund-raising appeal, Evans blamed the U.S. for Israel's economic woes: "Because of America's encouraging Israel to give up the Sinai and its oil [they lost, he said, $1.7 billion] and because of Israel's assistance to America through defense of the Middle East, Israel is on the verge of economic collapse." He said Reagan was "hesitant" to "alleviate Israel's great pressures."

The Evans theme linking America's survival to Israel was echoed in a full-page ad for the National Political Action Committee, a pro-Israel fund-raising organization, in the December 18, 1983, *New York Times*. It proclaimed that "Israel's survival is vital to our own," and "Faith in Israel strengthens America."

Radio and television broadcasts by Jim Bakker, Kenneth Copeland, Roberts, Swaggart and others routinely proclaim the sanctity of Israel through scriptural quotation, usually from the Old Testament, and then reinforce it with political and strategic arguments supplied by the broadcaster.

The arguments find a considerable audience. Most estimates place the number of evangelical Christians in the United States in the neighborhood of 30 million. Jerry Falwell's "Old Time Gospel Hour" is aired on 392 television stations and nearly 500 radio stations each week. Former Israeli Prime Minister Menachem Begin describes Falwell as "the man who represents twenty million American Christians."

Nor is the American style of evangelistic programming confined to U.S. shores. Its pro-Israeli message is now broadcast from the Middle East itself. The High Adventure Holyland Broadcasting Network of George Otis has maintained the Voice of Hope radio station in southern

Lebanon since the first Israeli invasion of Lebanon in 1978. He describes it as an effort "to bring the Word of God to an area that has not had the Word of God in many centuries." Otis named his broadcast ministry after his personal conviction that "Jesus [is] high adventure"; but over the last several years the station has been actively involved in adventure of a more secular sort.

The late Major Saad Haddad, before his death the Lebanese commander of the Israeli-backed militia which controlled southern Lebanon prior to the Israeli invasion in 1982, frequently used the Voice of Hope to broadcast his military objectives, including threats against civilians. Evangelist Otis, overlooking grim aspects of Haddad's rule, described Haddad as a "born-again" Christian who was a "good spiritual leader" to the people of southern Lebanon. The U.S. State Department confirms that Haddad often carried out threats to shell civilian areas, including the city of Sidon, "without previous warning." Haddad rationalized these attacks as reprisals against the Lebanese government for not meeting his demands for salary payment. (The Lebanese government ceased paying the salaries of Haddad's forces after he was dishonorably discharged from the Lebanese army).

In the spring of 1980, Haddad forces used five U.S.-built Sherman tanks in an attack on a Boy Scout Jamboree near the city of Tyre, killing 16 boys. Haddad's gunners also shot down a Norwegian medivac helicopter which arrived to help the wounded. The scout gathering, which was sponsored by the Christian Maronite Church, was just beyond the limits of the "Free Lebanon," or "Haddadland," the area controlled by Haddad's Israeli-backed army. Haddad announced at the time that such attacks would continue until the Lebanese government provided more electricity to this area and recognized Haddad schools.

With the support of both Israel and the remaining Christian forces in the south, High Adventure Ministries is going ahead with plans to establish the Star of Hope television station in southern Lebanon. Otis himself describes the Israeli support as "a miracle": "Did you ever think we would see the day when the Jews would push us for a Christian station?" Yet since a television station will assure more effective communication with the public—for military and other purposes—Israeli approval seems more the product of sound strategic thinking than of divine intervention. Like the Voice of Hope before it, the new Star of Hope will be financed through tax-deductible contributions of money and equipment from donors in North America.

Through such endeavors, American evangelical broadcasting supports the Israeli government indirectly by emphasizing the moral and religious commitment to the Jewish state which many Americans already feel and, directly, by broadcasting in the Middle East messages which promote the military objectives of Israel and its Lebanese allies.

Jerry Falwell periodically conducts tours of Israel for "born again" Christians. Although Falwell is careful to avoid the appearance of money flowing from Israel to Moral Majority, former Israeli Prime Minister Menachem Begin demonstrated his commitment by arranging for a jet plane to be sold to Falwell's organization at a substantial discount.

Besides Falwell, there are many other Christian groups offering Israel their support. In eastern Colorado, more than ten churches coordinate an annual "Israel Recognition Day" involving films, lectures, cultural exhibits and sermons reaching more than 25,000 parishioners. The National Christian Leadership Conference for Israel (NCLCI) holds an annual conference in Washington attended by more than 200 delegates representing Christian groups from all over the United States. As Dr. Franklin H. Littell, president of NCLCI, has noted, "Concern for Israel's survival and well-being [is] the only issue that some of the organizations ever cooperated on."

Other publicized events have included a "Solidarity for Israel Sabbath" at Washington's Beth Shalom Orthodox Synagogue in October 1982—in which evangelical leaders and local rabbis joined to "build bridges" and coordinate their efforts in behalf of Israel—and the "National Prayer Breakfast in Honor of Israel," which has become an annual event in the nation's capital.

The third such breakfast conference, given February 1, 1984, attracted over 500 ardent supporters of Israel, most of them Christians. The setting was brightly decorated with Israeli flags and symbols, including apples bearing Star of David stickers. The printed program for the affair carried an impressive list of political and evangelical leaders, including Edwin Meese III (unable to attend, it was announced, because of his just-announced nomination as attorney-general), Meir Rosenne, Israeli ambassador to the United States, and representatives from the National Religious Broadcasters and other conservative Protestant groups. Congressman Mark Siljander of Michigan, a member of the Middle East Subcommittee, delivered a stirring reaffirmation of evangelical solidarity with Israel: "It's not that we are anti-Arab. We seek peace in God's plan."

The breakfasts are coordinated by The Religious Roundtable, a group which describes itself as "a national organization dedicated to religious revival and moral purpose in America," yet one of its primary purposes is advancement of the Israeli cause. Edward E. McAteer, president of the group, is known in the Washington area as a partisan speaker and editorial writer on behalf of Israel. He uses the religious format of his organization to back such political stands as closer U.S.-Israeli strategic cooperation, restriction of U.S. arms sales to Arab states, and transfer of the United States embassy in Israel from Tel Aviv to Jerusalem. In 1984 McAteer was an unsuccessful candidate in Tennessee for the Senate.

Writing in the *Washington Post* on January 2, 1984, McAteer supported the Israeli intervention in Lebanon, likening opponents of the invasion to "the pre-med student who proposed removing only half a cancerous growth [the PLO] because of the blood generated by surgery." Considering the fact that the invasion led to staggering civilian casualties, this crusading knight of The Religious Roundtable certainly cannot be accused of fear of blood.

Perhaps inspired by Mike Evans Ministries, the prayer breakfast committee created its own Proclamation of Blessing for Israel. Issued in the name of "America's 50-million-plus Bible-believing Christians," it included a curious mixture of religious and political/military points:

A call for "Strategic Cooperation" with Israel is followed by an appeal to "the God of Israel, Who through the Jewish people, gave to the world of Scriptures, our Savior, Salvation and Spiritual blessings";

Scriptural selections affirming the divine right of the Jews to the Land follow language rejecting of "dual loyalty" charges against American Jewish supporters of Israel;

A call for the transfer of the U.S. embassy to Jerusalem is accompanied by an exhortation that "the Scripturally-delineated boundaries of the Holy Land never be compromised by the shifting sands of political and economic expediency."

Cooperation between Jewish and conservative Protestant groups has an important impact in the political sphere. At a recent address in Israel, Jerry Falwell declared that "The day is coming when no candidate will be elected in the United States who is not pro-Israel." Although the Moral Majority has not had 100 percent success in putting its favorites in power, candidates for high office, regardless of their own religious inclinations, now often feel compelled to address the issues on the evangelical political agenda. Israel ranks high among these.

Falwell's Moral Majority broadens its power base through voter registration drives in every state, the result that many members of the House and Senate—such as Siljander and Jepsen—welcome in order to emphasize the religious foundation of their political support for Israel.

Many conservative Christians see a theological basis for this support, as they ascribe to Israel a prominent role in the interpretation of Christian doctrine. On the one hand, it is maintained that Israel deserves Christian support because it exists as the fulfillment of biblical prophecy. Old Testament passages are most often quoted in defense of this view. On the other hand, many Christians back Israel because they believe the Jewish people remain, as they were in biblical times, the chosen nation of God. The same advocate will often cite both arguments. The prophecy argument is held by the most conservative fundamentalist groups, such as the Moral Majority, and has received more public attention, but the covenantal view is probably held by a larger segment of America's 40 million conservative Christians.

Dr. Dewey Beegle of Wesley Theological Seminary commented on the differing views of Israel held by American Christians in his 1978 book, *Prophecy and Prediction:* "All Christian groups claim to have the truth, but obviously some of these views cannot be true because they contradict other intepretations which can be verified."

Like many biblical scholars, Beegle has concluded that the scriptural basis which pro-Zionist Christians often cite for the establishment of modern Israel does not withstand close scrutiny. His conclusions can be broadly summarized in two basic propositions:

First, the prophesied return of the nation of Israel to Palestine was fulfilled by the biblical return from Babylon, and has nothing to do with twentieth-century Israel.

Second, the covenant through which God promised Israel "the land" was not permanent but conditional; it was abrogated in biblical times when Israel failed to be obedient to God's commandments and thereby forfeited the promise.

But the issue is not whether the scholarship of Beegle or the Moral Majority is the more sound, but the importance of open debate of such difficult issues. Here again the experience of Beegle is revealing. Because his book treated the controversial issue of modern Israel and its relations to biblical tradition, many publishers, even those who had handled previous works by this scholar, declined to publish it. One of these told him bluntly: "Your early chapters on the biblical matters of prophecy and prediction are well done. The only chapter that seriously disturbs us is number 15 on 'Modern Israel Past and Present.' " Beegle was informed that his views on Israel, which accept the legitimacy of the modern Jewish state though not on biblical grounds, would be "bound to infuriate" many readers.

Yet the fact that a book or a point of view is controversial is not, at least in the United States, usually grounds for rejection. Dr. Beegle views Christians and Jews who disagree with him in this way: "We know that these people think alike and feel alike and are going to help each other. It's perfectly natural. All I'm saying is we ought to have just as much right on the other side to speak out openly and put the

information out there." His book finally was published by Pryor Petten-
gill, a small firm in Ann Arbor, Michigan.

Many Christians who are neither fundamentalist nor evangelical
are also inclined to accept the supposed counsel of prophecy as
justification for Israel's dominant role in the Middle East. The president of the United States appears to be among their number.

President Reagan, in his October 1983 telephone conversation
with AIPAC executive director Thomas A. Dine, turned a discussion of
Lebanon's present-day problems into a discourse on biblical prophecy:

I turn back to your ancient prophets in the Old Testament and the signs foretell-
ing Armageddon and I find myself wondering if . . . if we're the generation
that's going to see that come about. I don't know if you've noted any of those
prophecies lately but, believe me, they certainly describe the times we're going
through.

Reagan's views are not unprecedented, even in the Oval Office.
His views reflect the wide credence given to biblical prophecy—and its
use to justify Israel's existence.

A Puzzling Paradox

Yet, recognizing Israel as the fulfillment of biblical prophecy implicates the Christian—and even more so the Jew—in several paradoxes.
First, conservative and "premillennial" Protestants have traditionally
sought to convert Jews to Christianity, and relations between the two
groups have often been less than cordial. Jews instinctively mistrusted
Southern Baptist Jimmy Carter in 1976 because, as Jewish author
Roberta Feuerlicht writes, "In Jewish history, when fundamentalists
came, Cossacks were not far behind."

Ironically, the Christian groups most likely to accept a biblical
basis for supporting Israel are also those most likely to feel the necessity of Jewish conversion to Christianity, an extremely sensitive issue
to Israelis. Dan Rossing, director of the Department for Christian Communities in the Israeli Ministry of Religious Affairs, states the problem
succinctly: the evangelical "theological scheme clearly implies that
Jews have to become Christians—clearly not today, but some day."

Many evangelical organizations carry on missionary activities in
the Middle East, particularly in Israel, which are strongly opposed by
many Israelis. The evangelists openly proselytize, seeing conversion of
the Jews as another precursor of the times which the "recreation" of
Israel in 1948 is said to foretell.

The International Christian Embassy in Jerusalem, an organization which works to foster support for Israel in twenty nations, is one

of a number of evangelical organizations which have come under fire recently for missionary activities inside Israel. The "embassy" was opened in Jerusalem in October 1980 as a gesture of "international Christian" support for the controversial transfer of the Israeli capital to that city from Tel Aviv.

Despite expressing political support for the state of Israel, the International Christian Embassy has devoted some of its efforts to the conversion of Jews to Christianity, becoming controversial in the eyes of many Israelis.

In Israel, Orthodox Jews have been active in pressing for legislation banning foreign missionaries and organizing opposition against them. Despite the monetary support and goodwill brought to Israel by these organizations, they are widely regarded as Trojan horses. There have even been physical attacks on their members.

The dilemma faced by the Israeli government in dealing with Christian groups like the International Christian Embassy is essentially the same as that faced by American Jewish groups in forming their relations with conservative Christian groups in the United States. While spokesmen within Israel, such as Rabbi Moshe Berliner, decry the inherent threat to Judaism posed by proselytizing fundamentalists—"Are we so gullible as to take any hand extended to us in friendship?"—the Israeli government under both Begin and Shamir has offered an emphatic reply: "Israel will not turn aside a hand stretched out in support of Israel's just cause."

In November 1980, Jerry Falwell was awarded a medal in recognition of his steadfast support of Israel. The award came at a New York dinner marking the hundredth anniversary of the birth of Zionist leader Vladimir Jabotinsky and was made at the behest of Prime Minister Begin. Opposition to the presentation was intense. Henry Siegman, executive director of the American Jewish Congress objected to "the way [Falwell] conducts his activities and the manner in which he uses religion." In Israel, the *Jerusalem Post* quoted Alexander M. Schindler, former chairman of the Conference of Presidents of Major American Jewish Organizations, as saying that it was "madness and suicide if Jews honor for their support of Israel right-wing evangelists who constitute a danger to the Jews of the United States."

What Schindler meant was illustrated by a remark Falwell had made at a Sunday service in his own Liberty Baptist Church in Lynchburg, Virginia. He declared that God did not "hear Jewish prayers." He later expressed regret over this remark, but for many Jews it confirmed their suspicion that Falwell was more interested in their conversion than the security of Israel. His protestation that "the Jewish people in America and Israel and all over the world have no dearer friend than

Jerry Falwell" has not made Jewish leaders forget his fundamentalist religious bias against Judaism, yet they openly continue to cultivate the support of American evangelicals in backing Israel. The paradox is striking.

New View from Mainline Churches

The pro-Israel alliance between American Jews and conservative Protestants comes at a time of friction between the Jewish community and the mainstream American Christian community. The friction has increased recently with the widespread objection among Christians to the Israeli invasion of Lebanon.

In September 1981, United Methodist Bishop James Armstrong issued a letter to Indiana United Methodist ministers in which he sharply criticized the "Falwell gospel" and the "Moral Majority mentality." He pointedly observed that

Israel was seen as God's "chosen people" in a servant sense. Israel was not given license to exploit other people. God plays no favorites.

Christian concern over events in the Middle East, particularly the suffering of Palestinian refugees, has been a source of tension between Jewish and Christian groups for some time. Though traditional efforts toward ecumenical cooperation between American Judaism and the mainline churches continue—as reflected in the recent announcement by the American Jewish Congress that a new Institute for Jewish-Christian Relations was being established to study the common Judeo-Christian scriptural heritage—the larger denominations have in recent years begun to view the Middle East in a new light.

The mainline churches focus more and more on the need to respect the human rights of the Palestinian refugees, as reflected in a series of church policy statements which show more sympathy for the plight of these refugees than many Jewish groups find acceptable. The United States Catholic Conference, United Presbyterian Church, United Methodist Church, American Baptist Churches, United Church of Christ, and others have called for mutual recognition of the Israeli and Palestinian right to self-determination, Palestinian participation in peace negotiations and Israeli withdrawal from lands occupied in the 1967 war. Several of the churches have identified the PLO as the legitimate representative of the Palestinian people.

As Father Charles Angell, S.A., associate director of Graymoor Ecumenical Institute, has observed, for the American churches to commit themselves to such an "evident clash between their position and that of the state of Israel abroad and the majority of the American

Jewish organizations at home" represents a break with the past. He feels that the "fundamental shift" occurred after the 1973 war, when Christians responded sympathetically to appeals for a peaceful settlement from the Arab side.

Members of the Jewish community have largely received the statements of the mainline churches as threats to their religious rights. Despite more than forty official statements by Protestant and Catholic organizations in the past two decades condemning anti-Semitism as un-Christian, Christian officials who assert the right of all peoples—not just Israelis—to territorial security and a decent standard of living are accused by the Israeli lobby of anti-Semitism.

Christian churches have been accused of "self-delusion" in opposing both anti-Semitism and at the same time Israeli government policies which restrict or violate the human rights of Palestinian refugees. Even confirmed humanitarian and pacifist groups like the Quakers have been branded anti-Semitic for urging greater restraint and mutual understanding upon all of the contending parties of the Middle East. Journalist Ernest Volkmann even sought to pin the anti-Semite label on the Reverend William Howard, president of the National Council of Churches, for his criticism of the June 1981 Israeli air strike against the Osirak nuclear reactor in Iraq.

The paradox thus becomes compounded: mainline Christians who accept the legitimacy of the Jewish faith but question some policies of the Jewish state are branded anti-Semitic, while evangelical Christians who back Israel but doubt the theological validity of Judaism are welcome as allies.

The experience of the National Council of Churches is instructive. An NCC insider describes the relationship between the council and the American Jewish community as "the longest case record of Jewish influence, even more than in government." For many years no one in the Jewish community had serious complaints about the council. Whenever disagreement arose, the Jewish leadership demanded—and usually received—prompt action. As a former NCC official described it, Jewish leaders would come "en masse with the heads of departments of about half a dozen different Jewish agencies and then really lay it out. They felt that they had a special right to get direct input to the council leadership."

A Committee on Christian-Jewish Relations, long a part of the council hierarchy, gives special attention to fostering cooperation and understanding between Christians and Jews in the United States. In addition, Inter-Faith, a division of the NCC devoted to humanitarian programs, was, despite its ecumenical title, until recently composed solely of Jewish and Christian groups.

The Committee on Christian-Jewish Relations has traditionally been known to share whatever information or new council materials it considered important with the American Jewish Committee. This practice was troubling to some council officials, as the American Jewish Committeee is not a religious body. Although it maintains a religious affairs department, it is mainly a lobbying organization. Jewish organizations of a primarily religious nature, such as the Synagogue Council of America, are not so closely involved in the workings of the council. But because top-level administrators at the NCC are understandably sensitive about the charge of being anti-Israel or insensitive to Jewish concerns in any council actions or publications, the oversight of NCC activities and literature—up to the point of accepting long critiques of proposed materials from the American Jewish Committee—has been accepted as standard procedure.

A representative of one of the largest Protestant denominations observes that the American Jewish Committee had "much more effect" on the content of National Council study materials than his office, even though his denomination accounted for the purchase and distribution of three-quarters of these publications.

After several years of mounting Jewish criticism—during which the council had debated but failed to adopt a number of resolutions on the suffering of Palestinian refugees—the NCC decided in December 1979 to issue a Middle East policy statement. As Allan Solomonow puts it, "because of strong Jewish criticism it became apparent that the NCC, which up to that point did not have a clear stand on the Middle East, had to have one." The consensus was that "the only way to limit criticism was to say exactly what you feel about these issues." But the Middle East policy statement which ultimately appeared was nevertheless unacceptable to many American Jewish groups.

Declaring that "the role of the National Council of the Churches of Christ in the U.S.A. is to seek with others peace, justice and reconciliation throughout the Middle East," the controversial final section included a call for control of arms transfers to the Middle East and an appeal for "reciprocal recognition of the right of self-determination" by the government of Israel and the PLO.

The Anti-Defamation League of B'nai B'rith, which had not presented its views in open forum, quickly denounced the statement as "a naive misreading of the contending forces and issues in the Arab-Israeli conflict which can have mischievous consequences."

Pro-Israel writers and commentators seized upon the policy statement as an example of growing anti-Semitism within the NCC—despite the clear emphasis of the text on secure peace for all peoples and denunciation of violent acts on every side. Journalist Ernest Volkman, in his book *A Legacy of Hate: Anti-Semitism in America,* somehow manages to cite the policy statement as the prime example of "an indifference to American Jews that has occasionally strayed into outright anti-Semitism." *The Campaign to Discredit Israel,* the "enemies list" assembled by AIPAC, goes to the length of claiming that "some segments of the National Council of Churches" are tools of a "systematic effort" to attack Israel's image in the United States.

A high-ranking NCC official at the time summed up the matter this way: "For years no one in the Jewish community had any serious complaints about the National Council; and then when they started to have political decisions that ran afoul of conventional pro-Israeli opinion, all of a sudden it became anti-Semitic and suspect."

Critics do not like to note, however, that the policy statement recognized the right of Israel to exist as a "sovereign Jewish state" rather than a "sovereign state" as some on the panel preferred. Butler identified this as "one of the most hotly debated phrases in the policy statement," because some members of the drafting committee refused to vote for the completed document unless it specified the Jewish identity of Israel.

The document also explicitly reaffirms the long and continuing close relationship between the Jewish community and the National Council of Churches.

God's Empire Striking Back?

As interest in the Middle East and humanitarian concern for the Palestinian refugees becomes more widespread among Americans of all religious persuasions, many Jewish groups and their pro-Israel allies are more adamant in rejecting open discussion as a means to broader public understanding. Under such pressures, even activist religious groups which are involved in campaigning for social justice and world peace often grow timid when the Middle East becomes a topic of discussion.

The Sacramento Religious Community for Peace (SRCP), a group which works to foster ecumenical cooperation in support of peace and social issues, in October 1983 organized a major symposium on "Faith, War and Peace in the Nuclear Age" at the Sacramento Convention Center. A large number of religious organizations, including the Sacramento Jewish Relations Council, co-sponsored the symposium under the auspices of the SRCP.

In early September, as publicity for the symposium was being arranged, the Sacramento Peace Center (SPC), another well-established local activist group, asked that a flier publicizing its memorial service for victims of the refugee camp massacres in Lebanon be included in the SRCP mailings for the symposium. Since it is routine for peace organizations in the area to cooperate in this way, Peggy Briggs, co-director of the peace center, was shocked to be informed that the flier could not be included in the promotional mailing.

The SRCP told Briggs that the Jewish Community Relations Council—the strongest local Jewish group and a major participant in SRCP activities—had made it known that if the flier appeared in the mailing, Jewish participation in the symposium would be withdrawn. This would have meant not only diminished support from the large local Jewish community, but also the loss of a rabbi scheduled as one of the keynote speakers.

Helen Feeley, co-director of the SRCP, further informed the Peace Center that no literature prepared by the SPC Middle East task force could be displayed during the proceedings. In discussing the matter later, Feeley was emphatic: "The Middle East task force has absolutely inflamed the Jewish community here, because they do not uphold the right of Israel to exist. That material is just inflammatory."

Greg Degiere, head of the SPC Middle East task force, protested that his group does recognize Israel's right to exist. He pointed out that the SPC calls for an end to war in the Middle East, respect for the human rights of all persons in the region and mutual recognition between Israel and the PLO.

The prohibition on discussion of the Middle East, along with the restriction on the Peace Center's right to distribute information, was accepted as the cost of Jewish participation in the symposium. Lester Frazen, the rabbi who served as a keynote speaker and thus helped provoke the issue, had unusual credentials for a showdown over free speech. He had boldly asserted his own First Amendment right at the outset of the 1982 Israeli march into Lebanon. He was among the leaders of a Sacramento march consisting mainly of fundamentalist Christians who expressed their joyous support for the invasion with a banner proclaiming: "God's empire is striking back!" Yet Frazen and his backers denied the Sacramento Peace Center the right to memorialize the victims of that invasion or to call for a negotiated end to killing on both sides.

In light of this background, it is not surprising that although the official title of the gathering was "Faith, War and Peace in the Nuclear Age," the agenda failed to address conflicts in the Middle East—in the region many observers believe to be the most likely center of nuclear confrontation. As Joseph Gerson, peace secretary for the American Friends Service Committee in New England observes, "The Middle East has been the most consistently dangerous nuclear trigger. Presidents Truman, Eisenhower, Johnson and Nixon all threatened to use nuclear weapons there. . . ."

The Uproar over Palm Sunday

Despite Jewish-fundamentalist cooperation and the pressures brought to bear against those who publicly advocate negotiation and reconciliation in the Middle East, a few religious leaders have had the courage to speak out. Foremost among them is the Very Reverend Francis B. Sayre, who took the occasion of Palm Sunday, 1972, to raise a number of questions to which American Christians are still debating the answers.

Throughout his twenty-seven years as dean of National Cathedral in Washington, the hearty and dramatic Dean Sayre took controversial stands on a wide variety of public policy issues. In the early fifties he fired some of the first salvos in the campaign to discredit McCarthyism. Declaring the Wisconsin senator's followers "the frightened and credulous collaborators of a servile brand of patriotism" brought Sayre a torrent of hate mail, but the possibility of criticism never caused him to shy away from speaking out on issues that stirred his conscience. He worked as an early advocate of civil rights for blacks, and in the sixties and seventies he stood in the forefront of opposition to the Vietnam War.

Dean Sayre is the grandson of Woodrow Wilson, and his father had been a diplomat, law professor and eminent Episcopalian layman. Sayre continued the family tradition of leadership, relishing his position as leader of the cathedral's influential congregation. Offered a government post by the newly installed Kennedy administration in 1960, his reply was swift: "No thanks. I already have the best job in Washington."

He once described his role as dean of the cathedral as a "liaison between church and state" and as a platform for "moral guidance" for government leaders. He explained his activism with characteristic candor: "Whoever is appointed dean of a cathedral has in his hand a marvelous instrument, and he's a coward if he doesn't use it."

On Palm Sunday 1972, Dean Sayre used his prestigious pulpit to deliver a sermon which was perhaps the most powerful—and certainly one of the most controversial—of his career. He spoke on Jerusalem, identifying the ancient city as a symbol of both the purest yearnings and darkest anger of the human heart. Historically, he proclaimed, both extremes were embodied in events of the single week between Jesus's triumphal entry into the city and His crucifixion.

Amidst the pageantry and exultation of Palm Sunday, Jerusalem was the emblem of all man's dreams: a king that will someday come to loose us from every bondage; dream of peace that shall conquer every violence; holiness of heaven driving out the dross of earth.

But just as Jerusalem symbolized "man's yearning for the transcendently good," so did it demonstrate his capacity for "hateful evil":

Her golden domes are also known as 'the Place of the Skull.' . . . Jerusalem, in all the pain of her history, remains the sign of our utmost reproach: the zenith of our hope undone by the wanton meanness of men who will not share it with their fellows but choose to kill rather than be overruled by God.

Having recognized Jerusalem as a portrayal of "the terrible ambivalence of the human race about truth, about himself, about God," Sayre spoke compassionately about the meaning of Jerusalem for the people now living in Israel:

Surely one can sympathize with the loving hope of that little state, which aspires to be the symbol, nay more: the embodiment of a holy peoplehood. For her, Jerusalem is the ancient capital; the city of the Temple that housed the sacred Ark of the Covenant. To achieve a government there is . . . the fulfillment of a cherished prayer tempered in suffering, newly answered upon the prowess of her young men and the skill of her generals. Around the world Hosannah has echoed as Jewish armies surged across the open scar that used to divide Arab Jerusalem from the Israeli sector.

Yet Dean Sayre's sermon was fired by a troubled sense that since the military victory of 1967, five years before, something had gone terribly wrong.

By 1972 Jerusalem was completely under Israeli control. But, to Dean Sayre, mankind's moral tragedy had been reenacted in Israeli treatment of the city's Arab population. As he saw it, the dream had been tarnished:

Now oppressed become oppressors. Arabs are deported; Arabs are imprisoned without charge; Arabs are deprived of the patrimony of their lands and homes; their relatives may not come to settle in Jerusalem; they have neither voice nor happiness in the city that after all is the capital of their religious devotion too!

Addressing the moral consequences of the Israeli annexation of Jerusalem, Dean Sayre quoted Dr. Israel Shahak—a Jewish survivor of the Nazi concentration camp at Belsen, a professor at Hebrew University, and a dissenter from Israeli policy—who branded the annexation "an immoral and unjust act," and called for recognition that "the present situation of one community oppressing the other will poison us all, and us Jews first of all."

Sayre explained that Israel's treatment of the Arabs mirrored "that fatal flaw in the human breast that forever leaps to the acclaim of God, only to turn the next instant to the suborning of His will for us."

He was not the only Washington clergyman to express a theme critical of Israel that day. Dr. Edward Elson, pastor of the National Presbyterian Church and chaplain of the U.S. Senate, chided "those Christians who justify Israel's actions in Jerusalem on the basis that they are the fulfillment of prophecy." And the Armenian Orthodox legate to Washington, Bishop Papken, called on Israel to recognize that "Jerusalem belongs to all men."

But because of his reputation and eminent position in American religion, Sayre was singled out to bear the brunt of the criticism. Rabbi Joshua O. Haberman of the Washington Hebrew Congregation reported to Sayre that the sermon was "so distressing to the Israel government that there had even been a cabinet meeting on the subject—what to do about this minister who had been friendly always to the Jews but who was so misguided." The response was not long in coming. Two leaders of the Washington Jewish Community Council issued a statement denouncing all three sermons and taking particular exception to the address of Dean Sayre. Drs. Harvey H. Ammerman and Isaac Frank said Jews, Christians and Moslems "freely mingle in the reunited city and live and carry on their work in peace." They characterized the Sayre sermon as "an outrageous slander."

Their position received support in a *Washington Post* editorial which called Sayre's sermon "an intemperate denunciation of current Israeli policy in Jerusalem." The *Washington Post* editors objected to Sayre's assertion that "even as [Israelis] praise their God for the smile of fortune, they begin almost simultaneously to put Him to death." They found the statement "painfully close to a very old, very familiar line of the worst bigotry."

An angry editorial letter in the *Washington Post* dismissed Sayre's sermon as "non-factual garbage":

This churchman illustrates well the typical liberal gentile bleeding-heart attitude to the Jews—we'll commiserate with you as long as you're dependent on our goodwill for your survival, and we'll weep for you when you are slaughtered every few years by our coreligionists—but Lordy, don't you start winning and controlling your own destiny! The hell with them, I say.

Several such letters appeared in the Washington press in the weeks after Palm Sunday, yet few challenged Sayre's central contention that

Israeli policy did not grant equal treatment to Arabs and Jews living in Jerusalem. The situation in Jerusalem was a matter of fact, subject to relatively easy refutation—or confirmation—through inquiry. Yet Sayre's critics, in the manner of the *Post* editors, largely confined their attacks to the tone and lack of "temperance" in his sermon. Sayre received widespread criticism, not for being wrong, but for being a forthright critic of unjust Israeli policies and therefore, in the eyes of some critics, anti-Semitic. Despite his long career of humanitarian activism, partisans of Israel sought to discredit Sayre himself since they could not discredit his arguments. Writer Ernest Volkman charged that Sayre demonstrated "mindless pro-Arabism [which] had undone many years of patient effort to improve relations between Christians and Jews."

David A. Clarke of the Southern Christian Leadership Conference wrote to defend Sayre: "I do view with some distrust the emotional rebuttals which follow any question of the propriety of Israeli conduct." He likened such emotionalism to the initial reaction against those who first challenged long-established concepts of racial superiority. Referring to U.S. policy in the Middle East, he expressed gratitude "that one of such intellectual integrity as Dean Sayre has given a differing view so that our perspective will not be one-dimensional."

But influential Christians remained divided in their reaction to the speech. Some shared Sayre's troubled disapproval of Israeli policy in the Holy City. Others continued to invoke the spectre of anti-Semitism.

The Reverend Carl McIntire, an outspoken Protestant fundamentalist, took exception to Sayre's sermon in a letter published in the *Washington Star.* He and Sayre had clashed previously, when McIntire had sought to disrupt a rally against the Vietnam War at the Washington Cathedral and Sayre had personally ushered him away from the gathering. "The liberals represented by the dean have long since departed from the historic Christian view concerning Israel and Jerusalem," proclaimed McIntire. Describing the 1967 war as "a thrilling example of how to deal with aggressors and the forces backed by Communism," he invoked scriptural justification for Israeli possession of conquered territory:

It is for those of us who believe the Bible to be the Word of God [to] come now to the assistance of our Jewish neighbors. What God has given them they are entitled to possess, and none of the land which they have won should be bartered away.

Some mainline clergymen joined in the fundamentalist outcry over the Palm Sunday sermon. Two leaders of the Council of Churches of Greater Washington issued a public statement declaring it "distressing and perplexing that men of goodwill should choose the start of this holy week for both Christians and Jews to make pronouncements which would inevitably be construed as anti-Judaic."

Two Catholic clergymen—an official of the Secretariat for Catholic-Jewish Relations and a director of the United States Catholic Conference—joined in an attempt to discredit Sayre. First they questioned the propriety of Sayre's quoting Israel Shahak, a dissident, to substantiate his charges of Israeli injustice in Jerusalem: "Is it not too close to the old anti-Semitic stratagem of using passages from the Hebrew prophets in order to scold Jews?" More significantly, they asserted that they had "failed to find any evidence of Israeli oppression" during a recent trip to Jerusalem.

Yet an article at the same time in *Christianity Today* reported a quite different reaction from the editor of the *United Church Observer*, an official publication of the United Church of Canada. The Reverend A. C. Forrest praised Dean Sayre for "the courage, knowledge and insight to speak prophetically about one of the most disturbing situations in the world today." Citing United Nations reports on Jerusalem, he said Sayre's charges "are kind of old stuff to anyone who's done his homework or traveled enough in the Middle East."

Support for Sayre was voiced by Jesuit educator Joseph L. Ryan of Georgetown University. Explaining that he spoke in response to the injunction of Pope Paul—"If you wish peace, work for justice"—Father Ryan cited statements by the Pope and by Catholic leaders in several Middle Eastern countries expressing concern about Israeli actions in Jerusalem and about the misery of Palestinian refugees. He pointed out that Israeli oppression of Christians and Muslims in Jerusalem was documented by publications of the Israeli League for Human Rights and the United Nations. "There is no dearth of evidence," he wrote. "If the public raising of these cases of oppression is shocking, the reality is incomparably more shocking."

Father Ryan reserved his strongest language for criticizing unquestioning Christian supporters of Israeli policies:

Further, a few Catholics and Protestants propagate the insinuation that to be anti-Zionist (that is, critical of Israel) is to be anti-Semitic. In their anxiety to wipe out racism, these spokesmen go to extremes. This insinuation which they try to make widespread hinders, instead of helps, the development of proper relations between Christians and Jews, and inhibits the free and open discussion of fundamental differences for Americans as citizens of their country and of the world community is essential in the search for justice and peace.

Dean Sayre remained largely detached from the tempest he had stirred on Palm Sunday. His only public action was to state through an aide that he would not retract any of his comments. Years later he acknowledged that, while he had given previous sermons on the plight of the Palestinian refugees, the 1972 Palm Sunday address was his first direct criticism of Israel. "Of course I realized that it would make a big splash," he said. "But if you put it more mildly, as I had [previously], it made no dent at all. So what are you going to do?"

Prior to the controversial sermon, Sayre had enjoyed high standing with the American Jewish community. A local Jewish congregation, at Sayre's invitation, held services in the cathedral until its synagogue was built. Jews respected him for the work he had done as president of the United States Committee for Refugees. In this capacity he had worked to resettle Jews from Jordan, Syria and Lebanon. As an Episcopal minister in Cleveland after World War II, he had been head of the diocese's committee to settle refugees, many of them Jews, from Eastern Europe.

The sermon had personal implications. Sayre and his family experienced a campaign of "very unpleasant direct intimidation" through letters and telephone calls. On a number of occasions, when his children answered the phone they were shouted at and verbally abused. The phone would ring in the middle of the night, only to be hung up as soon as a member of the Sayre family answered. "Even when I went out, I would be accosted rudely by somebody or other who would condemn me in a loud voice." Such harassment continued for about six months, Sayre said, "even to the point where my life was threatened over the phone; so much so that I had the cathedral guards around the house for a while."

The ecumenical spirit between Sayre and community rabbis was strained again six months after the sermon. When eleven Israeli athletes were killed at the 1972 Olympic Games in Munich, while being held capture by the radical "Black September" guerrillas, Dean Sayre shared the shock and revulsion felt around the world. Together with rabbis and other Jewish leaders in Washington, he immediately began to plan a memorial service in the cathedral.

Three days after the tragedy Israeli warplanes attacked Palestinian camps in Syria and Lebanon, killing 40 people. Sayre then told the rabbis of his intention to "make this a more general service than just for victims of Arab killing," memorializing the dead Palestinians as well.

Confronted with this prospect, the rabbis did not participate after all. There were, however, a number of Jews among the approximately 500 persons who attended the broadened memorial service. They heard Dean Sayre describe the Arab guerillas as "misguided and desperately misled" victims "of all the bitterness their lives had been surrounded with since birth, bitterness born of issues left callously unresolved by any international conscience."

He condemned the Israeli retaliation: "An eye for an eye, tooth for tooth is the rationale of that violence, by which I am desolate to think the government of Israel has sacrificed any moral position of injured innocence." The Dean invoked the broader historical and humanitarian view which had marked his Palm Sunday sermon in words which might well be repeated for every victim of Middle East violence:

I perceive that the victim of the violence which we mourn today is not only a latter-day Jew upon the blood-stained soil of Germany, nor yet the Arab prisoner of an equally violent heritage. The victim is all of us, the whole human race upon this earth.

Despite these words, unexceptional in their Christian message, Sayre was treated as though he somehow was a preacher of extremism. His career never had quite the shine it had before his forthright words on the Middle East.

Now in semiretirement on Martha's Vineyard, an island off Cape Cod, Sayre serves as chaplain at the local hospital but has no regular church responsibilities. One morning in 1983, I delayed his project for the morning—digging clams—to ask if the controversial Palm Sunday message had had any effect on his career. Still robust in voice and spirit, Sayre answered without hesitation: "Yes, very definitely. I knew it would. It's not popular to speak out. I don't like to speculate about it, because no one knows what would have happened. But I think I was a dangerous commodity from then on, not to be considered for bishop or anything else."

"I Felt I Had to Do Something"

The American religious community has seen few figures with the stature of Dean Sayre willing to speak out forcefully for peace and justice for all Middle East peoples. At the time of the Palm Sunday sermon in 1972, he was one of the most prominent spokesman of American Christianity: a powerful and intellectually gifted man wielding the authority of Washington Cathedral's prestigious pulpit. Despite the price Sayre paid for his courageous stand, younger voices are emerging which express similar resolve and depth of commitment.

The Reverend Don Wagner, a Presbyterian from Chicago, has risen quickly to the forefront of those within the religious community who seek to educate the public on realities in the Middle East and to counter the religious bias which often obscures awareness of those realities. His experiences have also brought him firsthand acquaintance with the intimidation which such efforts call forth.

Wagner first became involved in public debate over the Middle East while serving as associate pastor of a large Presbyterian church in Evanston, Illinois. He was at the time, in his own words, "very pro-Israel." In the wake of the first oil crisis, in 1974 the young pastor helped organize a series of speakers within the church, alternating between pro-Israeli and pro-Arab points of view. He felt the series would aid his parishioners to understand better this unprecedented event. Wagner was quite surprised when, halfway through, he began receiving pressure to stop the series. A barrage of anonymous telephone calls threatened picketing outside the church and more severe, unspecified reprisals if the series continued.

Wagner did not stop. In the end, however, the series was marred by the refusal of two Jewish members of the final panel to take part. They announced a half-hour before the scheduled discussion that the presence of an Arab academic on the panel rendered the event anti-Semitic and that they consequently refused to dignify it with their presence. They implied that Wagner had deceived them about the make-up of the panel and the nature of the discussion, although the topic of the discussion and the list of participants had been publicized well in advance.

Wagner suspected that these men had been pressured to quit the conference by their rabbis. This suspicion was reinforced later when he learned that many of the earlier telephone calls had also been from members of the local Jewish community. One of the callers even told him directly: "I am a Jew, and this kind of activity is very anti-Semitic. For a Christian to be doing this is unconscionable." This was an eye-opening experience for Wagner. He discovered, as have others who have dared to speak out and become involved, that one need not actually criticize the Jewish people or the state of Israel to be labelled anti-Semitic. Simply raising questions about Middle East issues and assuming that the answers may not all be obvious is enough to evoke the charge.

Wagner first traveled to the Middle East in 1977. He paid his own way but traveled with representatives of the Palestine Human Rights Campaign (PHRC), an organization concerned with the protection of Palestinian rights. After spending time with refugees and other residents in Beirut, the West Bank and Jerusalem, Wagner felt his long-standing sympathy for the displaced Palestinian refugees growing into a strong personal imperative. "I felt I had to do something," he recently recalled.

After his return to United States, he learned how difficult it could be to "do something." Shortly before his departure for the Middle East, Wagner had arranged a church speaking engagement for Dr. Israel Shahak, a prominent Israeli critic of government policy. He returned to discover that the senior minister of his church had acceded to pressure from local rabbis to cancel the Shahak engagement without informing either him or Shahak. The senior minister explained that the local rabbis had convinced him that it would be "in the best interests of the church and Jewish relations" if the appearance of such a well-known critic of Israeli policy were cancelled.

Undeterred, Wagner became increasingly active in speaking up about the Palestinian plight, offering Sunday morning prayers for the refugees, promoting more educational activities, and even bringing Palestinian Christians to his pulpit to speak. His activities led not only to a continuation of public criticism and pressure but also to problems within the staff of his own church as well. One associate frequently referred to him as "the PLO pastor," and staff friction grew as Wagner proceeded with plans for the First LaGrange Conference, (LaGrange I), named for the Illinois town in which it was held in the spring of 1979.

This conference, like LaGrange II which followed in May 1981, was aimed at raising awareness of the Palestinian refugee situation among American church groups and leaders. Both meetings were attended by a broad ecumenical body of Christians, including Evangelical, mainline Protestant, Roman Catholic and Orthodox. The first conference was jointly sponsored by PHRC and the Middle East task force of the Chicago Presbytery. The second was sponsored by PHRC and the Christian peace groups Pax Christi and Sojourners. The theme of these conferences was summed up in the title of LaGrange II: "Toward Biblical Foundations for a Just Peace in the Holy Land."

After a series of speakers and panels, each conference issued a statement. These two documents have become a topic of debate within the American religious community. The statements stress the common humanity of Arabs, Jews, and Christians and call upon the American Christian churches to be more active in spreading information and promoting reconciliation and peace. Specifically, the churches are enjoined to "encourage dialogue with other Christians as well as Jews and others concerning the priorities of peace in the Holy Land" and to "inform and educate their people of the historical roots of the Israeli Palestinian conflict."

The participants in LaGrange I and II made a significant step in ecumenical cooperation for greater public understanding of the Middle East. Unfortunately, the opponents of cooperation and understanding were also in attendance.

Prior to the convening of LaGrange I, the Chicago Presbytery received pressure from the local chapter of the Anti-Defamation League, led by associate director Rabbi Yechiel Eckstein, to withdraw Presbyterian sponsorship of the conference. There were telephone calls, an extensive letter-writing campaign, and finally meetings between Jewish leaders and members of the church hierarchy.

The elders of the church stood by Wagner, but the Jewish community promptly passed judgment on the conference. The day before the conference convened, the ADL issued a press release condemning its "anti-Semitic bias."

Efforts to discredit the conference did not end there. The slate of speakers had been planned to include Father John Polakowski, a noted writer on the Holocaust and active Zionist. The morning of the conference Father Polakowski sent a registered letter to Wagner announcing his withdrawal from the conference. He had been fully informed as to the nature of the conference and the identity of many of the other speakers, but he denounced the conference as unfairly biased against the Israeli perspective. He fulfilled his own prophecy. His decision to deprive the conference of his own perspective caused the Zionist view to be underrepresented at LaGrange I.

LaGrange II witnessed a virtual repeat of the same tactic. Rabbi Arnold Kaiman had agreed to address a section of the conference entitled "Religious People Talking from Their Perspectives." He had been invited to speak partly because of his long-standing personal friendship with Ayoub Talhami, co-convenor of the conference. Talhami had discussed the planned conference with Rabbi Kaiman in detail, even sending him a draft copy of the conference flier, and, of course, the rabbi was aware of the previous conference. The day of the conference Kaiman sent a special delivery letter to Wagner, Talhami and others announcing his withdrawal from the conference. The letter denounced Talhami and the convenors of the conference for having "misled" and "deceived" him. Talhami felt that the letter was intended mainly for Kaiman's congregational board, both because the chairman of that board was a co-addressee of the letter and because the accusations of deceit were so preposterous.

Whatever his reasons, Kaiman went beyond a personal refusal to speak and repudiation of the conference. He provided copies of his letter to reporters, so that the withdrawal of a pro-Zionist could be publicized before the conference could issue its statement.

To Wagner, the last-minute withdrawals of Polakowski and Kaiman after it was too late to schedule other pro-Israel speakers suggested that these supporters of Israel were more concerned with discrediting opposing points of view than with stating their own in an atmosphere of free and open debate. These withdrawals added color to subsequent ADL charges that the LaGrange Conferences were "anti-Israel conferences" or "PLO gatherings," despite the balanced character of the statements which emerged from the conferences.

However, the most disturbing incident to emerge from LaGrange I and II did not involve attempts to discredit the conferences themselves, but false charges made against one of the participants.

Sister Miriam Ward, a professor of humanities at Trinity College in Vermont and a Catholic nun, has a long record of humanitarian concern for Palestinian refugees. By her own description, her role in LaGrange II was modest. "I had doubts about whether I could justify the expense of going," she recently recalled. Sister Miriam moderated a panel discussion and received an award for her humanitarian endeavors. Like Mr. Wagner, she knew from experience the price of speaking out on Palestinian questions. Her activities had also attracted hate mail and personal innuendoes. Still, she was not prepared for the smear which resulted from her participation at LaGrange.

Sister Miriam was singled out for a personal attack in *The Jewish Week-American Examiner,* a prominent New York City Jewish publication. The June 21, 1981, issue gave prominent coverage to a scheme to disrupt Israeli policy on the occupied West Bank which Sister Miriam had supposedly advanced at the conference. The article claimed that she had urged that "churches finance a project with staff in the U.S. and fieldworkers in Israel and the West Bank for the purpose of 'spying on the Israelis.'" She was reported saying, "By the time the Israelis caught on to what was going on and expelled a fieldworker, they [presumably Sister Miriam and her co-conspirators] would have a replacement ready." The *Jewish Week* article added that "the proposal was accepted without dissent, and ways of obtaining church funds for it were discussed."

The report was a complete fabrication. No one at the LaGrange Conference had suggested such a plan, least of all Sister Miriam, and she was stunned when Wagner telephoned from Chicago informing her of the printed allegations. She had always shunned publicity for her humanitarian activities, and felt intimidated and intensely alone at being singled out for attack. "I was physically ill for some time," she recalls, "and could not even discuss the matter with other members of my religious community."

After pondering how—and whether—to respond, she finally sought the advice of a prominent biblical scholar then guest-lecturing at Trinity College. He advised her to see an attorney about the possibility of legal action. The attorney was sympathetic and agreed to take at least preliminary action free of charge. After several letters from the attorney elicited no response from the newspaper, the same scholar—himself a prominent member of the New York Jewish community—personally telephoned the editor. Sister Miriam feels that it was his call that impelled the editor to act.

In January 1982—more than six months after the original charges—a retraction was finally printed in *The Jewish Week-American Examiner.* The editors admitted that, "on checking, we find that there is no basis for the quotations attributed to" Sister Miriam. They explained that the story had been "furnished by a service" and "was not covered by any staff member of the *Jewish Week.*" In their retraction, the editors added that they were "happy to withdraw any reflection upon" Sister Miriam.

Yet, as Sister Miriam discovered, the published apology could not erase the original charge from the minds of all readers. Later the same year, a Jewish physician from New York was visiting Burlington as part of a campus program at Trinity College. In a conversation between this woman and another member of Sister Miriam's religious order, the name of the biblical scholar involved in Sister Miriam's case came up. The nun mentioned that he had recently visited Trinity at the invitation of Sister Miriam.

Recognizing the name from the original *Jewish Week* article, the physician repeated with indignation the accusations made against Sister Miriam. She had not seen the retraction. The visitor was quickly informed that the charges were false. Sister Miriam cited this as an example of why she is convinced that the damage to her reputation can never really be undone. "It's the original thing that does the harm. I just don't want it to happen to anybody else."

Chapter 10

Not All Jews Toe the Line

In its efforts to quell criticism of Israel, the pro-Israel community's first goal is to still Jewish critics. In this quest it receives strong support from the Israeli government.

Every government of Israel gives high priority to maintaining unity among U.S. Jews. This unity is regarded as a main line of Israel's defense—second in importance only to the Israeli army—and essential to retaining the support Israel must have from the United States government.

American Jews are made to feel guilty about enjoying safety and the good life in the United States while their fellow Jews in Israel hold the ramparts, pay high taxes, and fight wars. As Rabbi Balfour Brickner states: "We hide behind the argument that it is not for us to speak our minds because the Israelis have to pay the price."

For most Jews, open criticism of Israeli policy is unthinkable. The theme is survival—survival of the Zionist dream, of Judaism, of Jews themselves. The fact that the Jewish community in the United States has produced little debate in recent years on Middle East questions even within its own ranks does not mean that all its members agree.

In private, many American Jews hold positions in sharp disagreement with official Israeli policies. The differences are startling. A 1983 survey by the American Jewish Committee revealed that about half of U.S. Jews favor a homeland for the Palestinians on the West Bank and Gaza and recommend that Israel stop the expansion of settlements in order to encourage peace negotiations. Three-fourths want Israel to talk to the Palestine Liberation Organization if it recognizes Israel and renounces terrorism. Only 21 percent want Israel to maintain permanent control over the West Bank. On each of these propositions, the plurality of American Jews takes issue with the policies and declarations of the Israeli government.

A plurality also holds that American Jews individually, as well as in organized groups, should feel free to criticize Israeli policy publicly. Of those surveyed, 70 percent say U.S. Jewish organizations should feel free to criticize. On this question, even Jewish leaders say they welcome criticism: 40 percent say organizations should feel free to criticize; 37 percent disagree. This means that only one-third of the leaders say they want to stifle organizational criticism of Israel. The vote by individual Jews for free and open debate is even stronger. Only 31 percent declare that American Jews individually should not criticize Israeli policy publicly; 57 percent disagree. On this question, leaders and non-leaders vote exactly alike.

The results of the survey are not easily reconciled with the facts about public dissent. While American Jews say they strongly oppose some Israeli policies and believe that organizations and individuals should feel free to criticize these policies openly, the simple fact is that public criticism is almost non-existent. The views expressed in the survey must be regarded more as a "wish list" than a statement of principles which the people surveyed actually try to carry out.

In public, Jewish organizations in the United States support Israeli policies with a unanimity that is broken only in rare circumstances. They either give open support or remain silent. The leaders of B'nai B'rith and the American Israel Public Affairs Committee (AIPAC) expressed guarded support for President Reagan's Middle East peace plan immediately after it was announced in September 1982, but these expressions occurred before the Israeli government had stated its position. Once Israeli opposition was known, these organizations dropped the subject.

"Trampled to Death"

Of the more than 200 principal Jewish organizations functioning on a national scale, only the New Jewish Agenda and its predecessor, Breira, have challenged any stated policy of the Israeli government.

In return for their occasional criticism of Israel's policies, the two organizations were ostracized and kept out of the organized Jewish community. Breira lasted only five years. Organized in 1973, its peak national membership was about 1,000. Named for the Hebrew word meaning "alternative," it called on Jewish institutions to be "open to serious debate," and proposed "a comprehensive peace between Israel, the Arab states, and a Palestinian homeland that is ready to live in peace alongside Israel." Prominent in its leadership were Rabbis Arnold Jacob Wolf, David Wolf Silverman, Max Ticktin, David Saperstein, and Balfour Brickner.

The counterattack was harsh. *The National Journal* reports that

Briera was "bitterly attacked by many leaders of the Jewish establishment" and that a Breira meeting was "invaded and ransacked" by members of the militant Jewish Defense League. Some members of Breira came under intense pressure to quit either the organization or their jobs. Jewish leaders were warned to avoid Breira or fund raising would be hurt.

Israeli officials joined rabbis in denouncing the organization. Carolyn Toll, a reporter for the *Chicago Tribune* and formerly on the board of directors of Breira, quotes a rabbi: "My bridges are burned. Once you take a position like this [challenging Israeli positions], the organized Jewish community closes you out." Officials from the Israeli consulates in Boston and Philadelphia warned Jews against attending a Breira conference.

Breira came under attack from both right and left within the Jewish community. A pamphlet branding some of its members as "radicals" was quoted by Jewish publications and later distributed by AIPAC. Breira was accused of being allied with the radical U.S. Labor Party. An unsigned "fact sheet" suggested that it really was a group of Jewish radicals supporting the PLO. The *Seattle Jewish Transcript* said it was run by a "coterie of leftist revolutionaries" who opposed Israel.

Irving Howe, speaking at the final national conference of Breira in 1977, said the tactics used to smear the organization were an "outrage such as we have not known for a long time in the Jewish community." At the same meeting, retired Israeli General Mattityahu Peled, who was often boycotted by Jewish groups while on U.S. lecture tours, said, "The pressure applied on those who hold dissenting views here [in the U.S.] is far greater than the pressure on us in Israel. I would say that probably we in Israel enjoy a larger degree of tolerance than you do here within the Jewish community." Breira disbanded shortly afterward.

In December 1980, 700 American Jews gathered in Washington, D.C., to found another organization of dissenters, the New Jewish Agenda. Composed mainly of young liberals, it called for "compromise through negotiations with the Palestinian people and Israel's Arab neighbors" and opposed Israeli policies in the West Bank and Lebanon.

It was soon barred from associating with other Jewish groups. In June 1983, its Washington, D.C., chapter was refused membership in the Jewish Community Council, a group which included 260 religious, educational, fraternal and social service organizations. The council members voted 98 to 70 to overturn the recommendation of the group's executive board, which had voted 22 to five for admission. Irwin Stein, president of the Washington chapter of the Zionist Organization of

America charged that the group was "far out" and "pro-Arab rather than pro-Israel." Moe Rodenstein, representing the Agenda, said the group would like to be a part of "the debate" and added, "We're proud of what we're doing."

"It Is a Form of McCarthyism"

Like the Jewish organizations, individual Jews rarely express public disagreement with Israel policies, despite the broad and fundamental differences they seem to hold. The handful who have spoken up have had few followers and even fewer defenders. To Carolyn Toll, the taboo against criticism is powerful and extensive:

I believe even Jews outside the Jewish community are affected by internal taboos on discussion—for if one is discouraged from bringing up certain subjects within the Jewish community, think how much more disloyal it could be to raise them outside!

Toll laments the "suppression of free speech in American Jewish institutions—the pressures that prevent dovish or dissident Jews from organizing in synagogues, Jewish community centers, and meetings of major national Jewish organizations" and denunciations of American Friends Service Committee representatives as "anti-Semitics" and "dupes of the Palestine Liberation Organization" for insisting that "any true peace must include a viable state for the Palestinians."

A successful Jewish author suffered a different type of "excommunication" when she wrote a book critical of Israel. In *The Fate of the Jews,* a candid and anguished history of U.S. Jewry and its present-day dilemma, Roberta Strauss Feuerlicht explains that Zionism has become the "religion" for many Jews. This is why, she writes, that "opposition to Zionism or criticism of Israel is now heresy and cause for excommunication," adding that the idealism attributed to Israel by most supporters has been marred by years of "patriotism, nationalism, chauvinism and expansionism." She declares, "Israel shields itself from legitimate criticism by calling her critics anti-Semitic; it is a form of McCarthyism and fatally effective."

A year after its publication in 1983 by Times Books, the book was still largely ignored. The *Los Angeles Times* was the only major newspaper to review it. The publisher undertook no advertising, nor even a minimal promotional tour. Feuerlicht, the author of fifteen successful books, was subjected to what Mark A. Bruzonsky, another Jewish journalist, described as a "combination of slander and neglect." When copies sent to prominent "liberal Jews, Christians, civil libertarians and blacks" brought no response, Feuerlicht concluded, "It would seem that with universal assent, the book is being stoned to death with silence."

Other Jews who dare voice guarded criticism of Israel encounter threats which are far from silent. Threatening phone calls have become a part of life for Gail Pressberg of Philadelphia, a Jewish member of the professional staff of the American Friends Service Committee. In her work she is active in projects supporting the Palestinian cause. She reports that abuse calls are so frequent that "I don't pay any attention anymore." One evening, after receiving several calls on her unlisted telephone in which her life was threatened for "deserting Israel," in desperation she left the receiver off the hook. A few minutes later the same voice called on her roommate's phone, also unlisted, resuming the threats.

In my 22 years in Congress, I can recall no entry in *Congressional Record* disclosing a speech critical of Israeli policy by a Jewish member of the House or Senate. Jewish members may voice discontent in private conversation but never on the public record. Only a few Jewish academicians, like Noam Chomsky, a distinguished linguist, have spoken out. Most, like Chomsky, are protected in their careers by tenure and thus are able to become controversial without jeopardizing their positions.

"Dissent Becomes Treason"

Journalism is the occupation in which Jews most often and most consistently voice criticism of Israel. Richard Cohen of the *Washington Post* is a notable example.

During Israel's 1982 invasion of Lebanon, Cohen warned: ". . . The administration can send Begin a message that he does not have an infinite line of credit in America—that we will not, for instance, approve the bombing of innocent civilians."

In a later column, Cohen summarized the reaction to his criticism of Israeli policy: "My phone these days is an instrument of torture. Merely to answer it runs the risk of being insulted. The mail is equally bad. The letters are vicious, some of them quite personal." He noted that U.S. Jews are held to a different standard than Israelis when they question Israel's policies.

Here dissent becomes treason—and treason not to a state or even an ideal (Zionism), but to a people. There is tremendous pressure for conformity, to show a united front and to adopt the view that what is best for Israel is something only the government there can know.

In a world in which there are plenty of people who hate Jews, it is ridiculous to manufacture a whole new category out of nothing more than criticism of the Begin government. Nothing could be worse for Israel in the long run than for its friends not to distinguish between when it is right and when it is wrong.

Mark Bruzonsky, a persistent journalistic critic of these Israeli excesses, concludes, "There's no way in the world that a Jew can avoid a savage and personal vendetta if his intent is to write a truthful and meaningful account of what he has experienced."

Being Jewish did not spare the foreign news editor of Hearst newspapers from similar problems. In early 1981 John Wallach produced a television documentary, "Israel and Palestinians: Will Reason Prevail?" funded by the Foundation for Middle East Peace, a nonprofit institute established by Washington lawyer Merle Thorpe, Jr. His goal was a fair, balanced presentation of the problems confronting Israel in dealing with the Palestinians on the West Bank and Gaza. Public television broadcast the program without incident in Washington, D.C., New York and other major cities, but Jewish leaders in Los Angeles demanded an advance showing and upon seeing the film put up such a strong protest that station KCT inserted a statement disclaiming any responsibility for the content of the documentary.

Wallach received many complaints about the presentation, the most common being that it portrayed Palestinian children in a favorable light—some were blond and blue-eyed, and all attractive—a departure from the frequently negative stereotype of Palestinians. Before the film was produced, Israeli Ambassador Simcha Dinitz called Wallach, urging him to drop the project. When Wallach persisted, invitations to receptions and dinners at the Israeli embassy suddenly stopped. For a time he was not even notified of press briefings.

Wallach found himself in hot water again in 1982 when controversy erupted after a formal dinner he had organized to recognize Ambassador Philip Habib's diplomatic endeavors in Lebanon. Several cabinet officers, Congressmen and members of the diplomatic community attended the dinner. During the program, messages from several heads of government were read. Wallach asked Senator Charles Percy, chairman of the Foreign Relations Committee, to read the one from Israel's Prime Minister Menachem Begin to the audience. On Wallach's recommendation, Percy did not read these two sentences:

In the wake of the Operation Peace in Galilee, Phil Habib made great efforts to bring about the evacuation of the bulk of the terrorists from Beirut and Lebanon. He worked hard to achieve this goal and, with the victory of the Israel Defense Forces, his diplomatic endeavors contributed to the dismantling of that center of international terrorism which had been a danger to all free nations.

Moshe Arens, the Israeli ambassador, was furious. He sent an angry letter to Percy expressing his shock and stating, "Although I realize that you may not have agreed with its contents, . . . this glaring omission seems to me to be without precedent." He also wrote to Wallach, complaining of "unprecedented discourtesy" and calling the omission an attempt to "cater to the ostrich-like attitude of some of the ambassadors from Arab countries." Arens also wrote protest letters to the management of Hearst Corporation, which had picked up the tab for the dinner.

Wallach told another journalist the next day why he had recommended the omission: "I thought it was insulting to the Arabs [who were present] to have a message about war and terrorism at an evening that was a tribute to Phil Habib and peace."

Wallach said, "The irony was that, while I got lots of harsh, critical mail from those supporting Begin, I got no words of support or commendation from the other side. It makes one wonder—when there is no support, only criticism, when one risks his career."

Similar questions are raised by Nat Hentoff, a Jewish columnist who frequently criticizes Israel and challenges the conscience of his fellow Jews in his column for the *Village Voice*. During the Israeli invasion of Lebanon in 1982 he lamented:

At no time during his visit here [in the United States] was [Prime Minister] Begin given any indication that there are some of us who fear that he and Ariel Sharon are destroying Israel from within. Forget the Conference of Presidents of Major American Jewish Organizations and the groups they represent. They have long since decided to say nothing in public that is critical of Israel.

Hentoff deplored the intimidation that silences most Jewish critics:

I know staff workers for the American Jewish Congress and the American Jewish Committee who agonize about their failure to speak out, even on their own time, against Israeli injustice. They don't, because they figure they'll get fired if they do.

The threat of being fired was forcefully put to a group of employees of Jewish organizations in the United States during a 1982 tour of Lebanon. Israel's invasion was at its peak, and a number of employees of the Jewish National Fund—a nationwide organization which raises money for the purchase and development of Israeli land—were touring Lebanese battlefield areas. Suddenly, while the group was traveling on the bus, Dr. Sam Cohen of New York, the executive vice-president of the JNF, stood up and made a surprising announcement. A member of the tour, Charles Fishbein, at the time executive for the Washington office, recalls, "He told us that when we get back to the

United States, we must defend what Israel is doing in Lebanon. He said that if we criticize Israel, we will be terminated immediately."

Fishbein said the group was on one of several hastily arranged tours designed to quell rising Jewish criticism of the invasion. In all, over 1,500 prominent American Jews were flown to Israel for tours of hospitals and battlefields. The tours ranged in length from four to seven days. The more prestigious the group of visitors, the shorter, more compressed the schedule. Disclosing only Israeli hardship, the tours were successful in quieting criticism within the ranks of Jewish leadership and also inspired many actively to defend Israeli war policies.

"The Time May Not Be Far Off"

Peer pressure does not always muffle Jewish voices. A man who pioneered in establishing the state of Israel and helped to organize its crucial underpinnings of support in the United States later became a frequent critic of Israeli policy.

Nahum Goldmann is a towering figure in the history of Zionism. He played a crucial role in the founding of Israel, meeting its early financial problems, influencing its leaders, and organizing a powerful constituency for it in the United States. His service to Zionism spanned nearly fifty years. During World I, when Palestine was still part of the Ottoman Empire, Goldmann tried to persuade Turkish authorities to allow Jewish immigration. In the 1930s he advocated the Zionist cause at the League of Nations. During the Truman administration, he lobbied for the United Nations resolution calling for partition of Palestine and the establishment of Israel.

After the 1947 U.N. vote for the partition, unlike most Jews who were eager to proclaim the state of Israel, Goldmann urged delay. He hoped that the Jews would first reach an understanding with the Arab states and thereby avoid war.

He lamented the bitter legacy of the war that ensued. He wrote, "The unexpected defeat was a shock and a terrible blow to Arab pride. Deeply injured, they turned all their endeavors to the healing of their psychological wound: to victory and revenge." To the Israelis,

The victory offered such a glorious contrast to the centuries of persecution and humiliation, of adaptation and compromise, that it seemed to indicate the only direction that could possibly be taken from then on. To brook nothing, to tolerate no attack, cut through Gordian knots, and shape history by creating facts seemed so simple, so compelling, so satisfying that it became Israel's policy in its conflict with the Arab world.

When the fledgling nation was struggling to build its economy,

Goldmann negotiated with West German Chancellor Konrad Adenauer the agreement under which the Germans paid over $30 billion in compensation and restitution to Israel and individual Jews.

Yet he was bitterly condemned by some Israelis for his efforts. Philip Klutznick of Chicago, Goldmann's close colleague in endeavors for Israel, recalls the tremendous opposition, particularly from such extreme nationalists as Menachem Begin, to accepting anything from Germany. "At that time many Jews felt that any act that would tend to bring the Germans back into the civilized world was an act against the Jewish people. Feelings ran deep."

Goldmann's disagreement with Israeli policy toward the Arabs was his central concern. To those who criticized his advocacy of a Palestinian state, he responded,

If they do not believe that Arab hostility can some day be alleviated, then we might just as well liquidate Israel at once, so as to save the millions of Jews who live there. . . . There is no hope for a Jewish state which has to face another 50 years of struggle against Arab enemies.

Goldmann respected the deep commitment to the Jewish people of Israel's first prime minister, David Ben Gurion, but he regretted that Ben Gurion was "organically incapable of compromise" and that his "dominant force" was "his will for power." Goldmann's essential optimism and his instinctive striving to temper hatreds and seek compromise were qualities that distinguished him from so many of his contemporaries—on both the Arab and Israeli sides of the conflict.

"Goldmann might have been prime minister of Israel," Stanley Karnow wrote in 1980, "but he chose instead to live in Europe and act as diplomatic broker, frequently infuriating Israeli officials with his initiatives." Seeking an end to the Arab-Israeli conflict, he attempted to visit Cairo at the invitation of Egyptian President Nasser in 1970. But the Israeli government headed by Golda Meir resented his maverick ways and blocked the mission.

Goldmann was sharply critical of the Israeli government of Menachem Begin. He decried what he saw as Israel's denial of the original Zionist vision. He rejected the claim of some Israelis that they must occupy "Greater Israel" because it was promised to them by God. He called this thesis "a profanation."

Goldmann understood the need for U.S. support. He lived in the United States for more than 20 years and knew American Jewry well. In 1969 he wrote approvingly of Zionist political action in the United States: "It is not fair to single out Zionist pressure for censure. Democracy consists of a mutiplicity of pressure-exerting forces, each of which is trying to make itself felt."

Near the end of his life, however, Goldmann's views of the pro-Israel lobby changed. In 1980 he warned:

Blind support of the Begin government may be more menacing for Israel than any danger of Arab attack. American Jewry is more generous than any other group in American life and is doing great things. . . . But by misusing its political influence, by exaggerating the aggressiveness of the Jewish lobby in Washington, by giving the Begin regime the impression that the Jews are strong enough to force the American administration and Congress to follow every Israeli desire, they lead Israel on a ruinous path which, if continued, may lead to dire consequences.

He blamed the Israeli lobby for U.S. failures to bring about a comprehensive settlement in the Middle East. "It was to a very large degree because of electoral considerations, fear of the pro-Israel lobby, and of the Jewish vote."

He warned of trouble ahead if the lobby continued its present course. "It is now slowly becoming something of a negative factor. Not only does it distort the expectations and political calculations of Israel, but the time may not be far off when American public opinion will be sick and tired of the demands of Israel and the aggressiveness of American Jewry."

In 1978, two years before he wrote his alarmed evaluation of the Israeli lobby, *New York* magazine reported that Goldmann had privately urged officials of the Carter administration "to break the back" of the lobby: "Goldmann pleaded with the administration to stand firm and not back off from confrontations with the organized Jewish community as other administrations had done." Unless this was done, he argued, "President Carter's plans for a Middle East settlement would die in stillbirth."

His words were prophetic. The comprehensive settlement Carter sought was frustrated by the intransigence of Israel and its U.S. lobby.

President Ronald Reagan revived the idea of a comprehensive Middle East peace just four days before Goldmann's death in September 1982. A state funeral was conducted in Israel. As Klutznick, Israeli Labor Party leaders Shimon Peres, Yitzhak Rabin and others stood on Israel's Mount Herzl awaiting the great Zionist leader's burial alongside the five other former presidents of the World Zionist Organization, the conversation centered on the Reagan plan, which Prime Minister Begin had already rejected.

Symbolic of organized Jewry's reaction to Goldmann's life was the response of the Israeli government to his death. Begin gave permission for the burial but did not attend. In a strikingly empty commentary on the life of a man who had done so much to bring Israel into being and give it strength, Acting Prime Minister Simcha Ehrlich said only, "We regret that a man of so many virtues and abilities went the wrong way." It was a callous epitaph for one of Israel's great pioneers.

"You Must Listen When We Speak Ill"

At 7:45 A.M. the towering John Hancock Building in Chicago's downtown loop area was just beginning to come to life. On the fortieth floor were the offices of Philip Klutznick—attorney, developer, former U.S. secretary of commerce, president emeritus of B'nai B'rith, organizer and former chairman of the Conference of Presidents of Major Jewish Organizations, president emeritus of the World Jewish Congress. At that hour only Philip Klutznick was at work.

He was on the phone, seated on a sofa at one end of his spacious office, his back to a panoramic view of the building across the street where he and his wife make their home. On the walls were autographed photographs of the seven presidents of the United States under whom he has served.

This morning, in the fall of 1983, he was talking with Ashraf Ghorbal, Egypt's ambassador to the United States and a friend of many years. Ghorbal was preparing for a visit to the United States by his leader, Egyptian President Hosni Mubarak. He wanted to make sure the right people would be available to meet with him. The right people included Klutznick.

Klutznick's vigorous appearance and unrelenting pace belie his seventy-six years. His deep, rich voice echoes around the near-empty offices. His eyes smile through heavy glasses, and his firm, confident manner is that of a man in the prime of life.

But his apparent confidence about the flexibility of U.S. Jews belies his own experience working within—and outside—the establishment for sixty years. A visitor sharing coffee and conversation would never guess that this short, handsome, optimistic man—whose persistence and spirit helped to create Israel, pay its bills and provide its arms—had become, in the eyes of many Jews, a virtual castaway.

Measured by offices held and services rendered, his credentials in the Jewish establishment are impeccable. But in the eyes of most Jewish leaders, he is guilty of a cardinal sin: daring publicly to challenge Israeli government policy. This puts him at odds with the very Jewish organizations he did so much to bring into being.

He speaks from a base of confidence that includes business success, public office in both Democratic and Republican administrations, and high honors in the Jewish community. After seeing his savings wiped out by the Great Depression, he recovered, became a successful community developer, a millionaire, a leader of the Jewish community, and a diplomat.

In early years he worked to bring strength and unity to the Jewish community, a quest that took on urgency in 1942 when word arrived of Adolf Hitler's barbaric program to annihilate European Jews. Henry Monsky, an Omaha lawyer and president of B'nai B'rith, convened a meeting in Pittsburgh, inviting the membership of 41 major Jewish organizations. This gathering, identified as the American Jewish Conference, marked the first serious effort to unite U.S. Jews against the Holocaust.

"You know, we are an unusual group of people," Klutznick chuckles. "We fight over anything." This time the fight was over whether Jews would back the establishment of a national homeland. Monsky, the first committed Zionist to head B'nai B'rith, pulled the organization from its neutral stance into advocacy. When the conference met in early 1943 and cast its lot with Zionism, two of the largest Jewish organizations—the American Jewish Committee and the Jewish Labor Committee—walked out in protest.

"Anyway," Klutznick continues, "that meeting started a movement that stayed alive for four years." It also brought him for the first time in close association with Nahum Goldmann.

Klutznick and Goldmann wanted the American Jewish Conference to be permanent. In this effort, Klutznick battled to win the support of B'nai B'rith. "It was an enormous fight, and we lost," Klutznick recalls.

The bruises were still felt ten years later when Klutznick became president of B'nai B'rith. His first decision put him at odds with Goldmann, who wanted him to help re-create the American Jewish Conference. Despite his earlier effort, Klutznick now felt it would be divisive. "I looked him square in the eye and said, 'I'm not going to do it. If I tried it now it would split B'nai B'rith right down the middle. At this moment B'nai B'rith is too weak. I need these people together.' "

Klutznick told him he would "go all the way" on a program for a Jewish homeland, but he had what he believed to be a better plan for coordination of American Jews, an organization consisting of just the presidents of the major organizations. For one thing, the leaders needed to get acquainted with each other. "Believe it or not," Klutznick recalls, "many had attained these high positions without even meeting the presidents of other major organizations." Klutznick told Goldmann: "If we really want to do something, the presidents are the powerhouses." Goldmann agreed to the plan.

Klutznick's recalls changes: "The fact is during the 1950s people weren't as intense as they are now." As an example, he cites the Jewish response to the Eisenhower Doctrine, which pledged U.S. help to any nation in the Middle East threatened by international Communism. Israeli Prime Minister David Ben Gurion opposed a commitment that sweeping, arguing that it could lead to U.S. support for nations hostile to Israel. The Conference of Presidents of Major Jewish Organizations decided to support the U.S. position.

Klutznick recalls the confrontation. "I presided at that meeting, and we took the position that we should not oppose the president of the United States, and we didn't. In those days," he said after a long pause, "we could have those arguments. There was mutual tolerance."

Dealing with Israeli officials sometimes tested Klutznick's tolerance. In 1955 the U.S. was horrified at the Israeli massacre of Arab civilians in the Gaza raid, and Klutznick, as president of B'nai B'rith, reported the reaction to Jerusalem. He told Israeli Prime Minister Moshe Sharett: "Moshe, it was terrible. It wasn't the fact Israeli forces were defending Israel. It was the overwhelming response. It looked like a disregard for the value of human life."

After a pause, the prime minister answered quietly, "You know, Phil, I did not even know this was taking place. He [Defense Minister David Ben Gurion] did this on his own. I hope you will tell him what you told me." Klutznick met Ben Gurion the next day. "It wasn't long before he said, 'Phil, what was the reaction to the Gaza raid?' It was exactly the same question Sharett had asked, and I gave exactly the same answer."

Klutznick was astonished at Ben Gurion's response :

He stood up. He looked like an angry prophet out of the Bible and got red in the face. He shouted, 'I am not going to let anybody, American Jews or anybody else, tell me what I have to do to provide for the security of my people.'

When the prime minister stood up, Klutznick stood up too. Ben Gurion asked, "Why are are you standing up?" Klutznick answered, "Well, obviously I have offended you, and I assume that our discussion is over." Ben Gurion said, "Sit down. Let's talk about something else." Klutznick recalls, "That's the way it happened. So help me God. That's just the way it happened, and we had a wonderful talk." Klutznick says Ben Gurion could be as "tough or tougher than Begin," but when he had made his point he could go back to "being friends."

Klutznick had a similar experience years later with Prime Minister Begin. In the wake of the Camp David Accords, President Carter called in Klutznick and seven other Jewish leaders. The president said, "Look, I need some help. I think I can handle [Egyptian President] Sadat. We have an understanding, but I am not sure that I can convince

the Prime Minister [Begin]." One of the group interrupted and changed
the subject: "Mr. President, Israel is upset because there will be arms
sent to Arab countries. There is already a bill pending, as you know."
Then the next man said, "Can't you do something to make it more
comfortable for Israel?" Several men in a row spoke in a similar vein.

Klutznick noted Carter's irritation and undertook the role of
peacemaker:

Mr. President, I don't think we've quite got your message. There are all of
these requests for arms. I think what my colleagues are trying to say, if I may
interpret them, is whether there is some way to defer these requests until the
negotiations are over. I don't think it is for us with our limited knowledge to tell
you who should get arms and who should not.

He recalls, "I said that if the questions of arms sales had to be
answered during the Camp David negotiations, whichever way the
president answered them would be difficult." Klutznick says he added,
"And I am not here representing anybody except you, Mr. President.
Our country has to back you as fairly as it can."

Klutznick's remarks got the discussion back on the track Carter
wanted, but they were badly twisted in a news report published the
next day in Israel, where Klutznick was quoted as having told Carter
that he was at the White House meeting representing Egypt, not Israel.
He had, of course, said nothing of the kind and sent a cable to Begin
denying the story. The next day when reporters asked about the incident, Begin said simply, "I have received a cable from President Klutznick of the World Jewish Congress. He denies any such statement was
made, and that's the end of it."

But that was not the end of it. Klutznick flew to Israel in a few
days for previously scheduled meetings, including an appointment with
Begin. Klutznick recalls the frosty scene. It was the first time Begin did
not stand up and greet him with an embrace. Klutznick spoke first:

Look, Menachem, I know you are angry, but I'm the one that's angry and
entitled to be. When you told the press you got a cable from Klutznick and he
denies it and that's the end of it—is that the right thing to say? I say no. If
someone had said that about you to me, I would have said, 'I had a cable from
the Prime Minister, and the Prime Minister denies it. And I've known the Prime
Minister for a long time, and his word is good enough for me.'

Begin turned to his assistant and said, "Get that cable." He read a
cable from his ambassador to the United States which gave an inaccurate account of what Klutznick had told Carter, and asked, "What
would you have done?" Klutznick responded, "I would have fired the
ambassador. In his cable he wasn't writing about Phil Klutznick. He

was writing about the president of the World Jewish Congress. If he had any such information his first duty was to call me, not you. He never called me." Overcome with emotion, Begin stood and embraced his visitor.

Despite such shows of affection, Klutznick did not pull punches in his criticism of Begin's later policies and his recommendations on what the U.S. government should do. In 1981 he deplored the Israeli air attacks, first on the Iraqi nuclear installation and then in Lebanon. Later that year he traveled to the Middle East with Harold Saunders, a former career specialist on the Middle East who served as assistant secretary of state for Near Eastern and South Asian affairs under President Carter, former diplomat Joseph H. Greene, Jr., and Merle Thorpe, Jr., president of the Foundation for Middle East Peace. On returning, Klutznick joined in the group's conclusion that the Camp David peace process was not enough and that the Palestine Liberation Organization should be brought into negotiations.

Later in the year, when Saudi Arabia announced its "eight-point peace plan," Klutznick called it "useful" and argued that Israel at least "should listen to it."

All of these positions, of course, were violently opposed by Israel and its U.S. lobby. But Klutznick was not deterred. In mid-1982 in the *Los Angeles Times* and other major newspapers Klutznick wrote:

It is up to the Reagan Administration to face the realities of the Middle East as boldly as did the Carter Administration. The first step is to halt the conflict in Lebanon immediately and have Israel's forces withdrawn. This must be followed by an enlarged peace process that includes all parties to the conflict— including Palestinians. Only by doing so without apology and with determination can America pursue its own best interests, promote Israel's long-term well-being and protect world peace.

Despite public condemnation for these statements from the Jewish leadership in the United States, Klutznick privately received praise: "When I opposed the Iraqi raid, my mail from Jews was about four to one supportive, and about three to one when I proposed dealing directly with the PLO," he recalls. "But, you know, some of that support has to be discounted. There are people in the Jewish community who will assure me of their support even when they think I'm wrong."

Many more believed him wrong and said so. Abbot Rosen, Midwest director of the Anti-Defamation League in Chicago, rejected Klutznick's proposal to bring the PLO into the peace process and to establish a state for the Palestinians as "pie in the sky." He reported to the *Chicago Sun-Times* one of the lobby's tired cliches, "Under the present political circumstances, another Palestinian state, adjacent to Israel and Jordan, would provide an additional Soviet foothold in the region."

Robert Schrayer, chairman of the Public Affairs Committee of the Jewish United Fund of Metropolitan Chicago, joined the protest with another shibboleth: "Since no sovereign nation can be expected to negotiate its own destruction, Israel should not be pressured to negotiate with the PLO."

The *Near East Report,* a weekly newsletter published by the American Israeli Public Affairs Committee, editorialized against Klutznick's views, and accused him of promoting a "sinister canard" in calling the Palestinians "a special people in the Arab world, in some ways like the Jews were in the West following World War II."

The next year Klutznick took his crusade to Paris, where he joined forces with his old, ailing compatriot, Nahum Goldmann, and Pierre Mendès-France, a Jew and a former prime minister of France, in a plea to end Israel's war in Lebanon.

Klutznick's reason for going to Paris was to attend a meeting of the World Jewish Congress, but as soon as he landed, Goldmann, then living in Paris and critically ill, told him, "We've got to get fifty of the most distinguished Jews of the world to sign a statement to bring this war in Lebanon to an end." Klutznick responded, "But, first, let's see if we can write a statement."

Goldmann agreed and took up the subject at lunch the next day with Mendès-France, *Le Monde* correspondent Eric Rouleau, and Klutznick, agreeing to consider a draft statement the next day.

That night Klutznick, with the help of his aide, Mark Bruzonsky, wrote a brief statement which became the basis for the next day's discussion.

Klutznick recalls the scene, "Mendès-France is one of the best editors I've seen in my life. He would look at a word in typical French fashion in several languages, turning it around every which way. Four hours later, after sitting there fighting over every word, we had a statement."

Its conclusion was forceful:

The real issue is not whether the Palestinians are entitled to their rights, but how to bring this about while ensuring Israel's security and regional stability. Ambiguous concepts such as 'autonomy' are no longer sufficient, for they too often are used to confuse rather than to clarify. Needed now is the determination to reach a political accommodation between Israel and Palestinian nationalism.

The war in Lebanon must stop. Israel must lift its seige of Beirut in order to facilitate negotiations with the PLO, leading to a political settlement. Mutual recognition must be vigorously pursued. And there should be negotiations with the aim of achieving co-existence between the Israeli and Palestinian peoples based on self-determination.

When it was finished, Klutznick asked, "What do we do with the damned thing?" Goldmann said, "We've got to get those other fellows. Branch out and find them." Klutznick protested that there was not enough time and suggested that Goldmann and Mendès-France issue it in their own names. The former prime minister said, "I've never done anything like that. I don't sign statements with other people." Goldmann and Rouleau added their encouragement, and, finally, Mendès-France said, "I'll sign provided you can get an immediate answer from Yasser Arafat."

Isam Sartawi, a close associate of Arafat, was in Paris at the time and arranged this response by the PLO leader:

Coming at this precise moment from three Jewish personalities of great worth, worldwide reputation, and definite influence at all levels, both on the international scene and within their own community, that statement takes on a significant importance.

Klutznick took the podium at the meeting of the World Jewish Congress, then underway in Paris, to explain the declaration. The atmosphere, he recalls, was anything but cordial:

Heated is not the right word. If it had been heated it would have been better. It was sullen, solemn and bitter. I tried to have the delegates understand why we spoke up as we did. I told them it was the first such statement Mendès-France had ever made. And I said they also should know that Nahum Goldmann does what he thinks is right. And he's not been condemned just once. He's been condemned many times in the past by those who later chose to follow him.

The declaration brought headlines around the world, wide discussion, and some editorial praise. But it received little support among leading Jews and was largely rejected by Jewish organizations as "unrepresentative and unhelpful." It was Goldmann's last public statement. He died within a month, and a month later Mendès-France also died.

A few Jews helped Klutznick defend the statement. Newton N. Minow, a prominent Chicagoan who served in the Kennedy administration, praised Klutznick's "exemplary lifetime of leadership to Jewish causes and Israel" and "his independence and thoughtful criticism" in a column published in the Chicago *Sun-Times*. "As an American Jew pondering past mistakes, I believe that the American Jewish community has made some serious blunders in the past few years by choosing to remain silent when we disagreed with Israeli government policy."

Shortly after the Paris declaration, the world was horrified by the massacre of hundreds of civilians in the Sabra and Shatila Palestinian camps at Beirut. After four months of silence, Klutznick spoke at a luncheon in New York in February 1983. He launched a new crusade, pleading for the right of Jews to dissent:

We cannot be one in our need for each other, and be separated in our ability to speak or write the truth as each of us sees it. The real strength of Jewish life has been its sense of commitment and willingness to fight for the right [to dissent] even among ourselves.

In November, Klutznick took his crusade to Jerusalem, attending, along with forty other Jews from the United States and fifteen other countries, a four-day meeting of the International Center for Peace in the Middle East. Klutznick drew applause when he told his audience, which included several Israelis: "If you listen to us when we speak good of Israel, then you must listen to us when we speak ill. Otherwise we will lose our credibility, and the American government will not listen to us at all."

Despite his proven commitment to Israel, his leadership in the Jewish community and his unquestioned integrity, Philip Klutznick today is rejected or scorned by many of his establishment contemporaries. Two professionals in the Jewish lobby community, for example, say simply that Klutznick is not listened to any longer. One of them adds sadly, "I admire Phil Klutznick but he is virtually a non-person in the Jewish community." The other is harsh and bitter, linking Klutznick with other critics of the Israeli government as "an enemy of the Jewish people."

Charles Fishbein, for 11 years a fundraiser and executive of the Jewish National Fund, provides a partial explanation for the treatment Klutznick has received:

When you speak up in the Jewish community without a proper forum, you are shunted aside. You are dismissed as one who has been 'gotten to.' It's nonsense, but it is effective. The Jewish leaders you hear about tend to be very very wealthy givers. Some give to Jewish causes primarily as an investment, to establish a good business and social relationship. Such people will not speak up for a non-conformist like Klutznick for fear of jeopardizing their investment.

These thoughts echo that of Klutznick himself: "Try to understand. See it from their standpoint. Why should they go public? They don't want any trouble. They are a part of the community. They have neighbors. They help out. They contribute." He pauses, purses his lips a bit, then adds, "They have standing. And they want to keep it."

Klutznick smiles. "They say to me, 'You are absolutely right in what you say and do, but I can't. I can't speak up as you do.'" Another pause. "Maybe I would be the same if I hadn't gotten all the honors the Jewish community can give me."

He sees Washington policy as a major obstacle to reforming the lobby's tactics: "Let's not underestimate the damage that our own government does. Our government has been writing blank checks to Israel for a long time. As a result Begin would come over here for a tour, then go back home and say, 'What are you complaining about? I go to the United States, where the government supports me and all the leaders of the Jewish community applaud and support me.' "

"A Growing Gap in Our Liberal Tradition"

"Jews never had it so good as they've had in the United States," muses I. F. Stone, one of America's most respected Jewish journalists who calls himself a radical. Famous for his periodical, *I. F. Stone's Weekly,* which he issued for 19 years, and for his independent views, he discontinued the weekly because, as he says with typical self-mockery, he became "tired of solving the problems of the entire world every week."

Seventy-six years old and with eyesight so weak he has difficulty reading even large type, he is anything but retired. He is still a hero on campuses across the country and in liberal circles for his views on non-Middle East topics. Indeed, on those themes his following is enthusiastic. A recent lecture series on the trial of Socrates was a sell-out.

"Israel is on the wrong course," he says sadly, peering through the thick lenses of his eyeglasses. "This period is the blackest in the history of the Jewish people. Arabs need to be dealt with as human beings."

"I am gloomy about the future," he says. He can name no one with the promise to lead Israel out of its disastrous policies.

The conversation drifts to American Jews who dissent, and Stone recalls the day a publisher invited him to lunch and asked him to delete from a book he had written a passage recommending major changes in Israeli policy. The book, *Underground to Palestine,* deals mainly with Stone's experiences traveling with Jews from Nazi camps as they made their way through the British blockade to what is now Israel. The offending part was Stone's recommendation of a "binational solution, a state whose constitution would recognize the presence of two peoples, two nations, Arab and Jewish," to encompass all of Palestine. Stone refused to delete it, and as he wrote in the *New York Review of Books,* "that ended the luncheon, and in a way, the book. It was in effect proscribed."

According to Jewish journalist Carolyn Toll,

From then on, Stone, who might have been a hero on the synagogue lecture circuit as the first American newsman to travel with Holocaust survivors, was banned in any Jewish arena by leaders determined to close the debate on binationalism and statehood.

In Israel, where Jews establish their identity by birth rather than membership in an organization, Stone would be a full-fledged dissident. But in the American climate of insecurity about non-Jewish majority views, such arbitrary loyalty tests have not been challenged by the same Jews who vehemently champion others' rights to speak freely.

Two years later, Stone's book was published in Hebrew—in Israel—with the offending passage intact and read widely in the Middle East.

While he objects to the "excesses" of the lobby, Stone understands the motivations:

The Jewish people are apprehensive, fearful. They are afraid about the future. They feel they are at war, and many of them feel they have to fight and keep fighting.

He adds, after a pause, "When people are at war it is normal for civil liberties to suffer."

Stone sees a dangerous gap growing in this liberal tradition:

I find myself—like many fellow American intellectuals, Jewish and non-Jewish—ostracized whenever I try to speak up on the Middle East, [while] dissidents, Jewish and non-Jewish, in the Soviet Union are, deservedly, heroes.

But in the United States they are anything but heroes:

It is only rarely that we dissidents on the Middle East can enjoy a fleeting voice in the American press. Finding an American publishing house willing to publish a book which departs from the standard Israeli line is about as easy as selling a thoughtful exposition of atheism to the *Osservatore Romano* in Vatican City.

Those who speak up pay a price, says Stone, noting that journalists with long records of championing Israeli causes are flooded with "Jewish hate mail, accusing them of anti-Semitism" if they dare express "one word of sympathy for Palestinian Arab refugees."

In an essay in the *Washington Post* on August 19, 1977, Stone voiced his concern over "Bible diplomacy," particularly the effort to cite the Bible as the justification for Israel's continued control over the West Bank:

In the Middle Ages, as everyone knows, the Bible was under lock and key. The clergy kept it away from the masses, lest it confuse them and lead to schism and sedition. . . . Maybe it's time to lock the Holy Book up again, at least until the Israeli-Arab dispute is settled.

Two American Jews, Elmer Berger and Alfred M. Lilienthal, Jr., have much in common. From the very beginning they warned against Zionism, forecasting grave danger to Judaism in the establishment of a Jewish state. Without apparent trepidation they separated themselves from what has become the mainstream of Jewish thinking and devoted their lives to a lonely, frustrating and controversial crusade to alter the policies of the state of Israel. Long after Israel was established, broadly recognized and supported by the world community, they continued to make a case against the Jewish states. Both are often scorned as "self-hating Jews."

Both Lilienthal and Berger persist in their crusades despite attacks. The two are constantly on lecture tours, write extensively and appear at forums. They are as well known in the Arab world as in the United States, and more honored there than here.

In personality, the two have little in common. Lilienthal began as a lawyer, Berger as a rabbi. Lilienthal is a hard-hitting advocate in manner and speech. His mood shifts rapidly. Thoughtful and subdued one moment, he can be challenging the next. Berger, by contrast, is calm and unruffled, a patient listener. Even when his words thunder, his delivery is that of the soothing cleric.

Each has his audience, but neither has many outspoken disciples. The people who read the Lilienthal newsletter, "Middle East Perspective," and follow his activities may not be numerous, but his books are found in public and personal libraries throughout the country and are frequently cited in speeches and articles.

Rabbi Elmer Berger's circle may be smaller still—international audiences are hard to measure—but it appears loyal. When he sponsored a two-day seminar in May 1983 at the Madison Hotel in Washington, D.C., the gathering attracted over 200 people, principally journalists, scholars, clergy, public officials and diplomats. All had at least two things in common: an interest in the Arab-Israeli dispute and affection for Elmer Berger.

Lilienthal began his crusade against Israel soon after the government came into being in 1948 and at the age of seventy had not let up when I interviewed him in 1984. His 1949 *Readers Digest* article, "Israel's Flag Is Not Mine," warned of the consequences of Zionism. His first book, *What Price Israel?* in 1953 was followed by *There Goes the Middle East* in 1957 and *The Other Side of the Coin* eight years later.

In 1978 Lilienthal published his largest and most comprehensive work, *The Zionist Connection,* which focuses on the development and activities of the Zionist movement within the United States. An impressive 872-page volume studded with facts, quotations, anecdotes and, here and there, colorful opinions and interpretations, it was described by *Foreign Affairs* quarterly as the "culminating masterwork" of Lilienthal's anti-Zionist career.

By 1984, his crusade had taken Lilienthal to the Middle East twenty-two times and across the United States twenty-six times.

For all his longstanding and vigorous endeavors for the peaceful reconciliation of Jews and Arabs, Lilienthal remains a lonely figure, often shunned in the United States, even by those whose banner he carries the highest.

Lilienthal says some people kid him as being the "Man from LaMancha." And true to the characterization, he frequently brings audiences to their feet by quoting from the song which had Quixote "reaching for the unreachable stars."

His greatest accomplishment, he says, is getting "some Christians to have the guts to speak up on this issue." Formally excommunicated from the Jewish faith by a group of rabbis in New York in 1982, Lilienthal scorns the action: "Only God can do that. I still feel very much a Jew."

Chapter 11

Beyond the Banks of the Potomac

Efforts by the pro-Israel lobby to influence American opinion and policy most often focus on national institutions, particularly the federal government. Yet the lobby in its various forms branches out widely into American life beyond the seat of government on the banks of the Potomac River. Local political leaders, businesses, organizations and private individuals in many fields experience unfair criticism and intimidation for becoming involved in the debate over Middle East issues. Many on "Main Street" have paid a price for speaking out. Particularly distressing are instances of discrimination against Americans of Arab ancestry.

The Stigma of Arab Ancestry

Pro-Israeli PACs contributed nearly a million dollars to Senate races alone in 1982, and many members of Congress place a value on AIPAC support which is beyond accounting in dollars. The political activism of such groups is legitimate and accepted as part of the American political system; yet when Arab Americans attempt to become involved in the electoral process, they find doors closed to them.

On October 14, 1983, W. Wilson Goode was in the midst of a hard-fought campaign to become the first black Mayor of Philadelphia. The widely respected front-runner, popular with virtually every segment of the city's electorate, attended a fund-raising gathering one evening in the home of Naim Ayoub, a local businessman who had invited a number of friends—prominent academics, scientists, medical professionals and business leaders—to meet Goode and contribute to his campaign.

After a short social interlude, during which he was told of the discrimination often suffered by people of Arab ancestry, Goode expressed concern and declared, with feeling, "I renew my pledge to be mayor of all the people." Ayoub and his guests wrote checks to the Goode campaign. The candidate offered his thanks and departed. The total amount of the checks was $2,725, a small portion of the Goode campaign budget; yet it was enough to spark a heated controversy over Arab influence and the role of Israel in the campaign.

In the increasingly bitter final weeks of the campaign, Goode's main opponent tried to inflate the contribution into a scandal by disclosing that Ayoub was regional coordinator for the American-Arab Anti-Discrimination Committee—a nationwide organization dedicated to opposing discrimination against people of Arab ancestry. Goode, who had been courting the large Jewish vote in the crucial northeast wards by constantly reaffirming his support for Israel, responded by announcing that the checks from Ayoub and his friends were being returned. He explained: "I want to make certain that no one is able to question my support for the state of Israel."

Jewish voters were apparently satisfied with Goode's explanation of his "mistake," as he went on to win the election with overwhelming Jewish support. Yet as one Jewish Philadelphian later observed,

One need not support the entire program of the Anti-Discrimination Committee to share the shock and pain of many of its members and friends over such a highly publicized affront to one of its leaders acting in his private capacity. Full participation in the political process should never be restricted to those who espouse only that which is currently popular.

The Wilson Goode episode was the precursor of similar incidents involving Senator Gary Hart and former Vice-President Walter Mondale in their campaigns for the highest office in the land (see chapter four).

Arab Americans who have tried to maintain contact with their heritage have found unexpected difficulties. Anisa Mehdi, a news director with TV station WBZ in Boston, observes that it can be "a frightening thing" to be an Arab in America:

I grew up in New York City with a very politically active father. If there would be a commemoration of the anniversary of the Deir Yassin massacre, usually that date would coincide with the Israeli anniversary parade. Jews would be on Fifth Avenue and we would be on Madison Avenue.

There would be hundreds of thousands of people on Fifth Avenue and maybe ten of us on Madison Avenue. The point is there were at least 100,000 Arab Americans in New York City. Where were they? They were afraid to come out.

Arab ancestry can also be a liability outside politics, as Dr. George Faddoul, a specialist in veterinary medicine at the University of Massachusetts, can attest. Faddoul's origins are Lebanese, but he was born in Maine and has never had any interest in politics or international affairs. In 1974, Faddoul was working at the Suburban Experiment Station at Waltham, Massachusetts, a facility established by the university to service the farming community in the state. When the directorship came open, he decided to apply for it. After a distinguished career of more than 25 years, Faddoul felt that he deserved it and that such an administrative post would add an interesting new dimension to his work at the station.

Only one other applicant came forward, and a faculty committee voted 7 to 6 in Faddoul's favor. The rules of the university stipulate that only a simple majority is necessary, but the dean failed to appoint him. Faddoul's own investigation into the reasons revealed that there had been a number of slurs against him in the committee deliberations because of his Arab background. In the discussions Arabs were described as "worthless." Faddoul's assistant, who possessed only a bachelor's degree, was named acting administrative director of the station. Only after pressing his case for seven years did Faddoul receive the position.

Another person of Arab ancestry, Mahmoud A. Naji, has lived in the United States for 19 years. His wife and three children are all U.S. citizens. He owns his own home in the Chicago area and has an impressive record of gainful employment and civic involvement. He has never been arrested or charged with any wrongdoing. Still, for reasons which the U.S. Immigration and Naturalization Service will not disclose, he faces deportation from the United States.

Naji, a native of Jordan, was living in the Dominican Republic as a permanent resident at the time of the American intervention there in 1965. He was evacuated to the United States along with the other foreign residents of the island nation and at that time began his efforts to gain permanent residency status under U.S. immigration laws. Like many immigrants, Naji met with a number of administrative roadblocks and adverse rulings, but his persistence appeared to pay off as each was in turn overcome. His right to adjust his residence status was recognized by the INS district director late in 1980.

But in February 1981 his petition was again rejected by the INS regional commissioner for a previously unmentioned reason: he had been declared a threat to U.S. security and ordered to leave the United States.

Naji has been unable to learn the nature of the charges against him, except that the adverse ruling was based on "classified information which is relevant and material, and requires protection from unauthorized disclosure in the interest of national security." Inquiries by

Senators Charles Percy and James Abdnor and several House members have been unavailing.

Naji speculates that misunderstanding of his participation in several Arab American organizations has given rise to the undisclosed charges, although neither he nor any of these groups has ever been accused of any illegal or subversive activity.

"80 to 85 Percent . . . Are Terrorists"

Arab Americans in the Detroit area have learned about discrimination firsthand. In a June 1983 meeting at Detroit between U.S. Customs officials and airline officials concerning the processing of luggage, a senior Customs official declared that "80 to 85 percent of Arabs in the Detroit metropolitan area are terrorists and the rest are terrorist sympathizers."

This harsh accusation came after the arrest in 1983 of a 29-year-old Arab Canadian who tried to bring heroin in a false-bottomed suitcase through the Detroit-Windsor tunnel, and a vendetta in which Customs officials began to single out motorists who "looked Arab" for interrogation and automobile searches. In one case, an 18-year-old girl was strip-searched.

Though the Customs Service later apologized for the remark charging Arabs with terrorism—the offending official received only a reprimand—a local publication joined in the racial stereotyping. After the arrest of a military officer from the Yemen Arab Republic (North Yemen) for attempting to smuggle guns out of the United States, *Monthly Detroit* magazine carried a story entitled "The Mideast Connection: How the Arab Wars Came to Detroit." Though it cited no examples of Arab Americans being arrested for gun or drug-smuggling, the article portrayed the city's nearly 250,000 Arab Americans as a lawless and violent community.

"We Will Destroy You Economically"

Bias and intimidation assume many forms and know no geographical boundaries. Mediterranean House restaurant became an instant success after it opened in Skokie, a predominantly Jewish suburb of Chicago, in 1973. With an Arab cuisine and a mainly Jewish clientele, owner Abdel-Hamid El-Barbarawi—a Palestinian-born naturalized American citizen—held his staff to a strict "no politics" policy. He fired two employees for becoming involved in political discussions with clients.

At the peak of its success, Mediterranean House was recommended in all major Chicago dining guides and was frequently praised in newspaper articles. A growing business led Barbarawi to expand, opening several other restaurants under the same name in other areas.

On a summer night in 1975 a 6-foot pipe bomb was thrown through the window of the one in Morton Grove. No one was injured because the attack came late at night, but the restaurant was destroyed. Fire experts said the bomb was meant to "level the building."

Trouble returned a year later when Barbarawi and members of his staff emerged from his restaurant in Skokie about 3 A.M., discovering that one side of the building had been covered with posters proclaiming that "Mediterranean House food in your stomach is like Jewish blood on your hands," and "Money Spent Here Supports PLO Terrorism." The graphic impact of the posters' message was enhanced by red paint and raw liver thrown on the walls. Though the vandals were nowhere in sight, Barbarawi found the editor of the *Chicago Jewish Post and Opinion* taking pictures of the display. The editor said he just happened to be passing.

The next month, under the headline "Skokie Jews Unknowingly Funding Arab Propaganda," the periodical published an article which urged local Jews to boycott the restaurant, basing its recommendation on the fact that the Mediterranean House advertised on a weekly one-hour radio program called "The Voice of Palestine." Ted Cohen, author of the article, described the program as a source of "anti-Jewish propaganda."

Barbarawi points out that he advertised on six radio stations and also had commercials on several Jewish programs and an India-related program. "I was an advertiser, not a sponsor," he says. "I had never listened to the Voice of Palestine and was not interested in their editorial policy."

Publication of the Cohen article marked the beginning of the end for Barbarawi. A propaganda campaign was mounted against the restaurant. Leaflets urging local Jews to "Stop Paying for Arab Propaganda" were distributed door to door in Skokie. Large numbers of abusive calls and false orders forced Barbarawi to stop accepting orders by phone. One call threatened his life. In exasperation, Barbarawi interrupted a caller's invective with an anguished question: "Why don't you bomb the place like you did before?" The answer was chilling: "We wouldn't give you that satisfaction. We will destroy you economically. You will die while you are still living."

In a *Chicago Sun-Times* commentary, columnist Roger Simon conceded that Voice of Palestine broadcasts were not anti-Semitic, as Cohen had charged, but concluded oddly by agreeing that Jews should hold Barbarawi "responsible for where his money goes" and backed the *Jewish Post and Opinion* in calling for a boycott. Barbarawi feels that this commentary damaged business more than any other single factor.

Barbarawi appealed, to no avail, to local citizens of Arab ancestry, as well as to the local chapter of the Anti-Defamation League of B'nai B'rith to intercede with the Jewish community. He was told that ADL had nothing against him. Director Abbot Rosen stated personal sympathy—"It's terrible; you should sue"—but did not counter the hate campaign mounted by the *Jewish Post and Opinion* and the unseen callers.

Meanwhile Barbarawi saw his revenues drop from $40,000 a month to less than $7,000. As regular Jewish customers stopped coming, a number of non-Jews told Barbarawi that their neighbors were refusing to speak to them because they patronized his restaurant.

Facing financial ruin, Barbarawi in desperation turned to legal action, but high costs and repeated court delays finally forced him to abandon this last hope. In the end, the hate campaign of unseen enemies put him out of the restaurant business completely. After losing $3 million dollars, Barbarawi had $3 in his pocket when the local sheriff came to close down his restaurant.

Dick Kay, a reporter for Chicago television station WMAQ, summed up the fate of the Mediterranean House and its owner: "They really did a job on him, and it was the militant part of the Jewish community that did it."

An official of a Jewish organization faced still another form of pressure. In mid-1983, the Seattle chapter of the American-Arab Anti-Discrimination Committee (ADC) initiated a formal dialogue with the Jewish Federation of Seattle under the sponsorship of the American Friends Service Committee. Anson Laytner, head of the Jewish Federation, suddenly withdrew from the series, explaining to the Seattle ADC leader that his superior threatened his dismissal if he continued. He even asked that the ADC retract the report on the Seattle talks which had appeared in its national newsletter.

Such intolerance can also damage longstanding personal friendships. In mid-1983, author Stephen Green took the bound page proofs of his new book, *Taking Sides: America's Secret Relations with a Militant Israel,* to Edgar Bronfman, president of the World Jewish Congress and a close friend of the Green family for many years. Together the two men had scattered the ashes of Green's father after his death five years before. The young writer wanted to explain his reasons for writing the book, which discloses intimate U.S.-Israeli military relationships. Bronfman declined to see Green. He directed his secretary, whom Green has also known for years, to respond. Green recalls her words: "Mr. Edgar does not want to discuss this book with you, Steve. You've written it. It's your affair, and he doesn't feel he needs to discuss it with you." Green was devastated that the man he had known and respected for so long would refuse even to speak with him. He recalled with irony that years earlier Edgar's father had frequently upbraided his son for "not doing enough" for Israel.

Vanessa Redgrave: An Activist Playing for Time

The Middle East conflict has affected the career of Vanessa Redgrave, a British actress who is widely hailed as one of the foremost stage and screen talents of her generation. Yet her success in the United States has been limited by her long history of political activism. While many performers shy away from controversial issues for fear of damaging their careers, Redgrave has structured her life largely around her political passions. Her career has suffered accordingly.

Redgrave's apprehension was apparent on Labor Day, 1983 when I interviewed her in a backyard studio in a residential area of Boston. She had just cut a tape for a program directed to Arab Americans and was ill at ease. She spoke quietly of threats against her life, while glancing nervously through an open door. "I don't feel safe here," she said. "I've had so many threats."

Always controversial, Redgrave's opposition to the Vietnam war and sympathy for leftist causes led the U.S. government to refuse her a visa in 1971 when she wanted to come to the United States to discuss writing her autobiography and a possible motion picture. The refusal occurred despite the pleas of her publisher and the intervention of numerous public figures. Undeterred, she directed her activism increasingly toward support for the Palestinian people.

In 1978, the Jewish Defense League picketed the academy awards ceremony in which Redgrave received an Oscar for her supporting role in the movie *Julia*. The JDL was protesting her narration and financial backing of a documentary called *The Palestinians*, which included an interview with PLO chief Yasser Arafat. In her acceptance speech, Redgrave described the JDL picketers as "a small bunch of Zionist hoodlums whose behavior is an insult to Jews all over the world" and thanked the Academy for standing up to their intimidation. Many in the audience hissed and booed.

Another controversy arose in the summer of 1979 when it was announced that Redgrave would play the lead in a CBS-TV drama about Holocaust survivor Fania Fenelon, a member of the Auschwitz concentration camp orchestra who was spared death only to play music for other prisoners as well as camp officials. Many Jews were outraged that Redgrave was chosen for the part. Fenelon herself declared, "Vanessa Redgrave playing me is like a member of the Ku Klux Klan playing Martin Luther King." The network was criticized for keeping "an unusually tight lid on the names of sponsors" for the broadcast, in an attempt to avoid expected pressures on them to withdraw.

The two people most responsible for what one columnist called "the Vanessa thing" were Bernie Sofronsky, the CBS executive in charge, and Linda Yellen, the producer. CBS explained that it could not bow to pressure. Yellen responded to the criticism more directly:

I had always adored her as an actress, and I turned to her as the best person for the part. Basically, I was unaware of her politically. I never considered firing her for her political beliefs. That would have been anathema to me, given what I know about blacklisting and the McCarthy era. I believe her performance is extraordinary, and speaks for itself.

The critics were nearly unanimous in acclaiming Redgrave's performance. One asserted that it "may be the finest ever seen on television." But the excellence of the program did not quiet her detractors. The Simon Wiesenthal Center for Holocaust Studies in Los Angeles urged a nationwide boycott of the film, entitled *Playing for Time*, and some Zionist groups went even further by urging a boycott of products sold by its sponsors.

Obviously Redgrave's talents as an actress were not the real issue. As the *Los Angeles Times* cogently observed,

Her dazzling portrayal of a Holocaust survivor has no bearing on the controversy. . . . The principle involved is the simple one of keeping separate things separate—in this instance, separating the artist on the screen from the eccentric and grating political activist off the screen.

The difficulty in keeping this distinction clear was demonstrated again in 1982, when Vanessa Redgrave was designated to narrate Stravinsky's *Oedipus Rex* in a series of April concerts by the Boston Symphony Orchestra. In the face of a vociferous outcry by the local Jewish community, the orchestra cancelled the concerts without explanation. The announcement did not mention Redgrave by name, but as columnist Nat Hentoff pointed out, "There was no mystery. Wishing to offend as few people as possible—particularly during the spring fundraising season—BSO made its craven decision" not to do the performances with Redgrave.

Alan Dershowitz, a professor at Harvard Law School noted both as a Zionist and as a defender of civil liberties, defended Redgrave's statement that, "No one should have the right to take away the work of an artist because of political views."

Redgrave, who was awarded $100,000 damages, represents a complicated case, in that her political views are disagreeable to more than just partisans of Israel. Nat Hentoff quite properly invoked the wisdom of Justice Oliver Wendell Holmes to suggest how Americans should react:

> If there is any principle of the Constitution that more imperatively calls for attachment than any other, it is the principle of free thought—not free only for those who agree with us, but freedom for the thought we hate.

"A Consistent Pattern"

Efforts to stifle public debate on the Middle East focus to a great extent on the centerpiece of free speech in our country: the press. Over the years, support for Israel has become a requisite for respectability in journalism, just as it has in politics and other professions.

Edmund Ghareeb, a scholar who has written widely on the Middle East and the American media, observes that the media present "a rosy picture of Israel as the democracy in a sea of barbarians in the Middle East. . . ." On the other hand, the Palestinians are often referred to as "Arab terrorists," the Arab is portrayed as a camel driver, somebody who is a murderer, or something of this sort." Journalist Lawrence Mosher agrees: "They have stereotyped the Arab as an unsavory character with dark tendencies, and they have ennobled the Israeli as a hero."

Even *Time* magazine is guilty of perpetuating such stereotypes. In 1982 the magazine ran a four-color house ad with a photo of a sheik under a single-word headline: "Power." Columnist Richard Broderick described the sheik as "all you could want from an evil Arab— dyspeptic, garbed in traditional Saudi dress, he stares out at the camera with palpable malevolence."

Such stereotyping of Arabs is common in editorial cartoons. As Craig MacIntosh, editorial cartoonist for *The Minneapolis Star,* points out, "The Arabs are always in robes, the Palestinians always in 'terrorist' garb, with an AK 47." Robert Englehart, editorial cartoonist for the *Journal Herald* (Dayton, Ohio), agrees: "I could depict Arabs as murderers, liars and thieves. No one would object. But I couldn't use Jewish stereotypes. I've always had the feeling that I'm treading on eggs when I try to do something on the Middle East. . . ."

The Israeli lobby works diligently to keep journalists from rowing against the tide of pro-Israel orthodoxy. This mission is accomplished in part through carefully arranged, "spontaneous" public outcries designed to intimidate. Columnist Rowland Evans writes: "When we write what is perceived to be an anti-Israeli column, we get mail from all over the country with the same points and phrasing. There's a consistent pattern."

The ubiquitous cry of "anti-Semitism" is brought to bear on short notice, and it is this charge which has been most responsible for compelling journalists to give Israel better than equal treatment in coverage of Middle East events. Even former Defense Department official Anthony Cordesman was not immune from this charge when he wrote in 1977 an article for *Armed Forces Journal International* examining the Middle East military balance. Observing, for example, that the number of medium tanks requested by Israel for the decade 1976 to 1986 would approach the number to be deployed by the United States within the North Atlantic Treaty Organization, Cordesman questioned the need for ever-increasing U.S. military aid to Israel. For this straightforward assertion, the Anti-Defamation League of B'nai B'rith denounced the article as "anti-Israeli and anti-Jewish."

"Too Controversial and Fanatical"

Journalist Harold R. Piety observes that "the ugly cry of anti-Semitism is the bludgeon used by the Zionists to bully non-Jews into accepting the Zionist view of world events, or to keep silent." In late 1978 Piety, withholding his identity in order not to irritate his employer, wrote an article on "Zionism and the American Press" for *Middle East International* in which he decried "the inaccuracies, distortions and—perhaps worst—inexcusable omission of significant news and background material by the American media in its treatment of the Arab-Israeli conflict."

Piety traces the deficiency of U.S. media in reporting on the Middle East to largely successful efforts by the pro-Israel lobby to "overwhelm the American media with a highly professional public relations campaign, to intimidate the media through various means and, finally, to impose censorship when the media are compliant and craven." He lists threats to editors and advertising departments, orchestrated boycotts, slanders, campaigns of character assassination, and personal vendettas among the weapons employed against balanced journalism.

Despite this impressive list of tools for media manipulation, Piety draws from his own experience and blames the prevailing media bias more on editors and journalists who submit to the pressure than on the lobby which applies it.

Pressure began to build against Piety's employer, the *Journal Herald* of Dayton, Ohio, in the late sixties as his growing interest in the Middle East led him to write editorial pieces critical of Israeli policy. His editor received a long letter, hand-delivered, from the president of the local Jewish Community Council, along with a lecture on Middle East politics. A column asserting that American Jews "were being herded, and willingly so, into the Zionist camp" brought a lengthy response from the Zionist Organization of America and a delegation of six Jewish leaders to the paper for a meeting with the editorial board. A 1976 column on West Bank riots led Piety's editors to order him to write no more on the theme.

Upon writing another column in April 1977 on the anniversary of the Deir Yassin massacres in which Jewish terrorists under Menachem Begin murdered more than 200 Palestinian villagers, he was sharply rebuked by his editors. Editor Dennis Shere informed Piety that he had received orders—presumably from the corporate management—to "shut you up or fire you." Piety was subsequently told that he was "too controversial and too fanatical" and that he would not receive a promised promotion to editor of the *Journal Herald* editorial page. Under this pressure Piety left his position.

Mediawatch Blinks Out

During the summer of 1982, Minneapolis columnist Richard Broderick devoted several installments of his "Mediawatch" column—a weekly feature on media coverage—to exposing such inequities in American media coverage of the Israeli invasion. Among his findings:

Tapes purportedly of [Yasser] Arafat's 'bunker' and 'PLO military headquarters' being bombed aired over and over again while tape of civilian casualties wound up on the edit room floor. . . .

As Israeli ground forces swept through Southern Lebanon, the American press continued to employ the euphemism 'incursion' to describe what was clearly an invasion.

In local newspaper coverage, Broderick found:

While Palestinian and Lebanese civilians were being killed by the thousands, the *Minneapolis Star and Tribune* ran a front-page photo of an Israeli mother mourning her dead son.

Later that same day, another photo showed a group of men bound and squatting in a barbed-wire enclosure guarded by Israeli soldiers. The caption described the scene as a group of 'suspected Palestinians' captured by Israeli forces. Simply being Palestinian, the caption implied, was sufficient cause to be rounded up.

Broderick also used his column to relate scenes of horror witnessed by the Reverend Don Wagner, who had been in Beirut inspecting Palestinian refugee camps when the Israeli bombing began. Wagner saw a wing of the Gaza Hospital knocked down by the bombing and was in Akka Hospital while hundreds of civilian casualties were brought in. Wagner described his experiences to the Beirut network bureaus for NBC, ABC and CBS, but their reports beamed back to the United States were never aired.

While such examples of bias are disturbing, still more so are the consequences suffered by the journalist who publicized them. Soon after the "Mediawatch" columns on Israel ran in the *Twin Cities Reader*, movie distributors of Minneapolis—who collectively represent the largest single source of advertising for the paper—began telephoning editor Deb Hopp with threats of permanently removing their advertising as a result of the Broderick column. Hopp mollified them by agreeing to print, unedited, the thousand-word reply to the offending column. Contrary to usual policy, Broderick was not allowed to respond to this rebuttal.

Later in the summer, Broderick reported an attempt, as he saw it, by Minnesota Senator Rudy Boschwitz to manipulate public opinion through the local media. Boschwitz coordinated and appeared in a press conference with members of the American Lebanese League (ALL), an organization which endorsed the Israeli invasion. Boschwitz cited the testimony of league members in arguing that the people of Lebanon welcomed the Israelis.

Broderick quoted in his column a report by the nationwide American-Arab Anti-Discrimination Committee which described the league as "the unregistered foreign agent of the Phalange Party and the Lebanese Front. They work in close consultation with AIPAC, which creates for them their political openings." Senator Boschwitz, upset at seeing this information made public, castigated Hopp and Broderick in a lengthy telephone call. Three weeks later, Broderick was informed that his services would no longer be needed at the *Twin Cities Reader.*

"Frau Geyer" Under Fire

Concern over appearances and external pressure also led the Chicago *Sun-Times* to drop the regular column of veteran foreign correspondent and syndicated columnist Georgie Anne Geyer for several months during the 1982 war in Lebanon. The decision followed an outpouring of reader protest over Geyer's columns criticizing the war and Israeli policy. Letters assailed Geyer as "a well-known Jew hater," "an anti-Semite par excellence," and "an apologist for the PLO"—the sort of innuendos to which Geyer has grown accustomed during many years of covering both sides of the Arab-Israel dispute. She is frequently denounced in print and harrassed at lectures with similar charges. Geyer, whose worldwide journalistic coups have made headlines for years, told me that receiving "this endless, vicious campaign of calumny and insults because you write what you know to be impeccably true" is the most distressing aspect of her life as a journalist.

Editor Howard Kleinberg of the *Miami News* also suffered criticism for carrying Geyer's columns. He wrote in a 1982 editorial that

I cannot remember receiving more outside pressure on anything than I have about Georgie Anne Geyer's columns on Israel. . . . Geyer's antagonists have portrayed her not only as anti-Israel but anti-Semitic as well; 'Frau Geyer' some of them call her.

Aware of the violent response, Geyer suggested that Kleinberg too not publish her Middle East column for a while, but he was adamant: "I steadfastly have refused to bow to the pressure." He added: "We carry syndicated columns of contrasting viewpoints because it is the role of newspapers to provide a vehicle for the exercise of free speech."

Though the *Sun-Times* later resumed publication of her column and the criticism abated, Geyer finds that calling Middle East issues as she sees them exacts a personal price, noting sadly that her commentaries seem to have damaged permanently valued relationships with Jewish friends.

On and Off the "Enemies List"

Branding critics and thoughtful analysts as "enemies" is another familiar tactic of the Israeli lobby. Those singled out for inclusion on enemies lists—particularly *The Campaign to Discredit Israel,* published by AIPAC, and the ADL's *Pro-Arab Propaganda in America: Vehicles and Voices*—rarely take issue with lobby criticism, probably in the belief that a direct response would only give undeserved credibility to their detractors. But in December, 1983, a selective challenge to these enemies lists was offered by Anthony Lewis, a Jewish columnist who writes for the *New York Times.*

In two installments of his regular column, Lewis took issue with the inclusion on the 1983 lists of Professor Walid Khalidi, a professor at the American University, Beirut, and a research fellow at Harvard. Klalidi, recognized as a leading Palestinian intellectual, has long argued for a Palestinian state living in peace and mutual recognition with Israel. He had outlined his position in a 1978 *Foreign Affairs* article, subsequently receiving sharp criticism from extremist groups in the Middle East and elsewhere. Hence Lewis was "astonished to find Professor Khalidi's name on lists of supposed anti-Israel activists."

Lewis exposed the techniques used to implicate Khalidi in a putative campaign to discredit Israel. First AIPAC quotes him as saying in the 1978 article that Israel's existence is "both 'a violation of the principles of the unity and integrity of Arab soil and an affront to the dignity of the [Arab] nation.'" Khalidi in fact referred to this as an old view which has been discarded.

The book identifies Khalidi as a member of the Palestine National Council, a body which serves as a PLO parliament and claims that on one occasion he "narrowly escaped expulsion" from the PNC for supporting George Habash's radical Popular Front. Khalidi responds that he has never attended a PNC meeting "because of [his] lifelong commitment to complete independence from all political organizations." Lewis adds that Khalidi's views are the antithesis of George Habash's.

Lewis concludes: "Some people see his very moderation as dangerous. He is a Palestinian nationalist, after all, and one must not allow that idea to have any legitimacy." The *Times* published letters from both the ADL and AIPAC protesting the Lewis columns, and the ADL assigned a team of researchers to review previous Lewis columns in search of anti-Israeli bias. Lewis was also sharply criticized in the January 1984 issue of *Near East Report*, the AIPAC newsletter.

The Perils of Non-Orthodoxy

A New York businessman almost made an "enemies list," thanks to media coverage of his views. Jack Sunderland, businessman and chairman of Americans for Middle East Understanding, a national organization which issues scholarly reviews, made statements supporting Palestinian self-rule and an end to Israeli West Bank settlement construction during a trip to the Middle East several years ago. His remarks were widely reported in the U.S. and foreign media, and shortly after returning to his New York home, Sunderland learned that a man had visited several of his neighbors asking personal questions about his family, including his children's schedule and routes to and from school. Concerned for his family's safety, Sunderland engaged a private detective.

Working with FBI cooperation, the detective soon located a graduate student who admitted to the obtrusive questioning and also to illegally gaining access to computer information about Sunderland's finances and credit record. The student said he was an employee of B'nai B'rith and that Sunderland was being investigated as a prospect for inclusion on the organization's "enemies list." Faced with the student's confession, B'nai B'rith officials refused to meet with Sunderland personally but agreed not to mention his name in future publications. When the "enemies list" appeared in 1983, under the sponsorship of B'nai B'rith's affiliate, the Anti-Defamation League, the organization Sunderland heads was listed as a "vehicle" of "Arab propaganda." Several officers were mentioned by name but not Sunderland.

On a Saturday morning in 1977 producer Debbie Gage encountered peril of a different sort when she put on a one-hour program of interviews with local people of Palestinian origin on Minneapolis Public Radio. The station's switchboard was promptly swamped with calls demanding equal time for the Israeli viewpoint. Gage demurred, responding that she had decided to do her program because of the heavy coverage being given to the Israeli view in the local press. She saw her broadcast as "simply a small attempt to redress that imbalance."

The following Monday news director Gary Eichten informed Gage that her job would be terminated in three weeks and that a program devoted to pro-Israeli views would be aired the following Saturday. Eichten denied that he was pressured into doing the follow-up program, but, as station intern Yvonne Pearson observes, "If dozens of angry phone calls aren't pressure, I don't know what is."

Even when the media make an effort to ignore the dangers and resist pressure and bias, the price can still be high for those who speak out. James Batal, a man of Lebanese ancestry, was interviewed on Miami TV during the 1973 Arab-Israeli war. He was 72 years old at the time. Batal sought to explain the little-understood Arab view of the conflict. Following the broadcast of his interview, he received an abusive—and anonymous—phone call warning that his house would be burned down or bombed in retaliation for his remarks on television. Batal appealed to local police and the FBI, but was told that they were unable to provide protection. In desperation, he and his ailing wife closed their home and moved into a small apartment with her sister.

Grace Halsell, a noted writer on the Middle East, tells of a similar incident which took place in late 1983. While in Jerusalem, she visited Amal, a young Palestinian woman with whom she had become friends while living in Jerusalem some years before. An American TV journalist had asked to interview Amal while she was employed as assistant to the U.S. vice-consul in East Jerusalem, and her American boss had agreed to her being interviewed. But when the interview was shown, she was fired. She explains, "I was thought to be too pro-Palestinian. I had merely said, in answer to a question, that my family lived in a house where Israelis now live."

The consequences of publishing reports which do not convey such a congenial message can be even more drastic than loss of employment or public pressure from lobby groups. John Law, a veteran journalist who founded and edited the *Washington Report on Middle East Affairs,* a nonpartisan newsletter published by the American Educational Trust, once described the aim of the publication in these words:

It would like to see Middle East issues approached in a way that will benefit the interests of the people of the United States, while being consistent with their standards of justice and fair play.

On May 6, 1982, Law received a telephone call which threatened his physical safety and warned that he should "watch out." The following day John Duke Anthony, then an official of the American Educational Trust, was assaulted by two men near his home. One subdued Anthony by striking him on the head with a brick. The "muggers" took neither his money nor his credit cards—only his personal address book.

An editorial in the next issue of the *Washington Report* responded:

The man who threatened Mr. Law and the two men who assaulted [Mr. Anthony] were presumably hoping to deter them from doing their work. This is not going to happen.

"Conviction Under False Pretenses"

Opinions which depart from the pro-Israeli line cost a New York journalist his job in early 1984. For ten years Alexander Cockburn contributed the popular "Press Clips" feature to the *Village Voice* in New York. Though his topics and views were often controversial, his candor and originality were widely respected. One reader hailed him as "Guinness Stout in a world of Lite journalism."

In August 1982 Cockburn applied for and received a grant from the Institute of Arab Studies, located in Belmont, Massachusetts, to underwrite travel and research expenses for a book on the war in Lebanon. The grant was not secret. It was recorded in the IAS public report, but in January 1984 the Boston *Phoenix* published a long article exposing Cockburn's "$10,000 Arab connection." The article provoked a storm in the editorial offices of the *Voice.*

Editor David Schneiderman decided that Cockburn should receive an indefinite suspension without pay, but permitted him to reply in print. Cockburn defended the grant, contending that the IAS is a legitimate non-profit organization, founded "to afford writers, scholars, artists, poets and professionals an opportunity to pursue the full exploration of the Arab dimension of world history through their special field of interest." He argued that the bottom line of the matter was that he "didn't properly evaluate the climate of anti-Arab racism." The book grant, he felt, constituted an ethnically dubious "connection" because it was "Arab money."

Readers were outraged by Schneiderman's treatment of Cockburn, and many wrote to protest his "conviction under false pretenses."

It is sad that even in the United States, with its traditions of free speech, there are still people who, when it comes to Middle East issues, will use force and threats of force to try to prevent the dissemination of ideas they do not like.

Dow Jones Stands Firm

Major national media have not escaped these pressures. Organized letter campaigns are a favored tactic of pro-Israel groups. Lawrence Mosher, a staff correspondent for the *National Journal,* observes that such groups have

a seemingly indefatigable army of workers who will generate hundreds or thousands of letters to Congressmen, to newspaper editors, etc., whenever the occasion seems to warrant it.

. . . Editors are sometimes weighed down by it in advance and inhibited from doing things they would normally do if they didn't know that an onslaught of letters, cables and telephone calls would follow if they write or show such and such.

Mosher has himself experienced the pressures which speaking out bring. The *National Observer* of May 18, 1970, printed an article by Mosher on a hitherto little noticed court case then pending in Washington, D.C. The case involved Saul E. Joftes, a former high official of B'nai B'rith, who was bringing suit against the organization and its officers. The charge:

That the Zionists have used B'nai B'rith, a charitable, religious, tax-exempt American membership organization, to pursue international political activities contrary to the B'nai B'rith constitution and in violation of federal foreign-agent registration and tax laws.

Joftes had been especially disturbed at the "employment" by B'nai B'rith of a woman whose post was funded and controlled by the Israeli consulate in New York City. She was given the job of providing "saturation briefings" for Jews visiting the Soviet Union, but her main duty was to "channel information back to the Israeli government on who went to the Soviet Union and what Russians visited the United States." The woman, Mrs. Avis Shulman, observed that "Jewish organizations, particularly B'nai B'rith, are especially useful" as a "base of operation." Joftes was obliged to meet her request that "a subcommittee" be "invented with her as 'secretary' to give her a handle that could be relatively inconspicuous but meaningful."

The one-year employment of Shulman was but one aspect of what Joftes saw as the Zionist "takeover" of B'nai B'rith's international operations. He resented being compelled to develop the organization to serve policy mandates of the Israeli government, with "the identity of B'nai B'rith itself taking a secondary role in fostering the interests of a foreign power."

Mosher's article went on to discuss the broader issue of national versus extranational loyalties raised by Joftes's case, quoting the views of numerous national and international Jewish leaders. He disclosed the mechanisms through which tax-free donations from U.S. Jews were sent to Israel for purposes other than the designated "relief" and discussed the Senate Foreign Relations Committee hearings seven years before which had exposed and closed down an illegal Israeli propaganda operation in an organization called the American Zionist Council.

Shortly after the article appeared, the offices of Dow Jones, which owned the *National Observer,* were visited by Gustave Levy, senior partner in a New York investment firm, and a group of other Jewish leaders. The group did not dispute the accuracy of the article but protested its publication as an embarrassment and an anti-Jewish act. They questioned the motives of Warren Phillips, then vice-president of Dow Jones, in publishing the Mosher piece: "Why create public focus on this information?" Despite the pressure, Phillips stood behind his writer.

"Who Could Be Mad at Us?"

In its April 1974 issue, *National Geographic Magazine* published a major article entitled "Damascus, Syria's Uneasy Eden." The article discussed ancient and modern life in the Syrian capital, but a brief segment on the life of the city's small Jewish community caused a storm of protest.

Author Robert Azzi, a journalist with years of experience in the Middle East, found that "the city still tolerantly embraces significant numbers of Jews" and Sephardic Jews enjoy "freedom of worship and freedom of opportunity" although they live under a number of obtrusive restrictions, including strict limitations on travel and emigration. He had learned that about 500 Jews had left Syria in the years following the 1967 war, and that "reprisals against the families of those who leave are . . . rare."

A number of U.S. Jewish groups and many subscribers were out-raged by Azzi's portrait of Jewish life in Syria. A torrent of angry letters poured into the offices of the National Geographic Society pro-testing the "whitewash" of Syria's treatment of its Jewish citizens and the refusal of the editors to correct Azzi's "shocking distortions." Soci-ety President Gilbert M. Grosvenor later recalled that his offices re-ceived more than 600 protest letters. This correspondence was liberally seasoned with harsh charges, including "hideous lies," "disgraceful," "inhuman," "Communistic propaganda," and "as bad as Hitler's hatred for the Jews." One letter threatened Grosvenor's life. As the con-troversy grew, the Society even received a letter from Kansas Senator Robert Dole expressing concern over the issue and forwarding a longer letter from the Jewish Community Relations Bureau of Kansas City.

Unaccustomed to controversy, the *National Geographic* offices were shocked at the outcry raised over a small section of what had been seen as a standard article. Protestations by Grosvenor that the piece had been checked for accuracy by Western diplomats in Syria, the Syria desk officer at the U.S. State Department and even several rabbis—none of whom had found any problems with the text—were unavailing.

The criticisms culminated in a public demonstration by the Ameri-can Jewish Congress outside the Society's Washington offices in late June. Informed of the picketing outside the Society's opulent head-quarters, a receptionist was incredulous: "Are you kidding? Who could be mad at us?"

Phil Baum, associate executive director of the AJC, met with Grosvenor and declared that the picketing became necessary due to the refusal of *National Geographic* to acknowledge its "errors" in print. This was the first instance of picketing against the National Geographic Society since its establishment in 1888 to "increase and diffuse geo-graphic knowledge." As the picketers prepared to depart after marching in near 100 degree heat, one told a *New York Times* reporter, "The magazine doesn't print letters to the editor. This is our letter to the editor."

Grosvenor views the picketing basically as an AJC fund-raising event: "A simple matter of dollars out, dollars in. You can hire pickets on short notice around this town." Though some of the picketers ar-gued vehemently with *National Geographic* staffers who went out to speak with them, many were quite amiable. "We served coffee, dough-nuts and bagels to the picketers," Grosvenor recalls. "In fact I think we picked up a few new members from the group."

At the same time, Grosvenor did not ignore the pressure generated by Baum and the AJC. The Society decided to print an editorial com-menting on the episode—another "first" in the 86 years of the organization. Personally signed by Grosvenor, it conceded, "We have received evidence from many of our Jewish readers since the article appeared which convinces us that we unwittingly failed to reflect the harsh conditions under which that small [Damascene Jewish] community has existed since 1948. . . . Our critics were right. We erred."

Yet the society's "confession" contradicts events in Syria itself. The Syrian government banned the controversial article and declared author Azzi persona non grata for spreading "Zionist propaganda."

"A Mimeograph Machine Run Rampant"

During the same period, CBS-TV experienced a similar controversy over a "60 Minutes" segment dealing with the situation of Jews in Syria. The program, entitled "Israel's Toughest Enemy," was broadcast February 16, 1975, and featured correspondent Mike Wallace.

As his point of departure Wallace said, "The Syrian Jewish community is kept under close surveillance." He noted that Jews cannot emigrate, must carry special identification cards and must notify authorities when they travel inside Syria.

Despite such restrictions, Wallace concluded, "today life for Syria's Jews is better than it was in years past." Wallace backed this claim with a number of interviews with Jews who were making their way comfortably in Syrian society. The most striking of these was one with a Jewish teacher which included the following exchange:

Wallace: Where do all these stories come from about how badly the Jews are treated in Syria?
Teacher: I think that it's Zionist propaganda.

CBS was swamped with angry letters, and the American Jewish Congress branded the report "excessive, inaccurate and distorted." Protests were also sent to the FCC and the National News Council. As the complaints continued pouring in, Wallace realized that for the first time he had "come up against a conscientious campaign by the so-called Jewish lobby—against a mimeograph machine run rampant."

Wallace observed at the time,

The world Jewish community tends somehow to associate a fair report about Syria's Jews with an attack on Israel because Syria happens to be Israel's toughest enemy. But the fact is there is not one Syrian Jew in jail today as a political prisoner.

On 7 June "60 Minutes" again broadcast the segment on Syria, along with an account of the criticisms received and additional background on the film. The program also included a promise that Wallace would "go back and take another look" at the situation of Jews in Syria.

The second program, broadcast March 21, 1976, disappointed critics who expected the second report to prove their charges: instead, it confirmed the findings of the first. A Syrian Jew who had fled Syria at age 13 and lived in New York declared that Syrian Jews "in general are much more prosperous now than ever before."

Critics have since turned to attacking Wallace personally. In fact, AIPAC still bears a grudge nearly ten years after the original program. The February 1984 issue of *Near East Report,* the AIPAC newsletter, carried an anti-Wallace commentary by editor M. J. Rosenberg. He was disturbed by Wallace's observation in the January 8, 1984, edition of "Sixty Minutes" that "nothing affronts Syrian dignity and pride more than the fact that Israel has Syrian land, the Golan Heights, and Syria wants it back." Rosenberg responded that Wallace "mouths Syrian propaganda as if he were a member of the Ba'ath party's young leadership group." Recalling the controversy of 1976–1977, he wrote that "Wallace didn't learn much from that episode. After all, Mike Wallace is Jewish. Does he feel that he has to bend over backward to prove that he is no secret Zionist?"

"A Double Standard Toward Terror and Murder"

CBS radio became a storm center about the same time as the Wallace controversy. On its "First Line Report" White House correspondent Robert Pierpoint used this forum in March 1973 to make a controversial statement on events in the Middle East. Focusing on two recent incidents—a commando-style raid against Palestinian refugee camps 130 miles inside Lebanon and the downing of a Libyan commercial airliner which strayed over then Israeli-occupied territory in the Sinai Desert—Pierpoint commented on the differing American response to acts of violence committed by Israelis and by Arabs.

He observed that after the massacre of Israeli athletes at the 1972 Olympics Games in Munich, "the United States, from President Nixon on down, expressed outrage." Yet these two more recent acts by Israel had caused the death of more than a hundred innocent civilians, and there had been hardly a ripple of American response. Pierpoint's conclusion was blunt:

What this seems to add up to is a double standard in this country toward terror and murder. For so long Americans have become used to thinking of Israelis as the good guys and Arabs as the bad guys, that many react emotionally along the lines of previous prejudices. The fact is that both sides have committed unforgiveable acts of terror, both sides have killed innocents, both sides have legitimate grievances and illegitimate methods of expressing them.

Knowing that he had voiced an opinion rarely heard over network airways, Pierpoint was not surprised when CBS switchboards in Washington and New York were jammed for hours with protest calls after his broadcast.

The reaction grew so heated, in fact, that Pierpoint became concerned about the attitude of CBS management. Vice-President Sandford Socolow told him ominously, "Bob, you're in real trouble," and Gordon Manning, another CBS executive added, "It doesn't look good for you"—even though both men felt that the commentary had been professionally done and should be defended. When they walked into the Salant's office to discuss the matter, they quickly learned that Salant had already decided not to bow to the pressure. "Wasn't that a terrific broadcast Pierpoint did!" Salant declared, thus bringing the matter to a close within the CBS hierarchy.

For Pierpoint, however, the controversy lingered. He received over 400 letters on his broadcast, some labeling him "a vicious anti-Semite" and describing his report as "like Goebbels's propaganda machine." He later remarked that his commentary had caused him to be perceived as a "public enemy" by some Jewish Americans.

Soon after the "First Line Report" broadcast, Ted Koppel discussed the Pierpoint affair for ABC radio's "World of Commentary." Koppel cited the swift reaction of the pro-Israel lobby:

The Anti-Defamation League responded immediately. Regional offices of the ADL sent out letters the next day, enclosing copies of the Pierpoint report, and calling on friends of the ADL to send their protests to the local CBS affiliate station.

That kind of carefully orchestrated 'spontaneous reaction' disturbs me just as much coming from the ADL as it would from a politically partisan group. It is a tactic of intimidation. I hope that the Anti-Defamation League wasn't trying to get Robert Pierpoint fired, because he's a decent and responsible reporter. But I suspect he will think long and hard before he does another commentary that might distress the ADL—which is why I did this one. American newsmen these days simply can't afford to be intimidated—by anyone.

Affordable or not, the "tactic of intimidation" made its mark. Under pressure, Pierpoint dropped a chapter relating the details of the broadcast uproar and its aftermath from his book, *White House Assignment*. In the draft chapter Pierpoint wrote that "a very powerful group of Jewish businessmen and representatives of national Jewish organizations had demanded to see CBS news president Richard Salant" and that "a delegation of Jewish businessmen" called for a retraction by CBS affiliate station WTOP in Washington.

In the excised chapter, Pierpoint candidly explained its impact on his work as a newsman: "It was many months before I voluntarily discussed the Middle East on the air again." Recalling his decision, Pierpoint says Elisabeth Jakab, a book editor for the publisher, G. P. Putnam's, predicted that the controversial chapter would divert attention from the rest of the book: "She told me Jews are major book buyers and might boycott my book." Another Putnam staff member had similar advice: "Joel Swerdlow told me he didn't like the chapter, but he admitted he was emotional about the subject because he is Jewish. He suggested that I change the text or drop it." "Finally," concludes Pierpoint, "I gave in."

Indeed, Pierpoint admits that the intimidating pressure found its mark beyond his self-censoring decision on the book chapter:

Ever since that strong reaction, I have been more aware of the possibility of getting into arguments with listeners and viewers, and therefore sometimes when I had a choice as to whether to do a broadcast on a topic like that or go in another direction I probably went in another direction. You don't like to have constant arguments, particularly with people you may like and admire but don't agree with.

"Set Right This Terrible Thing"

During 1981 Patsy Collins, chairman of the board of King Broadcasting in Seattle, was subjected to severe criticism for a series of reports on Israel and the West Bank. Just before the Israeli invasion of Lebanon, she and a technical crew visited sites including Bir Zeit University in the West Bank, Hebrew University in Jerusalem, and the Israeli Knesset. They put together a series of eight four-minute segments, which were broadcast on the evening television news over eight consecutive days. The reports sought to portray the life of the Palestinians under Israeli administration. A closing thirty-minute documentary was planned.

Though public reaction to the reports was mild, the local heads of the American Jewish Committee and the ADL visited the station to "set right this terrible thing." They demanded and received a private screening of the final documentary before it was broadcast. Unable to cite any inaccuracies in the piece, they criticized its "tone and flavor." Among telephoned complaints was one accusing Collins of being in the pay of the PLO.

The Israeli consul general in San Francisco, Mordecai Artzieli, telephoned a stern demand that air time be provided to "refute the lies" in the program. The King stations in Portland and Seattle agreed to follow the closing summary with a 30-minute discussion between representatives of the Jewish and Arab communities moderated by a member of the broadcast company staff. The planned discussion did not materialize, however, as no Jewish group would agree to send a representative to share air time with an Arab American. Collins believes that the refusal to take part in the discussion was urged by Consul Artzieli.

Reflecting on her experiences, Collins concludes: "I don't think there's any Israeli or Jewish control of the media at all. It's influence; and people can be influenced only if they allow themselves to be influenced."

Criticism of Collins evaporated with the 1982 Israel invasion of Lebanon—during which Collins herself cited shortcomings in network coverage of the daily progress of the fighting. At the onset of the action, NBC was covering the attack on Lebanon not from Lebanon, but from Israel. Despite the courage of NBC crews in filming the progress and results of the Israeli advance to Beirut, film footage broadcast on the "NBC Nightly News" showed only Israel forces on their way to Lebanon. Moreover reports frequently described weapons used by Arabs as "Soviet-made," while the Israelis were never described as using "American-made" F-16s, or "U.S.-built" tanks.

Her comments paralleled those of Alexander Cockburn, who had noted in his *Village Voice* column how *New York Times* editors struck the word "indiscriminate" from foreign correspondent Thomas Friedman's August 3 report on the Israeli bombing of Beirut. The action violated usual *Times* policy. Friedman sent a lengthy telex expressing his outrage:

I am an extremely cautious reporter. I do not exaggerate. . . . You knew I was correct and that the word was backed up by what I had reported. But you did not have the courage—guts—to print it in the *New York Times*. You were afraid to tell our readers and those who might complain to you that the Israelis are capable of indiscriminately shelling an entire city. . . .

NBC Charged with Anti-Israel Bias

Despite the instances of pro-Israeli bias on the part of NBC cited by Patsy Collins, Alexander Cockburn, Richard Broderick and others, eight affiliates of the network in New York came under pressure in 1983 from partisans who alleged bias against Israel in "NBC Nightly News" coverage of the war in Lebanon. Americans for a Safe Israel (AFSI), a New York-based lobbying organization, filed petitions with the Federal Communications Commission to prevent the eight affiliates in New

York from renewing their broadcast licenses. AFSI director Peter Goldman described the NBC coverage as "deliberate distortion of the news," claiming that the network presented the war "in a manner favorable to the Arabs." Goldman's campaign against NBC—presented in a film entitled "NBC in Lebanon: A Study of Media Misrepresentation"—has been backed by the Committee for Accuracy in Middle East Reporting in America (CAMERA), a Washington-based group which focuses its efforts primarily against anti-Israel bias it finds in the *Washington Post*.

Lawrence K. Grossman, president of NBC News, called the AFSI charges "untrue and unfounded: The AFSI film distorted NBC News' coverage and selectively ignored important aspects of NBC's reports." He notes that the *Columbia Journalism Review* has praised the "overall balance" of NBC coverage, and *Washington Journalism Review* has criticized the AFSI film for "manipulation" of NBC's coverage of the war in Lebanon. Early in 1984 the FCC rejected similar AFSI petitions against seven NBC affiliate stations in New England, although the group did not relax its pressure. The petitions were revised and resubmitted.

Such attempts to stifle media coverage deemed uncomplimentary to Israel are augmented with a $2 million media campaign by Israel designed to "remind Americans that Israelis are 'nice, warm' people and not 'bloodthirsty militarists.'"

William Branigin of the *Washington Post* covered the same event, but his editors did not delete "indiscriminate" from his front-page report. During the same period, however, *Post* editors experienced an intimidating presence in their newsrooms.

Lobbyist in the News Room

Fairness in reporting Middle East events has been a special concern of the *Washington Post* over the last several years. Complaints from pro-Israel groups about its coverage of Lebanon—especially the massacres at Sabra and Shatila—led to the unprecedented placement of a representative from a pro-Israel group as an observer in the *Post* newsroom.

The idea arose when Michael Berenbaum, executive director of the Jewish Community Council of Greater Washington, council president Nathan Lewin, and Hyman Bookbinder, area representative of the American Jewish Committee, met with *Post* editors to inform them that the paper had "a Jewish problem." The meeting followed substantial correspondence between the *Washington Post* and Jewish community leaders. As an accommodation, executive editor Benjamin C.

Bradlee agreed to have Berenbaum observe *Post* news operations for one week, provided he not lobby or "interfere with the editorial process in any way."

Many members of the *Post* staff were unhappy at working under the surveillance of an outsider. News editor Karen DeYoung declared the idea "not the best in the world. . . . There's no question that someone following you around all day is an inconvenience."

Columnist Nick Thimmesch found the experience "very intimidating." He recalls a comment of one staffer which expressed the view of many: "Next thing you know, someone else will be in here."

Post ombudsman Robert J. McCloskey termed the week a "worthwhile experiment": "Irregular, yes, but so is the shelling newspapers are taking." Criticism from the Jewish community diminished somewhat as a result, but editors of other major newspapers were critical of the whole episode. *Boston Globe* editor Thomas Winship commented, "I understand the pressures the *Post* has been under from the Jewish Community Council, and I have sympathy for what the *Post* did, but I would hope personally that I would not do it." Robert Gibson, foreign news editor of the *Los Angeles Times,* questioned the fairness of the *Post*'s decision: "I honestly don't know how one could do it for Jews and refuse to do it for Arabs."

When Moshe Arens arrived in Washington as Israeli ambassador to the United States in February 1982, he initiated monitoring and evaluation of the coverage given to Israel in American newspapers. His scoring system showed that the *Washington Post* had distinguished itself as "by far the most negative" in reporting on Israel and the Middle East in 1982—the year of Israel's invasion of Lebanon. Arens noted with dismay that the massacre of hundreds of civilians in the Sabra and Shatila refugee camps in the fall of 1982 produced "a tremendous drop in the index, to the lowest point" since the beginning of the weekly survey.

Armed with a battery of graphs and charts, Arens presented his findings to Meg Greenfield, editor of the *Post* editorial pages. Greenfield, who ranks among the most respected voices in U.S. journalism, disputed the very premise of the ratings. She protested that the *Post* had fulfilled its "obligation of fairness" by having "as many of the important Arab and Israeli players as we could speak for themselves on our op-ed page." During the controversial Israeli invasion, commentaries by Israeli Foreign Minister Yitzhak Shamir, Abba Eban, Henry Kissinger, Alfred Friendly, Shimon Peres, and Arens himself had been printed. Two long editorials from respected Israeli newspapers had also appeared in the *Post.*

The *Boston Globe* was the only other paper contacted by Arens because of the low rating he gave its stories about Israel and the Middle East. Editor Winship recalls that Arens "started right off going after the American press on what he felt was very much a bias against Israel." He described the *Globe* as "one of the newspapers with the most negative attitide," and he made this view known to the local Jewish community.

Like Greenfield, Winship rejects the idea of the Israeli ratings system: "My feeling is that having such a list smacks of the Nixon enemies list and strikes me as pretty close to harassment of the media." *Globe* staff writer Ben Bradlee, Jr. describes the Arens study and his meetings with newspaper executives as "an unusually bold demonstration of Jerusalem's effort to put the American press on the defensive and make itself heard among opinion-shapers."

Pressure to "Stop the Ads"

Direct pressure to reject paid advertising unsympathetic to Israeli interests was applied beginning in late 1982 against major media in Maryland, Pennsylvania and the District of Columbia. The National Association of Arab Americans (NAAA), a Washington-based private membership organization, purchased radio air time in these areas for commercials questioning the U.S. government's decision to increase aid to Israel.

Typical of the messages was this one aired in Pennsylvania:

While there are more than 12 million Americans unemployed, with over half a million from Pennsylvania alone, Congress decided to give Israel two billion, 485 million of your tax dollars. Senator Arlen Specter [D-PA] is on the Senate Appropriations Committee that wanted to give Israel even more. Is funding for Israel more important than funding for Pennsylvania? Call your senators and ask them if they voted to give your tax dollars to Israel."

Thirteen Pennsylvania stations contracted to carry the NAAA message, but four of these cancelled the ads after only three days of an agreed-upon five-day run. Mike Kirtner, an ad salesman representing two stations in Allentown, informed the NAAA that its ads were being taken off the air because "they were getting a lot of calls, hate calls, and a lot of pressure was coming down on the station to stop the ads." Station management refused to comment on who was pressuring the station to take the ads off the air.

Mike George, salesman for an Erie station which canceled the ads, was more frank. He informed the NAAA that the station owner had been called by "a group of Jewish businessmen who told him that if he did not cancel the ads immediately, they were going to cause his radio and television stations to lose hundreds of thousands of dollars."

In Maryland the NAAA sponsored similar messages citing the prominence of Congressman Clarence "Doc" Long (D-Md) in supporting aid to Israel (see chapter one). Although the ads were aired on four stations in Washington and four in the Baltimore area, a number of stations rejected them as "anti-Semitic."

Later, in California the NAAA found stations in San Francisco, San Mateo, Berkeley and Santa Clara unwilling to carry the NAAA's paid message, despite editorial statements in some local newspapers supporting the NAAA's right to free speech. The stations offered no reason for their refusal.

Ron Cathell, communications director for the NAAA, is not surprised:

This has happened to us before. People have been threatened with financial losses to prevent them from having a talk show with us or running our ads. [But] it hasn't happened to this degree before. This week was really pretty stunning.

Cathell adds:

The only way to get [the Middle East conflict] resolved is to talk about it. And if we can't talk about it here in the United States, how do we expect them to talk about it in the Middle East?

Chapter 12

Repairing the Damage

In gathering material for this book I sought answers to troubling questions: Was my congressional experience at the hands of the Israeli lobby "just politics" or part of a broader attempt to silence criticism of Israeli policy? Do other Congressmen and officials of government encounter similar pressures? What about people in other occupations—on the campus, in business, the pulpit, the news rooms, in everyday life? The answers I found are not reassuring. They can be summed up in a single sentence: A dangerous erosion of free speech is occurring in the United States.

It is clear that many Americans do not feel they can speak freely on one of most complicated and challenging current issues: the Arab-Israeli dispute. The relatively few people who have ventured into this arena have found their cherished vision of the free and open society an illusion. Unlike other controversies, those on one side of the argument leave no room for honest disagreement. The only side that can be advocated with impunity is the Israeli side.

Those who criticize Israeli policy in any sustained way invite painful and relentless retaliation, and even loss of their livelihood, by pressure by one or more parts of Israel's lobby. Presidents fear it. Congress does its bidding. Prestigious universities shun academic programs and grants which it opposes. Giants of the media and military leaders buckle under its pressure. Instead of having their arguments and opinions judged on merit, critics of Israel suddenly find their motivations, their integrity, and basic moral values called into question. No matter how moderate their criticism, they may be characterized as pawns of the oil lobby, apologists for Arab terrorists, or even anti-Semitic.

The charge of anti-Semitism is a worrisome one, particularly because its use is becoming more widespread. Listen to Ben Meed, president of the American Gathering of Jewish Holocaust Survivors: "Years

315

ago they used to call it anti-Semitism. Today they call it anti-Zionism, but actually it's the same thing." In other words, by his definition, if you are against Israel, you are against all Jews.

In its latest usage, the term anti-Semitism stands stripped of any reference to ethnic or religious descent, signifying nothing more than a refusal to endorse all policy decisions of the government of Israel. As such, it no longer refers to a despicable social phenomenon—classic anti-Semitism—but is a charge employed by pro-Israel partisans as a weapon. Although no longer used to describe only the ethnic and religious bigotry which originally gave the word meaning, Israel's most spirited supporters have found that the mere accusation of anti-Semitism is enough to silence most critics. It has been a powerful factor in stifling debate of the Arab-Israeli dispute, causing many people in the United States, religious and secular, to censor their own speech, not on the basis of truth but rather on how their remarks will be construed by Israel's lobby, a particular group with a strong vested interest in silencing critics.

The lobby has already attained strength far beyond the level its numbers would suggest. Those active in its ranks constitute a tiny part of the population of the United States, but their demographic concentration in states critical to deciding national elections, combined with their unique ability to mobilize campaign resources and public opinion, gives them influence in the political process far out of proportion to their numbers. Even more significant is the remarkable commitment and devotion which lobby partisans bring to their cause. They give generously of their time, money and energy. Many are leaders in government, public information, education and politics. Their activities are supported by the government of Israel, openly through its embassy in Washington and consulates in our major cities and clandestinely through the extensive operations that Mossad, Israel's foreign intelligence service, undertakes throughout the United States.

The lobby's success in stifling dissent is shocking, particularly in Congress. Polls show that a plurality of American Jews—and of the American people as a whole—oppose certain Israeli policies. Normally this division would be reflected in the statements and voting records of their legislators. But on this issue, the views of these pluralities are not represented. In fact, the gulf between the expressions in Congress on the Arab-Israeli dispute and the views held by private citizens is probably greater than on any other topic.

The lobby has made free speech a casualty by skillful use of our free institutions. In most cases, it stays carefully within the letter of the law, but it abuses the spirit of fairness and tolerance that is so vital to public debate, effectively denying those who oppose its policies the constitutional right to free speech. It's one thing to know before you speak out that people will disagree with you. It's quite another to know they will seek to discredit you and destroy your reputation. To say the least, the threat of this kind of retaliation curbs the open exchange of ideas that is essential to the development of sound policy in a democracy.

The result is that most people come to consider Middle East issues "too hot to handle" and keep their views to themselves. They see what happens to their bolder colleagues and hesitate to voice their opinions. They censor themselves out of fear that the Israeli lobby will censure them if they do not.

The damage to U.S. institutions is clear. What may not be clear is why the lobby came into being and pursues its intimidating activities with such zeal.

Its origin and motivation can be summed up in just one word: fear. Many Jews are afraid, and their fear is understandable. Remembering Adolf Hitler's terrible program, which exterminated six million Jews, they see Israel as a place of refuge, perhaps the only one, if such horror should someday return. A resident of Potomac, Maryland, Perry J. Saidman, expressed this fear in a letter to the editor of the *Washington Post:*

Nearly all Jews believe that the survival of Israel is synonymous with the survival of Judaism. This is easy to understand in view of the Holocaust, since Jews in the diaspora now know that the only country that will not refuse them during the next Holocaust will be the Jewish state of Israel.

To Saidman, and to many other Jews, another holocaust is entirely possible, especially if criticism of Israel goes unpunished. To such people, the Holocaust is not only a historical event but a personal ordeal in which relatives or family friends were ruthlessly destroyed.

Fear of future ordeals is deep-seated. During his earliest shuttle diplomacy mission to the Middle East, Secretary of State Henry Kissinger, musing privately over the possibility that unwise policy by Israel might someday provoke a wave of anti-Semitism in the United States, said to a colleague, "I worry about my son when he grows up— a Jew in America." A Jewish woman who voted for Jesse Jackson in the 1984 Michigan primary election was warned by her outraged brother, "You will die someday in a gas chamber."

Jewish ties to Israel are powerful and intimate for other reasons, too. Beyond being a place of ultimate refuge, Israel is the physical repository of Judaism, the fulfillment of age-old Jewish dreams and the symbol of Jewish resilience and achievement. Equally important, it is linked by family ties to American Jews, most of whom have relatives and other acquaintances there and feel keenly the sorrow of Israeli families who have suffered death or injury in conflicts with Arabs.

These ties are deepened and made urgent by Israel's own sense of insecurity. Despite its unmatched war machine and expanding military capability, Israel remains at war with all its neighbors except Egypt. The nation is widely seen by its citizens and other Jews as struggling for survival in a vast and growing sea of hostile Arabs. It is a tiny country, only about nine miles wide at one point. This bleak prospect keeps military forces on a constant state of alert, produces in many Israelis a siege mentality and causes them to accept restrictions on civil liberties that they would consider anathema in other circumstances. The press, both Israeli and Arab, is censored, and Arab populations, especially in the occupied areas of the West Bank and Gaza, have their liberties restricted and are often brutalized.

This siege outlook pervades not just Israel but much of the U.S. Jewish community. Because Israel remains at war, many U.S. Jews feel they too are at war. Worried about Israel's survival in a generally inhospitable world, they accept tactics which stifle dissent in their own communities and throughout America as necessary measures which, in their view, enhance the likelihood that the United States will continue to serve as Israel's lifeline.

And, indeed, the United States is Israel's lifeline. Most observers feel that Israel could not have won the 1967 war without U.S.-supplied weapons. In the 1973 war, Israel's survival was in question until the United States undertook two extraordinary measures: ordering its own forces to a high state of alert worldwide in order to forestall a larger Soviet role in the war, and ferrying vast armor and supplies to Israel in an intercontinental airlift. The rescue operation demonstrated Israel's loneliness. Faced with the necessity of refueling its air transport fleet during the long journey to Israel, the United States found Portugal the only nation among our allies in western Europe willing to permit the use of its bases for this purpose. If another war with Arab states should occur—and many Jews feel it is only a matter of time—most Jews are convinced that Israel's prospects will be bleak without unqualified United States help.

For many concerned Jews, establishing the conditions which assure continued U.S. backing is a task which merits the highest priority—and one that justifies extraordinary measures. Consciously or not, leaders of the pro-Israel lobby accept the impairment of free speech in the United States as a price that must be paid to assure Israel's survival.

Whenever anti-Israel or pro-Arab expressions appear, the lobby's response is usually prompt and overwhelming. The aim is to protect

Israel from all criticism, but the tactics go beyond legitimate response to argument. They are varied and sometimes ugly: smear and innuendo, complaints to superiors at the workplace, mention in published "enemies lists," ostracism, hate mail, anonymous phone calls, threats to one's personal safety, and, in a few cases, physical attack. This is a process which most Americans know only second hand. We recognize it and never cease to condemn it in the Soviet Union and in other totalitarian societies; yet it recalls an ugly chapter from our own past as well.

Thirty years ago we knew it in a more virulent form as McCarthyism. After a shameful delay, we finally found the will to expose it, denounce it and put a stop to it. Now, as then, the people most ridden by fear are the ones most intolerant of dissent. In their zeal to silence critics they employ extreme measures.

Few are aware that these measures—and the fear that made them so effective—have found their way back into our political process. In new hands now, in response to a different issue, the tools of intimidation are wielded less visibly, less crudely, but no less effectively. And those who wield them are driven by a similar conviction of moral righteousness. The process is less visible because, unlike Senator Joseph McCarthy of yesterday, today's would-be enforcers of political conformity often shun the limelight. Despite its success, the pro-Israel lobby is little known. It prefers to avoid public attention and scrutiny, working behind the scenes, motivating other individuals or institutions to take the lead.

The lobby works diligently in the wings and the corridors to provide Israel with uncritical support. Whatever Israel undertakes is characterized as helpful to the United States, an attitude that makes criticism of Israel "un-American" and therefore unthinkable. Its partisans have defined the terms for discussing Middle East issues so rigidly that debate itself is excluded. "If you are not for us," its members say, "you are against us." There is no middle ground. Issues are painted in black and white. The gray area where truth is often found is considered too dangerous.

Driven by deep-rooted fears, activists for Israel create fear in others. In conducting interviews for this book, time and again I found professors, politicians, business leaders and others anxious lest their identity as a source of information become known. One said, "If my name gets into this, my career will be ended." When a university administrator supplied me a document issued by the American Jewish Committee, he warned, "You must never tell anyone—not anyone—where you got this." Others said, "I applaud what you are doing and would like to help, but I am afraid." A Texas professor, after suggesting a source of information in Arizona, pleaded, "Please forget you made this call." A businessman said: "I am taking a big chance in telling you this. I hope I can trust you to keep this confidential." A scholar who supplied details of his own encounters with lobby pressure, called in anguish, "I can't let you publish that information after all. I fear for my very life." A well-known retired diplomat, now providing consulting services part-time in Washington, encouraged me to write this book, but withdrew his offer to write a public endorsement when he learned this would upset his major client. "I'm embarrassed to admit it," he said ruefully, "because my decision is an example of the intimidation which is the central theme of your book."

I was struck by the fact that many of the people who dare to speak out have personal income that is not jeopardized by their forthrightness. Most academicians who speak out are protected in their careers by tenure. So, too, J. William Fulbright, Adlai E. Stevenson III, George W. Ball, Dean Francis B. Sayre, Philip M. Klutznick, Rabbi Elmer Berger, Alfred M. Lilienthal, Jr., speak from a base of financial security.

Public awareness of this critical erosion of free speech is especially important at this time when the Middle East looms as a possible arena of superpower confrontation. Today, more than ever before, the American people—Jews and non-Jews alike—must examine the lobby's methods openly, hold it accountable for its actions and insist on the right of all to be heard.

In the months ahead life-and-death decisions must be made concerning the role of the United States in the Arab-Israeli dispute, and these should emerge from an atmosphere of civility in which arguments are heard and judged on their merits, without labelling or emotionalism. The dispute is a ticking bomb that grows steadily more dangerous. Renewed fighting in the Middle East would carry the risk of increasing U.S. military involvement, as well as escalating political and economic costs. Recent conflict in the Middle East has claimed the lives of 264 Marines, and even after our military withdrawal from Lebanon more than 1,000 U.S. troops remain stationed near the border between Egypt and Israel as a peacekeeping force. Israel and Syria, as well as several other neighboring states, are engaged in an accelerating buildup of highly destructive new weapons, and no reconciliation of their mutual hostility is in sight.

If our citizens, whether in private life or public office, are able to hear only one side of the issue, they are seriously handicapped as they attempt to define intelligently their interests and set wisely the policies to be followed. From a fettered and unbalanced dialogue truly awful decisions may emerge.

In a democracy, the position taken by a large citizens' group—like those making up the Israeli lobby—must, of course, be taken into account. The United States, in addition to its moral interest in the survival of Israel, has a legitimate reason and an obligation to act in accordance with the wishes of its citizens, so long as the preferences of a particular special interest group do not violate the interests of the majority. But this does not require blind conformity. Surely one can criticize Israeli policies without being anti-Israel, just as one can criticize American policies without being anti-American.

Getting free speech off the casualty list requires realism, attention and commitment on the part of us all. As a starter, we must disenthrall ourselves from the false notion that the Israeli lobby is "bigger than life." Its members are neither superhuman nor especially blessed with the truth. The lobby consists of a relatively small group of people, not more than 200,000 at the most, and the core activists who keep things rolling are but a fraction of that total. Although its leaders are highly professional and highly committed, these same qualities can be found in other citizens. The lobby raises a lot of money and marshals broad support, but it cannot prevail over an informed and determined majority of our citizens.

Knowledge is power—as the lobby well knows—and the best way to demolish its façade of invincibility is to understand its tactics. It is often able to create a false impression of numbers. For example, several years ago one hundred identically worded telegrams were sent to Senator Adlai E. Stevenson of Illinois, protesting against legislation he was proposing. The telegrams bore serial numbers in sequence, indicating that they were ordered by a single individual even though each carried a different name. During the same period, Senator Abraham Ribicoff of Connecticut received twenty-eight telegrams. All carried identical wording and were charged to the same telephone number in Hartford, but each bore a different name as the sender.

Even two or three telephone calls can create the image of substantial constituent protest, even though the few actually placing the calls may be the sum total of protesters. Only a few telephone calls persuaded fourteen freshmen Congressmen in 1983 to take the exceptional step of changing their votes on legislation providing aid to Israel. These calls would have had far less impact if counterbalanced by even one call expressing the opposite view to each wavering Congressman. When Congressmen hear only one side of an issue by mail, telegram, telephone call, personal visit—or in public debate—they naturally assume there actually is only one side worth considering.

My own defeat in 1982 is often cited as an example of the lobby's power. It need not be so viewed. My margin of defeat was so narrow, less than one percent of the total votes cast, that it could be blamed entirely on any one of several other political and economic developments: redistricting, which added large new Democratic areas to my district; the recession, which caused record unemployment in Decatur, my largest new city; or a general downturn in economic conditions, which caused unrest throughout the district, especially among farmers.

Yet for understandable reasons, the Israeli lobby claimed responsibility for my defeat. In fact, the lobby's principal role was in simply supplying my opponent with extraordinary amounts of money. Under the circumstances my vote total could be cited as a moral victory. Despite the many varied challenges, I nearly won. Money from Jewish sources poured in against me, but my supporters matched these contributions.

I was subjected to this nationwide attack because I was the only critic of Israeli policy on the Congressional scene. In the future if just a few brave souls speak out on Capitol Hill at the same time, the lobby will face multiple problems and cannot therefore focus exclusively on the defeat of just one of its critics.

Until now, the lobby has been effective mainly because it has had the field of Middle East policy largely to itself. It has no serious competition in the corridors and chambers of government. Other highly professional, committed people are needed to counter its arguments, challenge its theories and match its enthusiasm in the public arena.

The lobby's influence rests mainly on mythology which a reasonably broad educational program can readily destroy.

For example, the lobby has successfully promoted the myth that an oil lobby, sometimes called an Arab oil lobby, operates in the United States, menacing our institutions of higher education. Jerome Bankst, research director for the Anti-Defamation League in New York, warns: "Our main concern is the possibility that academic freedom will be compromised. We're concerned that there could be Arab influence on the objectivity of teaching at these universities and discrimination against Jewish faculty." Bankst uses the word "Arab" as a negative stereotype, a form of bigotry that would evoke cries of outrage if one were to substitute the words "Jewish" or "Israeli" for the word "Arab."

While Arab governments and oil companies have contributed to educational projects, this money has not been used as a device to harm scholarly objectivity. Research for this book disclosed no instance in which oil interests attempted to impair academic freedom or influence selection of faculty. Considering the enormous damage done to academic freedom in recent years by Jewish activists, as chronicled in earlier chapters of this book, Bankst's warning might more suitably be directed against his colleagues in the Israeli lobby.

Nor does the "oil lobby" attempt to control U.S. policy toward the Middle East. The late Evan Wilson, a specialist in the Middle East, concluded that the oil companies exert little or no pressure on U.S. policymakers. Professor Seth Tillman of Georgetown University corroborates Wilson's assertion:

Supporters of Israel sometimes cite the major oil companies as participants in the 'Arab lobby,' but the allegation does not stand up under close scrutiny. Outside the realm of energy costs, uses, and taxation, the oil companies have in fact been chary of taking public positions on Middle East issues, much less of pressing these on Congress.

The lobby also benefits from other public misconceptions.

• There is the unfounded reputation that the lobby can deliver a powerful Jewish constituency on election day. Few Congressional districts have a constituency that is more than one percent Jewish. In only twelve states do Jews make up as much as three percent of the population. Even making adjustment for the fact that a higher percentage of Jews vote on election day than non-Jews, they can be crucial only in extremely close races.

• Few people are aware of the magnitude of aid to Israel. They do not know that one-fourth of all U.S. aid worldwide goes to that one country—the equivalent of $750 a year for each Israeli man, woman and child. This unawareness has added importance in light of the general disfavor of the U.S. public toward foreign aid.

• Most citizens have little knowledge about U.S. policy in the Middle East. If constituents held House and Senate members closely accountable for their positions on aid to Israel, for example, substantial changes in either membership or positions might soon occur. In the spring of 1984, 379 Congressmen voted for a $250 million gift to help Israel enlarge its own fighter aircraft industry. Only 40 Congressmen voted no. Given the importance of the U.S. aircraft industry to the U.S. economy, not to mention the heavy deficit in the U.S. federal budget, the vote to provide a substantial direct subsidy to foreign competition was extraordinary. Constituents could reasonably demand that the 379 explain why they supported this unprecedented subsidy.

• The Israeli lobby has the Middle East policy field largely to itself. To help correct this extreme imbalance, Americans of Arab ancestry need to discover the ingredients of successful political action. Democratic Congressman Merwyn L. Dymally of California observes that most ethnic Americans do not engage in lobbying activity because they do not understand its importance. Nor do they, he adds, have a "sense of political philanthropy." American Jews give generously of both money and energy to political candidates while Arab Americans rarely give either. Although the Arab American population at two million is one one-third the size of the Jewish population, this base is sufficient to provide enough people, financial resources and commitment to offset substantially the activities of the Israeli lobby.

In assessing the strength of the Israeli lobby, it is important to remember that a majority of American Jews disagree on important points with the policies of the Israeli government and the work of its lobby. A few thousand highly motivated citizens willing to work together and acquire the sense of political philanthropy Dymally mentions could profoundly influence public discourse.

The activities of the American-Arab Anti-Discrimination Committee and the National Association of Arab Americans are signs of progress, but neither group has established a program rivaling the grassroots activism that gives the Israeli lobby influence even where Jewish numbers are small. A dramatic illustration of this weakness occurred in June 1984 when the forty House members who voted for the amendment cutting U.S. aid to Israel's fighter aircraft industry were smothered with protests from pro-Israel activists but received almost no calls or letters supporting their action. In the wake of that experience, the forty Congressmen are unlikely to support similar amendments in the future.

People of Arab ancestry often shy away from asserting their interests. One day on the floor of the House of Representatives I asked James Abdnor, a Republican from South Dakota who is of Lebanese ancestry and now serves in the Senate, to join me and several other Congressmen in signing a letter protesting Israel's use of U.S.-supplied weapons in Lebanon. Abdnor paused and said, "Oh, I'd better not— because of my nationality." I did not sense that he was trying to hide his ancestry; rather, he just did not want his colleagues to think he was parading it. In contrast, Jewish members of Congress rarely fail to take a stand for Israel.

The U.S. Jewish community, acting alone, could retrieve free speech from the casualty list, and this action would be consistent with the great Jewish tradition of supporting civil liberties and opposing intimidation and oppression. Indeed, some of the most thoughtful and outspoken critics of Israel are Jews. But they speak out as individuals. They are not seen as Jewish leaders.

More voices of individual conscience would be welcome, but the greatest need is for forthright statements by leaders of Jewish organizations. Philip M. Klutznick set a courageous example in 1958 when, as chairman of the Conference of Presidents of Major Jewish Organizations and president of B'nai B'rith, he supported the Middle East Resolution recommended by President Dwight Eisenhower, despite strong opposition by Israel's prime minister. In 1982 the leadership of B'nai B'rith, after responding warmly to President Reagan's September Peace Plan, fell silent once Israel's Prime Minister Menachem Begin announced his opposition.

Nowhere is free speech more restricted in America than within the organized Jewish community. Jewish leaders are afraid to speak out against Israeli policy or even defend the right of others to do so. They look the other way when lobby activists stain the reputation of Israel's critics through misuse of the term "anti-Semitism."

Few Jews expressed concern over the 1983 decisions by AIPAC and the Anti-Defamation League to publish "enemies lists" or spoke up in 1982 against the flood of smear and innuendo against Adlai E. Stevenson III when he campaigned for governor of Illinois. A few leading Jews haltingly voiced concern for a while over the brutal 1982 Israeli attack against Beirut, but under lobby pressure most of them changed positions, either defending the war or saying nothing. American Jews flocked to dinners in 1983 featuring former Israeli Defense Minister Ariel Sharon, despite his own responsibility for the circumstances a few months earlier that led to the massacre of Palestinians at the Sabra and Shatila refugee camps. Few Jews speak up for academic freedom at Palestinian universities on the occupied West Bank, where Israeli troops routinely arrest students and order the schools closed on the slightest pretext.

In part, Jewish silence results from ignorance. Unfortunately, Israel and its lobby attempt to shield U.S. Jewish leaders from harsh reality when they visit Israel. These leaders usually see only selected places and people, have no opportunity for candid conversations with Arabs in the occupied territories, and return to the United States unaware of the brutality of the Israeli occupation.

The manipulation of Jewish leaders continues in the United States, where they receive a constant stream of messages and visits from Israeli officials and other lobbying agents. These U.S. leaders would render a great service to their fellow Jews, as well as to their country, by insisting on setting their own agenda when they visit the Middle East—having private discussions with Arab leaders inside and outside Israel, and interviewing Palestinians to learn what life is like in the West Bank. This would help to sweep away stereotypes and prejudices that infect both sides.

But ignorance cannot excuse Jewish silence on lobby excesses that occur in this country. During the University of Arizona's three-year ordeal at the hands of Carol Karsch and the Tucson Jewish Community Council, Jews were silent. With the exception of Professor Jerrold Levy, they said nothing and did nothing when blind loyalty to the Israeli cause damaged academic institutions. Several officials of national Jewish organizations privately said that Karsch had gone too far, but they complained only to each other. If just a few people, local or national, had joined Levy in protesting publicly, the excesses might have ended.

The danger in the Karsch "success" reaches beyond Tucson. While the tactics she used were designed and carried out locally, they may be used elsewhere. One "success" inspires others and, indeed, chapter seven demonstrates that this fanaticism—reflecting the mania that produced the Salem witch-hunts in early U.S. history—is already spreading.

Most Jewish Americans will be troubled by the examples of fanaticism reported in the pages of this book. But if they react by keeping their concerns to themselves, they permit the fanatics to create the impression that all American Jews are joined in a plot to alter our schools and other institutions of our society in order to shield Israel from criticism and stigmatize its Arab neighbors.

Chapter eleven recounts episodes involving people in various occupations widely scattered throughout the country. Many of them have one thing in common: they were harassed and stigmatized for their ethnic heritage—which happens to be Arab. If Jews suffered the same treatment, a national uproar justifiably would ensue, and people of all faiths would join in the protest. Yet despite their memory of similar mistreatment, Jews, with few exceptions, remain silent—as do most other Americans—at discrimination against Arabs.

Their silence is but a part of the unwillingness of Americans generally to discuss troubling issues arising from the Arab-Israeli conflict. This larger conspiracy of silence engulfs much of the U.S. Christian community as well. Some conservative Christian leaders accept, even rejoice in, the violence and shedding of blood to serve Israel's political ends. After the Israelis used U.S.-supplied F-16 aircraft to strike against the Iraqi nuclear reactor, evangelist Jerry Falwell congratulated Israel on "a mission that made us very proud that we manufacture those F-16s." Similarly, evangelist Mike Evans proclaimed as "a miracle" the safe return of all Israeli aircraft from strikes against unfortified targets in the commercial heart of Beirut—raids which resulted in countless civilian deaths.

As moral leaders the clergy have a duty to champion the oppressed and denounce racism, but few church leaders have challenged the inaccurate and inflammatory misuse of the term "anti-Semitism" or the ugly stereotypes applied generally to Palestinians and other Arabs. Instead, they duck controversy and thus strengthen the position of those who wish no debate at all. Many defer to Israel's historic claims out of convenience rather than conviction.

For centuries the region has held many religious and ethnic groups, and the issues which divide them are complex. The application of biblical principles will certainly aid in the quest for peace, but as the Reverend Jesse Jackson has advised, "We shouldn't try to use the Bible as a real estate guide." Solutions are simply not that easy. The way to discerning the divine plan for the Middle East certainly involves meditation and prayer, but in a free society like ours, we should also be able to enjoy the benefit of insights gained and shared through free and open debate in an atmosphere of tolerance and recognition of common purpose.

Public officials cannot escape a major responsibility to promote free discussion of Middle East policy. Chief among them, of course, is the·president of the United States. Zbigniew Brzezinski, national security adviser in the Carter administration, observes:

Success depends very much on the willingness of the President to have a confrontation with the lobby. If the issue is drawn in terms of whether the President will be supported or not, most presidents will be backed by Congress.

House and Senate members have a similar responsibility. My own experience notwithstanding, most Congressmen could survive even a sustained attack by the Israeli lobby. But, like other politicians, they crave public approbation, and, in this regard, they don't respond just to the threat of losing an election. They respond first to the threat of losing a supporter, for whatever reason. Thus, as long as pro-Israeli activists care enough to threaten to withhold approbation while others are indifferent, the situation cannot change. To most Congressmen, taking a controversial position which might leave them standing alone—even in their own party—just does not make sense.

From this, I must conclude that public officials are unlikely to take the initiative to restore healthy discourse. Reform must come from citizens at the community level.

All Americans—not just Jews, Christian clergy, Arab Americans and politicians—have a stake in promoting open debate of Middle East policy. Our young people will have to assume the military risks of our present policy, and all citizens must share in meeting the other costs: the budgetary outlays and, more important, the damage to our institutions. All citizens, therefore, should demand accountability from those who seek and serve in federal office, insisting that they take positions and then defend them.

On the 1984 presidential and congressional campaign trails the Arab-Israeli dispute was a non-issue. Except for brief statements by presidential candidates Jesse Jackson and George McGovern, no candidate for any federal office challenged basic U.S. policies in the Middle East—at least not loudly enough to receive national attention. Even those considered "shoo-ins"—those running unopposed for election—made no recommendations for course changes. The 1988 elections were the same.

More surprising, not even an echo was heard bemoaning the unprecedented $3 billion grant that is going to Israel, as well as the $2.1 billion to Egypt, at a time when popular U.S. domestic programs are being cut. Candidates and public officials are silent on these issues because their constituents permit them to be silent. The arena in which reform must occur is not Capitol Hill in Washington but Main Street, in suburbia and in rural America.

Fortunately, the open character of the U.S. political system places the process of effective challenge within everyone's reach.

Congressmen and candidates for Congress are accustomed to answering specific questions on public policy from the League of Women Voters, organized labor, business councils and other interest groups. Furthermore, most Congressmen and candidates respond to such questions during public meetings. If they are pressed during their candidacies or public service, most will eventually take a position on a carefully defined issue. They can duck and dodge only so long.

As the Israeli lobby has proven, a small number of highly committed people can have substantial effect on public policy. Partisans of Israel press early and often through the American Israel Public Affairs Committee, political action committees, other organizations and as individuals. They seem never to sleep, guarding Israel's interests around the clock.

Those citizens who favor a more balanced U.S. policy in the Middle East based on fundamental ideals of justice and peaceful settlement of international disputes, like the pro-Israel activists, may work through established organizations and supplement this work with personal activity. If they bring a high level of commitment to these endeavors, candidates and officials will respond. The majority of Congressmen resent heavy-handed tactics by the Israeli lobby and will welcome constituent pressure to modify their habit of voting for whatever Israel wants.

This process of challenge would help not just the United States, but the interests of Israel as well. The usual objection to a more conciliatory Israeli policy is that Israel possesses no margin for error—that any concession to Arabs, particularly Palestinians, will endanger the country's existence. Yet national security is not exclusively—or even principally—a military proposition. The survival of Israel does not entail simply the retention of a specified number of acres of land. In the modern era a hill or river no longer provides security from attack. As Nahum Goldmann, pioneer in the creation of Israel and first president of the World Jewish Congress, observed:

In a period when warfare is based on supersonic airplanes and missiles, the importance of borders, from a security point of view, has not disappeared but has greatly decreased.

True security arises more from the values and ethical principles, the way of life, which give a country its character. Military policy must serve the principles which the country seeks to live by and keep alive, and the security of a democracy like Israel—or the United States—is preserved more effectively through respect for the ideals of freedom and democracy than through demonstration of the force of its arms. Thus an atmosphere conducive to free discussion in the United States will also improve the scene in Israel, where opponents of government policy often declare that uncritical support provided by the United States only strengthens the hand of the hard-liners who oppose negotiations and advocate narrow military solutions to complex social and political problems.

Israel's problems are, however, unique. The layers of mutual distrust, bitterness and hatred that separate Israel from its neighbors are so numerous and deep that the parties cannot be expected to overcome these barriers without substantial outside encouragement and help. With that in mind, I introduced in several different Congresses a resolution under which the United States would guarantee Israel's pre-1967 borders within the context of a comprehensive settlement which would end the state of war, establish normal diplomatic relations among all parties, and extend the right of self-determination to the people living in territory under Israeli military occupation. I felt that this proposal, if adopted by the United States, would provide the necessary incentive to bring Israelis and Arabs together and provide the best hope for enduring peace in that region.

But U.S. policy in the Middle East must be tested first and foremost by our own national requirements. In this process, Israel must be an important consideration but not the only one. On a number of issues

United States interests are not identical to those of Israel. Considering the differences in history, region, culture, and international responsibilities, this is not surprising.

Interests and policies differ sharply, for example, on nuclear weapons policy. In order to discourage the proliferation of weapons and carry out treaty obligations, the United States provides a "nuclear umbrella" over many nations. It encourages all nations in the Middle East to ratify the Nuclear Non-Proliferation Treaty under which signatories pledge not to acquire nuclear weapons. Israel has refused to ratify the treaty and carries forward nuclear research and development in secrecy at Dimona, where experts believe it has clandestinely produced a number of nuclear warheads.

During the 1973 Arab-Israeli war, Israel attempted to shoot down a U.S. reconnaisance aircraft which overflew Dimona, even though the U.S. at the same time was ferrying arms to Israel. Admiral Thomas L. Moorer, chairman of the U.S. Joint Chiefs of Staff at the time, reports that Israel picked up the aircraft on its radar, identified it correctly as a U.S. SR-71 and "ordered its fighter planes to down it." Israel considers secrecy that important when it comes to Dimona. Fortunately, Moorer adds, "The plane was flying too high for the Israeli fighters to reach," and it returned safely.

While Israel may be convinced that it must take extreme measures to shield its nuclear facilities, such a policy is in conflict with our government's long-standing commitment to prevent nuclear proliferation in the Middle East. Nuclear weapons policy is but one of the fundamental differences which separate the United States and Israel. Other obvious ones are the occupation of territory taken by force of arms and relations with Israel's Arab neighbors.

In fashioning our policies toward the Middle East, we must recognize that we will differ with Israel on important issues while cooperating fully on others. Former Secretary of State Dean Rusk observes, "Israel has demonstrated over and over again that it is not a satellite of the United States. It is just as important for everyone to recognize that the United States is not a satellite of Israel."

Our goal must be decency, fair play, and security for all parties in the region. In particular, we must demonstrate our concern for the Palestinians in the West Bank and Gaza who have lived under Israeli military occupation for more than twenty-two years. All through our history, we have recognized self-determination as the most fundamental aspect of democracy. It is hallowed in our traditions, and on several occasions the United States has taken the ultimate step, going to war in order to promote, among other objectives, self-determination for the people in Western Europe, Korea and Vietnam. It is inconsistent, to say the least, for the United States to advocate self-determination for everyone except Palestinians. While we should not—and need not— use military force to demonstrate our concern for the Palestinians, we must avoid uncritical support of Israel's military policies which deny human rights to these people and degrade the great moral traditions of Judaism—lest our own nation's moral values suffer.

Indeed, the United States can serve Israel best by regaining its position as the respected advocate of even-handed policies that are fair to all parties. There is already a realization by many Israelis that their democracy will best be preserved, not through unquestioning support by the United States, but through thoughful analysis and free debate by all—Jews as well as non-Jews. U.S. support could go far in furthering the goal of a comprehensive Middle East peace, but it cannot be applied effectively so long as the lobby, as the voice of the U.S. Jewish community, demands that the United States give unquestioning support to the sterile military view of national security now current in Israel.

As Washington columnist Richard Cohen warned during the Israeli war in Lebanon in 1982:

The age-old dream of an Israel that incorporates the very best of Judaism, the dream that propelled kids like me out of the house with a cannister for the Jewish National Fund, is turning very slowly into a nightmare.

For the American Jewish community to defend the indefensible would only isolate it from the American community at large and transform a moral force in this country into nothing more than a lobby.

Our concern must reach beyond the damage being done to the moral force represented by our Jewish community, even though all citizens suffer as this force withers. All Americans must recognize the broader threat—the damage being done to our cherished institution of free speech as citizens fear to speak out on Middle East policy.

We could hardly do better than follow the vision—and heed the warning—which Israeli writer Amos Oz offers for his own country:

If there are people who could 'cure' us of the curse of pluralism, and open, with a strong hand and an outstretched arm, the eyes of whoever does not see the light as they do, then there is bound to be an ugly, even a dangerous, struggle. [But] if the confrontation is a matter of lobbying, with recognition of the legitimacy of differing positions and a willingness to be persuaded, then there will be fertile, creative tension.

Throughout history, the greatest threat to our society has come from within: the tendency of fearful people to trample on the rights of their fellow citizens. Abraham Lincoln warned that those who, in the name of national security, "destroy the spirit that prizes liberty as the heritage of all men in all lands everywhere" have effectively "planted the seeds of despotism around your doors." Democracy cannot function in an atmosphere in which citizens fear to speak out.

If one powerful group can succeed in inhibiting free expression on a particular topic, others inevitably will be tempted to try the same in order to advance their favorite causes. If the great institutions of education can be forced to ignore challenges to academic freedom on one subject, they will be fair game on other subjects. If a great newspaper can be pressured into letting the agent of a lobby look over the shoulders of editors as they prepare coverage of the war in Lebanon, other lobbies have a precedent on which to base similar demands. If a Catholic nun and an Episcopalian dean can be vilified as anti-Semitic because they apply religious principles to the tragedy of the Middle East, and if these same principles can be bent to political ends, religious freedom everywhere is endangered. If a lobby can force government officials into ignominious silence in one vital area of public policy, other parts of the body politic could be similarly disabled.

In short, when a lobby stifles free speech nationally on one controversial topic—the Middle East—all free speech is threatened.

Chapter 13

America's *Intifada*

When the first edition of this book appeared in 1985, I had little reason to expect that voices at the community level would soon begin a healthy discourse concerning U.S. policy in the Middle East. Heard only from scattered places in the countryside during 1986, the voices have steadily become louder and more numerous, suggesting the beginnings of America's own uprising.

The populist uprising known as the Palestinian *intifada* began in the Israeli occupied West Bank and Gaza in 1987, and, of course, it reaches far beyond America's *intifada* in violence, intensity, and human misery. The one in the occupied territories is broad, deep, and powerful—shaking Israeli society to its roots. The one in America, by contrast, is only beginning and is perhaps tentative. But, despite their vast difference in form, process, and effect, the movements continue in both places, reinforcing each other and challenging the status quo with growing strength.

In the territories occupied by Israel, the Palestinian movement responds to violations of human rights that are visible, brutal, and often lethal. After living for twenty-two years in degrading circumstances under the Israeli gun and waiting vainly for outside sympathizers to redress their grievances, Palestinians have literally taken matters into their own hands—throwing rocks and setting fire to tires in one of history's most spontaneous rebellions. They demand reform and often pay with their lives.

In the United States, the threat is to the integrity of institutions, not to life itself. The American uprising comes from citizens who, for the first time, see the dark side of Israel—radically different from past images. They see a foreign state that infiltrates and corrupts the U.S. political process, hires spies to steal classified documents, lies repeatedly to our highest officials, reneges on solemn promises, and, to an alarming degree, undercuts our national security interests to suit its own purposes. Still worse, they see an Israel that violates brutally the human rights of the Palestinians it holds in captivity.

Their concern is deepened by the spectacle of U.S. inaction amid this human tragedy, the failure of our government to respond to the agony of Palestinians in the occupied territories, where Israel—using U.S.-supplied weapons—meets the uprising with measures that leave hundreds dead, thousands maimed and homeless, and thousands more imprisoned without due process. They are shocked to find the U.S. government, universally recognized as Israel's military and financial patron, kept under the Israeli thumb as firmly as the Palestinians themselves.

These alarmed citizens conclude that Israel, long regarded as our most devoted friend and ally, at times betrays our friendship and subverts its own principles and ideals. They respond by taking in hand pens, petitions, and ballots—not rocks—and by igniting fires of public conscience.

As readers of preceding chapters must recognize, Israel, like other states, has always had shady corners it tried to hide. From its earliest days it spied on the United States, manipulated our political system, made illegal use of U.S.-supplied weapons, and often brutalized its Arab neighbors.

But until America's *intifada*, the searchlight of publicity rarely illuminated these infractions. A vigilant nationwide watch by Israel's friends in the United States stifled most critical reports and commentary, while carefully-regulated tours of the Holy Land and a torrent of publicity about Israel's positive achievements served to perpetuate the faulty vision of an unblemished, gallant outpost of human rights and democracy.

Accustomed to criticism of their own government and society but not of the Jewish state, those taking part in this U.S. uprising see for the first time an Israel with warts and scars. The elaborate public relations mechanism that for years kept only the attractive side of Israel before American eyes now finds itself overwhelmed by the sheer volume and diversity of Israeli misdeeds.

"Aid Dollars Into the Pockets of Traitors"

The first nationwide shockwave that revealed Israel in an untrustworthy posture emanated from a bizarre spy case, one of the most extraordinary in American history. Jonathan Jay Pollard, Jr., 31, a Navy counterintelligence analyst, was arrested in November 1985 for stealing classified documents as a paid spy for Israel.

"We have a moral problem," a former official of Israel's principal spy agency, Mossad, said when he learned of the arrest. "You can't take the money of the United States, and then use that money to buy information about that country." Immoral or not, that is exactly what happened.

Before the arrest, the prosecution of Israeli espionage had been taboo at the Federal Bureau of Investigation despite long-standing evidence that placed other federal employees under suspicion. Like officials at the State Department, where a senior diplomat describes as "fantastic" the level of spying for Israel, FBI officials habitually chose to look the other way, viewing pro-Israel political influence as great enough to make attempted prosecution an exercise in futility.

The FBI "knew of at least a dozen incidents in which American officials transferred classified information to the Israelis," according to Raymond W. Wannal, Jr., a former assistant director of the FBI. None was prosecuted. The files gathered dust.

John Davitt, a career official and former chief of the Justice Department's internal security section, says: "When the Pollard case broke, the general media and public perception was that this was the first time this had ever happened. No, that's not true at all." He adds that, during his tenure, only the Soviet Union did more spying in the United States than Israel.

Pollard's thievery, however, was so gross and frequent it could not be ignored. On several occasions he took large boxes of classified documents from the Pentagon, abusing flagrantly his "courier" clearance.

In the wake of Pollard's arrest, William Safire, a columnist who rarely criticizes Israel, warned, "The stark fact is that if the espionage charges hold up in court, American aid dollars will have been channeled by Israel into the pockets of American traitors. That will blow up, not over."

Supporting this forecast is the volume of publicity the case continues to produce. From the day of his arrest until this writing, aspects of the scandal have appeared frequently in nationwide headlines and newscasts.

As it came to light, the Pollard case had all the trappings of a fiction thriller—free luxury trips to faraway places, expensive gifts for the spy's wife, shady spymasters who handled the cash and stolen documents, dashes to elude surveillance teams, and finally arrest just steps away from political asylum—in the Israeli embassy.

The spy deal was cut in the summer of 1984 when Pollard, an ardent Zionist, met Aviem Sella, an Israeli aviation hero who doubled in espionage. He promised Sella military secrets in return for $1,500 a month compensation. The process began with a flourish. Pollard and his wife, Anne, 26, traveled first class to Paris for a luxury holiday and meetings with Sella, as well as with Rafael Eitan, the famous Israeli Nazi-hunter and spymaster who gave the Pollards $10,000 to cover expenses. Anne received a sapphire ring worth $7,000 from their hosts. They were also introduced to Joseph Yagur, a member of the Israeli embassy staff in

Washington who subsequently became Pollard's main "handler."

Returning to Washington, Pollard stole documents from U.S. military files about three times a week and delivered them for copying to either Yagur or Irit Erb, another embassy employee.

The next spring, the Pollards enjoyed another $10,000 luxury trip— this time to Israel—where Jonathan received an Israeli passport under a new name, a raise in pay to $2,500 a month, and a promise that the pay would continue for the next nine years. He was informed that a Swiss bank account had been established in his name.

Six months later—just over a year after the espionage began—the operation fell apart. FBI agents stopped Pollard for questioning in the parking lot near his Washington work station. Pollard broke away long enough to telephone his wife and, with the code word "cactus," warned her to remove all stolen documents from their apartment. While he returned for further questioning by the agents, Anne gathered remaining papers and took them in a suitcase to Erb's residence.

Shaken by the interview, Pollard asked Yagur for guidance. He suggested that the Pollards "lay low" for awhile, elude their FBI surveillance, and then find political asylum at the Israeli embassy. On November 21, 1985, they made the break but failed to shake their surveillance. They were refused asylum just inside the embassy gates and arrested as they left the property. Meanwhile, Yagur and Erb left for Israel.

After Pollard's arrest, embarrassed Israeli officials apologized for the spying. They denounced it as an unauthorized "rogue" operation unknown by anyone at cabinet level, and offered full cooperation in a U.S. investigation. They pledged that "those responsible will be brought to account."

Secretary of State George Shultz warmly accepted the apology, and the State Department quickly attempted a cover-up. Shultz sent a team headed by legal adviser Abraham Sofaer, an ardent Zionist who maintains a home in Israel, on a brief investigation there. Returning, Sofaer falsely reported that Israel had provided "full access" to all persons with knowledge of the facts. Within a month of the arrest, the department announced that Israel had returned all stolen documents and that the United States had resumed sharing intelligence with Israel "in all fields." The "matter," for the State Department, was now closed.

"More Damage Than Terrorists Could Dream Of"

Elsewhere, the "matter" was far from closed.

At the Justice Department, U.S. Attorney Joseph E. diGenova pressed the prosecution vigorously, and the case remained in the headlines for more than three years, giving the American people frequent reason to question Israeli cooperation and reliability. For example, the Pollard spy ring, far from being a "rogue" operation, reported to the highest levels of the Israeli government, including the Defense Ministry.

The "return" of stolen documents was a mockery. Of the thousands copied by the Pollards, Israel bothered to return only 163 and, given its appetite for top secrets, surely retained extra copies of these as well.

Instead of cooperating, Israel stonewalled attempts by U.S. Justice Department to investigate the spy ring, refusing to permit key officials to be interviewed either in the United States or Israel. One U.S. official, reflecting on the Sofaer mission, said, "The question is whether we got the truth. Quite frankly we didn't."

The two Israelis who had the most prominent roles in the spy episode were "brought to account" by the Israeli government in a curious way. Each won higher position.

Colonel Aviem Sella, identified by Pollard as his first principal "handler" and later indicted by a U.S. court for complicity with Pollard, was later promoted to commander of Israel's Tel Nof air base, usually the last rung in the command ladder before becoming air force commander. As a further reward, Israel refused to permit Sella to return to the United States for prosecution. Rafael Eitan, the man who headed the spy program, received similar "punishment"—appointment as the chief executive officer of Israel's largest state-owned company.

The promotions inspired embarrassing headlines and a delegation of Jews flew to Israel, urging the government to rescind the decisions. In the face of these protests, Sella resigned as air base commander but later quietly assumed a posh job at Electro-Optic, a major defense corporation. When they learned of this latest salute to Sella, the outraged editors of *Defense News*, a respected publication, called for a $200 million cut in Israeli aid each year until the U.S. government has recovered the full cost of the Sella-Pollard espionage.

The case returned to prime news coverage on June 4, 1986, when Jonathan Pollard, after engaging in extensive plea-bargaining interviews, pleaded guilty to conspiring to provide U.S. military secrets to the Israelis, and Anne to conspiring to receive and embezzle government property.

In return for Jonathan Pollard's cooperation, the prosecution did not ask for a life sentence, but the judge, Aubrey Robinson, impressed by a forty-six-page memorandum from Secretary of Defense Caspar Weinberger, selected that punishment nonetheless. He sentenced Anne Pollard to five years.

Weinberger wrote that the thievery caused "substantial and irrevocable harm," risking the lives of U.S. agents and creating the danger that "U.S. combat forces, wherever they are deployed in the world, could

be unacceptably endangered through successful exploitation of this data."
He added that Pollard had "both damaged and destroyed policies and
national assets which have taken many years, great effort, and enormous
national resources to secure."

In the wake of sentencing, Israel doubled Pollard's pay. The same
government that earlier denounced the affair as an unauthorized "rogue"
operation now deposits in Pollard's bank account $5,000 each month,
assuring the Pollards a comfortable life in Israel if he is released for good
behavior.

The imprisonment of the Pollards, U.S. officials believe, has not
ended Israeli espionage in the United States. Most of the secret information, as in the past, is furnished by U.S. citizens without compensation.
One official complains, "Mossad is the most active foreign intelligence
service on U.S. soil."

For years Israel has been able to learn virtually every secret about
U.S. foreign policy in the Middle East. Reporter Charles Babcock of
the *Washington Post*, basing his estimate on a 1979 CIA report and recent
interviews with more than two dozen current or former U.S. intelligence
officials, concludes, "This remarkable intelligence harvest is provided
largely, not by paid agents, but by an unofficial network of sympathetic
American officials who work in the Pentagon, State Department, congressional offices, the National Security Council, and even the U.S. intelligence agencies."

Meanwhile, Pollard became a cause celebre in both the United States
and Israel, where public protests against his sentence were organized
and legal defense funds raised. These funds were only a pittance, as the
Israeli government provided most of the $200,000 that American law-
yers for the two Pollards collected.

Alan Dershowitz, a Harvard professor and an attorney for Pollard,
cited Weinberger's assessment of U.S. security damage as the main reason
why the court ordered a life sentence, which Dershowitz considered excessive, and challenged Weinberger to prove that Pollard's thievery actually harmed U.S. security.

It was a limp challenge, because the public record already disclosed
overwhelming evidence of damage. Items stolen by Pollard included photographs of security-related installations taken by high-flying U.S. surveillance planes, sensitive data on laser technology and U.S. weapons,
secret information on naval forces, mines, and port facilities in the Middle East, and the text of a large handbook nicknamed the "bible," which
contained strategies the U.S. Navy would use if attacked. The stolen documents were voluminous enough, the court was told, to fill a box six by
six by ten feet in dimension.

Israel made quick use of the secrets. Information provided by Pollard enabled Israeli warplanes to evade U.S. naval and air surveillance in the Mediterranean during their October 1985 air strike against the Tunis headquarters of the Palestine Liberation Organization. The precision-like attack, first dismissed by President Ronald Reagan as "legitimate self-defense" but later denounced by other administration officials, left nearly one hundred dead, mostly Tunisian civilians, and the PLO headquarters in shambles.

The gravest harm to U.S. interests occurred when the Soviet Union acquired documents stolen by Pollard, perhaps all of them. The Soviets acquired the data through two separate secret channels. Israel opened one of them directly, offering U.S. secrets in an attempt to influence Moscow's policy on Jewish emigration. Using some of these same contacts, the KGB, Moscow's intelligence service, opened the other channel without the knowledge of Israeli leadership, establishing a spy network within Mossad.

These shocking revelations came in a news report distributed by United Press International on December 13, 1987. The author, Richard Sale, reported that the Soviet Union had breached Israeli intelligence and that information stolen by Pollard "was traded to the Soviets in return for promises to increase emigration of Soviet Jews to Israel." A State Department source told Sale, "It began as a straight data-for-people deal," but through it the Soviets "penetrated the Israeli defense establishment at a high level."

This new scandal belied Pollard's excuse that, in helping Israel, he did not hurt the United States. U.S. intelligence sources said stolen documents reaching Moscow by this route included "sensitive U.S. weapons technology and strategic information about the defense forces of Turkey, Pakistan, and moderate Arab countries, including Saudi Arabia."

Soviet acquisition of documents stolen by Pollard was discussed during an urgent review of the scandal by CIA, FBI, and other U.S. intelligence officials: "One of the guys was commenting that if Pollard had stolen the stuff, at least it was going to a U.S. ally, but a CIA guy spoke up and said that if Mossad was involved it meant that copies of everything were going to [the KGB's] Moscow center."

The Israel-Moscow spy link enabled "highly placed" Soviet "moles" to penetrate Mossad, the most serious blow to Israeli intelligence in twenty years. One U.S. intelligence analyst fixed the blame on "right-wing Jews" in Israel. U.S. agents first learned of the Israeli-Soviet spy link when information stolen by Pollard was "traced to the Eastern bloc."

The reported diversion of stolen documents to Moscow made headlines in nine newspapers but competing news services and television networks ignored it. The *New York Times* and the *Washington Post* printed not a word.

In another episode, Israel used data stolen by Pollard as the basis for a proposed military strike. Alarmed by the possibility that Pakistan might be building its own nuclear weapons—a concern shared by India—and armed with satellite photographs stolen by Pollard that showed a secret nuclear facility, Israel officials approached New Delhi in June 1985 with a daring plan. They urged that the two governments destroy the facility in a joint air attack. India refused.

The Pollard case continued to make headlines. In April 1988, Israel refused to let Howard Katz visit the United States for questioning. In June, two committees of the Israeli parliament, previously citing "lies, whitewash, and contradictions," closed their official report on the Pollard affair by blaming senior officials of both Labor and Likud parties but recommending no action.

From all this, columnist Safire concludes, "The Pollards in America, and their spymasters in Israel, have done more damage to their respective countries than any terrorists could dream of doing."

Safire's assessment is not overdrawn. The damage to the United States is incalculable in security terms, causing consternation in many friendly capitals, especially in Arab states, which must now assume that both Israel and the Soviet Union have all the military information useful to them that is possessed by the United States.

CIA officials agonize over the possibility that Pollard may have compromised the way the United States gathers intelligence and enabled Israel to crack secret U.S. codes.

The damage to Israel, too, is incalculable. As the American people learn the awesome extent of damage—especially the transfer of highly sensitive data directly to the Kremlin—they inevitably will rethink America's Israeli connection. Citizens, Jewish and non-Jewish alike, who, in their innocence, believed the Jewish state to be honest, open, and trustworthy in all its U.S. dealings are already expressing their outrage.

"You Can't Let Jews Be Tried By Gentiles"

Pollard's accomplices are not the only people the government of Israel shields from prosecution for crimes committed in the United States. Headlines in June and July 1988 reported that Robert S. Manning, 36, a Los Angeles-born member of the Jewish Defense League who is wanted in connection with a 1980 mail bomb murder of a California woman, is also a prime suspect in the October 1985 bombing that killed Alex M. Odeh, 41, who was employed part-time as the west coast director of the American-Arab Anti-Discrimination Committee.

Odeh, a quiet, scholarly father of three young children and a naturalized citizen born in Palestine, became a bomb victim twelve hours after he praised PLO chairman Yasser Arafat as a "man of peace" during an evening interview on a Los Angeles television news program. During the program he deplored the killing of Leon Klinghoffer, brutally murdered the day before aboard the Achille Lauro cruise ship in the Mediterranean. But Odeh asserted, "The media has mistakenly linked the (Klinghoffer murder) with the PLO."

When Odeh opened the door of the committee office the next morning, he triggered a blast that nearly severed his body and ripped through the office suite. In a similar occurrence earlier in 1985, two policemen were critically injured trying to defuse a bomb left at the door of the organization's Boston office. Manning was also suspected in that bombing.

Manning, a self-styled demolition expert, is also wanted in connection with two bombings aimed at men suspected as former Nazis. Along with three other suspects in the Odeh murder, he now lives in Kiriat Arba, a Jewish settlement in Israeli-occupied West Bank territory where followers of Rabbi Meir Kahane congregate. Kahane is a founder of the U.S. Jewish Defense League and heads Israel's anti-Arab Kach party, a group so radical it could not receive permission to field a slate of candidates in Israel's November 1988 general election.

Kahane's party, however, retains great political strength. Its influence, and that of other right-wing forces in Israel, is one reason that Manning and his cohorts have not been arrested. Many Israelis, including some of Kahane's supporters, view Jews who kill PLO supporters as heroes, not criminals. They try to frustrate the prosecution of Israelis who engage in anti-Arab crime. For example, when twenty-eight Gush Emunim terrorists were convicted in 1985 of bomb and grenade attacks against the West Bank Arabs, protests generated by right-wing elements were so heavy that all but seven have since been set free.

This type of pressure is so great that Israel's officials refuse to cooperate with the FBI's long-standing effort to secure telephone and travel records so that the agency can keep track of the movement of JDL members like Manning to and from the United States. In fact, despite his indictment in the United States, Manning served recently in the Israeli Defense Forces as an active duty reservist near Nablus in the occupied West Bank. The California prosecutor, Assistant U.S. Attorney Nancy Stock, is not optimistic about securing Manning's extradition, because no one has been extradited from Israel for thirty-two years. She says, simply, "The record speaks for itself."

Another fugitive, Richard K. Smyth, owner of Milco International, indicted in California for illegally exporting nuclear triggering devices to Israel, jumped bail in 1985 and, after rumors of kidnapping and murder, turned up in Israel.

A senior Israeli official explains, "There's a sort of feeling here that you can't hand a Jew over to be tried by Gentiles. It has to do with 2,000 years of Jewish history, of Jewish persecution at the hands of Gentiles."

"Zone of Danger" for "Enemies of Israel"

Public relations experts who specialize in protecting Israel's image in the United States have a busy life.

In December 1985, FBI Director William H. Webster, noting Odeh's murder, warned that Arab Americans had entered a "zone of danger" and were targets of violence by groups seeking to harm "enemies of Israel." In an annual report three years later, the Justice Department reported 160 episodes of violence or harassment of Arab Americans. Concerning attacks on Arab-American groups, Mordechai Levy, who heads the Jewish Defense Organization, a group denounced by other Jewish organizations, adds a militant note, "We aren't claiming credit, but it couldn't happen to better people, more deserving people." Former Senator James G. Abourezk, national chairman of the American-Arab Anti-Discrimination Committee, comments, "The authorities are finally beginning to realize that we've been brought into a war situation against our will."

Examples of some recent Israeli "image" problems:

• Despite public protests, Maj. Gen. Amos Yaron, reprimanded and stripped of command for his role in the 1982 massacres that left over eight hundred dead in Palestinian camps in Beirut, was welcomed to Washington four years later as Israeli's new military attache. Yaron, the senior Israeli officer on the scene at Sabra and Shatila, had failed to stop the commander of Lebanese Christian Phalangist forces from ordering the massacre of women and children in the camps.

• In July 1986, network television news reported that U.S. Customs Service and Justice Department officials were investigating charges that Israel illegally smuggled U.S. technology to build cluster bombs, which, when detonated, release hundreds of small explosives. The United States has prohibited the export of these bombs since 1982, when Israel violated agreements by using them against civilians during its invasion of Lebanon. The Reagan administration apologized for the publicity surrounding the allegations, and, as one of its last acts, resumed shipments of the bombs to Israel in late 1988.

• Americans watched with astonishment the treatment Israel accorded its citizen, Mordechai Vanunu, a nuclear technician who moved to

England and furnished classified information about Israel's nuclear facilities to the *London Times*.

The Mossad used female attraction to lure Vanunu from London to Rome, then abducted him from a Rome street and hustled him to Israel for trial in secret. While being hauled off in a Jerusalem van, Vanunu provided a bizarre finale to the drama by displaying to reporters through a van window a message written on the palm of his hand, "kidnapped in Rome." He received an eighteen-month sentence for divulging state secrets.

For defenders of Israel, a greater—and graver—public relations challenge lay ahead.

"Shoot on Sight"

Just as the Pollard spy scandal, which damaged the U.S. image of Israel as nothing before in history, receded from the headlines and evening newscasts, the American people began to receive daily glimpses of even more shocking Israeli behavior. This time the offensive conduct was in response to a popular uprising that has become historic in its spontaneity and sustained power.

Beginning in December 1987, Palestinians, principally women and young people, began expressing their opposition to Israel's control over their lives in the West Bank and Gaza by pelting stones at the occupying forces. The Israeli occupation had entered its twenty-first year with no end in sight. Nearly unanimous in their loyalty to the Palestine Liberation Organization and its leader, Yasser Arafat—long outlawed by Israel—and weary of waiting for outsiders to address their grievances, the protesters took to the streets, harassing military personnel with stones and blocking streets with piles of burning tires.

The grievances that produced the uprising are overwhelming. Life for 1.7 million Palestinians is rigidly controlled—even the planting of a tree or the digging of a well requires an Israeli permit—and the thousands of Palestinians who have jobs in Israel, most of them menial, must return each night to their homes in the occupied territories. Israel has permitted no elections there since 1976, and today every community except Bethlehem is governed by a mayor chosen by Israeli authorities.

Although they have not enjoyed independent statehood for centuries—they were successively under Ottoman, British and Jordanian control—Palestinians now find Israel threatening all hope for national identity.

The threat comes from relentless policies that make almost every aspect of Palestinian life miserable. Especially damaging is the Israeli program of constructing Jewish settlements at strategic points scattered throughout the West Bank and Gaza, a process that began within months after Israel conquered the territories in the June 1967 war. These settlements keep expanding in number and size, encompassing more and more arable land, and shrinking the space on which the growing population of Palestinians must struggle for existence. Efforts by the world community, led by the United States, to persuade Israel to return conquered Arab territory in exchange for peace agreements, have succeeded only in the Sinai, a desert area returned to Egypt under the Camp David Accords.

The Likud party, which has dominated Israeli politics since 1977 and negotiated the deal with Egypt, has defiantly opposed any land-for-peace arrangement with the Palestinians, contending that the West Bank and Gaza historically belong to Israel and are not subject to bargaining. Leaders of the party, including Prime Minister Yitzhak Shamir, were prominent in acts of terrorism against Arabs during the early days of Israeli statehood. These included the massacre of Deir Yassin village and the bombing of the King David Hotel. Even its present-day partner in the governing coalition, the Labor party, talks less and less in favor of land-for-peace, because each new settlement built in the occupied territories is seen as a step toward ultimate annexation.

The settlements have become flashpoints of controversy. Populated by heavily-armed militants, the settlements now total 110 in the West Bank, encompass 55 percent of the land area, control 70 percent of the water resources and have an aggregate population of 67,000. Nearly a million Palestinians live on the remaining 45 percent of the land with only 30 percent of the water. Even more painful is the situation in Gaza, one of the world's most heavily populated areas, where 2,500 Jews live in settlements that occupy 35 percent of the land, while 650,000 Palestinians are crowded into the remainder. Israel plans to build eight additional "flashpoints" in the near future, and the U.S. government, although opposed to the plan and possessing ample leverage over Israel, does not force the issue. When Israel went ahead in March 1989 with the first of the new settlements, the Bush administration uttered barely a word.

In its own powerful way, the uprising forces the issue—not just the question of new settlements but harmful facets of military occupation, posing an unexpected challenge that the Israeli military machine—one of the world's strongest—has been unable to master.

Protests grow in intensity as military measures become more harsh. In 1988, Israeli Defense Minister Yitzhak Rabin authorized his troops to arrest and imprison Palestinians for up to six months without due process in any form, and prisons soon bulged with over four thousand Palestinians. He announced a policy of "force, might, and beatings" to put down the uprising. This gave Israeli troops authority to club unarmed civilians even to the point of fracturing bones, and prison officials, in clear violation of international convention, began routine beatings of those in prison. Three months later, a team of U.S. physicians reported that several thousand Palestinians had suffered bone fractures.

In the wake of sporadic fires, Israeli civilians were authorized to "shoot on sight" anyone seen carrying a fire bomb.

The brutality of the repression is such that a growing number of Israeli soldiers refuse to serve and mass demonstrations within Israel are commonplace. In May 1988, American Ambassador Thomas Pickering notified Israel that the United States is "deeply opposed" to Israel's "harsh measures," including "deportations, administrative detentions, and the destruction or sealing of houses . . . without due process," but the diplomat served no ultimatums or even warnings. In July, 350 Israeli scientists, academics, and retired generals, protesting the violation of Palestinian human rights and warning that these violations will damage Israel's principles and idealism, publicly urged their government to withdraw from the occupied territories.

The most significant result of the uprising, from the standpoint of the American people, is its intense and sustained coverage by television networks. For more than two decades, the Palestinians had experienced repeated humiliations, even torture, but news of these harsh measures rarely received attention in the U.S. media. Now, reports of Israeli brutality, including a running total of killings, have become daily fare. Television viewers see homes of suspected protesters blown up, young Palestinians beaten, and women and children dragged off to prison.

For the first four months of the uprising—until Israeli authorities kept journalists from areas of greatest protest—the coverage was close up and vivid. One unforgettable sequence, filmed by a CBS cameraman hidden inside a building, showed two Israeli soldiers using rocks to engage in a prolonged beating of a young Palestinian, finally fracturing one of his arms. Broadcast worldwide, the episode probably made the greatest impact of any single event. When Palestinians in Gaza killed a soldier by dropping a concrete block on his head, Israeli troops fractured the skull of a six-year-old girl and shot to death a twenty-year-old man.

Israel's use of clubs, tear gas, bulldozers, gunfire, indiscriminate arrests, deportations, curfews, closing of schools and universities, and even torture seems to quicken, not quell, the spirit of the protesters.

With all its horror and sacrifice, the uprising has brought a profound unity and self-confidence to families in the occupied territories. Women and children have new respect, as they stand with adult males on the ramparts of resistance and often lead the charge against offending Israelis.

A Quaker Palestinian who helps young people suffering from stress in Gaza, reports, "Women now have equal rights. Period." She witnessed an episode in which a group of unarmed women overwhelmed two soldiers until a nine-year-old Palestinian they were beating could escape. Visiting a ten-year-old recovering in a hospital from stomach wounds inflicted by a plastic bullet, she was shocked by the intensity of his response when she asked, "Could I look at your wound?" Pointing first to his stomach, then to a shoulder wound sustained in an earlier altercation with Israeli troops, his face beamed with pride as he asked eagerly, "Which one?"

"Troops Used Clubs to Break Limbs"

In the wake of mounting international criticism, Israel nonetheless employed still tougher measures. Rabin authorized the use of plastic bullets in situations that are not life-threatening, making gunfire more prevalent and harmful, although the army acknowledged later that the bullets, far from being non-lethal, caused forty-seven deaths during the first four months of their use. Responding to complaints about killing, blindness, and other injuries from the plastic ammunition, Rabin said, "The rioters are suffering more casualties. That is precisely our aim."

Some behavior is barbaric. The cameras did not record a near-tragedy in which four Palestinians, deliberately buried alive by an Israeli-manned bulldozer, miraculously survived when dug out by neighbors. Meanwhile, leaders of the uprising have dealt harshly with those suspected of disloyalty. Thirteen Palestinians accused of conspiring with Israeli authorities have been murdered.

Nor do journalists escape Israeli-inflicted violence. Bob Slater of *Time* magazine, chairman of the Israeli foreign press association, reported more than one hundred attacks on foreign journalists during the first four months of the uprising.

Here and there are touches of humor: the owner of a Nablus ice cream shop, forced by Israeli soldiers to open for business in the winter, remonstrated, "But nobody here buys ice cream in the winter," and the NBC commentator who remarked, "Here you see Israel's new open door policy," as the news film showed an Israeli truck using chains to break open the locked shutters of a Palestinian shop.

Otherwise, it is grim business. Although journalists are now kept from direct coverage of protest areas, news of the violence filters out, partly from U.S. citizens who visit the occupied territories. Rev. John B. Jamison, returning to his Springfield, Illinois, Methodist pastorate, after living four weeks in a village near Bethlehem, says, "I find that I cannot keep silent. I have to speak out." Similar responses come from

Americans who have traveled to the scene of the uprising under the sponsorship of the American-Arab Anti-Discrimination Committee.

America's media coverage of the uprising has inspired widespread editorial criticism of Israeli brutality, letters to editors, and even a few complaints from Capitol Hill, where comments critical of Israel are almost unknown. In March 1988, over two thousand Arab Americans marched in protest past the White House, while a few blocks away, in a rare public sign of sympathy for Israel, about three hundred Jews chanted outside the Washington offices of ABC, expressing their resentment over the network's vivid coverage of the uprising.

In April 1988, Ted Koppel, in an unprecedented television event, broadcast his popular "Nightline" program live from Jerusalem in a week-long series devoted entirely to the uprising. The series included filmed history and discussion, presented from both Israeli and Arab viewpoints. The climaxing program featured a debate between panels of Israelis and Palestinians separated by a low wall—described by *Washington Jewish Week* as "a town hall meeting of people who don't recognize each other's existence." According to *Washington Report on Middle East Affairs*, the series "set a new high-water mark in balanced U.S. media coverage of this divisive half-century-old dispute, which so many mainstream American editors and commentators have just wished away." It enabled many Americans to consider the Arab-Israeli dispute for the first time in an arena of civil discourse.

King Hussein of Jordan gave the uprising new importance in July 1988 and focused its political objectives when he abandoned all Jordanian claims to the West Bank and announced his support for Palestinian statehood. This eliminated from the diplomatic scene the "Jordanian option," a proposal to solve the Palestinian problem by establishing a confederal link between Amman and the West Bank—a possibility that United States and Israeli officials had mentioned frequently and hopefully.

The American response to Israel's repression reached a powerful and surprising new level when, shortly after the inauguration of President George Bush, the State Department, in its sharpest criticism ever, devoted twenty-one pages of its annual worldwide report to Israeli human rights violations. In sharp contrast to the mild references of previous years, the report used plain language: 366 Palestinians killed; including 13 by beating and 4 from tear gas; over 20,000 wounded, and "about 10,000" imprisoned; 36 deported in violation of the Fourth Geneva Convention. Eleven Israelis have been killed and 1,100 others injured in the course of the uprising. These figures represent the victims in just one year.

The report charged Israel with "forcing prisoners to remain in one position for prolonged periods, hooding, sleep deprivation, and cold showers," practices employed to elicit "false confessions" as the basis for lengthy prison terms. "There were five cases in 1988 in which unarmed Palestinians in detention died under questionable circumstances or were clearly killed by the detaining officials."

"Troops used clubs to break limbs and beat Palestinians who were not directly involved in disturbances or resisting arrest," the report went on. "Soldiers turned many people out of their homes at night, making them stand for hours . . . At least 154 houses of Arabs were demolished or sealed . . . prior to trial and conviction."

In an exceptional reference, the report said that some human rights violations occur in Israel itself, "where Arab citizens of Israel, who constitute 17 percent of the population, do not share fully in the rights granted to, or the duties levied on, Jewish Israeli citizens."

Although congressional reaction consisted mainly of complaints that the State Department did not fully "understand" Israel's problems, two key committee chairmen spoke up. Senator Patrick Leahy (D-VT) and Representative David Obey (D-WI) warned that foreign aid might be jeopardized if Israel's maltreatment of Palestinians continues.

Copley newspapers joined a nationwide chorus of editorial criticism with these words, "Until Israel figures out how to defuse the Palestinian unrest in ways consistent with the Jewish state's democratic values and traditions, it will risk losing far more than just the uprising." Gerald G. Toy, a retired actuary in Portland, Oregon, puts it bluntly, "Israel is giving Jews a bad name."

"The Deadly Silence Has Ended"

Meanwhile, other powerful, historic currents added force to the American tide of sympathy for Palestinian statehood. An unprecedented political movement conceived and organized early in 1988 by Dr. James Zogby, a street-smart Arab-American activist and articulate former univer-sity professor, altered the national political landscape as it moved slowly but surely through the Democratic presidential nominating process.

It reached national media attention in February when more than two hundred Democratic party caucuses in Iowa, inspired mainly by supporters of the presidential candidacy of the Rev. Jesse Jackson, approved resolutions backing self-determination for Palestinians. These resolutions did not mention statehood, but declared the right of people living in the occupied territories to decide their political future without outside interference. Similar resolutions were soon approved by more than one hundred caucuses in Texas.

The Zogby forces continued their successes at the state level, where the more precise goal of statehood was endorsed by Democratic party conventions in Washington, Vermont, Maine, Oregon, New Mexico, and Illinois. Resolutions supporting self-determination won approval in Texas, Minnesota, and Iowa.

In Illinois, the pro-Palestinian forces won mainly by catching establishment Democrats asleep. Two hundred pro-Jackson delegates from Chicago converged unexpectedly on Springfield, the state capital, where they surprised party regulars at the convention by swiftly winning approval of a resolution endorsing "the rights of Palestinians to safety, self-determination, and an independent state," as well as Israel's right to live within secure borders. Approval occurred so late in the deliberations that pro-Israel forces from north Chicago who normally control party positions on Middle East questions had no time to counterattack. But that did not end their efforts.

With the convention adjourned, State Senator Vincent Demuzio, Democratic state chairman, responded to pressure from outraged Jewish delegates by charging Jackson supporters with "irresponsibility" and warning that the resolution would threaten Democratic success by dividing the party. In desperation, he considered taking an informal poll by telephone, through which the party's state central committee could somehow delete the resolution from the platform, but, confronted with its obvious illegality, dropped the scheme. Instead, the party made no reference to the offensive resolution in its annals. The record of its approval survived only in newspaper accounts of the proceedings.

Zogby moved the statehood issue to national center-stage in Atlanta in June 1988. There he gained unprecedented official approval for the question of Palestinian statehood to be debated before the Democratic platform committee and then, the next month, before the full convention, after agreeing, on each occasion, that he would not press the issue beyond a voice vote. *The Washington Jewish Week* called the debate "quietly historic." It was historic but not quiet. For the first time in history, the emotion-packed question of Palestinian statehood, a theme anathema to most Zionists, became the topic of open debate at a national gathering of a major U.S. political party.

In televised deliberations before the platform committee, Zogby noted "a greater awareness and sensitivity in this country on the question of Palestinian rights." When the issue reached the convention floor, Zogby and Congressman Mervyn Dymally of California, speaking for Palestinian statehood, squared off against Senator Daniel Inouye of Hawaii and Congressman Charles E. Shumer of New York before the convention hall audience dominated by delegates waving pro-Palestinian posters. An acrimonious debate raged for twenty minutes, with full coverage by all television networks creating an enormous audience, probably the largest ever to hear a discussion of Palestinian rights. Inouye rejected the Palestinian resolution as "an enormous kick in the teeth of American interests in that part of the world." When Shumer tried to dismiss Zogby's arguments as "clever but duplicitous," booing became so loud that Speaker Jim Wright, chairing the convention, had to bang the gavel for order. Dymally declared, "I am proud of this debate. This is history. Jesse Jackson and his call for peace and security can be heard."

Zogby summed up, "The deadly silence on Palestinian rights has ended. Peace in the Middle East is too important to be left without a principled debate. What is so clear today is that Israeli peace and security and Palestinian peace and security are interdependent." Denouncing Israel's treatment of Palestinians, Zogby declared to a wildly cheering convention hall, "We are already winning. We don't need a vote today."

Pro-Palestinian delegates rejoiced, citing the debate itself as a significant victory. Salam Al-Maryati, a member of the California delegation staff, looking over the vast sea of Palestinian posters, declared, "It looks like Palestine for president!" Fifteen hundred of the 5,500 delegates signed a pro-statehood petition circulated on the convention floor, and a network-sponsored poll showed that a majority of the delegates would approve Palestinian statehood if the vote were secret. Pro-Israel delegates blamed the support on "the Palestinian uprising's effect on public opinion"—as though that isn't what is supposed to happen in a democracy.

The Jewish Journal of Los Angeles saw challenges still ahead: "There is a growing sense in political circles that the pro-Israel forces were outgeneraled by Jim Zogby," and predicted that Zogby, "not one to rest on his laurels," will soon "launch a nationwide campaign to generate state and local resolutions similar to the defeated platform plank."

Zogby continues his political activism for Palestinian statehood and other Arab-related issues, as executive director of the Arab American Institute, a Washington-based group that encourages citizens of Arab ancestry, Republicans and Democrats alike, to engage in partisan activity. One of his achievements is the formation of Democrats for Middle East Peace, which consists of over one hundred Arab Americans and Jewish Americans who served as delegates, alternates, and standing committee members at the 1988 Democratic national convention.

Palestinian statehood showed remarkable support in two referendums on election day, November 8, 1988. In the communities of Cambridge and Newton, Massachusetts, voters approved, 53 to 47 percent, a proposition supporting both self-determination and statehood for Palestinians and an end to U.S. financial support for Israel's occupation of the West Bank and Gaza. In San Francisco, statehood won the support of one-third of the voters.

"The Ball Is in the American Court"

As the post-convention presidential campaign—totally lackluster on the Arab-Israel conflict—came to a close in November 1988, the Palestine Liberation Organization brought to top billing internationally the statehood issue that the Jackson forces had advanced months earlier on the U.S. domestic scene. A series of surprising developments won broad new support for the Palestinian cause and diminished, perhaps demolished, the negative stereotype that has long handicapped the PLO cause in the United States.

In Algiers, executive committee chairman Yasser Arafat persuaded the Palestine National Council—the PLO's congress—to take two historic, controversial steps: first, to endorse United Nations resolutions 242 and 338 as the basis for peace negotiations and, second, to declare the existence of a Palestinian state encompassing the occupied territories of the West Bank and Gaza.

These decisions proclaim PLO acceptance of a new Palestinian state side-by-side and at peace with Israel and the abandonment of the organization's long-standing commitment to "one democratic state for all of Palestine," in which Israel would cease to exist.

The decisions offer hope for better days to both the Palestinians in the uprising and their Israeli masters. The statehood proclamation provides a practical, worthy political objective behind which those engaged in the Palestinian *intifada* can rally and, equally important, the promise to the Israelis that the turmoil, so threatening to Jewish values and traditions, can be ended without sacrificing Israel itself.

They provide a powerful impetus, as well, to the uprising in America, where many citizens sympathetic to Palestinian grievances have long been troubled by the PLO's insistence that Israel must disappear when the new Palestine comes into being. Support for the survival of Israel is so pervasive in the United States, that, forced to choose between Israel and a new Palestine, most Americans—including those deeply supportive of Palestinian rights—would choose Israel. Actually, in recent years the PLO has finessed this grim choice, approving at Palestine National Council meetings several resolutions that show clear support for a two-state solution, while remaining ambiguous at other times.

The Algiers resolutions, of course, do not stop criticism of Arafat, Palestine's new president. Critics question his ability to control his own members, citing occasional cross-border attacks on Israel and other "terrorism." These episodes reflect the wide assortment of splinter groups within the PLO organization—some strongly opposed to the Palestine National Council's decisions—and the dispersal of the Palestinian population throughout the Middle East.

In making his announcement in Algiers, Arafat declared, "Our political declaration contains moderation, flexibility, and realism, which the West has been urging us to show. We feel now that the ball is in the American court."

A few weeks later, the U.S. Secretary of State hit the ball back in another development of historic importance that improved the PLO's public standing in the United States. It occurred just a few days before the close of Ronald Reagan's presidency. After a dismal December, during which Secretary of State George Shultz, acting against the advice of most of his advisers, prohibited Yasser Arafat from addressing the United Nations in New York, Shultz gave in to mounting international pressure. He shocked the world by announcing that the United States would begin direct talks with PLO officials.

The decision came as a surprise even to the American-Israel Public Affairs Committee, Israel's powerful lobby in Washington, an organization that traditionally not only keeps close tab on all Middle East developments but normally has a big voice in making U.S. policy in that region. It learned of the decision only an hour before Shultz's public announcement.

Quiet but effective work by Egyptian President Hosni Mubarak made the difference. On the telephone frequently with Arafat and Shultz during the tense weeks following the Algiers declaration, he persuaded each to accept changes in wording that finally produced the U.S. decision to talk with PLO representatives. Although protesting that he had already met every requirement, Arafat gave a final, convincing clarification in a press conference in Stockholm. The respected New York attorney Rita Hauser, prominent in the work of the American Jewish Committee, sat at Arafat's side and imparted a unique Jewish respectability to his position.

The U.S. decision to open direct talks and the PLO decisions at Algiers gave the Palestinian organization a promising new image in the United States. Public opinion polls showed rising support for Palestinian statehood, and, at the same time, lessening support for Israel.

A February 1989 *Washington Post*-ABC survey reported that a majority of Americans—56 percent—characterize Israel as an "unreliable ally" of the United States, the highest negative rating since the poll began eight years ago. Only 44 percent expressed a favorable view of Israel—one percentage point less than the 45 percent who viewed the Soviet Union positively.

"Not a Single Pro-Israel Letter in Six Months"

Other less visible events and activities reinforce America's uprising. The American-Israel Public Affairs Committee lost its aura of invincibility when its 1988 campaign endeavors failed to either unseat Senator John Chafee of Rhode Island or reelect Senator Lowell Weicker of Connecticut. The organization, registered to lobby for the interests of Israel, also found itself prominently on the defensive when the CBS "Sixty Minutes" television program, a report in the *Washington Post*, and a complaint filed by a group headed by former Ambassador George W. Ball charged the lobby with engaging in illegal partisan activities in federal general elections.

The lobby has retained enough influence on Capitol Hill, however, to inflict heavy damage on the U.S. arms industry. The staggering economic burden it has imposed came prominently to public attention in October 1988. The retiring secretary of defense, Frank Carlucci, charged that Israeli opposition to selling arms to Arabs had cost the United States economy "tens of billions of dollars worth of jobs," not to mention the cost in terms of lost political influence in the Arab world. His comment came just before Saudi Arabia announced it would buy $36 billion in fighter planes from Britain and mobile missiles of undisclosed value from the People's Republic of China.

Carlucci's statement followed a precedent-breaking speech in which Senator Chafee, addressing his Senate colleagues, incurred the ire of Israel's lobby by deploring congressional disapproval of arms sales to Arab states. In recent years, Congress, bowing meekly to lobby pressure, has routinely blocked these sales or imposed restrictions no self-respecting government would accept. On one such occasion, Senator Barry Goldwater expressed a vain plea, "I hope this is the last time that we are subjected to the intense pressure, money and threats of another country."

Secretary Carlucci's "tens of billions of dollars worth of jobs" figure is a conservative appraisal. The fifteen-year loss may rise as high as $260 billion. This figure is based on losses caused by Israeli opposition to the sale of arms to Saudi Arabia alone. The estimate is derived by compiling the aggregate value of the sale of merchandise and services that normally occur as the result of basic arms sales. When the total value of arms sales to other Arab states—lost as the result of Israeli opposition—are added, the cost to the United States economy rises still higher. The *London Economist* estimates that Israel's lobbying against arms sales to Arab states cost the U.S. economy as much as $20 billion in 1986 alone. Opponents warn that arms sales tend to escalate a dangerous build-up of arms in the Middle East, but the U.S. decision to sell, or not, has little to do with the pace of escalation. As recent events prove, Arab states need not look to the United States as a source of weapons and equipment.

The loss to the United States in political and security terms cannot be measured. Leaders of Arab states, embarrassed publicly by repeated congressional rebuffs, will be less dependent on U.S. spare parts and training as they look to Britain and other countries for arms. As this process continues, the United States will still need to protect its own vital national interests in the region but will have fewer avenues through which it can influence the decisions of Arab states.

While U.S. jobs and international influence are being destroyed by lobby "money and threats," several Washington-based organizations are moving forward projects that improve public understanding of Arabs, Islam, and the political problems of the Middle East.

Two retired U.S. foreign service officers, Andrew I. Killgore and Richard H. Curtiss, founders of the American Educational Trust, launched in 1982 a highly successful monthly magazine, *Washington Report on Middle East Affairs*, and provide a growing book, film, and lecture service. Through newspaper advertising, they enlivened the 1988 political campaign by inviting voters to telephone a toll-free number and learn how much money, if any, pro-Israel political action committees provided to their local senators or congressmen. The organization answered more than four thousand calls.

Since 1983, the National Council on U.S.-Arab Relations, headed by Dr. John Duke Anthony, has conducted fifty-one study tours of Arab states, each ten to fourteen days in duration. These tours have provided firsthand knowledge of the region to more than five hundred political leaders and academicians in the United States.

The American Arab Affairs Council, headed by George Naifeh, a former U.S. foreign service officer, publishes a scholarly quarterly and organizes two-day conferences about three times a year on university campuses where professors, journalists, diplomats, and business leaders debate Middle East issues.

Fortunately, America's *intifada* is also being expressed in direct political action. Citizens of Arab ancestry, who number over four million, are beginning to assert themselves after years of political quietude.

The American-Arab Anti-Discrimination Committee, founded by former senator James Abourezk, the Arab American Institute, and the National Association of Arab Americans—all with increasing effect are providing Americans of Arab ancestry with opportunities to work together in order to influence public policy. United States citizens of Muslim faith, now approaching eight million, are making headway on the political front. They do so in a variety of ways—through new groups based on Muslim affiliation, as well as through membership in Arab-American organizations and direct participation in the activities of Republican and Democratic party organizations. The untapped potential of these citizens is enormous, as only a relatively few citizens of Arab ancestry or Muslim affiliation have been aroused to political action or even to organizational membership.

Also being heard on the political front are the voices of Jewish citizens who are alarmed at the damage Israel is doing to both the United States and to Judaism. Among the groups strongly criticizing Israeli policies are the New Jewish Agenda and the Jewish Committee on the Middle East. In a surprising development, Theodore R. Mann, prominent in the American Jewish Congress, has endorsed an Israeli think-tank proposal that contemplates a Palestinian state. Professor Jerome Segal of the University of Maryland is the author of a book, *Creating the Palestinian State: A Strategy for Peace*.

The *Jewish News* of New Jersey, the nation's largest Jewish weekly, reported in March 1989 a "sharp" increase in mail to Capitol Hill critical of Israel: "One strongly pro-Israel senator revealed that his office has not received a single pro-Israel letter in more than six months." In some Capitol Hill offices, mail critical of Israel outnumbered supportive mail by as much as eight to one. Heaviest criticism followed publication of the State Department report that charged Israel with widespread violations of human rights in its treatment of Palestinians.

"You Call the Big Contributors First"

No matter what their national origin or religion may be, citizens who are concerned about the damage being done by Israel's lobby to cherished national institutions, as well as to our national interests in the Middle East, can make a difference. As James Zogby demonstrated in the 1988 Democratic presidential nominating process, the commitment of just one individual can have great impact.

Each citizen can easily become an instrument of political action in the public arena—for example, as a monitor demanding equal time—or space—for response whenever news reports are unbalanced or biased, or, equally important, whenever the accusation of anti-Semitism is made recklessly. Success in these endeavors requires perseverance, as news editors tend to ignore or reject an initial request but, being human, will usually yield to pressure that is firmly but decently applied.

Citizens can also become committees-of-one, each following the political scene in Washington, keeping track of performance by representatives in both the House and Senate and, when circumstances suggest, challenging them with questions and advice. Even more effective are the messages delivered publicly during the "town meetings" that most congressmen conduct periodically for their constituencies.

Each person can also engage in political action in the partisan arena, undertakings that may be less conspicuous but often are more productive than public appeals. The first step is to establish a personal relationship with candidates seeking election, or reelection, to Congress by helping in their partisan campaigns, either with money or time, or both. Suggesting the importance of this relationship, Senator Paul Simon of Illinois, with surprising candor, recently told a reporter: "At the end of a busy day, you find a stack of yellow slips on the spindle, each a call-back request. You can't call them all. Which calls are you going to return? If there are any big contributors in the stack, you start with them."

Still better is group action. When like-minded people band together, the effect can be multiplied, as the supporters of Israel demonstrate every day. A group that demands equal time or space from the editor of a newspaper or the director of a radio or television program will usually get cooperation more quickly than an individual. And a congressman is certain to pay close attention to a viewpoint, whether expressed privately or at a "town meeting," if he or she knows that it represents a group of constituents.

The responsibility for political action should not be placed only on citizens with ethnic ties to the Middle East. The damage caused by Israel's lobby hurts citizens, like myself, who have no such ethnic ties whatever. Donald McHenry, United States Ambassador to the United Nations during the administration of Jimmy Carter, in effect, challenges all citizens with this somber warning: "Because of the [Israeli] lobby's influence, our government is unable to pursue its own national interests in the Middle East."

The task of breaking Israel's grip on U.S. policy-making is so urgent and crucial that it needs the support of many citizens. For this reason, I report with great satisfaction and high hopes the organization of a new lobby. With my support, a group of United States citizens experienced in business, foreign policy, and politics, has established the Council for the National Interest. Motivated, as the name suggests, by the national interest of our country in Middle East policy, it is in the process of organizing a network of citizens throughout the United States who will respond with political activism when opportunities and challenges arise. The organization seeks support in each congressional district. Those interested should address the Council for the National Interest, Post Office Box 53048, Washington, D.C., 20009.

This new organization provides a way for all citizens, regardless of religious affiliation or national origin, to speak out in an effective way. Those who participate can help advance the national interest in the Middle East and at the same time help repair the damage being done to our political institutions by the over-zealous tactics of Israel's lobby.

Sustained work throughout the countryside, I firmly believe, can transform America's embryonic *intifada* into successful political action of immense value to our nation. It has the prospect of extending, within a short period of time, a badly-needed freedom and vigor to the public discussion of U.S. policy in the Middle East. It can enable our government once more to pursue its own national interests as it deals with the complexities and hazards that seem to grow each day in the Middle East.

"We Shall Nobly Save, or Meanly Lose"

Have the uprisings in the occupied territories and in America brought the Arab-Israeli conflict to an historic watershed? Startling changes suggest that this may be the case.

The Palestine Liberation Organization recognizes the existence of Israel and pledges that the newly-proclaimed provisional State of Palestine will exist entirely within the West Bank and Gaza areas and remain at peace with Israel. Thus, the PLO carries, along with a handful of stones, the olive branch of peace, while Israel, once seen as a plucky little nation fighting for its life against brutal neighbors, is cast as the tyrant who breaks limbs and fires lethal weapons at defenseless civilians.

In Washington, changes are equally sweeping. Although reiterating its opposition to an independent Palestinian state, the U.S. government conducts direct talks with the PLO and publishes a document citing in great detail Israel's widespread violation of Palestinian human rights. The United States declares that Israel has no sovereign rights to the West Bank and Gaza. The U.S. Secretary of Defense denounces Israel's lobby for blocking Arab arms sales that could bring "tens of billions of dollars in jobs" to American workers. Considering the record of the previous twenty-five years, during which each succeeding United States administration avoided almost all public criticism of Israel and provided the Jewish state with increasing levels of cooperation and support, these developments are astounding.

The changes beyond the banks of the Potomac are also remarkable. The chilling taboos of yesterday seem to be eased. Here and there, one can express a sympathetic word about Palestinians or denounce Israel's policies of repression without being accused of anti-Semitism.

For the first time, Palestinian statehood is an acceptable topic for discussion on many editorial pages, on radio and television talk shows, and on campuses. In an editorial, *USA Today* calls for Palestinian "independence." Statehood is even debated during a presidential nominating convention and within Jewish organizations. The scandalous behavior of Israel leads many Jews to agonize publicly over what is happening to the once-glistening principles and idealism of the Jewish state.

Do these happenings and trends herald a lasting change in the politics of the Middle East and in the terms of discourse in the United States? Or, is the American *intifada* only a passing phenomenon that will vanish as the inevitable Israeli public relations counterattack takes shape?

The answers to these fundamental, urgent questions will be found mainly in the American countryside, not on the banks of the Potomac, or even in the capitals of the Middle East. Our countryside remains the primary field of battle where the great struggles for peace and justice in the Middle East will be settled.

America's *intifada* has been the basic cause of changes in government policies in Washington, Tunis, and Jerusalem—not the other way around. This uprising created the domestic atmospherics that motivated the PLO to make its historic declarations in Algiers and Stockholm, led Egypt's President Mubarak to become the behind-the-scenes conciliator, prompted U.S. Jews like Rita Hauser to embrace the PLO, and, ultimately, produced the agreement for direct talks between the United States and the PLO.

The events do not reflect a newly-developed courage, conviction, or vision on the part of U.S. leaders. They, and their predecessors, have known all along what should be done. Missing, until recently, has been the assurance of public support for a confrontation with Israel. America's *intifada* provides this essential political base, but this positive trend in U.S. policy can be expected to continue only as long as the American uprising exerts pressure.

Public memory is abysmally short. For example, the April 1989 ABC-Washington Post poll showed that Israel's approval rating had returned to 59 percent—where it was before the uprising. If the people of the United States should lose interest in the agony of the Palestinians or in the threat Israel's lobby poses to the integrity of our cherished institutions, further progress toward peace is unlikely to occur. U.S. talks with the PLO will dwindle off to nothingness. Radicals will inevitably gain strength in both Israel and within the Palestinian movement, and the Middle East will once more become a ticking bomb, posing awesome danger to the entire world.

Intimidation and ignorance, the twin obstacles to peace with justice in the Middle East, seem less formidable than before, but the extent of ignorance is still staggering. How many of your neighbors are aware that the U.S. treasury sends a gift of $3 billion to Israel each year? How many of them know that Israel hired a spy to steal our country's most precious military secrets, traded some of these secrets to the Soviet

Union, paid the spy's legal defense costs when he was arrested and prosecuted, then doubled his pay when he went to prison? How many realize that the weapons Israel uses to bomb villages in southern Lebanon and to kill and brutalize defenseless Palestinian civilians are provided free of charge by the U.S. government?

The greatest struggles lie ahead. The government of the United States must assert, at long last, its own national interests in the Middle East.

Israel's policies are giving a bad name to America, not just to the Jewish state. The world views our nation—accurately—as Israel's essential partner in its military adventurism and its suppression of human rights. America must clear its good name of this complicity. Opening talks with the PLO and challenging Israel's right to the occupied territories are a good beginning, but only a beginning.

The next logical U.S. steps: declare that the people in occupied territories have the right to self-determination and, if they choose, independent statehood; demand that Israeli forces cease the detention of Palestinians without due process, as well as halt the beatings of Palestinians, the destruction of their homes and the use of plastic bullets and other lethal weapons against them; demand that new Israeli settlements in the occupied territories be prohibited. The United States has ample leverage with which to force compliance with these demands.

At some point—the sooner, the better—the United States must issue a clear ultimatum: notify the Jewish state that all U.S. aid will cease unless Israel, in exchange for border guarantees, withdraws its forces from Arab territories. This would be a bold step, but, with each passing day, the immoral burden of complicity in Israel's misdeeds becomes heavier.

Only Washington can deliver these demands in credible terms, because only Washington serves as Israel's lifeline; no Israeli government could defy an ultimatum from its sole benefactor and survive. And only citizens in the American countryside can persuade Washington to act.

The challenge is awesome, but, once informed and aroused, the American people have shown a remarkable capacity to rise above any difficulty. The words Abraham Lincoln wrote 125 years ago to a nation convulsed in civil war ring clearly today as a challenge to the American people: "We, even we here, hold the power and bear the responsibility. We shall nobly save, or meanly lose, this last best hope of earth."

Perhaps today's challenge is not the last hope, but surely it is the best. Circumstance has placed squarely on us the opportunity, as well as the responsibility, to rescue ourselves from impending calamity. And, in making a stand for basic human rights in the occupied territories, we will also be liberating ourselves from the heavy hand Israel's lobby lays on our cherished political institutions here at home. We must bestir ourselves, for the opportunity may be fleeting.

Notes

CHAPTER ONE: KING OF THE HILL

26 A former Congressman: Paul N. McCloskey, address before Conference on "U.S. Economic and Policy Challenges in the Arab World," sponsored by American Arab Affairs Council, Birmingham, Alabama, March 4, 1983.

26 A professional: A number of professionals in pro-Israel lobbying groups provided information for this chapter but, fearing an adverse impact on their future careers, preferred to remain anonymous.

26 This was illustrated: James G. Abourezk, interview, July 27, 1984.

26 No major Jewish: See *New York Times*, September 7, 1982. M. J. Rosenberg, editor of *Near East Report*, stated in an interview on September 5, 1983, that his publication does not publish criticism of Israeli policies lest this be construed as a schism within the pro-Israel Jewish community.

27 "At the State": Letter to the author from Don Bergus, July 10, 1984.

27 Stephen S. Rosenfeld: *Present Tense*, Spring 1983.

28 Certainly Israel: See *Washington Post*, September 27, 1983.

28 The White House: Interview with confidential Capitol Hill source.

29 Nine of the: *Richmond Times-Dispatch*, October 2, 1983.

29 The *Post* quoted: White House Press Release, October 18, 1983.

29 A candid tribute: John K. Wilhelm, statement to the Board for International Food and Agricultural Development, January 5, 1984.

31 In November: Interview with confidential Capitol Hill source.

31 In mid-March: See *New York Times*, March 15, 1984.

31 One development which: See *Washington Post*, April 10, 1984; also see *Wall Street Journal*, July 19, 1984.

31 At the time: Interview with confidential source.

31 After he rejected: The United States had engaged in indirect talks with the PLO during the Israeli invasion of Lebanon in 1982 and earlier during the Carter and Nixon administrations.

36 Paul Weyrich, who: *National Journal*, May 13, 1978.

38 As they voted: *Congressional Record*, October 3, 1984, page H10961; hearings, Trade Subcommittee, Ways and Means Committee, May 22, 1984.

38 Chairmanships: *Mideast Observer*, November 15, 1984.

42 Pro-Israel PACs: *Mideast Observer*, November 1, 1983; *Wall Street Journal*, August 3, 1983. Also in the highest range were doctors, milk producers, realtors and automobile workers.

43 Richard Altman: *Jewish Exponent* (Philadelphia, Penna.), November 11, 1983.

44 Golder explains: Stephen D. Isaacs, *Jews and American Politics*.

47 A non-Jewish: Ibid.

47 After the 1982: *Wall Street Journal*, August 3, 1983.

49 Columnist Nat Hentoff: *Village Voice*, June 14, 1983.

49 After the 1982: Thomas A. Dine, address before Jewish community leaders, Austin, Texas, November 1982.

49 Later, when he: *Yedi'ot Aharonot* (Jerusalem), November 27, 1984.

CHAPTER TWO: STILLING THE STILL, SMALL VOICES

50 In offering: *Congressional Record*, June 5, 1980; also see *Near East Report*, June 11, 1980.

51 "Friend and foe": Paul N. McCloskey, interview, May 10, 1983.

51 Representative James Johnson: *Congressional Record*, June 5, 1980.

52 This was true: See *New York Times Magazine*, April 18, 1971.

52 The wrong decisions: McCloskey, address to the Kenna Club, Santa Clara, Calif., August 13, 1982.

52 He charged it: Paul N. McCloskey, *Truth and Untruth, Political Deceit in America*.

52 Although the Californian: See McCloskey, *Truth and Untruth, Political Deceit in America*.

52 McCloskey agonized over: See *HaKol* (Stanford University), March 1981

52   McCloskey knew war's: See *New York Times Magazine*, April 18, 1971; also see *New York Magazine*, June 14, 1971.
52   He later explained: McCloskey, interview, May 10, 1983.
52   For protesting the: *New York Magazine*, June 14, 1971.
52   "At least fifty": Ibid.
53   He was twice: *San Jose Mercury*, October 23, 1978.
53   As a college: McCloskey, interview, May 10, 1983.
53   He reminded a: Letter from McCloskey to Earl Raab, August 11, 1981; also see *HaKol* (Stanford University), March 1981; also see *Heritage Southwest Jewish Press* (Los Angeles, Calif.), July 17, 1981.
53   McCloskey also vigorously: *Los Angeles Times*, August 2, 1981.
53   Still, McCloskey had: Ibid.
54   One of the: *Redlands Daily Facts*, April 11, 1981.
54   On the other: *San Francisco Examiner*, August 17, 1981.
54   A few days: *San Francisco Examiner*, August 26, 1981.
54   An article in: *B'nai B'rith Messenger* (Los Angeles, Calif.), August 7, 1981.
54   The charge was: Letter from McCloskey to *B'nai B'rith Messenger*, October 21, 1983.
54   The *Messenger* published: *B'nai B'rith Messenger* (Los Angeles, Calif.), October 2, 1981.
54   In an interview: Douglas Bloomfield, interview, October 8, 1983.
55   The *Messenger* charged: *B'nai B'rith Messenger* (Los Angeles, Calif.), August 7, 1981.
55   Another Jewish publication: McCloskey, interview, May 10, 1983; also see *Palo Alto Times-Tribune*, August 17, 1982.
55   An article in: *Heritage and Southwest Jewish Press* (Los Angeles, Calif.), August 7, 1981.
55   One of a: *San Francisco Examiner*, August 15, 1982.
55   Josh Teitelbaum, who: McCloskey, interview, May 10, 1983.
55   McCloskey's views on: See *Sacramento Bee*, December 17, 1982.
55   One former supporter: *Los Angeles Times*, August 2, 1981.
56   In the closing: See *Congressional Record*, August 11, 1982.
56   On September 22: *Congressional Record*, September 22, 1982.
56   In the closing: *Congressional Record*, December 21, 1982.
56   "Many of my": McCloskey, interview, May 10, 1983.
56   Ken Oshman, president: Ibid.
57   McCloskey accepted a: Ibid.
57   The group distributed: The memorandum, dated March 1, 1983, was headed: "To ADL regional directors from Justin J. Finger."
57   McCloskey accepted an: Letter to McCloskey from David Marks of the Guest Professorship Board of ASSP; also see *Stanford Daily*, November 9, 1982.
57   His own remuneration: See *Washington Post*, July 28, 1983.
57   Howard Goldberg: *Stanford Daily*, February 8, 1983.
57   Student leader Seth: See *Stanford Review*, May 25, 1983.
57   According to a: *San Jose Mercury News*, May 27, 1983.
57   One student, Jeffrey: *Stanford Daily*, April 29, 1983.
58   Responding, Professor Hubert: Letter to Jeffrey Au from Prof. Hubert Marshall, April 19, 1983.
58   McCloskey reacted sharply: *San Francisco Chronicle*, May 5, 1983.
58   The *San Francisco:* Ibid.
58   By mid-May: See *Washington Post*, July 28, 1983.
58   McCloskey told the: *Peninsula Times-Tribune*, July 27, 1983.
58   In September 1983: McCloskey, address before the International Conference on the Question of Palestine, Geneva, Switzerland, September 1, 1983.
59   Andrew Young resigned: *Washington Post*, August 16, 1979.
60   To show support: *Washington Star*, August 21, 1979.
60   Fauntroy said he: *Washington Post*, August 21, 1979.
60   While Terzi said: Ibid.
60   "I don't think": Ibid.
60   Prominent Jewish businessman: Ibid.
60   In an attempt: *Washington Post*, August 22, 1979.
60   Howard Squadron, president: Ibid.
60   Some said they: *Washington Star*, August 23, 1979.
60   Fauntroy said: "In": *Washington Post*, August 23, 1979.
61   The *Washington Post:* Ibid.
61   The validity of: *Washington Post*, August 27, 1979.
61   It didn't cripple: The Rev. Walter Fauntroy, interview, July 26, 1983.
61   As they departed: *Washington Post*, September 17, 1979.
61   Fauntroy recalls the: *Washington Post*, September 24, 1979.

61   Jews in the United States: See *Washington Post*, September 18, 1979; *Washington Star*, September 24, 1979.
62   The controversy deepened: *Washington Post*, September 23, 1979.
62   Rabbi Joshua Haberman: Ibid; also see *Washington Post*, October 29, 1979.
62   At a news: *Washington Post*, September 23, 1979.
62   Before the vote: *Washington Post*, January 26, 1980; February 7, 1980; February 21, 1980; March 9, 1980.
62   In an editorial: *Washington Post*, January 30, 1980; January 31, 1980.
62   Fauntroy called the: *Washington Post*, February 1, 1980.
63   The amendment was: See *Washington Post*, March 20, 1980.
63   Fauntroy's Middle East: *Washington Post*, October 16, 1979; also see *Washington Post*, October 24, 1979.
63   Some black leaders: *Newsweek*, October 22, 1979.
63   Before leaving for: *Washington Post*, October 17, 1979.
63   Other blacks supported: *Washington Post*, October 16, 1979.
63   "Any civil rights": Ibid.
63   Even before these: *Washington Post*, October 12, 1979.
63   Fauntroy added that: *Washington Post*, October 16, 1979.
63   Announcing her intention: *Washington Post*, May 15, 1982.
63   A month later: *Washington Post*, June 29, 1982.
64   Both candidates gave: *Jewish Week* (Washington, D.C.), July 1–7, 1982.
64   The challenger's campaign: See *Washington Post*, November 6, 1980.
64   He agreed with: *Washington Post*, August 13, 1983; August 14, 1983.
64   Reflecting on the: The Rev. Walter Fauntroy, interview, July 26, 1983.
65   Michael Nieditch, a: *Jews Speak Out: Views from the Diaspora*, a pamphlet published by International Center for Peace in the Middle East (Tel Aviv).
65   Morris Amitay, then: Michael Nieditch, interview, September 24, 1983.
65   Republican Charles Whalen: Charles Whalen, letter to the author, February 17, 1984.
65   Richard Nolan, now: Richard Nolan, interview, February 17, 1984.
67   Afterwards he told: *Chicago Sun-Times*, October 17, 1981; also see *Houston Chronicle*, October 16, 1981.
67   Columnist Carl Rowan: *Washington Post*, October 25, 1981.
67   In the following: *Mideast Observer*, November 1, 1983.
67   As Stephen S. Rosenfeld: See *Washington Post*, May 12, 1983.
68   They based their: *New York Times*, January 11, 1977.
68   Zablocki dismissed the: *Congressional Quarterly*, January 15, 1977.
68   Zablocki declared that: *Washington Post*, January 11, 1977; also see *Washington Post*, December 17, 1976.
68   He told columnist: *Washington Post*, January 10, 1977.
68   Despite the lobby's: *New York Times*, January 19, 1977; *1977 Congressional Quarterly Almanac*.
68   An aide said: Interview with confidential source.
70   Solarz's zeal: Public meeting, Room 2200, Rayburn Building, Washington, September 26, 1984.
70   He asked Chairman Howard Wolpe: Ibid.
70   A veteran Congressman: Regard for the influence of pro-Israeli lobbying interests compelled the Congressman to request anonymity.
71   He says, "When": Mervyn M. Dymally, interview, March 8, 1984.
71   The first encounter: Ibid.
72   Dymally met the: Ibid.
72   Moreover, to make: Letter from Dymally to Barry Binder, February 29, 1984.
72   Carmen Warshaw, long: Dymally, interview, March 8, 1984.
73   While one staff: Ibid.
73   He told the: *Wall Street Journal*, August 3, 1983.
73   Whenever he complains: Dymally, interview, March 8, 1984.
73   Taking part in: Hearings of the Subcommittee on Europe and the Middle East, February 28, 1983.
74   At fund-raising: Interview with confidential source.
75   Dymally spoke: Hearings of the Subcommittee on Europe and the Middle East, April 12, 1983.
75   During the same: Ibid.
76   Asked for comment: *Washington Post*, May 11, 1983.
76   He warned that: Ibid.
76   Democratic Congressman George: Ibid.
76   But Kansas Republican: Ibid.

76   A lobbyist for: Confidential interview with a member of the Congressional liason staff of AID.
76   Pritchard, witnessing Israel's: *Washington Post*, May 11, 1983.
76   "I must confess": Mervyn M. Dymally, interview, March 8, 1984.
77   "What is tragic": Ibid.
77   Dymally notes that: Ibid.
77   Dymally believes the: Ibid.
78   Donald J. Pease: Donald J. Pease, interview, September 20, 1983.
78   The resolution provided: See *New York Times*, November 11, 1983.
78   When the roll: *Congressional Record*, November 8, 1983.
78   "The Jewish community": As with many other knowledgeable Capitol Hill sources, this Capitol Hill insider would speak candidly about the workings of the Israeli lobby only on the condition that he remain anonymous.
79   Silvio Conte, senior: *Congressional Record*, November 10, 1983.
79   Republican leader Bob: Ibid.
79   To Republicans Conte: Ibid.
79   When the roll: Ibid.
79   But the excuse: Ibid.
80   During debate of: *Near East Report*, May 11, 1984; also see *Washington Report on Middle East Affairs*, May 28, 1984.
80   Rahall recalls that: Nick J. Rahall II, letter to the author, June 6, 1984.
81   The "brave" Congressman: Ibid.
81   He received "less": Rahall, interview, June 8, 1984.
81   In all, 91: *Congressional Record*, September 28, 1983.
81   A veteran Congressman: Interview with a confidential Administration source present at the discussion.
82   In late February: Interview with confidential source.
82   Asked to explain: Interview with confidential source.
82   Confronted by the: Interview with confidential source.
82   The panel approved: *Mideast Observer*, March 15, 1984; also see *Washington Report on Middle East Affairs*, March 5, 1984.
82   Written by AIPAC: Interview with confidential source.
82   In either form: See *Washington Post*, February 28, 1984.
83   When King Hussein: See *New York Times*, March 15, 1984; also see *Washington Report on Middle East Affairs*, April 2, 1984.
83   Meanwhile Democratic Congressman: Hearings of the House Subcommittee on Europe and the Middle East, June 7, 1984; also see *Washington Post*, April 27, 1984; also see *Near East Report*, August 17, 1984.
83   Democrat Larry Smith: Subcommittee Hearings, June 7, 1984.
83   Republican Larry Winn: Ibid.

CHAPTER THREE: THE DELIBERATIVE BODY
DECLINES TO DELIBERATE

84   This phenomenon: Hassan, Crown Prince of Jordan, interview, May 11, 1983.
85   Thompson, a Republican: See *Time*, September 20, 1982.
85   A crucial part: See *Jewish Chicago*, October 1982; also see *Chicago Sun-Times*, September 14, 1983; September 16, 1983.
85   Stevenson was attempting: See *Illinois Issues*, November 1977; *Nation*, December 11, 1976; March 3, 1979; May 5, 1979; *Foreign Affairs*, October 1974.
85   *Time* magazine described: *Chicago Magazine*, June 1979.
85   Effective in committee: *Chicago*, June 1979.
85   *Chicago Daily News:* November 1, 1974.
86   Although a "blue-blood": See *New York Times Magazine*, February 22, 1970; also see *Washington Post*, November 24, 1970.
86   During his second: *New Republic*, February 24, 1979; also see *Christian Science Monitor*, February 5, 1979.
86   "I'm going to": *Washington Post*, February 9, 1979; also see *Nation*, March 3, 1979.
86   Stevenson ultimately decided: Adlai E. Stevenson III, interview, June 9, 1983.
86   Several of the: Ibid.
86   Stevenson himself had: The Israel Bond "Man of the Year" designation was awarded to Stevenson on December 15, 1974, and recorded in the *Congressional Record*, January 10, 1975. The AJC in 1977 awarded Stevenson a commendation and a plaque for his work opposing the trade boycott against Israel. The Weizman Institute established the Adlai E.

Stevenson III Chair in endocrinology and reproductive biology in recognition of the Senator's steadfast support of the Institute and its work.

87   But trouble developed: *Jacksonville Journal Courier* (Jacksonville, Ill.), August 31, 1982. Though the Washington office of AIPAC had produced the defamatory document, an AIPAC spokesman at the time expressed displeasure at seeing AIPAC material thus used in a political campaign. Such political smear tactics have become less common for AIPAC under the more sophisticated leadership of present director Thomas A. Dine.

87   In fact, the: Adlai E. Stevenson, *The Middle East: 1976*, report to the Committee on Banking, Housing and Urban Affairs, United States Senate, on his study mission to the Middle East conducted between February 10 and February 25, 1976 (GPO, Washington, 1976).

88   The anti-Stevenson: *Congressional Record*, June 17, 1980; October 11, 1979.

88   In speaking for: *Congressional Record*, June 17, 1980.

88   After the vote: Stevenson, interview, June 9, 1983.

89   Stevenson was actually: See Rennan Lee Teslik, *Congress, The Executive Branch and Special Interests: The American Response to the Arab Boycott of Israel;* also Stan Marcus, interview, October 7, 1983.

89   For this achievement: Stevenson, interview, June 9, 1983.

89   The chairman of: Letter from Theodore R. Mann to Adlai E. Stevenson III, July 28, 1977.

89   *Jewish Chicago*, making: *Jewish Chicago*, October 1982.

89   A flyer distributed: *Jacksonville Journal Courier* (Jacksonville, Ill.), August 31, 1982.

90   The word was: See *Sentinel*, September 30, 1982; also see *Waukegan News Sun*, November 9, 1982.

90   The political editor: *Chicago Sun-Times*, June 27, 1982.

90   When Republican Senator: *Chicago Sun-Times*, September 14, 1982.

90   "I learned after": Stevenson, interview, June 9, 1983.

90   Phil Klutznick's daughter: Bettylu Saltzman, interview, June 16, 1983.

90   Stevenson's running-mate: Grace Mary Stern, interview, October 18, 1983.

90   "Many of my": Stevenson, interview, June 9, 1983.

90   In the end: *Time*, November 15, 1983.

90   Fed up by: *Chicago Tribune*, September 10, 1982.

91   The *Chicago Sun-Times: Chicago Sun-Times*, September 16, 1982.

91   Philip Klutznick, prominent: Stevenson, interview, June 9, 1983.

91   The election was: *Time*, November 15, 1982.

91   Stevenson asked for: See Illinois Supreme Court Docket No. 57637, Agenda 52, November 1982.

91   A post-election: *Waukegan News Sun*, November 9, 1982.

92   Campaign manager Joseph: *Chicago Sun-Times*, September 14, 1982.

92   Press secretary Rick: Rick Jasculca, interview, October 18, 1983.

92   Thomas A. Dine: *Present Tense*, Spring 1983.

92   Stevenson too believes: Stevenson, interview, June 9, 1983.

93   "When all of": *New York Times Magazine*, November 24, 1974.

93   Fulbright first gained: Haynes Johnson and Bernard N. Gwertzman, *Fulbright, The Dissenter.*

93   Because of this: Ibid.

93   Twenty-five years: *New York Times*, June 2, 1974.

93   His deepest and: See *Foreign Affairs*, Spring, 1979.

93   But Fulbright also: *Time*, June 10, 1974.

94   Fulbright put no: See J. W. Fulbright, *The Arrogance of Power.*

94   In 1963 Fulbright: *Congressional Record*, August 1, 1963.

94   Pincus recalls that: Walter Pincus, interview, November 14, 1983.

94   Both Fulbright and: Ibid.

94   The Fulbright hearings: See *National Journal*, May 18, 1970.

94   Despite his concern: *New York Times*, August 23, 1970. Also see *National Observer*, August 31, 1970; *New Republic*, October 10, 1970.

95   In 1971, he: *New York Times*, April 5, 1971; also see J. W. Fulbright, *The Crippled Giant.*

95   Appearing on CBS: "Face the Nation," April 15, 1973.

95   Six weeks after: *Washington Post*, May 31, 1973.

95   His criticism of: See *Christian Science Monitor*, January 24, 1974; *New Republic*, April 27, 1974; *Newsweek*, June 10, 1974.

95   Fulbright hadn't expected: J. William Fulbright, interview, June 3, 1983; also see *Saturday Review*, January 11, 1975.

95   Walter Pincus, who: Walter Pincus, interview, November 14, 1983.

96   The *New York Times: New York Times Magazine*, May, 1974; November 1974.

96   "I don't think": J. William Fulbright, interview, June 3, 1983.

96   Marked "confidential": Memorandum from the Washington office of B'nai B'rith, May 7, 1974.

96   In a speech: See *National Observer,* November 16, 1974.
96   His central concern: *Washington Post,* November 5, 1974; Fulbright, address at Westminster College, Fulton, Missouri, November 2, 1974.
96   Pondering the future: Fulbright, interview, June 3, 1983.
97   Yet the determination: *National Observer,* November 16, 1974.
97   Soon after he: James G. Abourezk, interview, August 1, 1984.
98   Blitzer's report: *Near East Report,* February 13, 1974.
98   The mailing: I. L. Kenen, letter to Ms. Carol V. Bernstein, February 25, 1974.
99   The next day: AIPAC later sent a memorandum to its Connecticut membership, as well as state leaders, denouncing Ribicoff for his attendance at the luncheon. (*Jewish Ledger* [Connecticut], March 23, 1978).
99   A major storm: See James Abourezk, *On Democracy and Dissent* (Middle East Affairs Council, 1977).
99   The Israeli lobby's: See *Boston Globe Magazine,* April 29, 1984.
100   This involvement began: Interview with confidential source.
100   The letter was: Interview with confidential source.
100   Over the years: Ibid.
100   Hathaway cooperated in: The letter was sent to President Ford on May 21, 1975. See Gerard G. Sheehan, *The Arabs Israelis, and Kissinger;* also see Richard H. Curtiss, *A Changing Image: American Perceptions of the Arab-Israeli Dispute.*
100   Ford, dissatisfied with: See *Washington Post,* March 8, 1978.
101   Three years later: Ibid.
101   Lobbying on both: See *Washington Post,* May 7, 1978.
102   The *Washington Post:* Ibid.
102   In the wake: *Washington Post,* April 22, 1978.
102   Concerning the book: Ibid.
102   Senator Wendell Anderson: Interview with confidential source.
102   In an interview: *Wall Street Journal,* March 13, 1978.
103   One of them: Interview with confidential source.
103   A staff member: Ibid.
103   Israeli officials opposed: See *Washington Star,* April 16, 1981.
103   Even before Reagan: Associated Press Wire Service, September 21, 1981.
104   Lobbyist Frederick Dutton: *Washington Post,* September 28, 1981.
104   The *Post* reported: Ibid.
104   Senator John Glenn: Associated Press Wire Service, September 21, 1981.
104   Syndicated columnist Carl: *Washington Post,* November 25, 1981.
104   When the Senate: *Boston Globe Magazine,* April 29, 1984; also see Seth Tillman, *The United States in the Middle East: Interests and Obstacles.*
104   His opposition to: *Washington Post,* July 9, 1973.
105   In a December: *Washington Post,* December 5, 1971.
105   Mathias was alarmed: See *Nation,* December 8, 1975; also see *Washington Post* November 26, 1975; February 15, 1976.
105   The late Clarence: Biography of Sen. Charles McC. Mathias Jr., prepared by the office of Sen. Mathias, June 1, 1978.
105   In fact, early: *Baltimore Sun,* December 3, 1980.
105   A resident of: *Washington Post,* June 2, 1974.
105   The controversial article: *Washington Post,* June 28, 1981.
105   The same year: *Baltimore Sun,* December 8, 1980.
105   As the *Baltimore Sun:* Ibid.
106   He was exhibiting: Biography of Sen. Charles McC. Mathias Jr., prepared by the office of Sen. Mathias, June 1, 1978; also see *Frederick Post* (Frederick, Md.), April 12, 1980; *Congressional Record,* December 18, 1979.
106   These qualities led: *Foreign Affairs,* Spring 1981.
107   The Baltimore *Jewish Times: Jewish Times* (Baltimore, Md.), July 3, 1981.
107   Arnold Blumberg, a: *Evening Sun* (Baltimore, Md.), July 13, 1981.
108   A prominent Jewish: *Jewish Times* (Baltimore, Md.), July 3, 1981.
108   Congressman Benjamin S. Rosenthal: *Baltimore Sun,* November 5, 1981.
108   Other critics expressed: Discussion of difficult issues involving the Middle East, Israel and American Jews, such as the AWACS sale to Saudi Arabia, always raises the issue of anti-Semitism on Capitol Hill. See *Washington Post,* November 29, 1981; *New York Times,* October 28, 1981; *Near East Report,* November 20, 1981.
108   A spokesperson for: *Jewish Times* (Baltimore, Md.), July 3, 1981; *Baltimore Sun,* July 6, 1981.
108   One critic, identified: *Jewish Times* (Baltimore, Md.), July 3, 1981.
108   Mathias dismissed the: Charles McC. Mathias, interview, August 3, 1983.

109   In his first: *Baltimore Jewish Times,* October 29, 1982.
109   His honeymoon: *Washington Post,* June 28, 1975.
109   That same year: *Jewish Times* (Baltimore, Md.), October 29, 1982.
110   A full-page: *Chicago Tribune,* July 21, 1983.
110   Although Percy: Confidential interviews, November 12, 1984.
110   By mid-August: *New York Times,* August 16, 1984.
111   By election day: *Washington Post,* December 7, 1984.
111   In addition: *Journal-Register* (Springfield, Ill.), December 8, 1984.
111   Former Senator: Chicago *Sun-Times,* November 5, 1984.
112   When the votes: *Journal-Register* (Springfield, Ill.), December 8, 1984, and *Washington Post,* November 12, 1984.
112   The Middle East figured: Paul Simon, interview, December 7, 1984, and *Journal-Register* (Springfield, Ill.), December 8, 1984.
112   Reviewing the impact: Interviews, Percy, November 13, 1984, and Simon, December 7, 1984.
113   AIPAC's Dine told: *Yedi'ot Aharonot* (Jerusalem), November 27, 1984.

CHAPTER FOUR: THE LOBBY AND THE OVAL OFFICE

114   It was a: Charles Bartlett, interview, November 1, 1983.
115   After learning of: Myer Feldman, interview, October 30, 1983.
115   Mr. and Mrs. Arthur: Confidential interview with informed source.
116   Zionists began: See John Snetsinger, *Truman, the Jewish Vote and the Creation of Israel;* also see Robert J. Donovan, *Conflict and Crisis: The Presidency of Harry S. Truman, 1945–1948;* Roberta Feuerlicht, *The Fate of the Jews.*
116   When Truman continued: Snetsinger, op. cit.
116   Two-thirds of: Feuerlicht, op. cit.
117   Their spokesman, Ambassador: Evan M. Wilson, *Decision On Palestine;* also see *Christian Science Monitor,* June 16, 1981.
117   In fact, pro-Israeli: Confidential observation of a person currently prominent in Middle East policy activities.
117   In fact, pro-Israeli: "At 6:11 P.M. on May 14, 1948—eleven minutes after the expiration of the British mandate and ten minutes after the coming into existence of the state of Israel—the White House announced American de facto recognition of the new state and its provisional government." (Seth Tillman, *The United States in the Middle East, Interests and Obstacles*).
117   Secretary of State: Evan M. Wilson, *Decision On Palestine.*
117   During a 1949: Quoted by Tillman, op. cit.
117   In September 1953: Stephen Green, *Taking Sides: America's Secret Relations with a Militant Israel;* also see Wilbur Crane Eveland, *Ropes of Sand: America's Failure in the Middle East.*
118   Predictably Eisenhower's decision: Green, op. cit.
118   Dr. Israel Goldstein: Ibid.
118   Eisenhower faced the: Ibid.; also see Tillman, op. cit.
118   Despite partisan assaults: Stephen D. Isaacs, *Jews and American Politics.*
119   Despite protests: Green, op. cit.; also see Kennett Love, *Suez: The Twice-Fought War.*
119   Informed that the: Ibid.
119   That night the: Ibid.
119   A determined President: Ibid.; also see Tillman, op. cit.
119   Dulles complained: Green, op. cit.
119   Eisenhower persisted, declaring: Ibid.
120   Although there is: See above, pp. 114–15; Isaacs, op. cit.
120   He approved for: Eveland, op. cit.
120   But Israel's military: Green, op. cit.
120   Friends of Israel: Ibid.
120   The latter often: So close was Johnson's friendship with the Krims that they were the first beyond the Johnson family to learn of the President's decision not to seek re-election in 1968. (See Donald Neff, *Warriors at Suez*)
120   In a September: Donald Neff, interview, May 23, 1984.
121   In early June: Green, op. cit.
121   Although Johnson's successor: See Stephen D. Isaacs, *Jews and American Politics.*
122   Privately, Nixon criticized: See Henry A. Kissinger, *Years of Upheaval.*
122   In July: Richard M. Nixon, interview, July 26, 1984.
123   The *Manchester Guardian: Manchester Guardian,* October 10, 1976.
124   He took the: George W. Ball, *The Past Has Another Pattern.*

124   Ball declined, believing: Ibid.
124   Ball was one: See *Foreign Affairs*, Winter 1975/76; *New York Times*, August 25, 1982.
126   Enlisted the year: *Washington Post*, July 11, 1982.
126   He admitted that: George W. Ball, interview, June 10, 1983.
128   A senior diplomat: Confidential interview with informed source.
129   Connally's campaign theme: See *Economist* (London), October 20, 1979.
129   He argued that: *New York Times*, October 12, 1979.
129   Connally became the: *New York Times*, October 22, 1979.
130   Henry Siegman, executive: *Washington Star*, October 13, 1979.
130   *Christian Science: Christian Science Monitor*, October 16, 1979.
131   Writing in: *The Nation*, November 3, 1979.
131   The *Washington Post: Washington Post*, October 15, 1979.
131   Within a few: See *Los Angeles Times*, December 29, 1974.
131   The New York Republican Committee: *Washington Post*, November 6, 1979.
131   The *Washington Post*, Ibid.
132   Columnist William Safire: *New York Times*, October 15, 1979.
132   But he had: See *Washington Post*, December 27, 1983.
132   Polls showed: Ibid.
132   In April 1983: Ibid.
132   After meeting with: See *Chicago Tribune*, December 5, 1983.
132   In addition: $300 million was to be spent in the United States for development of the Israeli
       Lavi fighter plane, while an additional $250 million was authorized to be spent in Israel. This
       $250 million, an unprecedented U.S. subsidy to a foreign industry, was the issue behind the
       Rahall amendment. See chapter two.
132   *Near East Report: Near East Report*, December 23, 1983.
132   In March, Reagan: See *Washington Post*, March 16, 1984.
133   Hussein told a: *New York Times*, March 15, 1984.
133   Mondale accused Hart: See *New York Times*, March 22, 1984.
133   Hart accused Mondale: Ibid.
133   When Donald McHenry: See *Washington Post*, March 2, 1980.
134   Three days later: *Washington Post*, March 5, 1980.
134   Both the nation: See *Wall Street Journal*, March 5, 1980; March 7, 1980; also see *Washington
       Post*, March 6, 1980; March 12, 1980.
134   Arabs were outraged: Ibid.
134   Sharon told Jews: Roberta Feuerlicht, *The Fate of the Jews*.
134   In November: See *Washington Post*, November 6, 1980; November 9, 1980.
135   In June 1984: Albert Joseph, interview, August 15, 1984.
135   Upon learning that: *Wall Street Journal*, March 23, 1984.
135   Hart's competitor for: *Los Angeles Times*, July 14, 1984.
135   As a Senator: *United States Senator Gary Hart on the Issues: Israel and the Middle East*
       (two-page summary prepared by the Hart presidential campaign, undated); also see *Near East
       Report*, January 13, 1984.
135   Senator Ernest Hollings: See *New York Times*, September 15, 1983; also see *Near East
       Report*, January 6, 1984; January 13, 1984.
135   In the past: See *Boston Globe*, February 15, 1983; February 20, 1983.
136   Bitten by the: Ibid.
136   In a speech: *New York Times*, September 14, 1983; also see *Washington Post*, September 15,
       1983.
136   One of Glenn's: Confidential interview with an Ohio Congressman.
136   The speech caused: Lucius Battle, interview, May 21, 1983.
136   McGovern called for: *New York Times*, February 4, 1979.
136   In a speech: Ibid.
136   The "Super Tuesday": *Washington Post*, March 14, 1984.
136   Jackson became controversial: *Washington Post*, October 6, 1979; also see *Rocky Mountain
       News* (Denver, Colo.), August 7, 1983.
137   By the time: *Washington Post*, October 12, 1984.
137   He immediately enlivened: See *Newsweek*, January 16, 1984.
137   He proclaimed, "The": Ibid.
137   In televised debates: See *Washington Post*, March 29, 1984; also see *New York Magazine*,
       January 9, 1984; *Sun* (Baltimore, Md.), February 6, 1984.
137   Jackson found himself: See *Chicago Sun-Times*, February 27, 1984.
137   Inspired by attacks: See *Washington Post*, April 7, 1984; April 8, 1984; April 15, 1984; April
       18, 1984, inter alia.
138   In advance of: Confidential interview with informed sources; also see *New York Times*,
       November 11, 1983.

CHAPTER FIVE: PENETRATING THE DEFENSES
AT DEFENSE AND STATE

139   "The leaks to": This chapter is based upon interviews with 17 present and former officials from the Department of Defense, the Department of State and the White House. Where considerations of career security permit, these sources have been identified.
141   Thomas Pianka, an: Thomas Pianka, interview, November 17, 1983.
141   Richard Helms, director: Donald Neff, *Warriors For Jerusalem.*
142   Les Janka, a: Les Janka, interview, August 16, 1983.
142   Zbigniew Brzezinski, Carter's: Zbigniew Brzezinski, interview, October 31, 1983.
146   "Our officers cannot": Israel is the only country where the U.S. permits such limitations.
147   On one occasion: Wilbur Crane Eveland, correspondence with the author, January 23, 1984.
148   Young recalls: Andrew Young, interview, May 10, 1983.
148   Young resigned as: See chapter two.
148   This denial: *Newsweek,* September 3, 1979.
152   The perpetrator was: *Washington Post,* March 2, 1977.
153   A few days: *Washington Post,* February 18, 1977.
153   When he read: James G. Abourezk, interview, August 1, 1984.
153   Abourezk tried unsuccessfully: Legislation was introduced in 1984 to provide Israel with open U.S. financing for its foreign aid activities. See chapter two.
154   The episode caused: Ambassador John C. West, interview, April 18, 1983; also see *New York Times,* April 20, 1980.
155   West recalls: *New York Times,* April 20, 1980.
155   If so, the: In the wake of the AWACS vote, the United States agreed to boost the level of aid to Israel by $300 million per year for a period of four years.
156   Before leaving his: *Washington Post,* January 24, 1981.
156   L. Dean Brown: L. Dean Brown, interview, January 1984.
158   Harold Saunders, a: Harold Saunders, interview, May 19, 1983.
159   Seelye pinpoints a: Talcott Seelye, interview, May 14, 1983.
159   Bryen was publicly: *Defense Week,* July 27, 1981; *Focus,* February 15, 1982; *New Statesman,* May 6, 1983.
160   During the controversy: *Washington Post,* April 6, 1978.
160   He later left: *Jewish Week* (Washington, DC), July 17–23, 1983.
160   Indeed a Justice: Memorandum from John H. Davitt, Chief of the Internal Security Section, Criminal Division, to Philip B. Heymann, Assistant Attorney General, Criminal Division.
160   An FBI summary: *In These Times,* April 27–May 3, 1983; *Atlantic Monthly,* May 1982.
161   Admiral Thomas Moorer: Admiral Thomas Moorer, interview, August 24, 1983.
163   During a visit: *DeLand Sun News* (DeLand, Fla.), August 11, 1983; also see *USA Today,* August 12, 1983.
163   The rifles in: *Washington Post,* August 10, 1983.
164   Les Janka: Janka, interview, August 16, 1983.

CHAPTER SIX: THE ASSAULT ON "ASSAULT"

165   The episode: Adm. Thomas L. Moorer, interview, August 24, 1983.
166   The *Liberty:* See James M. Ennes Jr., *Assault on the Liberty.*
166   Israeli Chief of Staff: *New York Times,* June 8, 1967.
166   At 6 A.M.: *U.S. Naval Institute Proceedings,* June 1978.
167   Admiral Donald Engen: Adm. Donald Engen, interview, August 29, 1983.
167   The planes: See Ennes, op. cit.
168   President Johnson accepted: *New York Times,* June 10, 1967.
168   Smith Hempstone, foreign: *Washington Star,* June 16, 1967.
168   The Pentagon staved: *U.S. News and World Report,* June 26, 1967; *Defense Electronics,* October 1981.
169   The court: *New York Times,* June 18, 1967.
169   Testimony completed, Admiral: Admiral Isaac Kidd, interview, October 7, 1983.
169   When finally released: Office of Assistant Secretary of Defense (Public Affairs), news release, June 28, 1967.
169   The censored summary: Ennes, *Assault on the Liberty.*
169   The report did: *New York Times,* June 29, 1967; also see *Washington Post,* June 30, 1967.

169   The *New York: New York Times,* July 1, 1967.
169   The *Washington Star: Washington Star,* June 30, 1967.
169   In early July: *New York Times,* July 7, 1967.
170   Lieutenant James M.: Ennes, interview, April 30, 1983.
170   Ennes discovered "shallowness": Ennes, *Assault on the Liberty.*
170   Ennes learned that: Ibid; see also *OPC Bulletin,* February 15, 1982.
171   The embassy message: Ibid.
171   Ennes believes this: See *National Review,* September 5, 1967.
171   Another request for: Ennes, interview, April 30, 1983.
171   It paralleled the: *Defense Electronics,* October 1981.
172   *Pueblo* Commander Lloyd: Cmdr. Lloyd N. Bucher, interview, April 10, 1983.
173   Bucher recalls how: Ibid.
173   Admiral Thomas L. Moorer: Moorer, interview, August 24, 1983.
174   Ennes quoted a: Ennes, *Assault on the Liberty;* also see *Pacific Northwest,* September 1982.
174   Admiral Moorer said: *Christian Science Monitor,* June 22, 1982.
174   Even tombstone inscriptions: *USS Liberty Newsletter,* December 1982.
174   A few days: White House memorandum from James U. Cross to Harry McPherson, June 20, 1967.
175   Responding to the: White House memorandum from Harry McPherson to James U. Cross.
175   While Washington engaged: Engen, August 29, 1983.
175   Yitzhak Rabin, military: Yitzhak Rabin, *Rabin Memoirs.*
175   Lyndon Johnson's own: President Lyndon Johnson, *Vantage Point.*
175   Although his signature: These understated numbers reflect estimates which appeared in some newspapers before the full casualty count was known. See *New York Times,* June 9, 1967; *Washington Post,* June 9, 1967.
176   Moshe Dayan, identified: Moshe Dayan, *Story of My Life.*
176   The cover-up; *Washington Post,* July 18, 1982; Ennes, interview, August 10, 1983.
176   The *Atlanta Journal:* Quotations taken from the dust jacket of Ennes, *Assault on the Liberty.*
176   Journalist Seymour Hersh: Letter from Seymour Hersh to Robert Loomis of Random House, 1979.
176   A caller: Ennes, interview, April 30, 1983.
177   As the result: *Middle East Perspective,* June 1981.
177   Talk show host: Ennes, interview, April 30, 1983.
177   At the invitation: Ibid.
178   After National Public: Ennes, interview, April 30, 1983.
178   Ennes's book may: Bucher, interview, April 30, 1983.
178   Later in 1983: *Jewish Veterans* (magazine), April/May/June, 1983.
178   Another retired officer: Moorer, interview, August 24, 1983.

CHAPTER SEVEN: CHALLENGES TO ACADEMIC FREEDOM

180   Coordinator Jonathan Kessler: Information on this and subsequent pages about AIPAC's Political Leadership Development Program is largely drawn from public remarks by Jonathan Kessler made at an AIPAC workshop in Washington, June 12, 1983, and literature distributed at the workshop; also see *AIPAC College Guide: Exposing the Anti-Israel Campaign on Campus; Near East Report,* August 10, 1984.
182   Edward Said, a: Edward Said, interview, July 20, 1983.
183   The Harvard Jewish: George Bisharat, former Harvard law student who helped organize the event, interview, June 21, 1983.
183   When this failed: *Harvard Law Record,* May 7, 1982.
183   Several members of: *Harvard Law Record,* April 30, 1982.
183   According to the: *Harvard Law Record,* May 6, 1983.
184   Noam Chomsky, world: Noam Chomsky, letter to the author, July 10, 1983.
185   When the monthly: James Schamus, interview, January 25; letter to the author, January 29, 1984.
185   The campus Jewish: *Daily Californian* (University of California at Berkeley), April 15, 1982.
185   The following week: *Daily Californian,* April 14, 1982.
185   The next day: *Daily Californian,* April 15, 1982.
185   While he was: James Schamus, letter to the author, January 29, 1984.
186   In an interview: *San Francisco Examiner,* October 25, 1982.
186   He told the: *Daily Californian,* October 20.
186   D'Anna was shocked: John D'Anna, interview, July 8, 1983.
186   He said that: *Arizona Daily Wildcat* (University of Arizona, Tucson), March 2, 1983.

187 Nevertheless, the day: *Arizona Daily Star,* March 4, 1983.
187 When the deadline: Copy of letter from United Zionist Institutions to "Business Concerns Advertising in the *Arizona Daily Wildcat* and All Ad Agencies in Tucson," dated March 15, 1983.
187 Beginning in the: Letter to the author from Willem A. Bijlefeld, Director of Hartford Seminary's Duncan Black MacDonald Center for the Study of Islam and Christian-Muslim Relations.
188 Ahmad says that: Eqbal Ahmad, interview, September 24, 1983.
189 S. C. Whittaker: S. C. Whittaker, interview, January 30, 1984.
190 The Washington-based: *Bryn Mawr-Haverford College News,* November 4, 1977, citing (without date) the *New York Times.*
190 "It was as": Kendall Landis, interview, June 17, 1983.
190 Haverford President Stephen: *Evening Bulletin,* (Philadelphia, Penn.), November 5, 1977.
190 The program would: *Bryn Mawr-Haverford College News,* November 4, 1977.
190 "This was to": Willis Armstrong, interview, June 22, 1983.
190 "There was never": Stephen Cary, interview, July 12, 1983.
191 Using material provided: *Phoenix* (Swarthmore College), November 2, 1977, p. 1.
191 Asked later about: James Platt, interview, July 27, 1983.
192 The Jewish Community: *Jewish Exponent* (Philadelphia, Penn.), November 11, 1977.
192 Finally, the Washington: Copy of Ira Silverman's confidential AJC memorandum dated November 28, 1977, p. 3.
192 Harrison Wright, a: Harrison Wright, interview, July 25, 1983.
193 Peter Cohan, a: *Phoenix,* February 8, 1978.
193 In a letter: *Phoenix,* November 9, 1977.
193 "I think the": *Bryn Mawr-Haverford News,* November 11, 1977.
193 In an editorial: *Philadelphia Inquirer,* November 9, 1977.
194 In a letter: Copy of letter from Armstrong to Friend dated April 11, 1979.
194 Haverford's provost at: Thomas D'Andrea, interview, July 29, 1983.
195 The dean of: Peter F. Krogh, interview, September 27, 1983.
196 John Ruedy, director: John Ruedy, interview, June 21, 1983.
196 The protest included: *Georgetown Voice,* November 1, 1977.
196 But Georgetown's executive: *Washington Post,* May 4, 1977.
196 "We don't mix": Ibid.
196 In his letter: *Chronicle of Higher Education,* September 25, 1978.
197 Arab Studies Director: Ibid.
197 According to the: *Washington Star,* July 27, 1978.
197 Father Healy refused: *Chronicle of Higher Education,* September 25, 1978.
198 An article in: *Washington Post,* September 9, 1980.
199 Healy said Libya's: *Washington Post,* February 24, 1981.
199 John Ruedy added: John Ruedy, interview, June 21, 1983.
199 Moreover, the day: *Washington Post,* February 25, 1981.
199 Healy told the: *Washington Post,* February 14, 1981.
200 In an interview: *Washingtonian,* October 1981.
200 One expression of: Peter F. Krogh, interview, September 27, 1983.
201 Says Fr. Ellis: Fr. Kail Ellis, interview, January 11, 1984.
203 Established in 1965: "CSIS in Brief," from inside cover of Center for Strategic and International Studies, Georgetown University, Publications 1983.
203 Scholarly participation: Ibid.
203 Former U.S. Ambassador: Letter of reference given Hameed by Akins, dated August 22, 1983.
203 Hameed was hired: Copy of letter of appointment, dated November 11, 1980.
203 That memo stated: Copy of CSIS memorandum, dated October 8, 1980.
204 Jordan sent back: Copy of telex from Jordan to Pat Denny, dated August 30, 1981.
204 Jean Newsom, when: Jean Newsom, interview, July 26, 1983.
204 But Trish Wilson: Trish Wilson, interview, August 2, 1983.
205 Research assistant: Paul Sutphin, interview, August 1, 1983.
205 Another of Hameed's: George Smally, interview, June 26, 1984.
206 In November: This account, from Hameed, was confirmed in substance by Amos Jordan in an interview April 5, 1984. Jordan specified that while Hameed's work was mentioned, it was "not central to the discussion" with Emerson.
206 In early December: Hameed's account. Jordan says he was interviewed "once" by Emerson and makes no mention of a draft.
207 Entitled "The Petrodollar": *New Republic,* February 17, 1982, p. 25.
207 Entitled "Georgetown Study": *Platt's Oilgram News,* February 18, 1982, p. 4.
208 The editor: Onnik Maraschian, interview, August 11, 1983.

208   The memo: Copy of CSIS memorandum "Re: Attached Platt's Oilgram Article," dated February 22, 1982.
209   In the secret version: *Draft of a Proposed Report: U.S. Assistance to the State of Israel,* prepared by the staff of the U.S. General Accounting Office (1983).
209   A week later: Amos Jordan states in a letter to the author dated April 12, 1984, that this incident occurred in October 1981, not in February 1982.
209   The new charge would: Jordan denies this, saying the new charge replaced the old. He also denies that the charge was made retroactive and says it was applied "to all project directors at the Center."
209   Wendt told Hameed: Hameed acknowledged a temporary deficit of about $12,000, which he had expected to cover through CSIS sales of his report.
210   Then, on March 5: The date and other details of the burglary are confirmed in the report of the Metropolitan Police Department, Washington, D.C., complaint number 109-933.
210   Several corporations: Hameed's account.

CHAPTER EIGHT: TUCSON: A CASE STUDY IN INTIMIDATION

212   In November 1980: Sheila Scoville, interview, July 7, 1983.
213   They told Dever: "Part II: History and Chronology," *Report on the Outreach Function of the Near East Center, Oriental Studies Department, University of Arizona,* prepared by the Tucson Jewish Community Council, Community Relations Committee.
214   The report questioned: Ibid.
214   It included reviews: *Report on the Outreach Function of the Near East Center.*
215   In May, 1982: Memorandum from Robert M. Gimello to Dr. Paul Rosenblatt, Acting Provost and Dean, May 13, 1982.
215   The four volunteers: *Arizona Post* (Tucson, Ariz.), May 21, 1982.
215   He dispatched a: Memorandum from Ludwig W. Adamec to Faculty, University of Arizona, re: "Censorship of Outreach Materials," August 9, 1982.
216   In a statement: Letter from Ludwig Adamec to Editor, *Arizona Daily Wildcat,* September 9, 1982.
216   After acknowledging the: Memorandum from Robert M. Gimello to Herman K. Bleibtreu, Dean of the Faculty of Social and Behavioral Sciences, September 24, 1982.
217   With this information: Letter from William G. Dever to Carol Karsch, October 29, 1982.
218   Instead, Carol Karsch: *Reply to the Department of Oriental Studies "Final Response,"* November 9, 1982.
219   In a letter: Letter from Dennis DeConcini to Kenneth D. Whitehead, Director, International Education Program, U.S. Department of Education, April 6, 1983.
219   Responding to the two: Letter from Edward M. Elmendorf, Assistant Secretary for Postsecondary Education, to Rep. James F. McNulty, March 29, 1983, and letter from Kenneth D. Whitehead (see previous reference) to Sen. Dennis DeConcini, April 15, 1983.
219   When Adamec learned: Letter from Ludwig Adamec to Henry Koffler, March 7, 1983.
219   When, despite these: Letter from Sen. Dennis DeConcini and Rep. James F. McNulty to Secretary T. H. Bell, May 13, 1983.
219   Secretary Bell responded: Letter from Secretary Bell to Sen. DeConcini of which duplicate was sent to Rep. McNulty, June 22, 1983.
219   In a letter to university: Letter from Ludwig Adamec to Henry Koffler, January 17, 1983.
220   The memorandum notified: Memorandum from Jack H. Murrieta to Mary Lou Tompkins, Teacher, Tucson Unified School District, May 4, 1983.
220   In a letter: Letter from Robert Gimello to Jack Murrieta, May 12, 1983.
221   The ACLU agreed: Letter from Helen Mautner, Associate Director, Arizona Civil Liberties Union, to Tom Castillo, President, TUSD School Board, May 19, 1983.
221   In a letter: Ibid.
221   The list of: Letter from Boris Kozolchyk to Henry Koffler, June 6, 1983, and letters from Saul Tobin, President, TJCC, to Henry Koffler, July 1 and July 5, 1983.
222   The newspapers quoted: *Tucson Citizen,* July 15, 1983.
222   Carol Karsch informed: Transcript of KUAT TV's public affairs program "Arizona Illustrated," July 15, 1983.
222   "But I couldn't": Sheila Scoville, interview, July 15, 1983.
222   He said that: Letter from Robert Gimello to Henry Koffler, July 15, 1983.
223   One teacher said: *Tucson Citizen,* July 15, 1983.
223   She said she: *Arizona Daily Star,* July 16, 1983.
223   A librarian who: *Tucson Citizen,* July 15, 1983.
223   In a statement: *Arizona Daily Star,* July 16, 1983.

224   In a joint: Transcript of KUAT TV's "Arizona Illustrated," July 19, 1983.
224   According to Scoville: Sheila Scoville, interview, September 5, 1983.
224   Gimello wrote to Ares: Letter from Robert Gimello to Charles Ares, September 7, 1983.
225   After learning that: Letter from Michael Bonine to Henry Koffler, September 20, 1983.
225   He wrote to: Letter from Ludwig Adamec to Charles Ares, September 7, 1983.
226   It seems not: Letter from Ludwig Adamec to Charles Ares, September 12, 1983.
226   TUSD Compliance Officer: *Arizona Daily Star*, July 15, 1983.
226   Its 11-page: *Investigation Findings—Near Eastern Center Outreach Program—University of Arizona, "Survey History of the Middle East,"* by Sylvia Campoy, Special Assistant for Compliance, Tucson Unified School District, September 13, 1983.
226   The *Arizona Daily Star*: *Arizona Daily Star*, September 16, 1983.
227   Adamec again wrote: Letter from Ludwig Adamec to the editor of the *Arizona Daily Star*, September 16, 1983.
227   The *Tucson Citizen*: *Tucson Citizen*, September 20, 1983.
227   The scholars: *Report to the President of the University of Arizona*, August 1, 1983.
229   Ares's report, to the: *Report to President Koffler on Outreach Program of Near Eastern Center*, by Charles E. Ares, Professor of Law.
231   Carol Karsch also: *Arizona Post*, October 7, 1983.
232   At a TUSD: *Tucson Citizen*, October 19, 1983.
232   At a faculty: Minutes of the Meeting of the Faculty Senate of the University of Arizona, October 3, 1983.
232   In a letter: Letter from Ludwig Adamec to members of the University of Arizona Faculty Senate, October 27, 1983.
233   In a memo: Memorandum from Myles Brand, Acting Dean, to Vice President Hasselmo, October 10, 1983.
234   Written by Gary: *Middle East Centers at Selected American Universities:* A Report Presented to the American Jewish Committee by the Academy for Educational Development, Dr. Gary Schiff, Project Director, 1981.
235   For its part: American Jewish Committee press release, September 16, 1981.
235   During the summer: Charlotte Albright, interview, June 21, 1983.
235   After attending a: Sheila Scoville, interview, May 16, 1984.
236   This professor: Richard Frye, interview, September 5, 1983.
236   Another Jewish professor: Jerrold Levy, interview, November 17, 1984.

CHAPTER NINE: CHURCH AND STATE

238   At "town meetings": Lee Hamilton, interview, August 2, 1983.
238   Many U.S. Christians: See Thomas Wiley, *American Christianity, The Jewish State and the Arab-Israeli Conflict* (Occasional Papers Series, CCAS, Georgetown University, 1983).
240   His views are: Speech reprinted in *Near East Report*, June 5, 1981.
240   Jepsen cited his: See *New York Times*, October 28, 1981.
240   Acclaimed in a: *Economist* (London), 3–9 March, 1984.
241   He has since: Mike Evans, letter to Mike Evans Ministries supporters, January 23, 1984.
242   "Did you ever": George Otis, letter to High Adventure Holyland Ministry supporters, undated.
243   As Dr. Franklin: *Near East Report*, November 20, 1981.
245   The prophecy argument: See Wiley, op. cit.; Dr. Dewey Beegle, *Prophecy and Prediction; The Link*, vol. 16, no. 4, November 1983.
245   First, the prophesied: See also Professor Alfred Guillaume in *Palestine and the Bible*, M. T. Mehdi, editor.
245   Second, the covenant: See also Bishop Jonathan G. Sherman, in ibid.
245   Dr. Beegle views: Dr. Dewey Beegle, interview, January 12, 1984.
246   President Reagan, in: White House press release, October 18, 1983.
246   Jews instinctively mistrusted: Roberta Fueurlicht, *The Fate of the Jews.*
246   Dan Rossing, director: *New York Times*, January 15, 1984.
247   The "embassy" was: *Near East Report*, December 16, 1983.
247   In Israel, Orthodox: *New York Times*, January 15, 1984.
247   The dilemma faced: The Friends of Israel Gospel Ministry, Inc., centered in Collingwood, New Jersey, is one of a number of American evangelistic organizations which take Jewish conversion as a primary goal. Its 1983 Mission Update report referred to more than 2,000 meetings on "Jewish evangelism, missions, prophecy and deeper life" conducted during the year, in addition to the distribution of nearly a million copies of its various publications.
247   While spokesmen within: *New York Times*, December 1, 1981.

247   Opposition to the: *New York Jewish Weekly,* Oct. 19, 1980.
247   In Israel the: *New York Times,* December 1, 1981.
248   He pointedly observed: *Atlanta Constitution Journal,* February 20, 1981.
248   Though traditional efforts: *New York Times,* January 15, 1984.
248   The mainline churches: See Ernest Volkman, *A Legacy of Hate.*
248   Several of the: The Middle East policy statements of eight of the leading U.S. Christian churches were collected in *Where We Stand,* a pamphlet published in 1977 by the Middle East Peace Project (Allan Solomonow, ed.)
249   Despite more than: Wiley, op. cit.
249   Christian churches have: Volkman, op. cit.; also see Alfred M. Lilienthal, *The Zionist Connection.*
251   Journalist Ernest Volkman: Volkman, op. cit.
252   Since it is: Peggy Briggs, interview, October 7, 1983.
252   In discussing the: Helen Feeley, interview, October 6, 1983.
252   Greg Degiere, head: Greg Degiere, interview, January 16, 1984.
253   As Joseph Gerson: *Nuclear Times,* February 1984, cited in *Palestine/Israel Bulletin,* March 1984.
253   Offered a government: *Life,* April 2, 1965.
253   He explained his: *Washington Post,* June 17, 1977.
253   On Palm Sunday: The 1972 Palm Sunday sermon and a number of statements reacting to it were collected in *The Jerusalem Debate,* a pamphlet published in 1972 by the Middle East Affairs Council (A. R. Taylor and J. P. Richaradson, eds.).
255   He was not: Ibid.
255   Their position received: Ibid.
255   An angry editorial: *Washington Post,* April 4, 1972.
256   Writer Ernest Volkman: op. cit.
256   David A. Clarke: *Washington Post,* April 8, 1972.
256   Describing the 1967: Dean Francis B. Sayre, interview, July 23, 1983; also see *Washington Star,* April 6, 1972.
256   Two leaders of: Taylor and Richardson, eds., op. cit.
257   First they questioned: *Washington Post,* April 4, 1972.
257   Citing United Nations: *Christianity Today,* April 28, 1972.
257   Support for Sayre: Rev. Joseph L. Ryan, press conference, April 6, 1972 (see *The Jerusalem Debate*).
258   "Of course I": Dean Francis B. Sayre, interview, May 25, 1983.
258   Three days after: Sayre, interview, May 25, 1983.
258   They heard Dean: Washington *Evening Star and Daily News,* September 11, 1972.
259   "I perceive that": Ibid.
260   He was at: The Rev. Don Wagner, interview, November 12, 1983.
262   He had been fully: Ibid.; Wagner, interview, February 3, 1984.
262   He had been invited: Ayoub Talhami, interview, February 6, 1984.
263   Still, she was: Sr. Miriam Ward, interview, February 6, 1984; Wagner, interview, February 3, 1984.
263   The article claimed: *Jewish Week-American Examiner,* June 21, 1981.
263   "I was physically": Ward, Ibid.
264   In January 1982: *Jewish Week-American Examiner,* January 14, 1982.
264   "It's the original": Ward, interview, February 6, 1984.

CHAPTER TEN: NOT ALL JEWS TOE THE LINE

265   As Rabbi Balfour Brickner: *Village Voice,* September 7, 1982.
265   A 1983 survey: See Stephen M. Cohen, *Attitudes of American Jews Toward Israel and Israelis: The 1983 National Survey of American Jews and Jewish Communal Leaders* (Institute on American Jewish-Israeli Relations, The American Jewish Committee).
267   The counterattack was: See Roberta Feuerlicht, *The Fate of the Jews.*
267   Jewish leaders were warned: *Progressive,* August 1979.
267   Carolyn Toll, a: Ibid.
267   An unsigned "fact sheet": Ibid.
267   The *Seattle Jewish Transcript:* Ibid.
267   Irving Howe, speaking: Irving Howe, *New Perspectives: The Diaspora and Israel.*
267   At the same: See Roberta Feuerlicht, *The Fate of the Jews.*
267   In December 1980: Ibid.
267   The council members: *Washington Post,* June 4, 1983.
267   Irwin Stein, president: Ibid.

268   To Carolyn Toll: *Progressive,* August 1979. Ibid.
268   Moe Rodenstein, representing: Ibid.
268   A successful Jewish: See *Washington Report on Middle East Affairs,* April 2, 1984.
268   The *Los Angeles Times:* Roberta Feuerlicht, interview, October 19, 1983.
269   A few minutes: Gail Pressberg, interview, November 4, 1983.
269   In a later: *Washington Post,* July 6, 1982.
270   Public television broadcast: John Wallach, interview, April 15, 1983.
270   For a time: Ibid.
271   "I thought it": *Washington Post,* December 14, 1982.
271   "It makes one": John Wallach, interview, April 15, 1983.
271   During the Israeli: *Village Voice,* June 29, 1982.
271   A member of: Charles Fishbein, interview, October 11, 1983.
272   He lamented the: See *The Autobiography of Nahum Goldmann,* trans. by Helen Sebba.
272   When the fledgling: See *The Jewish Paradox* by Nahum Goldmann.
274   In a strikingly: *Jewish Week,* (Washington, DC) September 2–8, 1982.
279   On returning, Klutznick: *Chicago Tribune,* December 3, 1981; see also *The Path to Peace: Arab-Israeli Peace and the United States,* published in 1981 by the Seven Springs Center.
279   When I opposed: Chicago *Sun-Times,* December 8, 1981; Klutznick, interview, September 19, 1983.
280   Robert Schrayer, chairman: Chicago *Sun-Times,* December 3, 1981.
280   The *Near East Report: Near East Report,* November 20, 1981.
280   Four hours later: Klutznick, interview, September 19, 1983.
280   The real issue: *Christian Science Monitor,* July 14, 1982.
281   Klutznick took the: Klutznick, interview, September 19, 1983.
281   A few Jews: *Chicago Sun-Times,* October 20, 1982.
282   "We cannot be": *Jewish Post and Opinion* (USA), February 23, 1983.
282   One of them: Interview with confidential source.
282   Charles Fishbein, for: Fishbein, interview, October 11, 1983.
283   "Jews never had": I. F. Stone, interview, April 24, 1983.
283   A recent lecture: See *Washington Post,* March 21, 1983.
283   According to: *The Progressive,* August 1979.
284   Proud to be: I. F. Stone, interview, April 24, 1983.
284   Stone sees a: *New York Review of Books,* March 1978.
284   But in the United": *New York Review of Books,* March 1978.
284   Those who speak: *Lincoln Review,* Autumn 1979.
286   His greatest accomplishment: Alfred M. Lilienthal, interview, May 24, 1983.

CHAPTER ELEVEN: BEYOND THE BANKS OF THE POTOMAC

287   Pro-Israeli PACs: *Wall Street Journal,* August 3, 1983; *Mideast Observer,* November 1, 1983.
287   On October 14: *Philadelphia Inquirer,* October 16, 1983.
287   After a short: *Philadelphia Inquirer,* October 19, 1983.
288   Yet as one: *Jewish Exponent* (Philadelphia, Penna.), November 11, 1983.
288   Anisa Mehdi, a: Anisa Mehdi, interview, September 4, 1983.
288   Arab ancestry can: Elaine Hagopian, interview, September 21, 1983.
289   Another person of: Mahmoud A. Naji, interview, April 16, 1984; see *Chicago Tribune,* July 13, 1975.
289   Naji, a native: Official correspondence between INS Regional Commissioner and counsel for Mahmoud A. Naji, February 13, 1981.
290   Arab Americans in: *ADC Bi-Weekly Reports,* April 1–15, 1984.
290   This harsh accusation: *Monthly Detroit,* February 1984.
290   Mediterranean House restaurant: Abdel Hamid El-Barbarawi, interview, September 7, 1983.
290   At the peak: See, for example, *Bilalian News,* October 7, 1977.
291   The next month: *Chicago Jewish Post and Opinion,* July 2, 1976.
291   In a *Chicago Sun-Times: Chicago Sun-Times,* November 11, 1977.
292   Dick Kay, a: Dick Kay, interview, September 15, 1983.
292   An official of: Eric Hooglund, interview, August 19, 1983.
292   In mid-1983: Stephen Green, interview, March 5, 1983.
293   Redgrave's apprehension was: Vanessa Redgrave, interview, September 4, 1983.
293   In 1978, the: *Los Angeles Times,* April 5, 1978.
293   Another controversy arose: *Midstream,* January 1980.
294   Fenelon herself declared: *New York Times,* September 25, 1980.

294   Yellen responded to: Ibid.
294   One asserted that: *Los Angeles Times,* September 28, 1980.
294   The Simon Wiesenthal: *Los Angeles Times,* September 28, 1980.
294   As the *Los Angeles Times:* Ibid.
294   The difficulty in: *Village Voice,* June 8, 1982.
295   Edmund Ghareeb, a: *Split Vision.*
295   Journalist Lawrence Mosher, a: Ibid.
295   Even *Time* magazine: *Twin Cities Reader* (Minneapolis, Minn.), July 1, 1982.
295   Such stereotyping of: Harold R. Piety, *Split Vision.*
296   Columnist Rowland Evans: *National Journal,* January 8, 1972.
296   Even former Defense: *Armed Forces Journal International,* October 1977.
296   For this straightforward: *Washington Post,* October 27, 1977.
296   Journalist Harold R.: *Journal Herald* (Dayton, Ohio), November 13, 1975.
296   In late 1978: *Middle East International,* December 1978.
297   A column asserting: *Journal Herald* (Dayton, Ohio), November 13, 1975.
297   Editor Dennis Shere: Harold R. Piety, letter to the author, July 27, 1983.
297   Among his findings: *Twin Cities Reader* (Minneapolis, Minn.), June 17, 1982.
298   Soon after the: Richard Broderick, interview, July 14, 1983.
298   Later in the: *Twin Cities Reader* (Minneapolis, Minn.), August 19, 1982.
298   Concern over appearances: Georgia Ann Geyer, interview, May 16, 1983.
299   She is frequently: Georgie Ann Geyer, *Buying the Night Flight;* see also *The Quill,* February 1983.
299   Geyer, whose worldwide: Geyer, interview, May 16, 1983.
299   Editor Howard Kleinberg: *Miami News,* April 4, 1983.
299   In two installments: *New York Times,* December 22, 1983; January 16, 1984; also see *Foreign Affairs,* July 1978.
300   The *Times* published: *Boston Globe Magazine,* April 29, 1984.
300   Jack Sunderland: Jack Sunderland, interview, June 3, 1983.
301   On a Saturday: *Twin Cities Reader* (Minneapolis, Minn.), July 1, 1982.
301   James Batal, a: Wafiya El-Hossaini, interview, April 17, 1983.
301   Grace Halsell, a: *Middle East International,* 27 January, 1984.
302   John Law, a: *Washington Report on Middle East Affairs,* May 17, 1982.
302   One reader hailed: *Village Voice,* February 7, 1984.
302   In August 1982: *Village Voice,* January 24, 1984.
302   Editor David Schneiderman: Ibid.
303   Lawrence Mosher: *Split Vision.*
304   Shortly after the: Lawrence Mosher, interview, November 16, 1983.
305   Society President Gilbert: Gilbert M. Grosvenor, interview, March 31, 1983.
305   The criticisms culminated: *New York Times,* June 21, 1974.
305   Grosvenor views the: Grosvenor, interview, March 31, 1983.
306   Personally signed by: *National Geographic,* November 1974.
306   CBS was swamped: Russell W. Howe and Sarah H. Trott, *The Power Peddlars: How Lobbyists Mold America's Foreign Policy.*
306   Wallace observed: *Christian Science Monitor,* March 19, 1976.
307   On its "First": "First Line Report," March 7, 1973.
308   Knowing that he: Robert Pierpoint, interview, March 8, 1983.
308   He later remarked: Robert Pierpoint, unpublished manuscript.
308   Affordable or not: Robert Pierpoint, interview, March 8, 1983.
309   Indeed, Pierpoint admits: Ibid.
309   During 1981 Patsy: Patsy Collins, interview, April 30, 1983.
310   Her comments paralleled: *Village Voice,* October 7, 1982.
310   Despite the instances: *Washington Report on Middle East Affairs,* May 28, 1984.
310   Goldman's campaign against: Goldman was featured as a panelist at the first national CAM- ERA Conference, held November 20, 1983 in Washington, DC.
310   Lawrence K. Grossman: NBC News Press Release, May 3, 1984; also see *Columbia Journalism Review,* November/December 1982.
311   Early in 1984: *Washington Report on Middle East Affairs,* May 28, 1984.
311   Such attempts to: *Minneapolis Star and Tribune,* April 3, 1983.
311   The idea arose: *Washington Journalism Review,* March 1983.
312   Columnist Nick Thimmesch: Nick Thimmesch, interview, April 11, 1983.
312   *Post* ombudsman Robert: *Washington Post,* October 6, 1982.
312   *Boston Globe* Editor Thomas: *Washington Journalism Review,* March 1983.
312   When Moshe Arens: *Washington Post,* November 10, 1982.
312   Greenfield, who ranks: *Washington Post,* November 12, 1982.
312   The *Boston Globe: Washington Post,* November 10, 1982.

313   He described the: *Jewish Week* (Washington, DC), November 4–10.
313   Like Greenfield, Winship: *Washington Post,* November 10, 1982.
313   *Globe* staff writer: *Boston Globe Magazine,* April 29, 1984.
313   Typical of the: *Sunday Call-Chronicle* (Allentown, Penn.), January 16, 1983.
314   In Maryland the: *Evening Sun* (Baltimore, Md.), November 4, 1983; *Washington Post,* November 7, 1983; also see *Washington Times,* November 2, 1983; *Jewish Exponent* (Baltimore, Md.), January 21, 1983.
314   Later, in California: *Times* (San Mateo, Calif.), November 1, 1982; November 9, 1982.
314   Ron Cathell: *Sunday Call-Chronicle* (Allentown, Penn.), January 16, 1983.

NOTES: EPILOGUE: REPAIRING THE DAMAGE

315   Ben Meed: *Washington Post,* May 2, 1983.
316   The lobby: *Boston Globe Magazine,* April 29, 1984.
316   Their activities: See chapter five (Penetrating the Defenses at Defense—and State).
316   Polls show: See Stephen M. Cohen, *Attitudes of American Jews Toward Israel and Israelis: The 1983 National Survey of American Jews and Jewish Communal Leaders* (Institute on American Jewish-Israeli Relations, The American Jewish Committee).
317   Its origin: See Seth P. Tillman, *The United States in the Middle East: Interests and Obstacles,* chapter four (Israel: the Politics of Fear). Also see *New York Times Magazine,* April 18, 1982.
317   A resident: *Washington Post,* May 2, 1983.
317   During his earliest: This incident and the one following are drawn from interviews with confidential sources.
317   Jewish ties: See *New York Times Magazine,* November 7, 1982; also see Cohen, op. cit.
318   The press: *Middle East International,* 23 December, 1983; *Miami Herald,* July 23, 1984; Amos Oz, *In the Land of Israel.*
318   This siege outlook: See chapter nine (Not All Jews Toe the Line).
318   Most observers: Donald Neff, interview, April 28, 1984.
318   In the 1973: See Neff, *Warriors For Jerusalem: The Six Days That Changed the Middle East.* Also see *Washington Post,* November 19, 1974.
318   Faced with: Admiral Thomas Moorer, interview, August 24, 1983.
318   For many concerned: See Richard Cohen, "When Jews Lose Their Tolerance for Dissent," *Washington Post,* September 26, 1982.
321   Surely one can: See Nat Hentoff, "The Continuing Silence of Most American Jews," *Village Voice,* June 7, 1983.
321   For example: *National Review,* May 13, 1978.
322   Jerome Bankst: *Boston Globe Magazine,* April 29, 1984.
323   The late Evan Wilson: Richard H. Curtiss, *A Changing Image: American Perceptions of the Arab-Israeli Dispute,* cited in *The Link,* January–March, 1984.
323   Professor Seth Tillman: Tillman, op cit.
323   There is the unfounded: See Stephen D. Isaacs, *Jews and American Politics;* also see *American Jewish Yearbook, 1980.*
323   This unawareness: See *Draft of a Proposed Report: U.S. Assistance to the State of Israel,* U.S. General Accounting Office (1983); also see Robert G. Kaiser, "The U.S Risks Suffocating Israel with Kindness," *Washington Post,* May 27, 1984.
323   Most citizens: Hyman H. Bookbinder, Washington representative for the American Jewish Committee has declared: "The greatest single thing going for American support for Israel is the fact that our American leaders—the President, Cabinet officials, Senators, Congressmen, national security advisers—have for 30 years consistently *said* that it is in America's interest. I do not contend that the great majority of Americans have themselves studied the issues . . . [or] come to their own conclusion. They have accepted a national verdict." (*National Review,* May 13, 1978)
323   In the spring: *Mideast Observer,* May 15, 1984.
323   Democratic Congressman Mervyn: Merwyn M. Dymally, interview, March 8, 1984.
324   American Jews: See *Jerusalem Post,* October 28, 1981.
324   The activities: Ibid.
324   Philip M. Klutznick: Klutznick, interview, September 19, 1983.
325   In 1982: Michael Nieditch, interview, September 24, 1983.
325   Nowhere is free: See Roberta Feuerlicht, *The Fate of the Jews,* also see Cohen, op. cit.; Hentoff, op. cit.
325   American Jews flocked: See Mike Royko, "Terror Is Telling," *Chicago Sun-Times,* October 3, 1982.
325   These U.S. leaders: See chapter one (King of the Hill).

325   Unfortunately: Interview with confidential source.
326   After the Israelis: Larry Neumeister, "Moral Majority Leader Says Begin Called Him Shortly After Reactor Raid," Associated Press Wire Service, July 6, 1981.
326   Similarly, evangelist Mike: Mike Evans, *Israel, America's Key to Survival.*
327   The application: the Rev. Jesse Jackson, interview, August 3, 1979.
327   Zbigniew Brzezinski: Zbigniew Brzezinski, interview, October 31, 1983.
329   As Nahum Goldmann: *Foreign Affairs,* Fall, 1978.
330   Israel has refused: See *New York Times,* March 16, 1976 ck.
330   During the 1973: Admiral Thomas M. Moorer, interview, August 24, 1983.
330   Former Secretary: Dean Rusk, letter to the author, May 25, 1984.
331   As Washington columnist: *Washington Post,* September 26, 1982.
331   We could hardly: Amos Oz, *In the Land of Israel.*
331   Abraham Lincoln warned: See Paul Findley, *Lincoln: The Crucible of Congress.*

CHAPTER THIRTEEN: AMERICA'S *INTIFADA*

335   The FBI "knew . . . *Washington Post,* June 3, 1986.
      In the wake of, *New York Times,* February 11, 1985.
337   Of the thousands, *Territory of Lies,* Wolf Blitzer, 1989.
      When they learned, *Defense News,* March 1989.
      Weinberger wrote, *Territory of Lies,* Wolf Blitzer, 1989.
      Reporter Charles Babcock, *Washington Post,* June 15, 1986.
338   These funds, *Territory of Lies,* Wolf Blitzer, 1989.
      Alan Dershowitz, Newark (N.J.) *Star-Ledger,* March 6, 1989.
      Items stolen, *Washington Post,* April 9, 1989.
339   Soviet acquisition, UPI dispatch, December 14, 1987.
      The reported diversion, interview, Richard T. Sale, November 16, 1988.
340   Headlines in June and July 1988, *Los Angeles Times,* June 25, 1988; July 30, 1988.
      CIA officials agonize, interview, Richard T. Sale, November 11, 1988.
341   Another fugitive, Richard K. Smyth, *Los Angeles Times,* July 30, 1989.
342   A senior Israeli official, *Los Angeles Times,* July 3, 1988.
      In December 1985, FBI director, *New York Times,* December 11, 1985.
      The Reagan administration, *Chicago Tribune,* July 24, 1986.
      Americans watched, *Washington Post,* November 28, 1986.
345   In May 1988, American Ambassador, *Washington Post,* May 21, 1987.
      In July, 350 Israeli scientists, *Washington Report on Middle East Affairs,* July 1988.
346   A Quaker Palestinian, interview in Cairo, January 23, 1989.
      Rev. John B. Jamison, interview, March 5, 1989.
348   Although congressional reaction, *Spotlight* newspaper, March 6, 1989.
      Copley newspapers, *State Journal-Register,* Springfield, Illinois, February 20, 1989.
      Gerald G. Toy, interview, February 28, 1989.
349   In Illinois, *New York Times,* June 23, 1989 and St. Louis *Post-Dispatch,* June 21, 1988.
      Zogby moved, *Washington Jewish Week,* July 21, 1988.
352   Quiet but effective, interview, President Mubarak, Cairo, January 22, 1989.
353   The retiring secretary of defense, *Washington Post,* October 22, 1989.
      On one such occasion, Congressional Record, June 5, 1986 S6801.
      The fifteen-year loss, *Washington Post,* March 25, 1989.
      The London, *Economist,* June 3, 1986.
354   United States citizens of Muslim, *Washington Post,* April 8, 1989.
355   In a surprising development, *Philadelphia Inquirer,* March 11, 1989.
      Professor Jerome Segal, *Creating the Palestinian State,* Jerome M. Segal, 1989.
      "One strongly pro-Israel . . . ", *Jewish News,* New Jersey, March 9, 1989.
356   Suggesting the importance, interview, April 26, 1989.
      Donald McHenry, interview, June 20, 1985.
357   In an editorial, *USA Today,* April 10, 1989.

Index

Abdnor, James, 290, 324
Abdul-Rahman, Hassan, 183
Abourezk, James, 30–31, 35, 97; and Israel-Arab negotiations, 97; in Rochester, N.Y., 98; at National Press Club, 98; and luncheon for al-Hout, 98–99; in Denver, 99; and subsidy to Hussein, 153
Abram, Morris B., 126
Abramson, Arthur, 235
Abshire, David, 204, 205, 206, 209
academic freedom, 180–237 passim, 322, 325, 332
Ackerman, Gary L., 82
Adamec, Ludwig, 213, 215–16, 219–20, 222, 224, 225, 227, 231, 232–33
Adelman, Lynn, 45
Adenauer, Konrad, 273
Ahmad, Eqbal, 188–89
AIPAC, 21, 23, 25–49 passim, 65, 98, 133, 144, 150, 157, 165, 187, 239, 246, 251, 266, 267, 280, 287, 298, 299, 300, 307, 325, 328; as part of Israel lobby, 25; influence on U.S. public policy, 25; presence in Congress, 51, college programs of, 58; and Dymally, 71, 73; and aid to Israel (1983), 78–79; and Lavi fighter, 80; and grant to Israel (1984), 82–83; in Stevenson campaign for governor, 87, 88, 92; and Hathaway, 100–101; and "spirit of 76" letter, 100–101, 106–7; and F-15 sale to Saudi Arabia, 102–3; and AWACS sale, 103–4; in Percy campaign (1984), 110–11, 112, 113; and attack on *Liberty*, 166; and *Assault on the Liberty*, 176; and academic programs, 180–81, 182, 184
AIPAC College Guide, 181, 182
Akins, James, 35, 203
Albright, Charlotte, 235
al-Hout, Shafiq, 98–99
Ali, Salim Rubyai, 2, 12; meeting with Findley, 7–8, 9, 10; overthrown, 11
Allen, James, 98
Allen, Richard, 158
Allen, Woody, 43
Al-Mazrui, Ghanim, 66
Altman, Richard, 43–44
American-Arab Anti-Discrimination Committee, 30, 81, 288, 292, 298, 324

American Baptist Churches, 248
American Educational Trust, 302
American Enterprise Institute, 164
American Farm Bureau, 38
American Friends Service Committee, 268, 269, 292
American Indian Law Students Association, 183
American Israel Public Affairs Committee, *see* AIPAC
American Jewish Committee, 26, 43, 60, 86, 89, 126, 131, 138, 191, 192, 194, 195, 231, 235, 265, 271, 276, 309, 311, 319; and academic programs, 180, 198, 199, 200; and NCC, 250
American Jewish Conference, 276
American Jewish Congress, 130, 247, 248, 271; on National Geographic documentary, 305; on "60 Minutes," 306
American Lebanese League, 298
American Professors for Peace in the Middle East, 203
American Zionist Council, 94, 304
Americans for Middle East Understanding, 300
Americans for a Safe Israel, 310–11
Amitay, Morris J., 45, 65, 100, 101, 110
Ammerman, Harvey H., 255
Anderson, Jack, 68, 150, 153
Anderson, John B., 127
Anderson, Warren, 102
Angell, Charles, 248–49
Angus, Jacob, 108
Anthony, John Duke, 302
Anti-Defamation League, 26, 35, 57, 98, 165, 176, 178, 184, 185, 192, 231, 235, 250, 262, 263, 279, 292, 296, 299, 300, 301, 308, 309, 322, 325
anti-Semitism, accusations of, 17, 33, 127, 131, 135, 137–38, 185, 249, 257, 260, 284, 296, 314, 315–16, 317, 327; against McCloskey, 59; against Stevenson, 90; against Fulbright, 94; against NCC, 250–51; against Sayre, 236; against LaGrange Conference, 262; against AFSC, 268
Arab Americans, 323, 324, 327; stereotypes of, 322, 327; discrimination against, 327
Arab-Israel conflict, 1, 21, 27, 40, 58, 128,